ALSO BY JONATHAN SCHELL

The Village of Ben Suc (1967)
The Military Half (1968)

THESE ARE BORZOI BOOKS
PUBLISHED IN NEW YORK BY ALFRED A. KNOPF

THE
TIME
OF
ILLUSION

THE
TIME
OF
ILLUSION

Jonathan Schell

ALFRED A. KNOPF · NEW YORK

1976

THIS IS A BORZOI BOOK
PUBLISHED BY ALFRED A. KNOPF, INC.

Most of the contents of this book originally appeared in *The New Yorker*.

Library of Congress Cataloging in Publication Data

Schell, Jonathan [Date]   The time of illusion.
Bibliography: p.   Includes index.
1. United States—Politics and government—1969-1974.
2. Watergate Affair, 1972-   I. Title.
E855.s36   1976   320.9′73′0924   75-35764
ISBN 0-394-40224-3

Manufactured in the United States of America

First Edition

For Ibs with love

CONTENTS

THE
TIME
OF
ILLUSION

PROLOGUE

I N THE COURSE of the last decade, the United States passed through a protracted internal political crisis that diverted the nation's energy and attention from virtually all other business, embittered every aspect of public life, and finally brought the American Constitutional system to the edge of a breakdown. The crisis had its origins in the intervention of the United States in a civil war in Indo-China —a move that, to the astonishment of the whole nation, grew in the space of a few years from a minor distraction in American foreign policy into an engulfing national obsession—and it reached its conclusion with the resignation of a President of the United States. No crisis in American political history came more unexpectedly than this one. And no crisis was more baffling to those who were caught up in it. At any given moment from the mid-nineteen-sixties until the early nineteen-seventies, most of the nation seemed to believe that the worst was over, with the result that the nation was repeatedly pitched from one phase of the crisis into the next without warning. In fact, so bewildered were Americans by what was happening to them and by what they themselves were doing that many came to believe that both in Indo-China and at home the United States had been overtaken by a wholly accidental and therefore wholly absurd fate. And when the crisis was unmistakably over, many voices were heard recommending that the nation try to forget about it immediately, as though people were ready to accept the notion that the events of recent years defied understanding in retrospect—just as they had defied anticipation and had defied understanding as they unfolded—and so were truly without any discoverable meaning whatever. Yet each phase of the crisis—the war abroad, the strife at home, and the systemic convulsion at the end —grew out of the preceding one, and all were episodes in a single story: a story that encompassed some ten years of American history. Today, looking back over events that no one foresaw, that no one fully grasped when they occurred, and that many would now like to forget, Americans are left still wondering where the trouble came from, what it did to the nation, and what, if anything, it was all for.

The crisis did not first emerge during the Presidency of Richard Nixon, but it came to a climax in those years, and it was his fall— anticipating the fall some nine months later of the regimes that the United States had supported in Vietnam and Cambodia—that marked the ending of the crisis. The Nixon Administration was characterized by, among other things, fragmentation. What the Nixon men thought was unconnected to what they said. What they said was unconnected to what they did. What they did or said they were doing at one moment was unconnected to what they did or said they were doing the next moment. And when they were driven from office, they left behind them not one but several unconnected records of themselves. First, there was the record of the Administration as it had presented itself to the public during its time in power. Second, there was the somewhat more complete record of the Administration as it was reflected in the press and on television in those years. And, third, there was the record of the Administration's multifarious covert activities, which was made known only later, as the Administration came to its premature end. Never in American history had as much information about an Administration in power been held in secrecy as was held in secrecy during most of the Nixon years. But never in the history of the world, perhaps, had as much been revealed about the workings of a government as was revealed about the workings of the Nixon apparatus during and after its fall. In a democracy, people must know what is going on, and know it immediately after it happens, if they are to make their judgments about where the country should be going and who should lead it there. In the Nixon years, information about public affairs came in bits and scraps, often out of sequence and after long delays; and the coherence and meaning of the public record was lost. Later, as the record of the Administration's covert activities was made available, some of the gaps were filled in, but by then the parts that had been learned earlier were fading from memory, and people were left with a pile of shreds. It was as though they had been invited to listen to a large orchestral composition, but then had heard each of the instruments separately, one after another, and with long waits in between. They had heard interminable notes, played hour after hour, but they had never heard the composition. In what follows, I will reconnect some of the fragments that are to be found in the various records of the Nixon Administration, in order—as a first step toward understanding what has happened—to make the experience whole; and I will offer some thoughts on the deeper and more enduring American political crisis, of which the Nixon Administration was only a part.

In November of 1968, when Richard Nixon was elected thirty-seventh President of the United States, the war had already installed itself at the center of the nation's political life. Wherever the shadow of the war had fallen—and it had fallen nearly everywhere—unity of purpose had been lost and hope had died. The political consensus on which President Lyndon Johnson had thought to build a program of reforms in American life had begun to fragment and dissolve.

Its base, the Democratic Party, had splintered into warring factions. A movement for racial justice that had gathered strength in the first part of the nineteen-sixties had grown angry and, on occasion, violent; its members, who had been at one with President Johnson on race, had divided with him on the war, and the ground for further coöperation had been lost. A program to eliminate poverty in the United States had been curtailed as federal funds were poured into the war effort. Even the booming, apparently unstoppable American economy was weakened by the enormous war expenditures. But although the war was unquestionably at the root of the nation's political disorders, what was at the root of the war itself was obscure. For one thing, it seemed that the war was as much a symptom of the disorders as it was a cause. No immediate peril had compelled the United States to go to war—certainly not the North Vietnamese. No Vietnamese force had ever posed any threat to America, and no Vietnamese had ever shown any desire whatever to fight a war against the United States. Nor had there been any clamor for war from the public. Rather, the American government had itself created the compulsion under which it labored in Vietnam. Events in Vietnam had taken on significance for the United States only insofar as American policymakers, guided by global strategic theories, had decided that they were significant. And yet when the government attempted to set forth these theories its explanations had been confused and contradictory. It was not that too few war aims were offered but, if anything, too many. One aim, the government said, was to promote the democratic system: America was in Vietnam to protect the freedom of the South Vietnamese against Communist totalitarianism. A second aim was to uphold certain rules of international conduct: America was in Vietnam to stop aggression. A third aim was to prevent other countries from falling to Communism, for the policymakers were convinced that if the United States permitted the Vietnamese revolutionaries to overthrow the regime in South Vietnam, a chain reaction would be set in motion in which the world's nations would fall to Communism one after another, in a long row, like dominoes (as a popular simile of our day has had it), until only the United States remained

free, and then, it was said, the United States, too, might fall:
America was in Vietnam, therefore, to protect its own security. A
fourth, and final, aim was to protect something that the policymakers called American "credibility." The word was a new one in
the political lexicon. It referred not to anything tangible but to an
image: an image of vast national strength and of unwavering determination to use that strength in world affairs.

Of all the war aims, the aim of protecting American credibility
proved to be the most durable. The defense of freedom and the
prevention of aggression had long been principles in American
foreign policy, but they had never been strictly adhered to, and the
United States had violated them rather often. Besides, it had become difficult after a while to maintain that the United States was
defending freedom in South Vietnam, inasmuch as it had soon become clear that there was no freedom in South Vietnam; and it had
been difficult to maintain plausibly that the United States was acting to prevent aggression in Vietnam, in view of the fact that all the
combatants but the Americans were Vietnamese. As for the domino
theory, it had grown out of the experience of another era—the era
in which Hitler was taking over Europe—and as the war in Vietnam
continued, men inside government as well as men outside had come
to the conclusion that the analogy between Europe in the nineteen-
thirties and Southeast Asia in the nineteen-sixties was, at best,
strained. The doctrine of credibility, however, was rooted firmly
in the experience of the modern period. It was rooted in the doctrine that formed the basis for all strategic thinking in the nineteen-
sixties—the doctrine of nuclear deterrence. For it was in the
credibility of the nuclear deterrent that the United States had
placed its hopes for survival in the nuclear age. The government
hoped that by creating a formidable impression of national strength
and will in the minds of the nation's adversaries it could deter them
from launching a nuclear attack. In its application to Vietnam, the
doctrine of credibility found expression in a revised version of the
traditional domino theory which might be called the psychological
domino theory. According to the traditional domino theory, each
nation that fell to Communism would endanger its immediate

neighbor; according to the psychological domino theory, the ill effects of a nation's fall would not necessarily be on neighboring nations but would be on nations all over the world, which by merely watching the spectacle would lose their confidence in the power of the United States. Allies, it was said, would be discouraged from relying on American power, and foes would be emboldened to challenge it. The United States would, in a word, lose credibility. In this thinking, Vietnam became a "test case" of the United States' will to use its power in world affairs. If the United States could not muster the "determination" to prevail in Vietnam, it was believed, then it would be showing, once and for all, that it lacked the determination to prevail in any conflict anywhere. And, since in the official view credibility was indivisible, a collapse of credibility in the sphere of limited conflict would cast doubt on the credibility of American power in other spheres of competition as well, including even the all-important nuclear sphere. Thus, according to the doctrine of credibility, the United States was engaged in a global public-relations struggle in which a reverse in any part of the world, no matter how small, could undermine the whole structure of American power.

By the mid-nineteen-sixties, the war had outlived every aim but the protection of credibility. In March of 1965, Assistant Secretary of Defense John McNaughton, who specialized in thinking through the rationale of American involvement in Vietnam, set forth the war aims in terms of percentage points, and he wrote that seventy per cent of the reason for being in Vietnam was "to avoid a humiliating U.S. defeat (to our reputation as a guarantor)." These words were, of course, a formulation of the doctrine of credibility. Only twenty per cent was "to keep SVN [South Vietnam] (and the adjacent) territory from Chinese hands." The word "adjacent" had reference to the traditional domino theory. And a mere ten per cent was "to permit the people of SVN to enjoy a better, freer way of life." In January of 1966, in another summation of the war aims, he wrote, "*The present U.S. objective in Vietnam is to avoid humiliation. The reasons why we went into* Vietnam to the present depth are varied; but they are now largely academic. Why we have *not withdrawn* is, by all odds, *one* reason. (1) To preserve our reputation as a guarantor, and thus to preserve our effectiveness in the rest of the world. We have not hung on (2) to save a friend, or (3) to deny the Communists the added acres and heads (because the dominoes don't fall for that reason in this case), or even (4) to prove that 'wars of national liberation' won't work (except as our reputation is involved)." By that time, maintaining "our reputation as a guarantor"—maintaining American credibility—was one hundred per cent of the United States' reason for being in Vietnam.

In the nineteen-sixties, then, policymakers in Washington had identified a strategic objective that in their view justified the tremendous price that the nation was paying for the war—a price that, as it turned out, included the embitterment of the nation's politics, the crippling of President Johnson's cherished domestic reforms, and the deepening crisis of the Constitutional system. But if the government was willing to wage war indefinitely for this objective, the public, it seemed, was not. One explanation of this unwillingness may be that the government had been strangely shy about rallying the public to its cause. Instead of trying to educate the public concerning the importance of the war, the government had consistently attempted to hide the true scope of the war effort. President Johnson had habitually spoken as though his fondest wish was to disengage from Vietnam. In the 1964 Presidential campaign, he had repeatedly indicated that he would never send American troops to fight in Indo-China, and he had been elected in a landslide over the Republican candidate, Senator Barry Goldwater, who had called for "victory" in the war. So profound was the government's conviction that the war effort was necessary that, when it found spontaneous support from the public lacking, it schemed to create incidents that could be used to stir up the public's wrath against the foe, and even went as far as to deliberately provoke the North Vietnamese into actions against American forces which could be used to justify escalation of the American effort. The United States had never gone to war in quite this way before. In past wars, American troops had gone into battle with the full, vocal support of the public behind them, but the American soldiers who were sent to Vietnam went into battle in silence, behind a screen of official evasions and deceptions. This time, the usual patriotic sentiments were not encouraged. How could they be? The government was pretending that the country was not at war.

A situation full of extreme danger for Constitutional democracy had arisen. The government, impelled by strategic objectives that the public did not understand, was moving deeper and deeper into an unpopular war on its own initiative. On both the political left and the political right, there was bafflement and distress. The challenge from the right came first, in the form of Barry Goldwater's Presidential candidacy. It gained the enthusiastic support of a large minority but then was turned back in the Johnson landslide. Goldwater had apparently given the public a fright with his talk of victory—and for a very good reason. A majority of the public evidently feared what the Administration also feared: that the measures necessary for a swift victory over the Vietnamese foe might draw the Chinese or the Russians, or both, into the war, and thereby precipitate a nuclear catastrophe. Johnson had capitalized on this fear during the campaign in an underhanded television commercial that first showed a little girl holding a flower in her hands and then showed a nuclear explosion and then urged a vote against Senator Goldwater. Nuclear dread, which had shaped the strategy of the war to begin with, was now shaping the public's reaction to the war. The public seemed to sense that in the nuclear age patriotic war fever might lead to pressure for reckless military action that could result in annihilation.

The challenge to the war policy from the left developed a few years later, and it proved to be more formidable. The left had no more taste than the right had for the drawn-out, if limited, warfare that the Johnson Administration was asking the country to support, but whereas the right wanted to end the war by winning it, the left wanted to end the war by withdrawing from it. If the right could see no reason for restraining the war effort, the left could see no reason for any war effort at all. (And some people took a position that combined the objections of the right and the left: they held that the country should "either win or get out.") A fateful gap had opened between the executive branch and the public. The people and their President had ceased to understand each other. The President, trapped in a world of his own by his inscrutable war aims, felt first misunderstood and then betrayed. He came to believe that what distressed the country was not his war policy but his personal style; he began to entertain the notion that a campaign to improve his public image would recapture his lost support. But, twist and turn as he would, he remained pinioned by the war. An atmosphere of rage began to seep through the White House. Bewildered by the breadth and persistence of the opposition to him, President Johnson became conspiratorial-minded. He began to imagine that the anti-war movement was in league with the Soviet Union, and to imagine that some of his aides were plotting against him. Image-making and political manipulation having failed, he turned, in his anger, to repression. The C.I.A., the Army, and the F.B.I. were sent out to spy on the domestic opposition. These moves were unknown to the people at large, but other repressive acts were soon on full public display. At the Democratic Convention in August of 1968, in Chicago, the police of a city controlled by Democrats went on a bloody rampage while the leaders of the majority faction of the Democratic Party looked on; the Convention hall swarmed with undercover agents, who harassed opposition delegates and newsmen; and the Convention proceedings were crudely and openly manipulated by the majority. An Administration was suffering from an affliction that was new in the American experience. Its symptoms were rage, isolation, secretiveness, and a proclivity for repressive action, and its cause was a war whose necessity only Presidents and their advisers, it seemed, were able to fully understand.

Meanwhile, the opposition to the Johnson Administration was deepening. The war-issue was at the heart of its protest, but many of its members were bothered by a great deal more than the war. The anti-war movement in the United States coincided with a youthful rebellion against established authorities which was worldwide. A number of observers, looking for some experience common to all young people which might help to explain this unexpected and apparently spontaneous world movement, noted the speed and impact of modern communications and also pointed out that the generation coming of age in the nineteen-sixties was the first to have grown up in the presence of nuclear weapons, and concluded that the threat of human extinction must somehow underlie their rebellion. If the young were upset in some general sense by the way the world they had inherited was arranged, it was hardly without reason, these observers remarked; and they suggested that if the new generation was absorbed in pleasures of the moment and tended to be uninterested in thought or in culture or in anything else that was meant to endure beyond a single generation, it might well be because they were the first generation to doubt that the human species had a future.

The question of human survival did not often arise in direct form in the strife of the nineteen-sixties, but it was in the air. For looming over the tumultuous American scene of those years was the remote and shadowy but all-pervading presence of the bomb. The bomb was lodged at the very center of the angry President's bloated power; the bomb was in the background of the government's obsession with the strange war in Vietnam; and the bomb had shaped the mood of the new generation. For some two decades, nuclear weapons had stood outside the flow of everyday business in the political world. Now it was as though they were coming closer, and were starting to pose their awful questions more insistently. Not yet overtly present in the mainstream of political thought and political action, they were indistinctly present as an atmosphere, and as the framework within which the events of the Nixon years would turn.

I.
UNITY

O<small>N</small> ELECTION NIGHT, a beaming President-elect Nixon went before the television cameras and said, "That will be the great objective of this Administration at the outset: to bring the American people together. This will be an open Administration, open to new ideas . . . open to the critics as well as to those who support us. We want to bridge the generation gap. We want to bridge the gap between the races. We want to bring America together." The generous tone of the President's remarks was widely welcomed, and to some it was a source of relief; for to a remarkable degree Nixon was a political unknown on the day he was elected to office. It wasn't for lack of exposure to him that the public did not know him well: he had been a prominent figure in national politics for twenty years, having served in the House of Representatives, in the Senate, and as Vice-President, and had shown himself to be, among other things, an uncompromising opponent of Communism wherever he might find it. But in the course of the Presidential campaign of 1968 he had made his politics unknown. During the campaign, he had drawn back from many of his old positions while putting forward few new ones, so that his campaign was a process of erasure more than of disclosure. On the issue of the war, he had consistently favored strong military action since at least 1954, when, as Vice-President, he had advocated direct American military intervention, but in the campaign he held that to take a position on the war at variance with President Johnson's would be irresponsible, and he therefore vowed to remain silent. In accepting the Republican nomination, he had said, "We all hope in this room that there's a chance that current negotiations may bring an honorable end to that war. And we will say nothing during this campaign that might destroy that chance." But, having said that, he went on to take the Democrats to task for the long duration of the war, and seemed to advocate putting an end to it even before the November election. "If the war is not ended when the people choose in November," he said, "the choice will be clear." And he said, "Those who have had a chance for four years and could not produce peace should not be given another chance." On the subject of how he would end the war, he said only, "How do you bring a war to a conclusion? I'll tell you how Korea was ended. . . . Eisenhower let the word go out— let the word go out diplomatically—to the Chinese and the North [Koreans]—that he would not tolerate this continual ground war of attrition. And within a matter of months they negotiated."

Mr. Nixon's statements on the war accorded with the clearly expressed wishes of the public, for by the fall of 1968 the country had made its decision to put an end to the war. The executive branch of the government, acting virtually on its own and by stealth, had made the decision to get the United States into Vietnam. The nation as a whole, using every available channel of public action and public debate, had made the decision to get out. In the spring of 1968, the anti-war movement had achieved a stunning victory: the retirement of President Johnson, who, in the face of strong opposition from Senator Eugene McCarthy in the early Democratic primaries, had suddenly announced that he would not run for reëlection, that he was calling a halt to the air and naval bombardment of most of North Vietnam, and that he hoped the cessation of the bombing would lead to peace talks with the Vietnamese foe. Then, only two months later, the movement had suffered an equally stunning reversal: the assassination of the man who in the course of the later primaries had become its principal political hope—Senator Robert Kennedy. Kennedy's assassination neutralized the movement as an electoral force; for the movement's strong suit in national politics had been its power to win victories in the Democratic primaries, and when Kennedy was killed the victories he had won, which would have given him his strength at the Democratic Convention, could not be transferred to another candidate. At the Convention in Chicago, what was left of the leaderless anti-war forces was defeated, and Vice-President Hubert Humphrey, a man who was linked in the public's mind with President Johnson's war policies, was sent into the field against Mr. Nixon. The anti-war movement, having retired one President, had been unable to offer a candidate of its own to the public in a national election. Nevertheless, the nation had gone through its convulsion and made its decision on the war, and Humphrey, too, now advocated an end to the war.

Mr. Nixon saw it as his responsibility to take no specific position on how the war should be ended, and on other matters, too, he was clear about his ends but vague about his means. He announced his support of racial equality but, apart from some references to a plan for promoting "black capitalism," did not propose any specific programs. He declared his intention of ending the wave of crime that had afflicted the United States in recent years, but his most often mentioned method of doing it was to "appoint a new Attorney General"—something that any new President who represents the opposition party does automatically. Bernard Nossiter, a staff writer for the Washington *Post*, wrote shortly before the election that Vice-President Humphrey's campaign lacked a theme. Mr. Nixon's campaign had a theme—which was to bring an end to the war and disorder of the Johnson years—but it lacked any clue to how he proposed to carry it out.

Nevertheless, the Nixon campaign strategy was a popular one, even among many observers who had not supported Mr. Nixon in the past. Some of these observers saw in his ambiguity an abandonment of an "old Nixon," whom they had not cared for, and the emergence of a "new Nixon," more to their liking. The "old Nixon" had been a vigorously partisan figure who sometimes engaged in ruthless or unfair tactics, such as accusing his opponent of virtual treason or putting out false campaign literature under his opponent's name, but the "new Nixon" was capable of saying, "I want the Presidency to be a force for pulling our people back together once again, and for making our nation whole by making our people one." In early October, the columnist Walter Lippmann, who had written of President Johnson that "the root of his troubles has been pride, a stubborn refusal to recognize the country's limitations or his own," gave compelling reasons for believing that the "new Nixon" was real. "I believe that there really is a 'new Nixon,' a maturer and mellower man who is no longer clawing his way to the top, and it is, I think, fair to hope that his dominating ambition will be to become a two-term President," he wrote. "He is bright enough to know that this will be impossible if he remains sunk in the Vietnam quagmire. Ending the war is indispensable if he is to become a successful President. And at home, he must, as he knows well, move out to find common ground with the active minorities who are dividing and might paralyze the nation." Lippmann went on to recommend a vote for Nixon. So widespread was the notion that Nixon had in effect re-created himself politically that few observers in the press looked to his past conduct in politics as a guide to his future behavior. And a country that only a few months earlier had watched the Democratic Convention in Chicago found Mr. Nixon's new tone a welcome contrast. Kenneth Crawford, a columnist for *Newsweek*, believed that Nixon wanted "to steer a middle course, emulative of the Eisenhower Administration," adding, "Indeed, restraint is the name of Nixon's game." And the columnist Joseph Kraft, apparently thinking along very much the same lines as Lippmann, wrote that a "crisis of authority" had arisen, and that the Democrats were "not yet ready to abandon the illusion that the world can be run from a single place" and so were "not equipped to back away from the true source of the crisis in authority." Therefore, he wrote, "it makes sense to vote for Richard Nixon and the Republicans." As he and millions of others saw it, a vote for Nixon was a vote for decentralization and modest aims after a period of inflated Presidential power and excessive national ambition.

Through most of the campaign, Mr. Nixon had enjoyed a wide lead in the polls. But in the final weeks his lead began to shrink, and his campaign underwent a sudden shift in tone. It seemed to break into several parts, and to begin to speak in several voices. One of them was the voice of Governor Spiro Agnew, of Maryland, Mr. Nixon's running mate. His language had been characteristically rougher than Nixon's, but now it reached new levels of stridency. On one occasion, when hecklers shouted "Humphrey! Humphrey! Humphrey!" at one of his campaign appearances, he retorted, "You can renounce your citizenship if you don't like it here, so why don't you leave?" And he added that when the Republicans took office, people like those hecklers were going to "dry up and disappear." Three days later, when Mr. Nixon encountered a disruption, he said, "I'm delighted to hear these differences." His response was in keeping with the tone he had tried to maintain in his campaign. In a major speech on the Presidency, for example, he had said, "It's time we once again had an open Administration. . . . We should bring dissenters into policy discussions, not freeze them out." But in the very last days of the campaign, when Agnew was accusing Humphrey of conciliating people who "condone violence and advocate the overthrow of the government," Nixon's own tone began to slip, and he aligned himself with Agnew's remarks by saying that Humphrey had a "personal attitude of indulgence and permissiveness toward the lawless." In another last-minute shift, he began to accuse Humphrey of being insufficiently concerned about military unpreparedness. "Let me tell you that I am the one who stands for a stronger United States and Mr. Humphrey who stands for a weaker one," he said now. He was making the point for the first time in the campaign.

These contradictions and abrupt reversals, which caused considerable puzzlement when they occurred, were to be explained partly by an unusual system of speechwriting that Mr. Nixon had adopted. Instead of choosing speechwriters who would achieve as much consistency in theme and style as possible in the speeches they wrote for him, he chose two of his principal writers for their ability to draft speeches in opposite styles. One of the two was Raymond Price, a former editorial-page editor of the *Herald Tribune*, and he wrote florid, inspirational, high-minded speeches. He was known around the campaign as Mr. Outside, because what he wrote was designed to please a broad range of people, and not just those in the narrow circle of Mr. Nixon's traditional supporters. He was also known as Nixon's "liberal" writer. The other principal speechwriter was Patrick Buchanan, formerly an editorial writer for the Saint Louis *Globe-Democrat*, who was the first full-time member of Mr. Nixon's Presidential-campaign staff; he wrote abusive, combative, vigorously partisan speeches, and produced what one former colleague called "bang-bang-socko stuff." He was known around the campaign as Mr. Inside, because his speeches were designed expressly to please the hard-core supporters. He was also known as Nixon's "conservative" writer. The candidate had established this two-track system because, as Buchanan explained a while later, he wanted to be free at any given moment to choose between "both viewpoints."

The campaign's change of tone as the election approached troubled many of those who had been pleased to see the emergence of a "new Nixon." They were afraid that his apparently magnanimous, conciliatory mood might be giving way to the harshness of the "old Nixon," and the country had had enough of anger in the White House under President Johnson. These doubts, however, were largely banished when, on Election Night, Nixon made his promises to run an open Administration and to bring the nation together.

The message coming out of the President-elect's entourage in the months between Election Day and Inauguration Day was of a piece with the theme he had set on Election Night. Mr. Nixon held a widely publicized meeting with Vice-President Humphrey and congratulated him on his campaign. He invited a delegation of black leaders to meet with him in his hotel suite in New York, and one of those who went reported afterward that the President-elect had promised to "do more for the Negro people than any President has ever done." Senate Majority Leader Mike Mansfield, encouraged by the President-elect's conciliatory mood, announced that he looked forward to a stronger role for the Senate in foreign policy during the Nixon years. (During the Johnson years, the Senate had declined considerably as a force in foreign affairs.) In an editorial titled "New Bipartisan Era?," the Washington *Post* wrote of Nixon, "He knows that if his Administration is to succeed in the sphere of foreign policy he will have to have the coöperation of the Democratic Congress, and especially of the Foreign Relations Committee, where the power to approve treaties and to confirm foreign-relations personnel is centered." It was learned that several Democrats were under consideration for high positions, including Cabinet posts. The President-elect also moved to reassure the nation in other ways about the Cabinet. In the Johnson Administration, the Cabinet, like the Senate, had lost much of its power, and the White House staff had grown in importance. During the campaign, Mr. Nixon had announced his intention of reversing the trend. He had said he wanted "a Cabinet made up of the ablest men in America, leaders in their own right and not merely by virtue of appointment—men who will command the public's respect and the President's attention by the power of their intellect and the force of their ideas." And in the course of a description of what he didn't want he had gone on to say, "Such men are not attracted to an Administration in which all credit is gathered to the White House and blame parcelled out to scapegoats, or in which high officials are asked to dance like puppets on a Presidential string."

Now, a little more than a month after the election, he announced, in a televised ceremony that had no precedent, his choices for the Cabinet. On a stage at the Shoreham Hotel, in Washington, the nominees sat in two rows facing the camera. Mr. Nixon stood at a microphone to one side, and praised the Cabinet as a group and then praised each man singly. "These are strong men, they're compassionate men, they're good men," he said. "I don't want a Cabinet of yes-men," he continued, and he said that each man would bring an "extra dimension" to his job. These assurances were all the more welcome because few of the new men were well known to the country and few had political bases of their own. On an earlier occasion, when the President-elect announced the appointment of Henry Kissinger, a Harvard professor, as his chief adviser on foreign affairs, he said, apparently in an effort to lay to rest any fears that Mr. Kissinger might grow too powerful, "I intend to have a very strong Secretary of State." His nominee for Secretary of State was William Rogers, who had served as Attorney General in the Eisenhower Administration but even so was not well known to the public. The President-elect also took steps to reassure the public that he meant to run a candid Administration. He appointed Herbert Klein, an old friend and long-time adviser, to serve as communications director in his new Administration, and Klein, at his first meeting with the press after his appointment, said, "Truth will become the hallmark of the Nixon Administration. . . . We will be able to eliminate any possibility of a credibility gap in this Administration." His words reinforced a promise that the candidate had made in his acceptance speech when he said, "Let us begin by committing ourselves to the truth—to see it like it is, and tell it like it is—to find the truth, to speak the truth, and to live the truth."

While the nation's eyes were fixed on the ceremonies attending the introduction of the Cabinet, the members of the new President's staff took their posts virtually unnoticed, as was suitable for men whose position was to be strictly subordinate in the new scheme of things. Scores of articles were written about the backgrounds and qualifications of the Cabinet Secretaries, but very little was written about the qualifications of the staff—except Mr. Kissinger, whose appointment was widely remarked on and widely applauded. The appointment of two men who had worked closely with Mr. Nixon for years and who consulted with him as regularly, perhaps, as any other members of his entourage—H. R. Haldeman, the new chief of staff, and John Ehrlichman, who would serve as the President's legal counsel—attracted relatively little attention. An article in the *Times* headlined NIXON RULES OUT AGENCY CONTROL BY STAFF AIDES said, "Sensitive to the possibility of empire building within his own small cadre of assistants, he plans instead to organize his White House staff in a way that will encourage and not inhibit direct communication between his Cabinet officers and the President." Rowland Evans and Robert Novak, two syndicated columnists who were reputed to have excellent sources within the budding Administration, confirmed the *Times* report. "The Nixon team hopes to change the whole character of the White House staff operation," they wrote. "What Nixon is driving for has eluded many Presidents before him: to use his own staff strictly as an information-gathering device and leave [to] his Cabinet all the major policy advice." Kissinger, in particular, they said, would be restricted to a modest role: "Kissinger will never propose or advocate a particular policy, but will only present 'options.'" And Haldeman, in a rare public pronouncement, told a reporter that there would be no dominant figure on the Nixon staff comparable to the man who headed the staff of President Eisenhower for six years in the nineteen-fifties. "There will be no Sherman Adams," Haldeman said.

The mood of the Inauguration was more sober and expectant than celebratory. In downtown Washington, some six thousand demonstrators chanted such slogans as "Peace now!" and "Work, study, get ahead, kill!" and "Four more years of death!"—a reminder of the torment that the country had just been through and now expected to leave behind. Already, they seemed like voices from another era— disgruntled remnants out to ruin the new atmosphere of peace and conciliation. The President's delivery of his Inaugural Address was solemn, as befitted one of the less exultant moments in the nation's history. Warning that "the American dream does not come to those who fall asleep," he advised Americans to "lower our voices," and to free politics "from inflated rhetoric that promises more than it can deliver; from angry rhetoric that fans discontents into hatreds; from bombastic rhetoric that postures instead of persuading." Apparently referring to his plans with regard to the war in Vietnam, he said, "The greatest honor history can bestow is the title of peace-maker." And concerning the racial question he said, "The laws have caught up with our conscience. What remains is to give life to what is in the law." Mr. Outside had done a good deal of the work on the speech, and some of the passages were rhapsodic in tone, and even seemed to fall into the category of "inflated rhetoric" that the President had just advised against. "We can build a great cathedral of the spirit—each of us raising it one stone at a time, as he reaches out to his neighbor, helping, caring, doing," the President said. And he closed with the words "We have endured a long night of the American spirit. But as our eyes catch the dimness of the first rays of dawn, let us not curse the remaining dark. Let us gather the light." If the tone of these remarks was out of keeping with the mood of the occasion, their content was welcome, and had the effect of confirming the generous and open mood of the new Administration. They seemed to indicate that the President was leaning toward the "viewpoint" of Mr. Outside. The next day, Chalmers Roberts, a staff writer for the Washington *Post*, wrote some lines that were characteristic of much of the reaction to the speech: "There was no note of partisan political triumph, no call to arms to win an unpopular war, no demand for a crackdown on dissent here at home. . . . In short, the new President's speech was intended to be in tune with the times and with the mood of the voters who put him in the White House. He had heard their voices, at least their majority voice, and he was reflecting it."

On Election Night, during the transition, and on Inauguration Day, President Nixon had seemed to be moving decisively to set the tone of his Administration. He would take special care to avoid the afflictions of the Johnson Administration in its last years. His would be a government of national unity. The war abroad and the strife at home were to be brought to an end. Where Johnson had been deceptive, the new President would be straightforward; where Johnson had been angry, he would be calm; where Johnson had been secretive, he would be open. New ideas would be welcomed, old enmities forgotten. The Cabinet would enjoy great independence, the staff would be subordinate, and the Congress would be restored to its rightful place as a co-equal branch in the conduct of foreign affairs.

A widespread conviction took hold that the country would now enjoy a period of national cooling-off under the leadership of a modest, unpretentious, hardworking, practical-minded Administration. Column after column, picking up the President's Inaugural theme, announced that the period of turmoil was over, and that the country was about to get back to what William Shannon, of the *Times*, had called, a few weeks before the Inauguration, "the known and familiar." Although many people were horrified by the record of the immediate past, they looked to the future with a touch of complacency. They tended to share the opinion of Ben Wattenberg, who had just left the White House after serving for two and a half years as an aide and speechwriter to President Johnson, and who, a day before the Inauguration, had written, in an article called "Upbeat Auguries Belie the Alarmists," "In all, we have lived through a somewhat gloomy time. Incessantly during the last year we heard from Democrats, Republicans, and independents alike that 'America faces its greatest crisis of a hundred years.' Is this uptight view of our future valid? . . . Nixon will be facing a series of new and developing situations. . . . It would seem as if these new situations would markedly change life in America—for the better." Among the favorable new situations he foresaw were a further increase in the number of blacks above the poverty level, an end to the war, and a decline of left-wing radicalism. Nothing that the Nixon people said belied such expectations. Concerning the mood of the new Administration, one columnist summed up the general impression when he wrote, "The incoming Nixon men seem relaxed and almost mellow. . . . There is none of the moralistic sense of good guys replacing bad guys."

However, if a cure for the political diseases that had afflicted the Presidency and the nation in the Johnson years was all but universally expected, the measures for effecting the cure had not been announced. Once the new President was installed in the White House, a period of waiting for specific policies began. As Joseph Alsop put it in the heading of a column in the Washington *Post* two days after the Inauguration, NIXON'S CALL FOR TRANQUILITY MUST BE MATCHED BY ACTION. The country waited to learn how the President was going to get the country out of the war, how he was going to stop the wave of crime, how he was going to do more for black people than any other President in history, and how he was going to bridge the credibility gap. During the first few months of the Administration, the Nixon men tended to evade these questions. In response to inquiries about their political philosophy, they tended to say only that they were "pragmatists" or "realists." When Henry Cabot Lodge, the President's appointee to the Paris peace talks on the Vietnam war, was asked for his views on the negotiations, he answered, "I'm not a hard-liner. I'm not a soft-liner. I try to be a realist." As a policy for ending the war, though, he proposed merely that the demilitarized zone between North and South Vietnam be neutralized; the North Vietnamese were uninterested, since the plan would require them to cut off supplies to their troops in the South. The Nixon men began to speak as if the disorders of the last few years had arisen because there had been too much philosophizing in government, and not enough action. At the Justice Department, for instance, Kevin Phillips, a young assistant to John Mitchell, who was the new Attorney General, described the problem of criminal justice as primarily administrative. "The main problem is that there is no real command system," he said. And he said, "Mitchell is a terrific administrator, and that's just what this place needs most." What it didn't need, Phillips went on, was idealists who made a lot of promises they couldn't fulfill. "It's time we got these hypocrites out of town and began administering," he said. Richard Kleindienst, the newly appointed Deputy Attorney General, said of Ramsey Clark, the outgoing Attorney General, "Ramsey Clark is a nice guy, but he just wouldn't act. As a result, the Ramsey Clark administration did a lot of theorizing about crime, but it didn't take action. We're going to act, and act fast."

The idea that a team of bright, efficient administrators was coming in to clean up a mess left by woolly-headed idealists and impractical philosophers was reinforced by a dizzying whirl of "reorganization," or "structuring," which soon got under way in the White House. For each national problem, it seemed, the White House had an administrative answer. New organizations began to proliferate. In foreign affairs, Henry Kissinger was placed in charge of a strengthened National Security Council, which would coördinate White House foreign-policy planning. In domestic affairs, Daniel Patrick Moynihan, a Harvard professor who had served in the Kennedy and Johnson Administrations, was made executive director of a Council on Urban Affairs. This council was described by some as a National Security Council for domestic policy; at the same time, George Romney, the new Secretary of Housing and Urban Development, was described as retaining full authority over his field. (If urban affairs was the new Administration's central domestic preoccupation, it may have been in part because urban renewal—what was often referred to simply as "the cities"—had become a lively and fashionable political issue in the late nineteen-sixties, and had been the subject of innumerable magazine articles, television specials, and university seminars.) Vice-President Agnew was placed in charge of a new organization, an Office of Inter-governmental Relations, which was to serve as a link between the federal government and state and local officials. And an organization called the President's Advisory Council on Executive Organization was set up to plan still more reorganization.

Toward the end of February, the President sent his first message to Congress on domestic affairs. Some of the Johnson Great Society programs, apparently, were to be continued, but others had fallen prey to reorganization. Hubert Humphrey was asked how he thought the Administration was doing after one month in office, and he answered that he thought it was doing well but had "no real program" yet. The wait for the Nixon policies continued.

Early in 1969, the President drew up contingency plans to cope with a possible uprising in the United States.

In February, the President set off on a grand tour of Europe. For days, the smiling face of the President as he arrived in one European capital after another filled the newspapers. The trip, like so many things he had done since taking office, was strong on atmosphere and weak on substance. He described the trip to five European capitals as a series of "working visits," and said he was going to Europe "to listen." Asked whether he had any broad aim in making the journey, he answered, "I am not going to Europe for the purpose of lecturing the Europeans, of telling them that we know best, and of telling them to follow us."

While the President was away, the fighting in Vietnam intensified, and upon his return from his European tour he was asked at a press conference whether the United States would renew the bombing of North Vietnam. Instead of replying directly, the President placed the blame for the intensified fighting on the North Vietnamese, and added, "I will only say, in answer to that question, that the United States has a number of options that we could exercise to respond. We have several contingency plans that can be put into effect." These were ambiguous words, and did not seem to jibe very well with his promises as a candidate to bring the war to a quick conclusion, but in the absence of any stronger suggestion that the President had changed his mind about ending the war the public remained unalarmed. Indeed, when the President was asked at his press conference whether the American public would endure the continuation of the war for many more years, he answered, "Well, I trust that I am not confronted with that problem when you speak of years." The President seemed to answer the questions put to him ably, and the *Times*, in an editorial exemplifying the friendly mood that now existed between the President and some of those who had not previously supported him called his performance a "tour de force." American casualties were in the hundreds each week, but in the new mood of reconciliation and calm that had been established by the President the country had taken its mind off the war and was already enjoying a postwar relaxation of tension. The President himself had ordered a study of what should be done with funds released by the war's ending. Mr. Kissinger was privately assuring journalists that the war would be brought to an end soon. Discussion of whether or not to grant amnesty to war resisters had begun. The newspapers—exhausted, like everyone else, by the war and everything to do with the war—had turned their attention with grateful relief to other issues: "the cities," the Middle East, the Atlantic Alliance. These were serious matters, but after the delirium of the war years they had an air of tameness and normality which was welcome. They were "the known and familiar." "Public pressure over the war has almost disappeared," one reporter wrote in early March. The *Times* was reflecting a consensus of many educators when, in February, it reported that only an end to the war stood "in the way of a dramatic escalation by President Nixon of the urban and egalitarian-minded Johnson policies" in support of federal aid to education.

In mid-April, the Republican National Committee released a statement that seemed to indicate that the anticipated pacification of American political life by the Nixon Administration had been successfully accomplished. "In his first ninety days," the committee announced, "President Richard M. Nixon has made a dramatic impact on the national spirit. With quiet dignity, efficiency, and purpose, he has visibly altered America's mood and has changed the direction of Government for generations to come."

In March, 1969, while the country was waiting to learn how the President was going to shape his broad aims into policies, he had taken the boldest action of his Presidency to date—but had taken it secretly. He had expanded the war in Indo-China. Ordering a military action of unprecedented secrecy, he launched a bombing campaign against enemy forces in Cambodia. To keep track of the secret bombing, the military was obliged to set up an improvised command system, outside ordinary channels, that extended from the Commander-in-Chief down to the pilots and bombardiers. Some high military officials knew of the bombing, and some did not; the Chairman of the Joint Chiefs of Staff did, for instance, but the Secretary of the Air Force did not. In the field, records were falsified or destroyed. No one ever sat down to figure out exactly how to handle the record-keeping, and the Chairman of the Joint Chiefs of Staff later said that a chaotic system of covert reporting "just grew up." Looking back on it afterward, General Creighton Abrams, the commander of American forces in Vietnam at that time, said, "From a purely administrative viewpoint . . . the whole thing had become too complicated. I could not keep these things [where the planes were bombing] in my mind, so I had to have specialists who kept them; and what we had to do for this case, and that case, and that case."

The secret project soon acquired a secret domestic arm. In early May, a story in the *Times* revealed that American planes were bombing Cambodia. The leak of secret information greatly worried the new President. The war was by far the most important issue facing the country, and the full story of the President's actions had the potential for disabusing the public of the idea that the Administration meant to end the war quickly, and therefore had the potential for destroying the atmosphere of "quiet dignity" and calm which the Administration was then claiming as one of its accomplishments. The President, H. R. Haldeman, and Henry Kissinger arranged to have certain of their own colleagues and five newsmen wiretapped, at least partly in the hope of discovering the source of the leak. (Kissinger supplied the names of several of his aides for tapping.) No Cabinet Secretaries were tapped, but several of the men closest to them were. They were William H. Sullivan, Deputy Assistant Secretary of State for East Asian and Pacific Affairs, and Richard

Pedersen, Counsellor of the Department of State, close associates of the Secretary of State William Rogers; Air Force Colonel Robert Pursely, a top military assistant to Secretary of Defense Melvin Laird; and James McLane, a White House aide with close ties to Robert Finch, the Secretary of Health, Education, and Welfare. The newsmen included Joseph Kraft and representatives of two of the most important news organizations in the country: Marvin Kalb, of CBS News; William Beecher and Hedrick Smith, of the *Times*. (The fifth newsman was Henry Brandon, Washington correspondent of the London *Sunday Times*.) Even though it was the leak that had spurred the program of surveillance, what it amounted to was about as effective a program of spot-checking the private conversations of official Washington as one could put together with a handful of wiretaps, provided that one did not go as far as to tap congressmen or Cabinet members or the chief editors of the news organizations. And, of course, whenever any of these people spoke with the people who were being tapped, one would hear them, too.

All the taps except one were carried out by the F.B.I., at the request of John Ehrlichman, without warrants. The exception was the tap on Joseph Kraft. That was placed by the chief of security of the Republican National Committee, with the assistance of a Secret Service employee, under the direction of John Caulfield, a retired New York City policeman. (Kraft did not, however, entirely escape the attention of the F.B.I. When he made a trip to Paris that spring, he was followed by William C. Sullivan, Assistant Director of the F.B.I., who arranged with local authorities for microphone surveillance of Kraft's hotel room.) Caulfield, whom Haldeman had hired after interviewing him at the Nixon campaign headquarters in New York, had as his primary duty supervising political investigations of the personal lives of potential candidates of the opposition party. (Ehrlichman had got his start in politics as a spy for Richard Nixon in the camp of a competing Republican candidate in the Presidential primaries of 1960.)

Leaders of democratic nations in wartime ordinarily have the comfort of knowing that their countrymen have freely chosen to share among themselves the terrible burdens of waging war. But

President Nixon, by secretly ordering the bombing of Cambodia, had in effect taken the entire burden of the war on his own shoulders. The tension, anger, rage, and grief of war, ordinarily diffused among a whole people, became compressed into the narrow zone of the White House. The President had turned the Oval Office into an emotional high-compression chamber. And if he soon began to regard the United States' success in the war as a matter of his personal vindication, and began to despise personally those who opposed him over the war, it may have been because the war was now literally "his war." He had made it so by excluding the public from knowledge of his plans. The President, by his own actions, had isolated himself from the country. The gap that had been opened between the public and the executive branch in the Johnson years had been opened again. But President Nixon's deceptions, although they were no greater in scale than President Johnson's, were different in kind, for when President Johnson escalated the war, the public had at least known that the war was being escalated, though it did not know by how much, whereas when President Nixon escalated the war, the public, owing to his assurances, believed that the war was coming to an end. In the United States in which the public lived, the war was almost over, and an open, trustworthy, even "mellow" White House was turning the nation toward peaceful pursuits. In the United States in which President Nixon lived, however, the war was growing, tension was building, and the level of suspicion had become so intense that he felt driven to spy on his own subordinates. The President had wanted to bring the country together, and he was bringing it together, but around an illusion—the illusion that the war would soon end. A country that was looking forward to imminent peace was being led by a President who was heading deeper into war. In his secret, embattled, isolated world, the country might be called upon at any moment to muster its determination for new military campaigns, but for the time being the determination was all his own. He had been in office less than four months.

As the war had continued, so had student protests against it. But in recent months the protests had taken a strange turn. Students had begun "occupying" buildings of their own universities. The strategy of the militant students who led these particular protests was complex. It was to try to provoke the university authorities into calling the police, who might then club and beat the students in the seized buildings, thus shocking and "radicalizing" the moderate majority of students by supposedly demonstrating that the power of the university rested on illegitimate force, just as the government's did in Vietnam. The strategy often succeeded. University officials often did call in the police, who often did club and beat the students, thereby radicalizing moderate students who might otherwise have kept out of it all. This sequence of events was repeated over and over around the country. To a public convinced that the war was coming to an end, the students' actions seemed not only illegal and outrageous but gratuitous. To many people, in fact, the war and the anti-war movement were like two symptoms of a single disease, and now that the people were convinced that one symptom—the war—was about to disappear, they were all the more eager to have this second symptom disappear, too. Now that the war was regarded by most people as "no longer an issue"—so the phrase went—the students seemed intent on prolonging the hated period of "national division" out of sheer perversity.

One important voice on the subject was the editorial page of the *Times*. "The crisis is nationwide," the *Times* editorialized in March. "It stems from the adoption of terroristic methods as a substitute for rationality." And in an editorial in May the *Times* wrote, "The left fascists are determined to rule or ruin. . . . The choice is now relatively simple. Either the administrators, faculty, and responsible student majority call the would-be professional revolutionaries to order, or the community at large will do so." The editorial was not a call to vigilantism. On the contrary, the *Times* was concerned for the independence of the universities and feared that student rebellion might provoke a repressive response—perhaps from the Nixon Administration. In other editorials, the *Times* advised the Administration to let university authorities handle the situation in the universities. The *Times,* of course, shared the general conviction that the war would soon end, and, having reported the belief of many educators that the Nixon Administration would then turn to the "dramatic escalation . . . of the urban and egalitarian-minded Johnson policies" in support of federal aid to education, it was perhaps afraid that the student rebellions would so anger the Administration as to jeopardize this happy turn of events.

The President, however, was attracted to the subject of student protest. His decision to expand the war and to expand it secretly had important consequences for his conduct of domestic politics. He had initiated new military campaigns, but how could he rally the people to victory when he had promised to end the war swiftly if it had not already been ended by Election Day, now six months past? But if President Nixon could not rally the people against the enemy abroad, he could vent the natural passions of a wartime leader on the anti-war protesters at home. The strong feelings building up in the White House, blocked from direct expression, could be displaced to this secondary object. And to the public the protesters were, if anything, more acceptable than the Vietcong as a target of Presidential anger, for unhappy though the public had grown with the war, it had perhaps grown even more unhappy with the rebellion against the war.

On March 20th, in Chicago, in an action that was bound to antagonize the anti-war movement, a federal grand jury, acting with the approval of John Mitchell's Justice Department, indicted eight leaders of the tumultuous demonstrations at the Democratic Convention in 1968. (Eight policemen were also indicted.) The demonstrators were accused of having violated a law recently passed by Congress which made it illegal to cross state lines to incite a riot. Soon the "Chicago Eight" became a *cause célèbre.* Two days after the indictments were handed up, the President, in one of the first major statements of his Presidency, addressed himself to the subject of student rebellion. He sounded an apocalyptic note. "It is not too strong a statement to declare that this is the way civilizations begin to die," he said. "The process is altogether too familiar to those who would survey the wreckage of history. . . . As Yeats foresaw, 'Things fall apart; the center cannot hold.' " As though heeding those who advised that the Administration stay out of university affairs, the President said that the federal government would not become involved. Then he immediately involved it, by announcing, in the same statement, that Secretary Finch, of H.E.W., had written a letter to the nation's college and university presidents. One section of the letter read, "I ask that you bring to the attention of your students the applicable provisions of these laws and advise them of the procedures you intend to follow in complying with them." (Finch was referring to recently enacted statutes that denied government loans and scholarships to students convicted of crimes in campus disorders.)

As the spring advanced, the Administration's tone grew more and more menacing. At the beginning of May, Attorney General Mitchell said, "This Administration has tried to be patient in the hope that students, faculty, and local officials working together would put an end to all this chaos, but the time has come for an end to patience." By June, the President was in a state of extreme excitement and alarm. He had already said more on this subject than on almost any other, although it was a subject that by his own account the federal government would leave alone. In early June, at a speech at General Beadle State College, in Madison, South Dakota, he said, "Our fundamental values [are] under bitter and even violent attack." And he went on, "We live in a deeply troubled and profoundly unsettled time. Drugs, crime, campus revolts, racial discord, draft resistance—on every hand we find old standards violated, old values discarded." Mentioning "the forces and threats of force that have racked our cities and now our colleges," he continued to raise the spectre of civil war in America, and, rattling the federal sword in advance, pointed out that if the students and the government should go to war the government would be the victor: "Force can be contained. We have the power to strike back if need be, and to prevail. . . . It has not been a lack of civil power, but the reluctance of a free people to employ it that so often has stayed the hand of authorities faced with confrontation." The next day, he spoke again, this time at the graduation exercises of the United States Air Force Academy. Declaring that in contemporary America "it's open season on the armed forces," he broadened his assault on the rebellious students to include another menace to the United States: "skeptics and isolationists." He meant members of Congress—most of them liberal Democrats—who had just recently begun to ask publicly when or if the war was going to be brought to an end. "The skeptics and isolationists . . . have lost the vision indispensable to great leadership," he said. And he said, "Our arms must be mighty, ready for instant action, so that no potential aggressor may be tempted to risk his own destruction. . . . When a war can be decided in twenty minutes, the nation that is behind will have no time to catch up. . . . The weak can only plead, magnanimity and restraint gain moral meaning coming from the strong." For a President who only four months earlier had promised peace and warned against "bombastic rhetoric that postures instead of persuading," these were rough words.

About a week after the President's speeches at General Beadle State College and the Air Force Academy, and several weeks after he had begun wiretapping newsmen, Cabinet aides, and White House aides, the Justice Department filed a brief in Federal Court in connection with the Chicago conspiracy trial which, after revealing that the government had used electronic surveillance to monitor the conversations of several of those who had been indicted, asserted that, even without a warrant, the government had the power to wiretap anyone who in its judgment was out to "attack and subvert the government by unlawful means." The members of Nixon's entourage had been preoccupied with the subject of wiretapping even before they came to power. In 1968, Congress had passed a law permitting the Justice Department to place wiretaps on American citizens in certain cases, provided that it first obtained a court warrant in each case. Attorney General Ramsey Clark, however, had declined to use this new grant of authority, because he considered it un-Constitutional. As a candidate, Mr. Nixon had made it clear that one of the things his Attorney General would do would be to make good use of the wiretapping power, and when Attorney General-designate Mitchell was asked at his confirmation hearing how his stewardship would differ from Clark's, he had answered that he would not shrink from using wiretaps. Now, in the court brief, the Justice Department was asserting a power to wiretap without first obtaining a warrant. The attorneys for the defendants in the conspiracy trial in Chicago were outraged, and they declared, "For the first time in American history, a member of the President's Cabinet has publicly—and proudly—stated that he has, in open violation of his oath of office, taken the law into his own hands." The Chicago defendants and their attorneys had no way of knowing, of course, that the President and, in some cases, the Attorney General had already ordered a program of warrantless wiretaps, not only against radicals who were thought to be out to "attack and subvert the government" but against newsmen and White House aides, and that the Justice Department's argument in court would provide, if not a legal justification, then, at least, an assertion of a justification, for the record, in case the wiretapping became known. The mere assertion in court that something is legal doesn't make it legal—even provisionally—but the Justice Department's claim set the stage for the Administration to argue one day that the courts had not yet ruled on the point.

In the early summer, the Administration turned its attention to domestic affairs, and the long-awaited specific programs began to emerge. On June 26th, Attorney General Mitchell went to Capitol Hill to testify against a renewal of the Voting Rights Act of 1965, which was due to expire in August of 1970, and to suggest a greatly weakened bill in its place. The Voting Rights Act had been one of the most effective pieces of civil-rights legislation passed in the Johnson years: under the act the registration of black voters in the South had gone up more than a hundred per cent in four years. Mitchell's testimony was the first of a series of moves by the Administration in the area of civil rights. The moves were not covert, but they were often presented misleadingly. The President began to act to weaken civil-rights programs while continuing to speak as though he supported them. When it had been made known that, as President-elect, he had promised to do more for black people than any President before him, his commitment had enjoyed wide support within his Administration. But earlier, during the fall campaign, he had announced that he opposed the use of the federal government's principal method of promoting integrated schools: enforcing federal desegregation guidelines by cutting off federal funds for schools that were out of compliance. On one occasion, he had said to a Southern television audience, "To use the power of the federal Treasury to withhold funds in order to carry [desegregation] out—then I think we are going too far." And he had implied that he would work to change that. This commitment, too, had found wide support in his Administration. The apparent contradiction between the two commitments had been one of the many ambiguities displayed by the "new Nixon" in late 1968. But whereas during that period the difference between his shifting points of view had been only a matter of words, the difference was now reflected in a sharp division of bureaucratic forces which ran from top to bottom of an Administration. For if the President had not made his position on civil rights clear to the public, neither had he made it clear to the executive branch. As spring passed into summer and no directive that would settle the matter came out of the Oval Office, each aspect of the Administration's civil-rights policy became an object of intense internal bureaucratic struggle. At issue was not merely whether to go forward with or to hold back on racial integration but whether to comply with or to break the law—or, as President Nixon had put it in his Inaugural Address, whether or not "to give life to what is in the law." In the matter of integrating schools, the law was unambiguous. In May of 1968, the Supreme Court had ruled that plans for desegregation must be carried out, and that the plans must be shown "realistically to work," and "to work now." Two warring factions took shape within the Administration. Favoring compliance were, among others, Secretary Finch, of H.E.W.; most members of the civil-rights office of H.E.W.; and most members of the civil-rights division of the Justice Department. Favoring noncompliance through delay were Attorney General Mitchell; the leaders of the Republican Party in the South; and some members of the White House staff. Mitchell, a former law partner of the President's, favored the Southern strategy, and he was known to be the most influential of the President's advisers. Among those who said so was Mitchell himself. During the campaign, he had met with a group of friendly congressmen and had told them, with a bluntness characteristic of him, "I'm running the show. I bring more business into the firm than he [Nixon] does. When I tell Dick Nixon what to do, he listens. I'm in charge." Political considerations weighed in on the side of noncompliance. The Administration saw very little hope of winning the votes of blacks, no matter what it did in regard to civil rights, but it hoped that by putting a "Southern strategy" into effect it could win the votes of Southern whites.

During most of the spring, the pro-compliance forces had had the upper hand, but by the beginning of summer the Mitchell forces had begun to prevail. On July 3rd, a week after Mitchell had given his testimony, a bulletin from H.E.W. and the Justice Department stated that federal guidelines for integration in 1969 would be enforced, but added that "in some districts there may be sound reasons for some limited delay." One civil-rights leader—Roy Wilkins, the head of the National Association for the Advancement of Colored People—accused the Administration of "breaking the law," and went on to say, "It's almost enough to make you vomit." In August, Finch capitulated, and joined in a plan to send Justice Department lawyers into court to oppose plans already drafted by men in his own department for the integration of thirty-three school districts in Mississippi. The chief technical expert on desegregation plans in the Office of Education, in Finch's own department, had assured the Fifth Circuit Court of Appeals that "each of the . . . plans is educationally and administratively sound," but now Finch reversed the Department's position, and wrote, in a letter to Chief Judge John Brown, of that court, that the plans "must surely, in my judgment, produce chaos, confusion and a catastrophic educational setback to the 135,700 children, black and white alike, who must look to the

41

222 schools of these Mississippi districts for their only available educational opportunities." The Justice Department followed this letter up by bringing witnesses to court to testify against the plans. A rebellion broke out in the Justice Department, and sixty-five of a total of seventy-four lawyers in nonsupervisory positions in its civil-rights division signed a letter of protest to Attorney General Mitchell.

By the fall, the public record abounded with words and actions of the Nixon Administration concerning the racial issue in the United States, and they showed the Administration to be involved in a full-scale retreat in the area of civil rights. The issue was one of those that had had a strong bearing on the President's promise to bring the country together; the division "between black and white" had always been included in the litany of the nation's divisions. Yet in the course of the summer the Administration's actions stirred very little interest and did next to nothing to dispel the impression that the White House really meant what it had said about bringing the country together. One reason may have been that, although a policy had clearly taken shape, it was never announced. In fact, Administration spokesmen had steadfastly denied that a retreat was under way. In April, Secretary Finch had stated that no change in the federal guidelines for integration was contemplated. In June, he had said there would be "no softening or modifying" of the guidelines, though he added that they were being reëvaluated to provide "a more realistic time approach." Attorney General Mitchell, who had worked all summer to weaken civil-rights programs, said in a mid-August speech that racial discrimination was morally, legally, and socially wrong, and had to be "substantially eliminated if we are to survive as a nation of free and independent people." Now, in September, the President said, "There are those who want instant integration and those who want segregation forever. I believe that we need to have a middle course between those two extremes." These statements and others like them apparently carried greater weight with the press and with the public in 1969 than the news of what the Administration was actually doing.

Soon the Administration's two major efforts to weaken civil-rights programs were blocked by other branches of the government. In October, the Supreme Court, in language that closely resembled its 1968 decision, ordered integration of the Mississippi districts "at once." And a few months later the Congress rejected the weakening modifications proposed by Mitchell and renewed the Voting Rights Act in a stronger form than ever. Oddly, the Administration, having testified against the act in the House, had failed to follow up with its usual lobbying efforts to block passage in the Senate. In its first moves on civil rights, therefore, the Administration had challenged the Congress not to renew an act that enjoyed great popularity with the members, and had been overruled; and it had challenged the Supreme Court to repudiate a clear ruling of only one year back, and had again been overruled. It had moved to undercut the two main pillars of the civil-rights movement, but in a manner that would predictably fail.

In July, a group of worried civil-rights workers had met with Attorney General Mitchell, and by way of reassurance he had told them, "You will be better advised to watch what we do instead of what we say." He apparently meant to suggest that the Administration's public statements would be deceptive, and certainly they were. But by the fall it was not what the Administration said that was upsetting the civil-rights workers—for had not Mitchell declared that racial discrimination would have to be "eliminated" if the United States was to "survive as a nation"? By then, it was clear that he would have been giving them sounder reassurance if he had added that the Administration's deeds would be deceptive, too, but that those at whom the deception was aimed would not be the civil-rights workers. Those to be deceived by the Administration's actions were the white Southerners who, disregarding the Administration's promises to give life to the law, rested their hopes on Administration moves—the moves that would predictably fail to halt integration. In the Administration's plans, the words would deceive the civil-rights workers, and the actions would deceive the Southern segregationists, and in the process the political onus for integration would shift from the executive branch of the government to the legislative and judicial branches.

An Administration policy on a major issue—race—had unfolded to a temporary conclusion. It revealed a convoluted style of action. The policy had been improvised through bureaucratic struggle, not planned in advance; it had emerged piecemeal, without formal explanation beforehand or elucidation afterward; it had challenged the law, and the challenge had apparently been meant not to succeed but to fail, and, in failing, to create a politically favorable public image.

On July 11th, fifteen days after Mitchell testified before the House Judiciary Committee against renewal of the Voting Rights Act, the Administration, in a move in a second important area of domestic affairs, proposed the District of Columbia Court Reorganization Act, a crime bill for the District of Columbia which had been drafted at the Justice Department and was widely understood to be a model for a national crime bill. (There was little change in the situation in Vietnam or elsewhere abroad during this period.) The D.C. crime bill (as the bill was soon referred to) contained, among its many provisions, one that would empower judges in the District to jail some criminal suspects for sixty days before trial, and one that would allow policemen to break into houses without showing a search warrant. The first provision, which came to be known as "preventive detention," would apparently suspend due process, and the second, which came to be known as the "no-knock" provision, would apparently violate the Fourth Amendment's protection against unreasonable searches and seizures. One Constitutional expert in the Senate—Senator Sam Ervin, of North Carolina—condemned the bill as a "garbage pail" of "repressive" legislation, and said, "This bill might better be entitled 'A Bill to Repeal the Fourth, Fifth, Sixth, and Eighth Amendments to the Constitution.'"

Until 1968, the issue of crime had never played an important role in Presidential politics. One reason was that the law assigns the task of criminal law enforcement to local authorities, not to the federal government. (This was why the Nixon Administration had found itself unable to intervene in the student disruptions.) Soon after taking office, the President and his men were reminded of the Constitutional limits of their powers in this field by Donald Santarelli, a young lawyer who had drafted many of the President's statements on crime during the 1968 campaign and was chosen by President Nixon to be Associate Deputy Attorney General in charge of the Justice Department's Office of Criminal Justice. In early 1969, Santarelli met with John Ehrlichman, Attorney General Mitchell, and the President, and told them that—as he later recalled the substance of his remarks—"the reach of the federal government's power in law enforcement did not penetrate to the state or local level . . . where most of the street crime people were afraid of existed." And since "the federal government simply did not have the machinery or authority to deal with crime in America outside of the District of Columbia," he told them, "in the rest of America, the only thing we could do was to exercise vigorous symbolic leadership." The idea of exercising "symbolic leadership" struck a responsive chord in the thinking of the President and his advisers. Whereas the men in the Johnson Administration had believed that the roots of crime were to be found in social conditions, and had looked to a combination of improvements in police work, reform of the penal system, and a wide array of social programs in poverty areas for remedies, the Nixon men believed that the roots of crime were in attitudes—in a moral climate they described as "permissive"—and that a change in attitudes was the remedy. Some of the blame for the spread of the permissive moral climate, they thought, lay with parents who, guided by modern theories of child-rearing, were too lenient with their children; some of it lay with "soft" educators; some of it lay with politicians who "encouraged" criminals by attributing crime to social conditions rather than to the criminals' moral failings; but most of it lay with the judicial system, and especially with the Justices of the Supreme Court. The Supreme Court had given the "green light" to "the criminal elements," Mr. Nixon had said in the campaign. He meant that by handing down decisions that affirmed or expanded the rights of criminal suspects—decisions such as the one in the case of Miranda v. Arizona, in which the Court had ruled that the police must inform all criminal suspects of their rights upon arrest, including the right to remain silent and the right to the presence of an attorney, and that the police must also warn the suspect that "any statement he does make may be used as evidence against him"—the Court had signalled an attitude of leniency toward criminals. The President had never argued that revision of the laws would enable prosecutors to convict and jail so many more criminals that the crime rates would fall. Rather, he apparently meant that statutes like the no-knock statute and the preventive-detention statute would serve as a "symbolic" warning—a red light—to the "criminal forces" (as the President phrased it). New, tough laws, he seemed to believe, would change the moral climate, and in the changed climate crime rates would fall.

If "symbolic leadership" was suited to what the Administration saw as the primarily moral nature of the problem of lawlessness, it was also suited to the public-relations needs of political strategy. Egil Krogh, a deputy counsel to the President with special responsibility for law-enforcement programs in the District of Columbia, later said to a reporter in reference to the Administration's crime bills, including the D.C. crime bill of 1969, "I would call them political law-and-order bills." As for no-knock and preventive detention, "the final legislation reflected the rhetoric of the 1968 campaign," he said; and he went on, "It was my view that while these bills would suggest a tough law-and-order demeanor by the Administration, the legislation itself did not provide an enhanced ability to the police departments or to the courts to reduce crime as such. The no-knock legislation struck me, and also Mr. Ehrlichman, as almost inherently repressive in tone. . . . Jerry Wilson [the police chief of Washington, D.C.] stated to me that he had adequate authority to enter a dwelling where there was a probable cause, and to legislate that power through the no-knock bill was unnecessary. . . . He viewed that more as a sort of law-and-order window dressing rather than as initiatives that would strike at the core of the problem. . . . The political purpose [was], by supporting this legislation, [to appeal to] the sense of anxiety and urgency felt [by some people concerning] the law-enforcement issue rather than really being directed at curbing a real problem." In the area of crime, as in the area of civil rights, the Administration was subordinating the substance of government to the image of government. In many past Administrations, images had been created to enhance policies; now policies were being framed to enhance images. Emergency measures were being taken not to meet emergencies—not to solve "a real problem"—but to seem to meet emergencies. One young aide, after working with the new Administration for a few months on anti-crime programs, came to the conclusion that "all government is seventy-five per cent P.R." In the area of crime, moves were designed to produce an image of "toughness"—even of repressiveness. Some observers at the time took note of the Administration's repressive tendencies, but few supposed that the Administration was elaborately scheming to make itself appear repressive. The D.C. crime bill resembled the Administration's move in civil rights in another respect, too: it was expected not to pass. The strategy was to propose a bill that the Congress was likely to turn down and then to blame Congress for its "soft" approach to crime. As an Office of Management and Budget paper titled "Crime Control and Law Enforcement: Political Position for 1970 Election" put it a few months later, "the Administration position in the crime field depends on our ability to shift blame for crime bills' inaction to Congress and concurrently to hammer home comprehensive Administration programs." In its efforts to weaken civil-rights legislation, the Administration had succeeded in failing, but this time it failed to fail. The Congress, apparently afraid of the political consequences of seeming to be "soft" on crime, passed the bill.

On August 8th, in a move in a third important area of domestic affairs, the President went on all three major television networks in prime time to propose a sweeping program called the Family Assistance Plan. Under the plan, outright grants of money on the basis of income would replace the tangled, heavily bureaucratized welfare system that had grown up under President Johnson. Unlike the civil-rights program and the crime bills, this program did seem to represent a significant attempt to carry through in action the

47

President's promise to bring the nation together in the realm of domestic policy, for the Family Assistance Plan was the sort of program that the President's opposition might be expected to approve. Once again, however, there was a gap between image and substance—between what the Administration said and what it did. The President was under heavy pressure from conservative quarters not to set up a program of "giveaways" that might undermine the recipients' will to find jobs, and, in an apparent effort to satisfy the conservatives, he called the program "workfare" in his speech. It was not a program of "guaranteed income," he said, and he added, "To put it bluntly and simply, any system which makes it more profitable for a man not to work than to work . . . is wrong and indefensible." In fact, the Family Assistance Plan was precisely a program of guaranteed income, and by introducing his new program in this confusing manner the President made a minor detail of the plan—a provision aimed at mildly penalizing recipients who did not work—seem to be its main plank. The debate that followed concentrated on that detail rather than on the central merits of the proposal. Liberals and conservatives both asked, "Is it really 'workfare'?" In liberal circles, the President's reputation as a man concerned with social justice was already low. An atmosphere in which Roy Wilkins was ready to "vomit" was a poor one for any social program of the President's. The directors of the California Community Action Program—an outfit that had been set up in the Johnson years and might be closed down under the new plan—were only a bit more heated than many others when they called the plan a "regeneration of domestic neocolonialism in dealing with the poor." Resistance from liberals in Congress was also based largely on the misapprehension that what the President had said about his bill was true, and that the federal government would soon be in the business of coercing people to perform menial tasks, probably at very low wages. The liberals had decided that the plan really was "workfare." Conservative objections, too, were focussed on the question of work requirements. The conservatives *wanted* strict work requirements, but they, unlike their liberal colleagues, quickly realized that the bill did not contain them. They understood that the plan was "workfare" only in name. Eventually, the combined opposition of liberals and conservatives killed the bill in the Senate.

When Attorney General Mitchell told the civil-rights workers to watch what the Administration did instead of what it said, he was giving them confusing advice, but if he had said the same thing in connection with the Family Assistance Plan, the advice would have been sound. For "workfare" was a liberal program in conservative clothing. The President acknowledged as much in an informal comment to Daniel Moynihan, one of the architects of the plan—and himself a strong believer in liberal programs put through in conservative disguises—saying, "Tory men and liberal policies are what have changed the world." But in the summer of 1969 the President's formulation held only for his welfare policy. In his strategy on civil rights, he was advancing a conservative program in liberal clothing. (In his policy on crime, he was cloaking a non-policy in a conservative disguise.) The advocates of civil rights, having waked up to what was happening in the case of civil rights, assumed Family Assistance to be more of the same. In his announcement of the plan, the President had again meant to fool the conservative half of his audience while winking at the liberal half. But the reverse occurred. The liberals were fooled, the conservatives were undeceived, and "workfare" was doomed.

By September, as the nation returned to work and school after the summer holidays, many vivid signs of a new, combative mood in the White House were on the public record. The President had delivered his menacing speeches on the subject of student protests, he had made his apparent attempt to repeal some of the civil-rights advances of the Johnson years, and he had proposed his harsh legislation for dealing with criminal suspects. The nation was not being brought together. Yet these signs somehow still failed to catch the nation's attention, and in early September James Reston could still write in the *Times* that the President was "toning everything down—talking softly, urging caution, bringing home some troops, cutting new Federal construction, lowering his voice, and advocating restraint and coöperation at home and abroad." In June, Mr. Nixon had announced an initial withdrawal of twenty-five thousand American troops from Vietnam. The notion that the war was ending and the country entering upon a more tranquil era had become something like an unshakable conviction. It was as though in 1968 peace and national unity had been settled upon as the theme for the next four years, and any events that failed to carry out the theme were deprived of their significance and were invisible. Somehow, an image had been fixed in place which mere events could not easily dislodge. The public, of course, was unaware that the President had paced his troop withdrawals from the war with bombing escalations of the war, and since the war had been at the root of the nation's turmoil, it was difficult for most people to imagine that the turmoil could continue while the war—they believed—was ending.

The Nixon Administration's apparent ability in the summer of 1969 to establish an image of itself, and even of the national life as a whole, that was sharply at odds with the facts marked a new stage in the public-relations revolution that had been under way in American politics for many years. The techniques of public relations had originally been developed in the business world, but politicians had soon recognized that they could be extremely useful in politics as well. In fact, their applicability to politics was, if anything, greater than their applicability to business. If nuclear weapons had been by far the strongest influence on politics in the postwar period, television—the most powerful machine for the establishment of images ever devised—had certainly been the second-strongest. For politics—and particularly electoral politics—was a dance of images in its purest form. When an advertising campaign persuaded a consumer to buy a product, the consumer then at least possessed something tangible against which to test the image. But when public relations persuaded a voter to put a politician in office, the voter was left with only another image against which to test his choice—the image propagated by the man in office. There were, of course, connections between the voter's experience in his own life and the politician's performance, but these were often vague or concealed. As a candidate for various offices, Nixon had learned that a wound to the image could sometimes prove mortal to its subject's chances for success—something that not only politicians but corporations, movie stars, publications, religious groups, revolutionary groups, and many others had found out from bitter experience. When he assumed the Presidency, he brought a team of public-relations experts to power with him. There was his chief of staff, H. R. Haldeman; his appointments secretary, Dwight Chapin; his press secretary, Ronald Ziegler; and one of his speechwriters, William Safire—and those were only a few of the men in his Administration with experience in advertising agencies and public relations. They all soon realized that the resources for image-making available to a President were incomparably greater than those available to a candidate. For one thing, a President could command unrivalled access to the channels of communication; his every gesture was news, and his speeches were often carried live on all three of the major television networks. For another thing, he could exert a profound influence upon the press and other independent sources of the public's impression of political events. Moreover, while casting the Presidential spotlight on some events (or non-events), he could shroud other events in secrecy. Most important of all, however, was his ability actually to shape events in order to promote images. By using the resources of government to compose scenes rather than to solve real problems, a President could build up an illusory world that not even the most determined reporters could tear down. In his first eight months, President Nixon, through the use of all these techniques, had established what amounted almost to a new form of rule, in which images were given precedence over substance in every phase of government. The secrecy surrounding the bombing of Cambodia and the warrantless wiretaps had turned out to be only the first steps in a far broader separation of image and substance in the Nixon Administration's conduct of its affairs. In each of those instances, a major action had simply been concealed. In other Administration policies, the relationship between image and substance became more elaborate. In its civil-rights policy, the Administration presented a conservative program as a liberal program. In its crime policy, it took actions that it knew were futile in order to create an appearance of effective action and to transfer the blame for inaction to the political opposition. In its welfare policy, it presented a liberal program as a conservative program, and the image was so convincing that the liberals joined the conservatives to defeat the program. But whether the Administration was saying one thing in public while doing the opposite in secret or was saying one thing in public while doing the opposite also in public, and whether it was cloaking liberal programs in conservative disguises or cloaking conservative programs in liberal disguises, and whether it was framing policy that was meant to succeed or framing policy that was meant to fail, the one constant was that it had broken the unity of word and deed which makes political action intelligible to the rest of the world.

After a summer of attending to domestic affairs, the nation's attention began to swing back to the war. That fall, many of the people who had actively opposed the war in 1968 began to grow impatient, and the first large cracks in the public's conviction that it had embarked on a period of peace and national unity appeared. On September 16th, the President announced the withdrawal of thirty-five thousand more troops from Vietnam. The number was not great enough to satisfy the anti-war movement, and plans were laid for demonstrations in Washington and other cities on October 15th. The anti-war movement had changed since the spring of 1968, when it was last heard from. The Presidential candidacies of Senator Eugene McCarthy and Senator Robert Kennedy, together with the retirement of President Johnson, had then given it political weight. And as it had entered electoral politics, a militant fringe had separated itself from the main body, and the main body had gained still more in political strength from other quarters. All at once, reports of the protest pervaded the news. The anti-war movement seemed to have burst out of its confines on the left-wing fringes of American politics and to have flooded the center. It had become respectable. Now, for the first time, an anti-war demonstration received qualified editorial support in major newspapers, including the *Times*. A poll showed that fifty-seven per cent of the public favored a withdrawal of all American troops from the war by a date certain—a position that the marchers supported and the President opposed. The protest on October 15th turned out to be an event of immense proportions. Forty thousand people marched peacefully in Washington; sixty-five thousand attended a series of rallies in New York; a hundred thousand marched in Boston; and smaller observances and ceremonies were held all around the country. The anti-war movement was older and tireder, but also broader, than it had ever been before. A second demonstration was planned for November 15th.

In the White House, tempers were rising. Had the President meant to withdraw from the war soon, as he had seemed to say in the Presidential campaign, the gathering strength of the anti-war movement might not have worried him. As it was, he felt obliged to strike back. The "basic need," he wrote in a memo to Haldeman in late September, "is *not* PR—it's PO." Not, that is, public relations but a Presidential Offensive. The need, he said in another memo, was for a "Nixon Big Charge." A Big Charge, of course, was a far cry from the advice he had given in January to "lower our voices." But whether one might call the incipient campaign PR or PO or a Big Charge, it was in fact public relations. On September 22nd, the President dictated no fewer than eight memoranda on the subject to H. R. Haldeman. He foresaw a fierce struggle just ahead. "I do not want to continue to slide along with what I fear is an inadequate response and an amateurish response to what will be an enormous challenge in the next two or three months," he wrote. In one of his memos, he listed some of the themes he wished his people to emphasize. "When we have our Public-Relations discussion on Saturday, I think we ought to put down five or six public-relations goals that we want to impress on the public consciousness," he wrote. They were "hard work, dignity, staff treatment (compared with Johnson), boldness in offering new programs, world leader restoring respect for United States [in] the world, RN family, and others that may come to mind." Nixon also had comments on public-relations efforts that had been set in motion already. "I have completed a very thorough analysis of the reports made by HK [Henry Kissinger] E [Ehrlichman] and Harlow [Bryce Harlow, a White House aide] which were submitted to me at San Clemente," he said. "On the four PR fronts, I asked for coverage. In general, I think I could sum up my reaction in this way—the only area where we really came through with a better-than-average grade (and here it was considerably better than average) was on Family Assistance and Welfare and the New Federalism. This was due to a plan executed and followed through. On the Foreign Policy front, on the Nixon Big Charge front, our record in the Congress and the others are performances considerably lower than average. . . . I have reached the conclusion that we simply have to have that full-time PR Director, who will have no other assignments except to bulldog these three or four major issues we may select each week or each month and follow through on directives that I give but, more importantly, come up with ideas of his own."

In the days just before and just after the October demonstration, Jeb Stuart Magruder, an aide of Haldeman's who specialized in matters having to do with the press, began to devise a "Game Plan" for the Nixon Big Charge. A special Planning Objectives group began to meet. The day after the demonstration, Dwight Chapin wrote a memo to Haldeman, in which he listed a number of steps that should be taken. In the period from October 20th to October 26th, "a full-fledged drive should be put against the media," he thought. It would involve "letters, visits to editorial boards, ads, TV announcements, phone calls. (In New York, the networks should be visited by groups of our supporters—the highest level—and cold turkey should be talked.)" Also, "A representative of the Justice Department and a spokesman for the F.B.I. should hold a press conference on Monday, October 20th. They would brief the press with documented information on the leaders of the two movements." (Chapin was speaking of the two groups who were sponsoring the demonstration in the capital in November—the Vietnam Moratorium Committee and the New Mobilization Committee to End the War in Vietnam.) Having prepared the ground with these and other measures, the time would be ripe, Chapin thought, for "the appearance of pro-Administration sentiment." He wrote, "It should be shown by all—each in their own way—but what they do must be visible. It does not have to be group-oriented—it can be as simple as everyone wearing a flag lapel pin, writing letters to Congressmen and so on. It might be an idea to ask the networks to tell it to Hanoi —what if the networks were set as the sounding board for the vast segment of American people who support the President and his peace efforts. Thousands of wires, letters, and petitions to the networks."

Around this time, too, Nixon began to shower his aides with scores of little memos ordering them to do something about news stories that had annoyed him. He had never cared for the men of the press, and he was given to remarking to his aides, "the press is the enemy." Two days after the march, Jeb Magruder collected and sent to Haldeman about twenty requests that the President had made in the past thirty days, and these, Magruder wrote in an accompanying memo to Haldeman, were perhaps only a third of the total number. Some of the President's requests were for sweeping action. In a memo to Klein he had asked that Klein (as Magruder described it in his memo) "take appropriate action to counter biased TV coverage of the Adm. over the summer." A memo sent to Patrick Buchanan was, Magruder noted, a "request for a report on what actions were taken to complain to NBC, *Time,* and *Newsweek* concerning . . . recent coverage on the Administration." Other requests from the President were highly specific. Many minute details of news coverage inspired memos to his aides. One of the memos was (again in Magruder's words) "President's request for letters to the editor of *Newsweek* mentioning the President's tremendous reception in Mississippi and last Sat. Miami Dolphin football game." Another was "President's request that we have the Chicago *Tribune* hit Senator Percy hard on his ties with the peace group." (The President seemed to believe he had control over the editorial policies of the *Tribune.*) Another, which had been sent to a White House aide named Alexander Butterfield, asked for "a report . . . from our

P.R. efforts following up the Friday press conference." And a memo to Patrick Buchanan asked that "appropriate columnists be informed of the extemporaneous character of Presidential press conferences."

Magruder had titled his memo to Haldeman "The Shotgun Versus the Rifle." The "shotgun" was the technique of peppering the press with scores of scattered complaints from the White House, and Magruder thought it ineffective. "When an editor gets continual calls from Herb Klein or Pat Buchanan on a situation that is difficult to document as to unfairness, we are in a very weak area," he wrote. The "rifle" was the technique of using "concentrated efforts" against "the media and other anti-Administration spokesmen," and Magruder preferred it. He had five proposals to make. The first was to "begin an official monitoring system through the F.C.C. [Federal Communications Commission] as soon as Dean Burch is officially on board as chairman." (Burch, a former aide to Senator Barry Goldwater, had been nominated for the chairmanship of the F.C.C., but had not yet been confirmed.) The second was to "utilize the anti-trust division [of the Department of Justice] to investigate various media relating to anti-trust violations." Magruder believed that "even the possible threat of anti-trust action . . . would be effective in changing their views." The third was "utilizing the Internal Revenue Service as a method to look into the organizations that we are most concerned about," for he believed that "just a threat of an I.R.S. investigation will probably turn their approach." The fourth was to "begin to show favorites within the media." And the fifth was to "utilize Republican National Committee for major letter writing efforts." In concluding, Magruder warned against the consequences of a failure "to use the power at hand to achieve our long-term goal, which is eight years of a Republican Administration."

Four days after the October demonstrations, Vice-President Agnew launched a ferocious attack on the leaders of the anti-war movement in a speech. He called them an "effete corps of impudent snobs who characterized themselves as intellectuals." Another demonstration was planned for November 15th, and the Vice-President described the organizers as "hard-core dissidents and professional anarchists," who were bent on holding a "wilder, more violent" demonstration than the one in October. Going on to give an explanation he had worked out of how young people were persuaded to join a demonstration, he said, "The young, at the zenith of physical power and sensitivity, overwhelm themselves with drugs and artificial stimulants. Thus, subtlety is lost and fine distinctions based on acute reasoning are carelessly ignored in a headlong jump to a predetermined conclusion." (Agnew, who derided people who "characterized themselves as intellectuals," himself used many intellectual-sounding phrases in his speeches.) In a speech at the end of October, Agnew, speaking of "arrogant ones" who "have a masochistic compulsion to destroy their country's strength whether or not it is constructive," said, "They rouse themselves to a continual emotional crescendo—substituting disruptive demonstrations for reason." Soon he began to employ some of the rhetoric usually associated with the European Fascist movements of the nineteen-thirties. He asserted that "anarchists and Communists," abetted by "ideological eunuchs," were, like "vultures who sit in trees" and "prey upon the good intentions of gullible men," perverting "honest concern to something sick and rancid." And, referring again to the "glib, activist element," the "impudent snobs who characterized themselves as intellectuals," he said, "We can, however, afford to separate them from our society with no more regret than we should feel over discarding rotten apples from a barrel." The Vice-President's speeches were something new in American politics. They were long, rambling sessions of abuse, apparently unconnected with government policies —sheer outbursts of angry feeling. They were not spontaneous outbursts, however. The Vice-President read them out verbatim from prepared texts, speaking in a flat monotone. President Johnson, toward the end of his term, had become so enraged with the opposition that he harbored the suspicion that they were literally traitors, but he had kept that idea to himself. Now President Nixon found himself thinking the same thoughts, but, unlike Johnson, he had discovered in his Vice-President an instrument for their public expression. Since the Inauguration, the Nixon White House had been evolving in two opposite directions. In many of its public pronouncements, the Administration portrayed itself as open, trusting, and conciliatory, and dedicated to unifying a divided country. But, especially in its covert actions, a new policy—almost a new Administration—had been taking shape. This Administration was angry, suspicious, and vengeful. Now, as the Nixon Big Charge began, with the Vice-President in the front rank, this other Administration burst suddenly into full view.

The Vice-President's rise in American politics had been swift and had involved some surprising twists and turns. In 1960, he had been a member of the Zoning Board of Appeals of Baltimore County, Maryland. He ran for Circuit Court Judge in Baltimore County that year and lost. Two years later, he ran for County Executive and won. In 1966, he ran for Governor of Maryland, against a Democrat who made open appeals to racist sentiment, and he won with a heavy crossover vote and strong support from the black community. His reputation was that of a liberal Republican. He supported the 1968 Presidential aspirations of Governor Nelson Rockefeller, of New York—who was also a liberal Republican at the time—until Rockefeller withdrew, that March, and he put through the first open-housing law in his state's history. But before his Vice-Presidential nomination he seemed to change his political stripe, veering sharply to the right. The change became evident after a riot in the black community in Baltimore in April. Agnew called moderate black leaders into his Baltimore office and angrily blamed them for the riot, saying they had not done enough to restrain more militant leaders—leaders he called "the circuit-riding, Hanoi-visiting, caterwauling, riot-inciting, burn-America-down type of leader." The moderate leaders were insulted, and many walked out.

As Agnew rose in politics, he worked out a system of bribes and kickbacks from contractors doing business with the state government. Sometimes the money, which in some years amounted to more than ten thousand dollars, was handed to him personally, in the form of cash in unmarked envelopes. At one point, he explained to an accomplice that such payments were part of "the system." (Now Agnew was attacking people who he thought wanted to tear down "the system.") As Vice-President, he continued to receive payments from some of the contractors, but, although his office was higher, the amounts were smaller. He also received a reduction in the rent of his Washington apartment, and received weekly deliveries of free groceries from a nearby supermarket.

As the Nixon Big Charge gathered momentum, its mood and objectives were reflected in a flurry of clandestine activity in the federal intelligence agencies and federal law enforcement agencies. Long before President Nixon had arrived in office, many of these agencies had already been engaged in spying upon and harassing domestic political groups—particularly those on the left. The F.B.I., for instance, had carried out some hundred break-ins a year against political targets in the United States during the nineteen-sixties. It had also engaged in widespread wiretapping, and had conducted a clandestine program, called "Cointelpro," of disrupting groups which the Director decided were subversive. A characteristic technique of this program was to send out poison-pen letters whose purpose was to have someone fired from his job or to ruin the relations between one political group and another. And, starting in the early nineteen-fifties, the F.B.I. compiled a "National Security Index" of the names of people to be locked up in the event that a national emergency were to be declared. The C.I.A., whose charter forbids it to engage in "internal security functions," had also been spying on the opposition at home and had also engaged in break-ins and wiretaps. On at least three occasions, it had placed taps on newsmen. Also, since the early nineteen-fifties, the C.I.A. had been monitoring and opening letters from Americans to people abroad. By 1959, the C.I.A. was opening some thirteen-thousand letters a year at one letter-opening station. In 1967 and 1968, as opposition to the war grew, and the civil-rights movement became militant, and as President Johnson developed his conviction that the domestic disorders were fuelled by foreign Communist support, the surveillance and harassment of domestic groups had greatly increased. The military intelligence agencies opened secret offices in several major cities in the United States and set about infiltrating the protest movements. And in those same years, local police departments in many cities expanded their operations against groups they had decided were subversive. At the C.I.A., in August of 1967, a "Special Operations Group," which later came to be called "Operation CHAOS," was set up to look into the question of whether protest groups in the United States were getting support from the nation's enemies abroad. On at least four occasions, the C.I.A. delivered reports on the question to President Johnson. On each occasion, the reports concluded that there was no such support. In spite of its consistently negative findings, Operation CHAOS expanded steadily, and as it expanded it began to concern itself with purely domestic matters. When President Nixon came to power, officials of his Administration were shown the reports; but President Nixon, like President Johnson before him, was adamant in his insistence that foreign support existed, and on June 20, 1969, he ordered still another report prepared. This report, titled "Foreign Communist Support to Revolutionary Protest Movements in the United States," failed, like its predecessors, to show that there was any such support. Nevertheless, Operation CHAOS continued to grow. The smaller the purpose it served, it seemed, the larger it became. In September of 1969, as the anti-war movement was building strength again, C.I.A. Director Richard Helms wrote and circulated an unusual memorandum to the heads of each of the directorates within the C.I.A. in which he instructed each division to coöperate with Operation CHAOS "both in exploiting existing sources and in developing new ones" and to give Operation CHAOS "necessary access to such sources and operational assets." In October, Operation CHAOS acquired the capacity to operate agents on its own within the United States, and it began to infiltrate the peace movement.

By the time President Nixon came to power, the various clandestine agencies of the federal government had made their presence strongly felt among dissident groups. They had become a noticeable element on the political scene. Most demonstrations, whether peaceful or not, now swarmed with agents of all kinds, and the leaders of the demonstrations were experiencing serious harassment as they tried to organize their activities. And in the summer of

1968, the Democratic convention itself had been all but overrun by countless "security" agents whose exact affiliations were never quite clear to the delegates. The clandestine domestic operations of the various agencies had grown up spontaneously within each agency over the years, often without the knowledge of the Administration in office, and were isolated from each other to a considerable extent. When the Nixon Administration came to power, however, it immediately set about forging links. On May 14, 1969, Attorney General Mitchell had met with C.I.A. Director Helms to discuss the gathering of domestic intelligence. The head of Operation CHAOS, Richard Ober, was promptly put in touch with Assistant Attorney General Jerris Leonard, the head of the Civil Rights Division, and James Devine, who, under Leonard, was head of the Interdivision Information Unit, which assembled information on domestic disturbances. Also, regular liaison was established between the Justice Department group and the C.I.A. group. Then in July, Ober helped Leonard establish relationships with military intelligence groups. In July, too, Tom Huston, a young White House aide, acting on behalf of the President, instructed another powerful government agency with a deep reach into the lives of citizens—the I.R.S.—to get involved in the business of spying and harassment. At Huston's instigation, a "Special Service Group" was set up to concentrate on "Ideological Organizations." The service this group performed was to take away an organization's tax-exempt status if someone in the I.R.S. or elsewhere in the government decided that its politics were wrong-minded. In addition, one of the group's "principal functions," Huston noted, was to "determine the sources of [the ideological organizations'] funds, the names of their contributors, whether the contributions given to the organizations have been deducted as charitable contributions, what we can find out generally about the funds of these organizations." And Huston noted, "We do not want news media to be alerted to what we are attempting to do or how we are operating because the disclosure of such information might embarrass the Administration."

Liaison between the intelligence agencies and law-enforcement agencies was also going forward at lower levels. The C.I.A. gave advice to local police departments regularly. In 1968 and 1969, police officials from Washington, D.C. attended several three-week seminars given by the C.I.A. in Washington on wiretapping, bugging, and lock-picking. And as the struggle that fall between the Administration and the anti-war movement deepened, the links between the C.I.A. and the local police were gradually elaborated and strengthened.

On October 30th, the Vice-President seemed specifically to revoke the theme of national unity. "If, in challenging, we polarize the American people, I say it is time for a positive polarization," he said. "It is time to rip away the rhetoric and to divide on authentic lines. . . ." And, as though to clarify the President's remarks in the campaign, he added, "When the President said 'bring us together' he meant the functioning, contributing portions of the American citizenry." No rebuttal was offered by the White House.

On November 2nd, Attorney General Mitchell went on television to say that the Vice-President's phrase "effete snobs" was, if anything, too kind a characterization of some of the anti-war demonstrators. The ones he had in mind were "active militants who want to destroy . . . some of the institutions of our government." A few days before, the President, who had temporarily held aloof from the Vice-President's attacks, appeared in public with Agnew and said, "I am very proud to have the Vice-President, with his Greek background, in our Administration, and he has done a great job for this Administration."

On November 3rd, the President, in a nationally televised speech that he had announced three weeks in advance, addressed himself to the subject that, more than any other, had fuelled the enmity between the President and his opposition: the war in Vietnam. (In Dwight Chapin's plan, the President's speech was to be the occasion for the surfacing of "pro-Administration sentiment.") He described immediate withdrawal from the war as the "popular and easy course" from a political standpoint. Expatiating on this, he noted, "After all, we became involved in the war while my predecessor was in office. I could blame the defeat, which would be the result of my action, on him—and come out as the peacemaker." But he rejected this course. He had a different plan for ending the war—one that he could not fully reveal to the public. It involved a "scheduled timetable" for withdrawal, but the timetable had to remain a secret. "I have not and do not intend to announce the timetable for our program, and there are obvious reasons for this decision which I'm sure you will understand," he said. He described his secret plan as one for ending the war, but the justifications he offered for it seemed to be justifications for staying in the war and winning it. An American "defeat," he said, would "inevitably" be followed by "massacres" of thousands of people at the hands of the Communists. Furthermore, "for the United States, this first defeat in our nation's history would result in a collapse of confidence in American leadership not only in Asia but throughout the world." Nor was that all: "Our defeat and humiliation in South Vietnam without question would promote recklessness in the councils of those great powers who have not yet abandoned their goals of world conquest."

As a candidate, Nixon had declined to discuss the war in great detail, yet when he mentioned it he had seemed to promise a swift withdrawal. Now he was speaking very differently. Now he was raising points that appeared to have escaped him entirely during the 1968 campaign. In fact, in describing the principal war aim as avoidance of "defeat and humiliation," he was reaffirming the aim that, more than any other, had inspired the Kennedy Administration and then the Johnson Administration to escalate the war through most of the nineteen-sixties. In the opinion of Assistant Secretary of Defense McNaughton, avoiding "humiliation" had been the whole aim of the American war effort. President Nixon was signalling that he, like Presidents before him, regarded the war primarily as a "test case." His aim of preserving "confidence in American leadership not only in Asia but throughout the world" and John Mc-

Naughton's aim of preserving America's "reputation as a guarantor" were the same thing. He was reaffirming the doctrine of credibility. In the fall, he had spoken more than once of an "honorable" peace. By "honor" he did not mean a quality that it would be nice to preserve for reasons of idealism and pride. He did not mean the honor of the offended gentleman. The word "honor" in this context was another synonym for "credibility." Yet even as he referred to the danger of "world conquest" he paradoxically asserted his intention of withdrawing American troops from the struggle. From the way he described the magnitude of the challenge, it sounded as though it would make better sense to send more troops in. The President, it seemed, meant to withdraw to victory. But in this anomalous behavior, too, President Nixon was following a long tradition. President Johnson and President Kennedy had also pursued aims of global scope with "limited" forces. In other words, President Nixon had not invented his dilemma; he had only sharpened its contradictions. It was a dilemma shaped by the requirements of nuclear strategy, for it was the nuclear dilemma that had given credibility its vast importance in American strategic thinking. By maintaining an *appearance* of great strength and great will, Presidents since the time of Kennedy had hoped to avoid the catastrophe for mankind which would occur if the nation's full strength should ever actually be used. In this scheme, the global public-relations war, in which Vietnam was regarded as the main front, acted as a surrogate for actual global warfare. The problem that Presidents faced was how to strike the right balance between belligerency and restraint. And for no President had it proved more difficult to strike the right balance than it had for President Nixon, because no President had faced the amount of opposition he faced in attempting to create the appearance of strength and will. Never had a President tried to achieve so much in the world with so little understanding or support from the people. If a gap had opened between the President and the public, its origin was here; for while he had been growing ever more determined to uphold the nation's image, the public had been growing ever more tired and confused. His solution was to try to take on himself the responsibility for pursuing the strategy. Since the demonstrations of will that were crucial to the policy were not forthcoming from the country, he apparently felt all the more obliged to make it clear to the world that his own will, at least, was firm.

In the closing passages of his speech, President Nixon turned his attention to the domestic scene. At the beginning of the speech, when he said that immediate withdrawal would be the "popular and easy course," he had seemed to acknowledge that the country still wanted to get out of the war quickly. But then he went on to define two groups of Americans—a "minority" who were trying to "impose" their point of view "by mounting demonstrations in the street" in order to end the war immediately, and a "majority" who, presumably, supported the secret plan whose existence he was now revealing. The Constitution, he said, required him to comply with the wishes of those he defined as being in the majority. "For almost two hundred years," he said, "the policy of this nation has been made under our Constitution by those leaders in the Congress and the White House elected by all of the people. If a vocal minority, however fervent its cause, prevails over reason and the will of the majority, this nation has no future as a free society." Having defined the movement against the war as an anti-democratic force that would, if it succeeded, overthrow the Constitution and put an end to freedom in America, he made a final appeal, not to the nation as a whole but to the part of it that supported him and that he said was a majority. "So tonight, to you, the great silent majority of my fellow Americans, I ask for your support," he said. In reference to others—the minority—he said, "North Vietnam cannot defeat or humiliate the United States. Only Americans can do that." His assertion marked a significant shift. He had identified a foe within the United States more dangerous to the country than the one it was fighting in Vietnam. As he now saw things, therefore, the war had two fronts—a primary front at home, where the government struggled against a foe who could not only overthrow the Constitution but also "defeat" and "humiliate" the United States, and a secondary front in Vietnam, where the government struggled against a less formidable foe, unable to accomplish any of these dread

65

things. He had already deployed forces on this primary front. His Administration had brought the indictment against the Chicago demonstrators. It had launched its covert attacks on the press. The Vice-President and other members of the Administration were giving the anti-war movement an almost daily lashing. The Nixon Big Charge was on. A year earlier, the war had been widely viewed as an international struggle that had some important domestic consequences. Now, in the eyes of the President, the war was a domestic struggle with some serious international consequences. Thereafter, the Vietnam war would be waged primarily in the United States.

President Nixon's reaffirmation of the doctrine of credibility disclosed in his foreign policy a practice that had come to govern most of his domestic policies: the practice of subordinating the substance of governing to the image of governing. For credibility was nothing other than an image—a "reputation," McNaughton had called it. What the strategists of the Vietnam war had always most feared was not the reality of defeat but the appearance of defeat, and what they had most wanted in Vietnam was not victory but victory's image. In fact, President Nixon's separation of word (or image) and deed (or substance) in the domestic sphere had merely extended a separation of word and deed in the foreign sphere which was of long standing. Such a separation had characterized the whole conduct of the Vietnam war since the beginning of the American combat involvement, as the record of the Kennedy and Johnson Administrations attested; and the effort to uphold the image of success in the face of increasingly evident actual failure was one of the reasons for the infamous credibility gap that had grown up between what the government said and what the people believed. The Nixon Administration, too, had been duplicitous in its statements regarding the war. But in its *mode* of governing, at least, a remarkable degree of consistency had emerged: at home and abroad, President Nixon was using the entire power of the federal government to protect and promote images.

Television and the press were, inevitably, major participants in any struggle to establish images, and in recent months the President had grown increasingly angry over their performance. On November 13th, Vice-President Agnew delivered the harshest and most insulting attack on the television networks that had ever been made by anyone in the top ranks of an Administration in power. The speech opened yet another front in the mounting Presidential Offensive. In tone, the speech combined the stilted, intellectual-sounding phrasing and the lurid abusiveness that had by now become the trademarks of a speech by the Vice-President. Again, the bone of contention was the war. The Vice-President concentrated his attacks on the networks' coverage of the President's recent speech. "Monday night a week ago, President Nixon delivered the most important address of his Administration, one of the most important of our decade," Agnew said. "His subject was Vietnam. His hope was to rally the American people to see the conflict through to a lasting and just peace in the Pacific." But the networks, Agnew thought, had tried to obstruct the President: "When the President completed his address—an address, incidentally, that he spent weeks in the preparation of—his words and policies were subjected to instant analysis and querulous criticism. The audience of seventy million Americans gathered to hear the President of the United States was inherited by a small band of network commentators and self-appointed analysts, the majority of whom expressed in one way or another their hostility to what he had to say." One network, he said, had "trotted out" Averell Harriman, President Johnson's chief negotiator in Paris. "Throughout the President's message, he waited in the wings," Agnew said. "When the President concluded, Mr. Harriman recited perfectly. . . . All in all, Mr. Harriman offered a broad range of gratuitous advice challenging and contradicting the policies outlined by the President of the United States." After claiming that the networks enjoyed "a monopoly sanctioned and licensed" by the government, Agnew suggested that the networks be "made

67

more responsive to the views of the nation," and he urged the public to write to the networks protesting their news coverage.

Never in the country's history had the executive branch meddled so deeply in the affairs of the press; and rarely had the partisan political inspiration of a campaign by the executive been more nakedly apparent. (The Vice-President was calling outright for an end to criticism of the President on the most controversial issue facing the nation.) The press, however, seemed more interested, on the whole, in taking up the substance of the Vice-President's remarks than in examining the propriety of his having made them. The networks set the tone for the response from many news organizations when, in a decision that had no precedent in the annals of coverage of Vice-Presidents, they ran his speech live in its entirety. During the weeks that followed, a large part of the press, at the Vice-President's prompting, plunged into self-examination. Little phrases from his speech, including "instant analysis" and "querulous criticism," at once became the stuff of daily discussion in columns and in news articles all around the country. The press and the networks seemed almost to welcome the opportunity to rethink their coverage of the Nixon Administration. Howard Smith, the commentator for ABC News, remarked, "I think Mr. Agnew had some good points, but I disagree with him about intent." Max Frankel, writing in the *Times*, called the issues raised by the Vice-President "complex indeed." Walter Cronkite, the CBS newsman, said that he agreed with the Vice-President that journalism was too heavily concentrated in New York. Many politicians welcomed the Vice-President's remarks. Hugh Scott, of Pennsylvania, the Senate Minority Leader, said, "I think the networks deserve a thorough goosing," and the Secretary of Housing and Urban Development, George Romney, said he believed that the Vice-President was acting as a "champion of the old culture that values historic and democratic principles." One of the few angry remarks came from the man whom the Vice-President had attacked most harshly—Ambassador Harriman, who said that the Vice-President's speech "smacked of a totalitarianism, which I don't like at all."

Around the time of the speech, other Administration officials made threatening moves against the press. A week before it was given, Dean Burch, who had been confirmed as chairman of the Federal Communications Commission, called up the television networks requesting transcripts of their "instant analyses" of President Nixon's speech of November 3rd—just as Jeb Magruder had suggested in his memo to Haldeman that Burch should do. (In fact, Burch asked for the transcripts at the White House's request.) A few days after Agnew's speech, Klein went on television to say that if the networks and press did not correct their bias against the President, then "you do invite the government to come in." These moves were out in the open.

There were, however, several things about the Vice-President's speech that the public did not know. Publicly, the President had been keeping himself at one remove from the Vice-President's attack on the news media, and there had been considerable debate in the press over whether the President concurred in the Vice-President's sentiments. Actually, the speech had been written mainly by one of the President's own speechwriters, Patrick Buchanan, and the President himself had added a few finishing touches. And after the Vice-President spoke the President had called up Buchanan to compliment him on his work. But Buchanan, of course, was only an instrument of the President, so when Vice-President Agnew called the President's speech "one of the most important of our decade," the President, in a process of hidden remote control, was praising himself.

Another thing that the public did not know was that a part of the "public reaction" to both the President's and the Vice-President's speeches had been concocted by the White House. Thousands of letters had poured into network offices after the attack on television coverage, and the networks, like the people who read about the letters in the following days, took them to be spontaneous and real. The evidence is strong that some of them had been produced by the system the President set up for having his aides write letters that would go out over the signatures of ordinary citizens around the country. The President was deeply involved in the details of these mailing efforts. As early as September, shortly after Senator

Edward Kennedy had criticized the Administration's war policy in terms similar to those used a few days later by Hanoi radio, the President recommended in a memo to Haldeman that "Buchanan's . . . group might get a major mailing-out to editors and columnists in Massachusetts and perhaps even nationally, just setting forth the Hanoi quote, or, better still, an editorial which takes that line. . . . The best place from which this could be mailed would be, of course, from Boston." Haldeman, too, took a strong interest in the rigged mailings and he wrote in a memo to Magruder that several people around the White House "will be responsible to work out a program over the next week for sending letters and telegrams, and making telephone calls to Senators, blasting them on their consistent opposition to the President on everything he is trying to do for the country. This program needs to be subtle and worked out well so that they receive these items from their home districts as well as other points around the country." By a similar system, telegrams of support had been sent to the President after his speech on the war. (Later, he had shown them to newsmen as evidence of public support.) At the same time, he had been putting together governmental machinery that would frighten or coerce television and the press into giving his Administration favorable coverage—into taking more careful note of the "tremendous reception" he had received at the Miami Dolphins football game, for instance. The President had set in motion an elaborate hidden machine for manufacturing the appearance of public enthusiasm for himself. He had begun by making a direct appeal for support in the traditional manner. Then he had sent himself rigged telegrams and letters of support. Then he had put the telegrams and letters on display before the public that had supposedly sent them. Then he had arranged to have the Vice-President praise him effusively. Then he had apparently had telegrams and letters sent to television networks and the press praising the Vice-President for praising him. He had become his own most ardent and prolific supporter.

While the Vice-President—surely the best "rifle" in the White House armory—was leading the charge against the television networks, the President was on Capitol Hill thanking Congress for its support of his war policy. He addressed each house of Congress, and once again he promised to end the war but spoke more in the manner of a leader rallying his people to victory. In the House of Representatives, he read a letter from a family whose son had been killed in Vietnam, in which the family said it supported "your plan to Vietnamize the war." The day before, the House had given strong support to a resolution praising the President's war policy, and the President now said that such support for "the policy of the President" was "in the great tradition of this country."

The President's attack on the anti-war movement had not sat well with its members. Indeed, his appeal to the "silent majority" seemed almost to have been designed to provoke them. On the fourteenth and fifteenth of November, hundreds of thousands of demonstrators streamed into Washington, and on the fifteenth the largest demonstration in the capital's history, amounting to several hundred thousand people (estimates varied according to the politics of the observers), was held in the grounds of the Washington Monument. The Administration was well prepared to meet them. The Interdivision Information Unit had met regularly in the days leading up to the march, and when the marchers arrived, the Washington Police Department and the C.I.A. had established a joint command for the collection of intelligence. One branch of the command was located in the headquarters of the Intelligence Division of the Washington Police headquarters, and the other was located at the C.I.A. headquarters.

President Nixon had come full circle. In 1968, the nation, through one of the most gruelling ordeals in the practice of democracy in its history, had made its decision to leave the war. Even the supporters of the war had seemed in 1968 to recognize the irresistible finality of that decision. As a candidate, Mr. Nixon, too, had seemed to acknowledge the electorate's mandate in his acceptance speech. And it may be that President Nixon had truly expected to bring the war to a rapid close. At any rate, millions of people who watched the President-elect on Election Night saying, "That will be the great objective of this Administration at the outset: to bring the American people together," had found him convincing; and when, in the months following, he had promised candor, openness, and a spirit of reconciliation there had seemed to be every reason to believe what he said. Not only the interests of the country but his own political interests seemed to call for the course he was announcing. Yet on entering office he had changed. The cautionary example of President Johnson had somehow lost its force. Before long, he had ordered the bombing of Cambodia in secret and had placed the warrantless wiretaps on the newsmen and the White House aides, and by the fall the Presidential Offensive was under way throughout the nation. The change was psychological, political, and strategic, but it centered on the issue of the war—and, more broadly, the issue of national security. When President Nixon arrived in power, it seemed, he entered a realm of complex and demanding global military strategy whose rigid imperatives caused him to reverse the promises he had made to the people during the campaign—the principal imperative being the one that had to do with American credibility, which had been so fateful for the Johnson men, and which had grown out of attempts to resolve the dilemma of how to frame a military policy in the shadow of nuclear war. It was as though at the very heart of American life in the nineteen-sixties, at the place where the President sat with his hand on the button, there was an isolate world of cold, abstract strategic theory which endured unchanged from Administration to Administration, regardless of any upheavals in the society at large. Presidents had, in a manner of speaking, discovered a second mandate, more powerful than the popular one, under which to act. By the fall of 1969, this other mandate, which had governed American life for nearly a decade, had prevailed again. The war had endured in defiance of the democratic process. And following in the war's train was the full array of afflictions, disorders, and distortions of the Presidency which seemed to be indivisibly bound up with the war effort: isolation, secrecy, deception, rage, repression. These, in turn, gave rise to renewed bitterness and division in the nation. Instead of the expected return of the "known and familiar," the nation was experiencing a revival of the alien and weird. In fact, by now the alien and weird had prevailed for so many years that they had almost become the known and familiar.

The manner in which the Administration reversed itself had been as remarkable as the substance of the reversal. It had come like a change in the political weather. No known events had precipitated it. No explanations were offered for it afterward. The President never alluded to any change. Rather, he and his spokesmen talked as though the new mood of the Administration had always been its mood. And the reversal was received in much the spirit in which it was offered. There was opposition, but very little wonderment, over the necessity of once again opposing an Administration on matters that the country thought it had laid to rest. In the "polarized" America whose revival the Vice-President had announced, people took up their old positions as if the promises of the year before had no binding force on the present. For nearly a year, most observers, friendly or unfriendly, had sought to judge the politics of the Administration in terms of what had been the prevailing issues in 1968: the war, race, "the cities," the rising crime rate. At first, the President had seemed, as he "reorganized" his government, to be striving to devise policies that were responsive to these issues. Observers had waited for him to fill in the missing pieces—the specific programs—that would give life to his portrait of a country that was unified and at peace. And pieces did fall into place, one after another, but the portrait, when it was done, turned out to be of a nation that was divided and at war. In seeming to fill in the details of one broad policy, he had quietly created another. The Administration had buried the old issues and brought forth new ones for itself to cope with: not the war but the legitimacy and popularity of the protesters against the war; not the policies and programs of the Administration at home but the way those policies and programs were being reported in the press. (As for "the cities," that issue, with its magazine features and television specials and panel discussions by academic experts, just disappeared in all the new excitement, and no one ever saw it again.) This unexpected revival and intensification of the divisions of the Johnson years could produce no fresh emotions: they had the stale, dead quality that comes with repetition; and behind the stridency of "positive polarization" was the ache of exhaustion.

It was a noticeable measure of the President's power that the Administration's assault on its opposition had thrown the opposition into disarray. But the President had exercised a prior and greater power: the power to frame the issues on which he would do battle with the opposition. Upon being elected, he had promised to "bring the American people together," and for nearly a year the country's perception of the Administration and of national politics as a whole had been ruled by this image, even in the face of mounting evidence that he was not attempting to make it a reality. Now he had, in effect, withdrawn this image and put forward its exact opposite— "positive polarization." The public's attention was directed away from the old issues that would bring it together, and toward new ones—issues that would tear it apart. The President, a single component of our politics, had exercised a conjurer's power to rearrange the national scene—a power to define and then to redefine national politics at his pleasure.

II.
DIVISION

I N HIS FIRST nine months in office, President Nixon had proved to be an even more dedicated combatant in the domestic political struggle over the Vietnam war than President Johnson had been. President Johnson had been bewildered and torn by the opposition to his war policy; if the nation had been in torment during his Presidency, his face had been the picture of that torment. One source of his difficulties had been the fact that the anti-war movement had deprived him of a large part of his natural constituency, for the divisions of those years ran down the center of the Democratic Party, destroying the consensus he needed if he was to put through his cherished domestic reforms. President Nixon was more single-minded and, in some ways, more consistent. To be sure, he had switched suddenly from a political line in tune with the national desire for peace and promoting a spirit of national unity to a political line justifying protraction of the war and promoting what Vice-President Agnew approvingly called "positive polarization"; yet the underlying drift of his policies, even during the early months (particularly in the growing area of his Administration's covert operations), was in the direction of division. He had begun to put together a political consensus, centering on the Republican Party— what he called the "silent majority"—that would exclude the protesters against the war and the supporters of civil rights. Moreover, he was persuaded that the principal established institutions of American political life, including the Congress, the Supreme Court, and, above all, television and the press, were impeding his communion with the new majority, and were thereby thwarting the majority's will. His first job, then, as he saw it, was to clear away this noisy, willful minority impediment.

As Christmas approached, the President announced the withdrawal of fifty thousand troops from Vietnam; added to the withdrawal of twenty-five thousand in June and a further withdrawal of thirty-five thousand in September, this meant that some four hundred and thirty thousand were left in Vietnam. On January 1, 1970, in his first official statement of the new year, the President voiced support of the movement to reduce environmental pollution. "The nineteen-seventies absolutely must be the years when America pays its debt to the past by reclaiming the purity of its air, its waters, and our living environment. It is literally now or never," Mr. Nixon said. An abatement of the "positive polarization" advocated by the Vice-President in the fall seemed to be in the works. (The Vice-President was off on a tour of Asia and the Pacific.) In his first State of the Union message, on January 22nd, the President's angry mood seemed to have given way entirely to the mellow—even glowing— mood of Election Night and the Inauguration. "The moment has arrived," he told a joint session of the Congress, "to harness the vast energies and abundance of this land to the creation of a new American experience, an experience richer and deeper and more truly a reflection of the goodness and grace of the human spirit." After calling for "equal voting rights," among other things, he said, "But we could still be the unhappiest people in the world without an indefinable spirit, the lift of a driving dream which has made America from its beginning the hope of the world. . . . Above all, let us inspire young Americans with a sense of excitement, a sense of destiny, a sense of involvement in meeting the challenges we face in this great period of our history." It seemed that Mr. Outside was back on the job.

The President's benign tone notwithstanding, the campaign to bring the press into line moved forward both in public and in private. In early January, the Justice Department subpoenaed the unused portions of a CBS film about the Black Panther Party. At the end of January, a second subpoena demanded that all the materials used in the production of the film, including tape recordings, be furnished to the Secret Service and the F.B.I. In early February, a federal grand jury looking into a rampage the previous October by a left-wing radical group—the Weathermen—in Chicago subpoenaed the notes of reporters for *Time, Life,* and *Newsweek,* and files of unused photographs as well, and a reporter for the *Times* received a similar subpoena. A federal grand jury is a body that is, ultimately, under the guidance of the Justice Department. Though a spokesman for the Justice Department denied that any new policy toward the news media was in effect, such subpoenas were virtually unprecedented, and behind the scenes, too, the efforts to get the media under control were progressing. The Administration was particularly upset by the coverage it was receiving from NBC news. In early February, H. R. Haldeman wrote to Jeb Magruder, "The need, probably, is to concentrate on NBC and give some real thought as to how to handle the problem that they have created in their almost totally negative approach to everything the Administration does. I would like to see a plan from you . . . just some specific thinking on steps that can be taken to try to change this, and I should have this by Friday." Haldeman was also unhappy about a program of rigged letters critical of liberal Republican senators, which had been instituted in October of 1969, and which he felt was not large enough. It consisted of letters to the senators which, like the rigged letters to the press, were written by White House aides and sent out over the signatures of ordinary citizens. The letter-writing effort was now called the silent-majority program. Of this silent majority, comprising those Americans who the President thought could be enlisted in support of his conduct of the war in Vietnam, Haldeman wrote to Magruder, "We have got to move now in every effective way we can to get them working to pound the magazines and the networks in counteraction to the obvious shift of the Establishment to an attack on Vietnam again."

Three days before the President delivered his State of the Union message, he placed the name of G. Harrold Carswell, a resident of Tallahassee, Florida, and a judge on the Fifth Circuit Court of Appeals, in nomination for Supreme Court Justice. Supreme Court nominations had a central position in the President's thinking on domestic affairs. It was to the Court that he had turned in the fall to give the South relief from the speedy integration of the public schools. The Court had, of course, rebuffed him unanimously, and had thus provided him with an opportunity to point out where the pressure for integration was coming from. "I believe in carrying out the law," he said soon after the Court's decision, "even though I may have disagreed, as I did in this instance." It was the Court, also, that he blamed for the rising crime rate, for it was the Justices of the Supreme Court, he said, who had given the "green light" to "the criminal elements." From the start, the President had maneuvered carefully in the area of Supreme Court nominations. In June of 1968, Chief Justice Earl Warren had announced his retirement from the Court, and President Johnson had nominated Associate Justice Abe Fortas to succeed him. But Fortas's nomination had run into opposition in the Senate from Republicans, from Southern Democrats, and from those who were disturbed by the revelation that while Fortas was on the Court he had accepted a substantial fee for conducting a seminar at a Washington law school; and in the fall Johnson had withdrawn the nomination. Fortas had remained on the Court, and Chief Justice Warren had agreed to serve until a successor was confirmed. In the spring of 1969, however, Fortas had got into more trouble, when it was discovered that he had agreed to accept an annual fee from a foundation. At that time, President Nixon's Justice Department had fed this information against Fortas to the Senate, and Attorney General Mitchell had lobbied with Chief Justice Warren to enlist his aid in obtaining the resignation of Fortas. Soon Fortas had resigned. President Nixon had then nominated his own Chief Justice, and later that spring his nominee, Judge Warren Burger, had been confirmed by the Senate. That summer, faced with the vacancy created by Fortas's resignation, the President had proceeded—as part of the Southern strategy —to nominate a conservative judge from the South to the Court. The nominee was Judge Clement Haynsworth, of the United States Court of Appeals for the Fourth Circuit. But in late November the Senate had rejected Haynsworth, in part because it discovered that he had once decided a case in which he might be thought to have a conflict of interest.

Judge Carswell was the President's second choice to fill the seat. The Senate, having just turned down a Supreme Court nominee, for the first time in forty years, was at first strongly inclined to accept almost anyone the President chose. Then, over a period of months, the senators learned a number of things about Carswell which gave them second thoughts. They learned that in 1948, while campaigning for the Georgia Legislature, he had said, "I am a Southerner by ancestry, birth, training, inclination, belief, and practice. I believe that segregation of the races is proper and the only practical and correct way of life in our states. I have always so believed and I shall always so act. . . . I yield to no man as a fellow-candidate, as a fellow-citizen, in the firm, vigorous belief in the principles of white supremacy, and I shall always be so governed." They learned that in 1956 he had taken part in the transfer of a golf course from municipal control to private hands, apparently to evade a Supreme Court ruling of a year earlier which required the integration of municipal recreation facilities. They learned that in an appearance before the Judiciary Committee of the Senate he had misrepresented the facts of his involvement in the golf-course matter—knowingly, it appeared. And they learned that his decisions on the bench had been reversed on appeal some sixty per cent of the time by superior courts—a rate of reversal more than twice as high as the average for other judges in the Fifth Circuit District Courts. As these and other damaging facts came to light, a conviction began to form, first in the legal community and then in the Senate, that Carswell was unfit for the Court. Louis Pollak, the dean of the Yale Law School, declared that Carswell had "more slender credentials than any nominee for the Supreme Court put forth in this century." The deans of several other prominent law schools and some two hundred former law clerks to Supreme Court Justices signed an open letter urging every senator to reject the nomination. Moreover, a strong feeling was growing that in nominating Carswell the President meant to degrade the Court as an institution of American life. One leading Republican senator later said of his conclusions at the time, "I learned that the Justice Department had rated Carswell way down below Haynsworth and a couple of other candidates. That made it clear that the choice of Carswell was vengeance—to make us sorry we hadn't accepted Haynsworth—and at the same time it was an attempt to downgrade the Supreme Court and implement the Southern strategy."

By late March, 1970, it looked as though the nomination might be defeated. The President took extraordinary action. He wrote a letter to Senator William Saxbe, of Ohio (the letter was made public by Saxbe), urging the nomination on the Senate. He brushed aside the objections that had been raised to Carswell's nomination, and, in addition to arguing the merits of the nominee, he argued Constitutional law. "What is centrally at issue in this nomination," he wrote, "is the Constitutional responsibility of the President to appoint members of the Court—and whether this responsibility can be frustrated by those who wish to substitute their own philosophy or their own subjective judgment for that of the one person entrusted by the Constitution with the power of appointment." And he wrote,

"What is at stake is the preservation of the traditional Constitutional relationships of the President and the Congress." He added, "The question arises whether I, as President of the United States, shall be accorded the same right of choice in naming Supreme Court Justices which has been freely accorded to my predecessors of both parties." Actually, of course, the Constitution does not give the President the sole power to appoint Supreme Court Justices. It specifies that "he shall nominate and by and with the advice and consent of the Senate shall appoint . . . judges of the Supreme Court." On April 8th, an affronted Senate rejected the nomination, by a vote of fifty-one to forty-five.

The President was deeply angered, and the next day he made his harshest attack on the Senate so far. "Judges Carswell and Haynsworth have endured with admirable dignity vicious assaults on their intelligence, their honesty, and their character," he said in a statement to reporters. "They have been falsely charged with being racist, but when all the hypocrisy is stripped away, the real issue was their philosophy of strict construction of the Constitution —a philosophy that I share—and the fact that they had the misfortune of being born in the South. . . . I understand the bitter feelings of millions of Americans who live in the South about the act of regional discrimination that took place in the Senate yesterday."

Probably no two issues could have been more unalike than the war in Southeast Asia and the nomination of Justices to the Supreme Court of the United States, yet the President's handling of them seemed to have been molded by a single pattern of response. He apparently regarded the two issues as expressions of an overriding issue that had preoccupied him more and more since he arrived in office: the issue of his authority as President. In November, he had imagined the anti-war movement to be a rebellion intended to overthrow the Constitution and usurp his authority as the Commander-in-Chief and the elected leader of the country, and now he imagined that the United States Senate intended to take away what he believed (incorrectly) to be his power of appointment. And in both cases misconstruing and exaggerating a threat to his Constitutional prerogatives had led him to overstep the bounds of the Constitution himself—first by suggesting that peaceful assembly by a "minority" was un-Constitutional, and then by claiming sole power of appointment. In much the same way, he had come to see the protection of the rights of criminal suspects as an unnecessary and dangerous curtailment of the powers of the police, and had proposed an apparently un-Constitutional bill—the crime bill—to deal with the situation. The President was finding usurpation on every side and was responding in kind. Even as the President's power expanded, a preoccupation with impotence was developing in the White House. This preoccupation had developed first in the foreign sphere, where the nation had attempted to reduce the executive's warmaking power, and was now spreading to the domestic sphere. And as the President's attention shifted from the specific details of each issue to the larger issue of the crisis of Presidential authority, he apparently felt confirmed in a deepening conviction that each obstacle he faced was due not to the inherent intractability of circumstances but to the machinations of his enemies. As issues were handled by the President, therefore, they became more abstract and more personal at the same time. They also became more apocalyptic, since in each small challenge the President saw a challenge to the whole edifice of his power.

In March, President Nixon secretly turned his attention to still another set of institutions that he had come to regard as a virtual enemy of his Administration: private foundations. "The President directed several of us to give thought to how to combat the institutionalized power of the left concentrated in the foundations that succor the Democratic Party," Patrick Buchanan wrote in a memorandum to the President on March 3rd. He offered recommendations of "an offensive and defensive nature." He wanted to "initiate a policy of favoritism in all future federal grants to those institutions friendly to us that want the work—and we should direct future funds away from the hostile foundations, like Brookings." (The reference was to the Brookings Institution, a research organization in Washington.) And he wrote, "Anti-Administration foundations should be cut off without a dime." His principal recommendation, however, was for the creation of a new institution, to serve as a tool of the Administration. It would be a right-wing "talent bank" and would secretly carry out Administration orders; for instance, it would help organize pressure against the press. A board of directors made up of front men would be used to disguise the Administration's control over the organization. As Buchanan put it, "the Board of Directors would run from right to center of the political spectrum," and "we would have to have people there who knew what was up and agreed to it; and then let the hand-picked staff run the thing." Then "we would have to lock it into the White House with probably two individuals at the top level—who had the ear of the President at all times—and who were intensely familiar with the Institute and its working." And, to maintain full secrecy, "some of the essential objectives of the Institute would have to be blurred, even buried, in all sorts of other activity that would be the bulk of its work, that would employ many people, and that would provide the cover for the more important efforts." Magruder had proposed using the Internal Revenue Service against the press and the television networks, and now Buchanan wanted to use it against the foundations: he wanted "a strong fellow running the Internal Revenue Division; and an especially friendly fellow with a friendly staff in the Tax-Exempt Office."

By creating a front group to act for the Administration in the public realm, and by getting the Internal Revenue Service and other federal agencies to "engage in combat" (as Buchanan put it) with existing foundations, the Administration hoped to advance what had now become its broad aim of undermining and dominating the principal institutions in the mainstream of American political life. Buchanan noted in his memo to the President, "We would be striking at the heart of the Establishment"—for the men of the Nixon Administration saw themselves as being at war with "the Establishment." (Haldeman's conviction that "the Establishment" was mounting a campaign against the President's war policies was another expression of this thinking.) The Nixon men wielded the overwhelming power of the Presidency. In the reckoning of most people, they now *were* "the Establishment." Yet they had come to see themselves as shabbily treated outsiders whose rights were constantly being encroached upon by "the Establishment." So they were striking back with all the means—covert as well as overt—at their disposal.

There were, then, at least two groups in America at the time who wished to destroy "the Establishment." One was a left-wing fringe of the anti-war movement. It had learned recently to despise "liberals"; and in order to destroy "the Establishment" its members often ran through the streets breaking windows and shouting until they were beaten up by policemen and thrown into jail. For a period of several months in late 1969 and early 1970, some of their number managed to plunge many universities into disorder. Also among the members of this left-wing fringe group were young people who had devised techniques of clowning and flamboyant theatrical "happenings" that attracted considerable attention on television and in the press. Yet the militant left had almost no public following, and was, in fact, generally despised. "The Establishment" easily weathered its attacks. By the spring of 1970, this group's influence had waned greatly. The other group that was out to destroy "the Establishment" in 1970 was a right-wing group. It was in the White House. It had been quietly eased into a position of great power—by a President who had run as a moderate. The names of its members—H. R. Haldeman, John Ehrlichman, Patrick Buchanan, and Jeb Magruder, among others—were barely known to the public. This group, too, despised "liberals." (There was something about the "liberals" that aroused visceral anger in Americans on both the left and the right during this period.) But whereas the left-wingers had only modest resources with which to attack "the Establishment," the men in the White House had the use of the Internal Revenue Service (if they could bring it under control), the Justice Department, the Federal Communications Commission, and every other federal agency that they could divert to their political purposes. Unlike their counterparts in the streets, they stood a fair chance of attaining their goal.

During the month of April, several of the President's top aides began to question whether the images that the Administration was promoting were the best ones available. John Ehrlichman, who now concerned himself primarily with domestic affairs, wrote on April 15th to Haldeman, "Among young business executives, among municipal officials and on the campuses we are epitomized by the Vice-President, the Attorney General, and Judge Carswell. We are presenting a picture of illiberality, repression, closed-mindedness and lack of concern for the less fortunate. . . . I do not sense any existing activity on the part of Herb Klein, or, for that matter, Ron Ziegler, to respond to this dilemma."

Haldeman showed the memo to Jeb Magruder, who soon wrote back, "Some time ago, we quietly set out to recruit Middle America, the Silent Majority, or whatever we choose to call it, into our camp. We have done a good job—and the images which the Vice-President and the AG project have been largely responsible. . . . Now to appeal to those outside Middle America (the young, the poor, the black, *most* of the Northeast, *all* of New York City, the 'student community,' much of the media, many of the 'opinion molders,' etc.) we have to send other emissaries. And that really is much of the problem: I do not think we have exploited the people in this Administration who project an image quite different than that of the Vice-President, the Attorney General, and Judge Carswell. I would propose that we develop a major strategy to publicize the fact the President has surrounded himself with bright, young, well-educated men who *care*. Men . . . who, while moderate, have hearts and consciences. Men like Moynihan, Ehrlichman, [Donald] Rumsfeld, [Peter] Flanigan, [Leonard] Garment, [John] Whitaker, and Haldeman." As an example of what he had in mind, he wrote, "What sophisticated young professional man (or his wife) would not be interested in, say, an *Esquire* picture-story on the life-style of a Dwight Chapin or a Ron Ziegler, men who daily meet with the President and are not yet middle-aged?" Magruder wanted to make it clear, however, that he was proposing a change of image only, and that the substance of policy would be left alone. This emphasis was not surprising, in view of the fact that most of what the Administration had been doing had been done with a view to projecting images in the first place. Speaking of Martin Anderson, a White House aide, Magruder wrote, "Who better than Marty Anderson can 'turn on' young people about draft reform?" The reason Anderson could do this was not that his views were more acceptable to the young than the views of others in the White House. "Young Metroamerica won't listen to Mel Laird, but they will to Marty Anderson," Magruder wrote, "not because Marty's any more liberal (he's probably *less* liberal than Laird) but because he's got more *hair*, a Ph.D., a sexy wife, drives a Thunderbird, and lives in a high-rise apartment."

In the margin of Magruder's memo, Haldeman wrote, "*Absolutely*. Really work on this."

In the country at large, decompression was under way. The psychological demobilization that had begun after the 1968 Presidential election and been interrupted by the sudden unleashing of "positive polarization" in the fall of 1969 seemed to have resumed. The Moratorium organizers, who had once promised to hold a demonstration on the fifteenth of every month until the war ended, dissolved their program. Here and there, a campus was disrupted as black students brought their grievances to the fore, but on the whole the campuses were quieter than they had been in 1969. Something essential to the outbreak of moral anger, pleasure-seeking, mystical withdrawal, faddism, and spontaneous political action known as "the Movement" had died, and the rebellious young were beginning to turn to more modest pursuits. They were melting back into an American life that had, for its part, been deeply altered by their brief career at the center of the nation's attention. The newspapers were saying that "the environment" was the new issue on the campuses, as though the indignation of the young were now a force of fixed intensity which would turn from issue to issue like a garden hose. But the young were growing tired of all the issues, and there were no signs that fashions of some new kind were about to replace the old ones. Nothing like that was emerging—no new politics, no new music, no new clothes. Just a rest. The war that had given birth to "the Movement" had outlasted it.

On the evening of April 20th, the President, as though in tune with the emerging national mood, announced in a television address that he would withdraw a hundred and fifty thousand additional American troops from Vietnam over the next year. The withdrawal would accompany a program of "Vietnamization," he said, which meant a program for training the South Vietnamese Army to take over the defense of its territory as the Americans left. Many of the people who opposed the war wished that he would withdraw more men and do it sooner, but they were tired of carrying signs in marches, and the President's mood seemed less deliberately provocative than it had in the fall. "Tonight, I am pleased to report that progress in training and equipping South Vietnamese forces has substantially exceeded our original expectations last June," he said in his address. "Very significant advances have also been made in pacification. . . . The decision I have announced tonight means that we finally have in sight the just peace we are seeking."

On Capitol Hill, however, a rumor making the rounds had caused some apprehension. In Cambodia, earlier in the year, the neutralist regime of Prince Norodom Sihanouk had been overthrown by pro-American military forces, and some senators had heard that the Administration might be planning to supply arms that the new regime had requested shortly after taking over, and perhaps troops as well. And on April 7th Secretary of State William Rogers had gone before the Senate Foreign Relations Committee and given the impression that the request was under consideration. On the other hand, he assured a House subcommittee that the Administration had no plans to escalate the war in Indo-China. "We recognize that if we escalate and we get involved in Cambodia with our

89

ground troops that our whole [Vietnamization] program is defeated," Rogers said.

On the evening of April 30th, President Nixon suddenly went on national television and informed an astonished nation that he had ordered American forces into Cambodia. "The time has come for action," he declared. He had decided to "go to the heart of the trouble." One reason for his action, he said, was his outrage at the enemy's having long violated the neutrality of Cambodia with impunity by setting up sanctuaries there. "American policy has been to scrupulously respect the neutrality of the Cambodian people," he claimed. "We have maintained a skeleton diplomatic mission of fewer than fifteen in Cambodia's capital, and that only since last August." And he said, "Neither the United States nor South Vietnam has moved against these enemy sanctuaries, because we did not wish to violate the territory of a neutral nation." Actually, of course, the United States had been secretly bombing Cambodian territory with B-52s for more than thirteen months. The American troops' objectives, he said, would be "cleaning out major North Vietnamese- and Vietcong-occupied territories" in Cambodia and, more dramatically, wiping out "the headquarters for the entire Communist military operation in South Vietnam." These were limited, purely military objectives. But the President also described vaster aims. He described them in what was, in effect, the fullest description of his vision of the world he had given since he entered the White House. "My fellow-Americans," he said, "we live in an age of anarchy both abroad and at home. We see mindless attacks on all the great institutions which have been created by free civilizations in the last five hundred years. Even here in the United States, great universities are being systematically destroyed. Small nations all over the world find themselves under attack from within and from without." All this, too, was at stake. For, the President said, "if, when the chips are down, the world's most powerful nation, the United States of America, acts like a pitiful, helpless giant, the forces of totalitarianism and anarchy will threaten free nations and free institutions throughout the world." And he said, "We will not react to this [the North Vietnamese] threat to American lives merely by plaintive diplomatic protests. If we did, the credibility of the United States would be destroyed." He added, "We will not be humiliated. We will not be defeated." But he went on to say that he did not mean to suggest that these immeasurable stakes rested solely on the progress of our arms in Cambodia. "It is not our power but our will and character that is being tested tonight," he said. That is, to read the future of the institutions that had been created by free civilizations in the last five hundred years one should not follow the bulletins from the battlefield in Southeast Asia but watch the reaction on the campuses, in the Congress, and in the press in the United States. The testing was not of the troops—not of our power. It was of the people at home—of the national will. In framing the issue this way, the President reaffirmed what he had said in a speech on the war which he had delivered almost six months earlier, on November 3rd —that only Americans could humiliate America. What happened here was primary; what happened in Southeast Asia was secondary. If the troops searching the Cambodian jungle for the Communist headquarters never found it, that would be unfortunate, but if the people at home failed to rally behind the President in his decision to send them on the search, it would be catastrophic. For it would show that the national will to unleash military force in the name of national objectives was broken.

Some of the President's deeper strategic thinking may have been revealed in a sentence he spoke a moment later: "If we fail to meet this challenge, all other nations will be on notice that despite its overwhelming power the United States, when a real crisis comes, will be found wanting." The Cambodian crisis, then, was not a "real" crisis. It was a test crisis. And therefore *what America revealed to the world about itself*—about its "will and character"—in the course of the crisis was more important than a tangible outcome. For if the crisis itself was not real, then the supposed attack on the Communist headquarters for the entire military operation in South Vietnam might not be real, either. It might be a stage prop designed to elicit the all-important expression of national resolve. Like so much that the President had done, at home and abroad, the invasion was more important for the appearance it created than for anything it might actually achieve. It was a lesson taught to a myriad unwilling students, among them other superpowers; rambunctious small powers, such as the Cubans and the Egyptians; shaky allies; and even domestic rebels. The people at home who were systematically destroying the universities would themselves learn something about what kind of President they were dealing with. And if it seemed paradoxical that with stakes like these in the balance the Administration was *withdrawing* from the war even as it expanded the war—indeed, in the President's telling, the Administration was expanding the war *in order to* withdraw from it—the paradox disappeared if one reflected that a display of national will did not necessarily require a clear-cut victory. In fact, as a stage for a display of national will an unpopular, shrinking war had some advantages, inasmuch as it would be an even more impressive feat for the nation to stomach the expansion of an unpopular war than for it to cheer on the expansion of a popular one.

The President went on to place his action in a historical context. He spoke of "great decisions" made by former Presidents. "In this room," he said (he was speaking from the Oval Office), "Woodrow Wilson made the great decisions which led to victory in World War I. Franklin Roosevelt made the decisions which led to our victory in World War II. . . . John F. Kennedy, in his finest hour, made the great decision which removed Soviet nuclear missiles from Cuba and the Western Hemisphere." But had history given Richard Nixon the opportunity to make a great decision in the Oval Office, too? He wistfully concluded that it might not have. "I have noted that there has been a great deal of discussion with regard to this decision that I have made, and I should point out that I do not contend that it is in the same magnitude as these decisions that I have just mentioned," he said. (Actually, there had been no discussion, since the country was now hearing about his decision for the first time.) And there was another difference, he continued, turning bitter. "In those decisions," he said, "the American people were not assailed by counsels of doubt and defeat from some of the most widely known opinion leaders of the nation." Unlike him, other Presidents had had "the Establishment" on their side.

In conclusion, he sounded a personal note, as he so often did now when he faced crises of public policy. He pointed out that his decision might make him a "one-term President." He was willing to take the consequences: "I would rather be a one-term President and do what I believe was right than to be a two-term President at the cost of seeing America become a second-rate power and to see this nation accept the first defeat in its proud hundred-and-ninety-year history." It was a manner of speaking which suggested that the test ahead would be, after all, not of America's will and character in facing a hostile world but of President Nixon's will and character in facing a hostile America.

President Nixon's speech was, among other things, the most comprehensive statement of the doctrine of credibility that had ever been made by an American President. Not only did he reconfirm the doctrine that had guided American policy since the time of President Kennedy and had controlled the conduct of American policy in Vietnam for almost as long but he expanded it enormously. He extended its application to events in the domestic sphere, and he stated plainly that American credibility was the thing that stood between the present political balance in the world and the "forces of totalitarianism" at home and abroad. Avoiding "humiliation" of the United States had, of course, been what Assistant Secretary of Defense John McNaughton described in early 1966 as the whole reason the United States had to go on fighting in Indo-China, and President Nixon had affirmed this in clear terms in his November 3rd speech. "Humiliation" in this scheme represented the loss of credibility. But President Nixon now took the logic of the doctrine one step further than the Johnson Administration had. He was speaking publicly of the danger that the United States would experience "defeat" in Indo-China. The word was one of the most inflammatory words in the political lexicon. Defeat, after all, was not the same as a mere failure or setback; it was the opposite of victory. It evoked white flags, troops throwing down their arms. It meant helplessness, and surrender to the will of an armed foe. Although to many in the nation the word seemed far out of proportion to any real danger that the United States faced in Indo-China, President Nixon was engaging in something more than oratorical excess when he used it. In traditional military terms, nothing like defeat was in the offing, but in terms of the strategic thinking that governed the policies of President Nixon something that might be called defeat was in fact at stake. For in his view, as in the view of his predecessors in the White House, American credibility was at stake in Indo-China, and the loss of credibility encompassed far more than any tangible losses of men or territory that might occur there. As McNaughton had put it, the aim of the war was to protect America's "reputation as a guarantor." And he had explicitly rejected the idea that the strategy had to do with turning back wars of national liberation as an aim in itself. The aim was not, he said, "to prove that 'wars of national liberation' won't work (except as our reputation is involved)." The policy was aimed at shoring up America's "reputation" in the very broadest sense, not at demonstrating a particular skill in a particular area of challenge. Therefore, not only was Indo-China a test case of the strategy of limited war but the strategy of limited war was a test case of the ability of the United States to meet challenges from any quarter. And the principal quarter from which challenges might come was, of course, the nuclear forces of the opposition. A tremendous—indeed, a limitless—burden had been placed on the strategy of limited war in general and on the Indo-China war in particular. In another age, objectives as large as these would no doubt have called for military efforts on a commensurate scale, and "great decisions" of the kind that President Nixon fondly recalled—decisions to unleash force on a far greater scale than he had released in the Cambodian action—might have been made. Military campaigns aimed directly at the main foes —at the Russians and the Chinese—rather than at their assumed proxies, the people of Indo-China, might have been launched. But in the nuclear age a ceiling had, for the first time in history, been placed on the profitable uses of violence. American Presidents were held to "limited" war. Only weak proxy-enemies, such as the Vietnamese rebels, were available for attack. Only little decisions were open to them. Yet through such limited war Presidents had to try to achieve the great global objectives for which great means had once been available. And credibility was the device by which small wars were meant to cast a long and fearful shadow. Thus, in speaking of "the great decisions which led to victory" President Nixon was obliged to use the past tense. And in another sentence, a moment later, he was obliged to remind the country where great decisions might lead if they were taken in our age: "We will avoid a wider war," he promised.

When President Nixon spoke of "defeat," therefore, he meant the defeat of military forces that were the only ones not ruled out by the fear of human extinction. It was solely by standing firm in these little crises—these test crises—that a "real crisis," which was to say a nuclear crisis, could be avoided. If President Nixon, theoretically the most powerful man in the most powerful nation in the world, was haunted by images of impotence—not only in foreign affairs but in domestic affairs, including matters as remote from foreign policy as crime legislation and the nomination of Supreme Court Justices—and if he had now come to conceive of virtually all his struggles at home and abroad as mere facets of a deeper crisis of Presidential authority, it may well have been because by far the largest component of his power (nuclear arms) was more a restraining, paralyzing influence than a source of strength. In his thinking, a momentous struggle was under way, and it was not only between the United States and Communism but between the President and those at home who would wrest from his hands the nation's chosen weapons for its defense in the nuclear age, and would thereby "defeat or humiliate" the United States even before the "real" struggle overseas began in earnest. And so it had become necessary, according to his way of thinking, to do what he had in fact been doing almost from the moment he arrived in office: make war against Americans.

Nearly as soon as the President had finished speaking, a large part of the nation did demonstrate its will—its will to get out of the war—

and it did so through something more than discussion. Civil disorders greater than anything previously seen in the United States in the twentieth century spread throughout the country. Dormant campuses exploded and began to go on strike. The protest this time had little to do with the old "Movement." It did not reflect a generation gap. On many—perhaps most—campuses, students and faculty were united against the war. Thirty-seven college and university presidents signed a letter pleading with the President to end it. For them, as for the President, the domestic stakes were now paramount. What they feared, however, was that if the war did not end, all possibility of restoring peace on their campuses and in American life generally might be lost. In other quarters, too, including the Republican Party organization, there was amazement and consternation. The House of Representatives, which had consistently supported the President in his war policy by means of resolution, now fell silent.

With the invasion speech, two disjunct worlds clashed: the world of the White House strategic thinking and the world of the country at large. The so-called credibility gap that had made its appearance during the Johnson Presidency had grown to a chasm. President Nixon had first escalated the war into Cambodia more than a year before, but then he had acted in secrecy. In doing so, he had taken the war's burden solely onto his own shoulders, and had, in effect, isolated himself from his people. Since then, the distance had steadily widened. The war issue had soured relations on his own staff to the point where he had decided to spy on many staff members, and by the autumn of 1969 it had soured his relations with a large section of the country to the point where he had launched a full-scale assault on Americans in all walks of life—Americans whom he now regarded as his enemies and as enemies of the country. In the walled-off White House, the pressure had been rising steadily for almost a year and a half, and now it was bursting out in a torrent of horrifying predictions and desperate measures poured forth without warning on national television by the President himself. In the world of global strategy in which the President lived, a sense of emergency had been steadily building, but in the world of public discourse in which the rest of the nation lived a sense of calm had been spreading. In the country at large, there were, of course, people of every political stripe, but the quality of the President's vision came as a jolt to almost all of them. In the President's vision, "anarchy," "defeat," "humiliation," and "totalitarianism" were in the offing; and the forces of darkness and the forces of light were locked in contention on every side—in Indo-China, in the universities, on Capitol Hill, in the courts, in the home. The country at large had been living in anticipation of "the just peace" that the President had promised only ten days before—not to mention "the lift of a driving dream" he had offered less than three months before that in his first State of the Union message. Now, in effect, Americans were having their first clear look at the man their President had become in his fifteen months in the White House. The shock was severe.

The day after the Cambodian speech, the President gave the country another glimpse of the full extent of his rage. He was speaking at a gathering of civilian employees in the Pentagon, and cut loose—extemporaneously, it appeared—on the subject of campus rebellion. The White House later released a transcript of his remarks. "You see these bums, you know, blowing up the campuses," the President said, and he rushed on, "Listen, the boys that are on the college campuses today are the luckiest people in the world, going to the greatest universities, and here they are burning up the books, storming around about this issue. You name it. Get rid of the war, there will be another one. Then out there we have kids who are just doing their duty. They stand tall and they are proud."

Two days after this, one public official who thoroughly agreed with the President—Governor James Rhodes, of Ohio—travelled to the town of Kent, in his state, where there had recently been student disorders at Kent State University, and, speaking of disruptions on campus, he announced, "We are not going to treat the symptoms. We are going to eradicate the problem." He said that "a group" numbering "three or four" was responsible for "the most vicious form of campus-oriented violence" in Ohio. Pounding a table, he said, "They're worse than the Brown Shirts and the Communist element and also the night riders and the vigilantes. They're the worst type of people that we harbor in America." He seemed to have picked up some language that Vice-President Agnew had used on the eve of the Cambodian action. The Vice-President, in his most intemperate attack on the anti-war movement so far, had invited the public to look upon the demonstrators as Nazi Storm Troopers or as members of the Ku Klux Klan, and to "act accordingly." On May 4th, the day after Governor Rhodes spoke, National Guardsmen shot fifteen students on the Kent State campus during a demonstration, killing four.

In a statement the same day, the President drew a lesson from the shootings: "This should remind us all once again that when dissent turns to violence it invites tragedy." That evening, the Vice-President called the killings "predictable and avoidable." He went on to attack "élitists" who regarded the Bill of Rights as a protection "for psychotic and criminal elements in our society," and observed that with leadership like this it was not surprising that "we have traitors and thieves and perverts . . . in our midst." In the country at large, the shootings triggered a national tumult of new dimensions. Campuses in the hundreds now went on strike. With American troops crossing new borders in Indo-China, and the President evidently in a world of his own in the White House, and four dead in Ohio, and colleges and universities all over the nation in a state of virtual revolt, and the Vice-President acting as if he were egging on the citizenry to new acts of violence, the nation seemed, for a moment, to be spinning out of control, perhaps irrecoverably. That Sunday, Max Frankel wrote in the *Times*, "America was a nation in anguish last week, her population divided, her campuses closed, her capital shaken, her government confused, her President perplexed." John Gardner, who had been Secretary of Health, Education, and Welfare under President Johnson, said in a speech, "Virtually all of us have failed in our duty as Americans. The failure goes to every level and phase of American life. . . . And while each of us pursues his selfish interest . . . the nation disintegrates. I use the phrase soberly: the nation disintegrates." A thousand lawyers from New York, many of them members of Wall

Street firms, arrived on Capitol Hill to lobby against the war. In the Senate, a serious drive to legislate an end to the war got under way.

Within the executive branch itself, Secretary Finch of H.E.W. declared that the Vice-President's inflammatory speeches had "contributed to heating up the climate in which the Kent State students were killed," and his Commissioner of Education, James Allen, told a meeting of four hundred applauding Office of Education employees that he could not support the President's war policies. At the State Department, more than two hundred and fifty employees signed a letter to Secretary of State Rogers protesting the Cambodian operation. A national unease that had been gathering around the person of the President crystallized. It found its most widely publicized expression in a letter to the President from his Secretary of the Interior, Walter Hickel. "About two hundred years ago, there was emerging a great nation in the British Empire, and it found itself with a colony in violent protest by its youth—men such as Patrick Henry, Thomas Jefferson, Madison, and Monroe, to name a few," Hickel wrote. "Their protests fell on deaf ears and finally led to war. The outcome is history. My point is, if we read history, it clearly shows that youth in its protest must be heard." And then, in an appeal whose implication frightened official Washington far more than the Secretary's thoughts on the President and the young, Hickel mentioned another group that must be heard by the President—his own Cabinet. "Permit me," he wrote, "to suggest that you consider meeting on an individual and conversational basis with members of your Cabinet." This advice raised an ominous question: If the President was out of touch with young people, and out of touch with Congress (whose advice he had not asked before he ordered troops into Cambodia), and out of touch with his Cabinet, then whom was he in touch with?

In his speech announcing the invasion of Cambodia, the President had said, "I promised to end this war. I shall keep that promise." And it was true that as he escalated the war with one hand, he was de-escalating it with the other. It was not in the name of an expanding, unbounded war effort that the country was being put through its worst ordeal in this century. The President was not rallying his people to victory. He was rallying them to endure a protraction of the announced liquidation of a war that the country had rejected. Withdrawal was tearing the country apart as escalation had never done: a dying war had been parlayed into a national convulsion.

The day after the killings at Kent State, as the tide of anger and dismay was rising, the President reversed his course. He met with several congressional delegations, and, whatever his military plans may have been when he announced his intention of going "to the heart of the trouble," he now announced that American troops would not penetrate more than twenty-one miles into Cambodia, and that they would be withdrawn within a period of from three to seven weeks. He reversed his mood, too. Three days later, on the evening of May 8th, he held a news conference, and when he was asked now about student protests against his decision to send American troops into Cambodia, he said, "I made the decision for the very reasons that they are protesting. And as far as affecting my decision is concerned, their protests I am concerned about; I am concerned because I know how deeply they feel." He also said, "You can be sure that everything that I stand for is what they want." In his Cambodian-invasion speech, the President had portrayed an "age of anarchy." Now, as a result of the invasion, something close to real anarchy had been unleashed in the land, but the President's vision had faded, at least in his public pronouncements. When he was asked whether the war, after it was over, would seem worthwhile to Americans looking back on it, he answered, "It's a rather moot question. . . . Only history will record whether it was worthwhile." The threat that had recently menaced the institutions that had been created by free civilizations in the last five hundred years had evaporated for the moment, too. The public justifications for the war, it now seemed, were of variable magnitude and intensity. It was as though there were a thermostat on the nation's war aims, which could be turned all the way up to stakes of apocalyptic proportions and turned down to near zero.

That night, the President was unable to sleep. Between nine o'clock in the evening and five o'clock the next morning, he made fifty-one phone calls, including eight to Henry Kissinger. Later, looking back on it all, Kissinger offered the opinion that the President had been "on the edge of nervous breakdown." On May 9th, a demonstration against the Cambodian action was to take place in Washington. At 5 A.M., the President decided to go out and meet his young adversaries face to face. He awakened his valet, Manolo Sanchez, who drove him in the early-morning darkness down to the Lincoln Memorial, where some young people were waiting for the day's events to begin. He approached a group of students, and opened the conversation with some small talk. He chatted about sports (football, surfing), and described the importance of travelling while you were still young. (The American West would be a nice place to start, he said.) Shifting to weightier subjects, he pointed out that at one time he had considered Winston Churchill "a madman." The young people were disconcerted, and some hours later, when the President was back in the White House, he told a reporter, "I doubt if that got over."

On the day the President was telling the country that he wanted just what the protesters wanted, construction workers in Lower Manhattan—as though following the advice given by the Vice-President ten days earlier to regard the protesters as Storm Troopers or as members of the Ku Klux Klan and to "act accordingly"— attacked a group of peaceful student anti-war demonstrators with their fists and tools, injuring about fifty of them. Men in business suits were seen directing the workers to their targets. The attack marked the first major incident of street violence between ordinary citizens over the issue of the war. Overnight, the term "hard-hat"—a reference to the construction workers' headgear—entered the language, signifying a generalized lower-middle-class anger against "liberals." On May 26th, President Nixon met with a delegation from the New York construction-trade and longshoremen's unions and informed them that he had found the actions of the union men on the streets "very meaningful." Peter Brennan, president of the Building and Construction Trades Council of Greater New York, and the other union men presented the President with a hard-hat bearing the legend "Commander-in-Chief," together with a statement in support of the President's war policy that said, in part, "The hard-hat will stand as a symbol, along with our great flag, for freedom and patriotism to our beloved country."

By the end of June, the troops had been withdrawn from Cambodia. They had not found a Communist headquarters, nor had they encountered the enemy on a large scale. As it turned out, the enemy, apparently having got wind of the invasion beforehand, had withdrawn deeper into Cambodia and set about training Cambodian insurgents in techniques for overthrowing their government. In the field in Southeast Asia, the most momentous military result of the invasion had turned out to be a takeover of some two-thirds of Cambodia by the insurgent forces. But in Washington the events in Cambodia went all but unnoticed. Washington was preoccupied with the uprising at home. From the start, the President, who had precipitated the crisis single-handed, had regarded the Cambodian invasion primarily as a domestic event, and it had turned out to be just that. The military results were unimportant to him, because what was being tested was "not our power" but our "will and character," and will and character could be tested only at home. Ordinarily, in wartime, it is the foe that tests the will and character of a people, and does so by posing a military threat. The Cambodian crisis was unique in that the President, not the enemy, was testing his people's character, and was doing it with a crisis that was a mere rehearsal for a "real crisis." The invasion, therefore, was not so much an invasion of enemy territory as an invasion by the President of what he took to be the soft, irresolute territory of the American character. President Kennedy and President Johnson had used Vietnam as a stage to demonstrate American credibility. President Nixon, ever since he came to office, had been using America as the stage. And if in recent years the White House and the country had grown apart, the President's foray out of the White House fastness into the nation in the form of a symbolic military invasion accompanied by fearsome rhetorical flourishes gave the inhabitants of each world a glimpse of the other. The President encountered a wrathful resistance whose depth he had not expected, and the resisters encountered, among other things, bullets. Both sides recoiled in shock. And after the brief scene of mutual bewilderment in the early morning on the steps of the Lincoln Memorial each side withdrew again into its own world.

In early summer, the President, returning to the calm and predictability of the executive branch, launched a fresh bout of "reorganization." The shakeup, with its hirings and firings and transfers of power, showed the President in command of affairs and helped calm fears that he might be losing his grip. And, like the first bout of reorganization, which had been launched when the President first arrived in office, it gave the country something of what William Shannon in 1968 had called "the known and familiar" to think about. Moreover, it gave the President a chance to expand his power in a new direction: over the agencies and Cabinet departments of his executive branch. The first bout of reorganization had been presented as action preliminary to the formation of policies, but now it turned out that what the action had been preliminary to was more reorganization: the system set up for domestic affairs in January of 1969 was scrapped in the early summer of 1970 in favor of a whole new set of institutions. The 1970 plan came from the President's Advisory Council on Executive Organization, headed by Roy Ash, who had had a hand in reorganization from the beginning. The Advisory Council had been ordered to work in total secrecy. Members had been forbidden to take documents home with them. They had been required to throw all the wastepaper of their work in "burn bags," whose contents were always incinerated. Even the Cabinet was kept uninformed of the impending changes. Finally, the President announced, when the plan was submitted to Congress, that two principal new institutions were being set up in the White House. They were, first, the Domestic Council, which would include the Vice-President, the Attorney General, the Secretary of Agriculture, the Secretary of Commerce, the Secretary of Health, Education, and Welfare, the Secretary of Housing and Urban Development, the Secretary of the Interior, the Secretary of Labor, the Secretary of Transportation, and the Secretary of the Treasury, and also the new Council on Urban Affairs, which had been established with such high expectations in 1969; and, second, the Office of Management and Budget, which would subsume the old Bureau of the Budget and would take an interest in almost all domestic programs from a budgetary point of view. In the second week of June, after the statutory sixty-day waiting period had elapsed without a congressional vote against the new plan, the President announced that it would take effect on July 1st. John Ehrlichman was placed in charge of the Domestic Council, and so became one of the two or three most important men in the executive branch. Every document on domestic affairs that was submitted for the President's attention was channelled through him. In the fall of 1969, Ehrlichman had been named Assistant to the President for Domestic Affairs, and a *Times* reporter had written, "Thus Mr. Ehrlichman was named to oversee the domestic policymaking machinery, and the question therefore arises, what do we know about him?" After giving a few details of Ehrlichman's background, the reporter concluded, "On balance, he is the sort of man to whom one would unhesitatingly grant power of attorney." The other new organization, the Office of Management and Budget, would be headed by George Shultz, who had resigned as Secretary of Labor, and who would now also be an Assistant to the President.

The Advisory Council proposed, further, a change in the independent regulatory commissions, whose effect would be to bring them under tighter White House control. Most of the existing commissions would be merged, abolished, fragmented, or reduced in size. The Interstate Commerce Commission, the Civil Aeronautics

Board, and the Federal Maritime Commission would be merged into one commission, headed by a single administrator; the five-member Securities and Exchange Commission would be replaced by a new agency, also headed by a single administrator; the five-member Federal Trade Commission would be abolished and its functions distributed among two new agencies; and the seven members of the Federal Communications Commission would be reduced to five. In other words, bipartisan voting boards, composed of commissioners who served for fixed terms specified by statute, and each of whom had to be confirmed by the Senate, would be replaced by strong chairmen who would be nominated by the White House, and would serve at the pleasure of the President without a fixed term of office. "The aim would be to center the making of policy in highly visible executives . . . and abandon the time-consuming pretense that the commissions can sit as courts and reach impartial judicial-type decisions" is how the *Times* explained the proposal. Actually, the "reorganization," which sounded so humdrum and was so boring to think about, was an immense part of a drive to concentrate power in the White House.

There were some people outside the White House who expected reorganization to inaugurate the mood of conciliation and calm that the President had once promised. Some of those who had applauded the Administration's idea of bringing the country together and deplored its later idea of "positive polarization," and who were pleased that the President had now said he wanted just what the demonstrators wanted, saw the new reorganization as a means of giving the Cabinet the access to the President which he had promised it even before he was inaugurated but which Interior Secretary Hickel had found lacking in the spring of 1970. They hoped that, following the President's reorganization, "a Cabinet made up of the ablest men in America, leaders in their own right and not merely by virtue of appointment—men who will command the public's respect and the President's attention by the power of their intellect and the force of their ideas," as the President had described the ideal Cabinet during the campaign, would now swing into action and would at last establish the tolerant, "open" Administration that the nation had thought it put in power in 1968. The President and his newly powerful advisers saw reorganization in exactly the opposite light. All three of the high Administration officials who had ventured to breathe a word of criticism of the Administration during the crisis—Hickel, Allen, and Finch—were marked for removal from their posts. (Within months, the sentences were carried out.) The crisis over Cambodia had confirmed the top men of the Administration in their picture of themselves as a beleaguered band trying to execute the President's policies in the face of the virtually treasonous machinations of a whole league of enemies. When the country, at the President's invitation, revealed its will and character in the uproar after the Cambodian action, the men in the White House had been deeply alarmed by what they saw. As John Ehrlichman later described the way he saw things, the White House was faced with the "problems of leaks, demonstrations, bombings and terrorism, public opinion, and congressional support." And, besides public opinion, terrorism, and the like, there was another problem, he said—"holdovers" in the executive branch, as Democrats who remained in their jobs after the change of Administration were known. Erlichman went on to say of the holdovers, "These people conducted a kind of internal guerrilla warfare against the President during the first term, trying to frustrate his goals. . . . The object was to create hostility in the Congress and abroad and to affect public opinion." Thus, in Ehrlichman's mind the holdovers within the Administration merged with the terrorists outside it. He said, "A similar threat . . . was posed by the combination of street demonstrations, terrorism, violence, and their effect on public and congressional support for the President's policy." Since arriving in office, President Nixon had developed the conviction that a powerful "Establishment" consisting of the Senate, the anti-war movement, the press, the television networks, and independent foundations was plotting to cripple the American Presidency and to destroy him personally at the earliest possible date, and now he had arrived at the conclusion that the federal bureaucracy, too, was in on the plot. The crisis of Presidential authority, he believed, now reached into his own executive branch. Reorganization was an excellent weapon for combat on the bureaucratic front. Through reorganization, the President could in a very short period create a bureaucracy within the White House which was wholly under White House control and whose functions would often duplicate those of the Cabinet departments. Then, in the long run, the Cabinet departments themselves could be staffed with politically loyal people. Patrick Buchanan, in proposing the front group disguised as a foundation which would carry on Administration activities seemingly outside the Administration, had suggested that one of its roles might be to train loyalists who could be moved into the State Department "five deep" after the 1972 Presidential election. Now it turned out that, in the absence of such a "foundation," the expanded White House staff was to be the training ground.

Reorganization also increased the power of the White House in relation to the Congress. White House control in the foreign sphere was already complete. Now, by removing domestic policy-making to the White House, the Administration turned power in the domestic sphere over to men who, unlike the Cabinet Secretaries, did not require Senate confirmation and could not, in the ordinary conduct of their duties, be required to testify on Capitol Hill. Moreover, under the old system the Cabinet departments, with their entrenched bureaucracies, were prone to alliances with Congress and subject to congressional influence, but the new policymakers in the White House would be independent. Under the new arrangements, it would be considerably harder for members of Congress to "substitute their own philosophy or their own subjective judgment" for that of the President, as he had said they did when the Senate had rejected the Carswell nomination. The diminution of congressional power would be good for the country, the White House men thought—for their attitude toward Congress was deeply contemptuous. Since going to work at the White House, Ehrlichman, for one, had had a good look at the legislative branch, and he had been shocked by what he found. He had seen drunken members "totter onto the floor," he told the Senate Select Committee on Presidential Campaign Activities in the summer of 1973, and he believed that others had been sucked into a "local culture which scoffs at patriotism and family life and morality just as it adulates the opposite." To let these degenerates, drunkards, and incompetents make policy would obviously be as inexcusable an abdication of Presidential responsibility as it would be to turn policy over to the guerrilla warriors in the Cabinet departments, not to mention the ones in the streets. So policy would not be made in the Congress or in the Cabinet department or in the streets—or, for that matter, in the Supreme Court, where strict constructionists would be keeping out of the President's way. It would be made in the White House.

To some people in Congress, and some people in the Cabinet departments, the process might look like a takeover from the top, in which the White House had set out to subjugate the independent centers of power in the federal government, but to the men in the White House it seemed an effort to put down an insurrection. To them, the coup looked like counterinsurgency war.

In the summer of 1970, the White House opened an "offensive" against Chet Huntley, the co-anchorman of the NBC evening news. Huntley had been quoted in *Life* as saying of Nixon, "The shallowness of the man overwhelms me; the fact that he is President frightens me." In mid-July, Lawrence Higby, an aide to Haldeman, wrote a memo to Magruder asking for "some creative thinking" on "an attack on Huntley for his statements in *Life*." Higby suggested a petition "calling for the immediate removal of Huntley right now." As it happened, Huntley was already retiring, but Higby wanted to press ahead with the attack. Huntley might be retiring, but there was still NBC to destroy. "The point behind this whole thing is that we don't care about Huntley—he is going to leave anyway," Higby wrote, and he added, "What we are trying to do here is to tear down the institution."

On July 9th, Haldeman wrote a memo to Magruder suggesting that another institution—the Harris poll—should be torn down. The Harris organization had taken a poll showing that seventy per cent of the students in American colleges were disturbed by American foreign policy. "Let's figure out a way to get some mileage out of this and some similar questions in the Harris poll and use them as a way of discrediting the Harris poll," Haldeman wrote, and he added, "There is a lot of dirty work that could be done here and should be."

In the period of intensive reorganization that followed the Cambodian action, the Administration's campaign against the press became more ambitious than ever. In the fall of 1969, Jeb Magruder had suggested moving from the "shotgun" technique to the "rifle" technique. Since then, the Vice-President had made his series of speeches attacking the news media; the system of rigged letters had been instituted; a method of arranging leaks and plants in the press had been devised; the Justice Department had subpoenaed the notes of reporters from many of the country's major news organizations; the Administration's Communications Director Herbert Klein had made threatening remarks (for example, he had characterized the Vice-President's attacks as a "physician-heal-thyself" warning); other government officials had threatened government intervention in broadcasting; and, within the Administration, White House staff members had been looking into the possibility of using the F.C.C., the Justice Department, and the Internal Revenue Service to bring the press and the television networks into line.

By mid-1970, the target was not one news organization or another but the news media as an institution. The aim, as Magruder put it in response to a request from Haldeman for a program of action, was to "generate a public reëxamination of the role of the media in American life." Instead of just tearing down NBC, "the focus of our effort should be to raise the larger question of objectivity and ethics in the media as an institution," Magruder wrote.

"To do this, we will have to turn objectivity into an issue and a subject of public debate." Like his superiors in the White House, Magruder was confident of the Administration's power to control the content of public debate. And, indeed, Magruder's plan illustrated one of the great strengths of the White House propaganda machine. Its power lay not so much in its ability to control what was said on a given issue as in its power to determine which issues were taken up for national debate. Sometimes a blistering speech by the Vice-President would be all that was necessary. In the fall of 1969, at his instigation, the television networks had already devoted their attention to the question of their "objectivity." In other cases, the fact that the President had taken up, or dropped, an issue would be reason enough for the networks and the press to take up, or to drop, that issue.

Magruder suggested several specific measures for making an issue of objectivity. One was to "plant a column" with a columnist "which raises the question of objectivity and ethics in the news media." Another was to "arrange for an article" on the same subject in a "major consumer magazine," which would be written by "Stewart Alsop, [William] Buckley, or [James] Kilpatrick." (The men in the White House had no doubt of their power to induce independent writers to write what the White House wanted them to write.) Another was to "arrange" for an article on objectivity to be written for a "prestigious journal," such as the *Columbia Journalism Review*. Another was to "ask the Vice-President to speak out on this issue." (He was already doing so.) Another was to "have Rogers Morton"—the chairman of the Republican National Committee—"go on the attack in a news conference." Another was to "have Dean Burch"—the chairman of the Federal Communications Commission—"'express concern' about press objectivity in response to a letter from a Congressman." Another was to arrange for a book-length "'exposé' to be written by an author such as Earl Mazo or Victor Lasky"—which, of course, could enable the men in the White House to "generate a massive outpouring of letters-to-the-editor." Another was to "form a blue-ribbon media 'watchdog' committee to report to the public on cases of biassed reporting." Another was to "have a Senator or Congressman write a public letter to the F.C.C. suggesting the 'licensing' of individual newsmen." Of such stuff were White House "offensives" made.

In no area was the White House more eager for reorganization than in that of domestic intelligence. The President might say he wanted the same thing as the people demonstrating against him in the streets, but privately he remained convinced that the "age of anarchy" he had announced in his Cambodia speech was continuing. In 1969, the Administration had sought to establish working links between the Justice Department and the C.I.A., among others; now, in June of 1970, the President ordered a "reassessment" of the government's intelligence-gathering activities at the highest level. Haldeman assigned Tom Huston, who had once been an Army intelligence officer, and who described himself as a "Jeffersonian Republican," to oversee the work. On June 5th, as the uproar over the invasion of Cambodia was subsiding, the President called in Director Helms of the C.I.A.; the Director of the F.B.I., J. Edgar Hoover; the head of the National Security Agency, Vice-Admiral Noel Gayler; and the head of the Defense Intelligence Agency, Lieutenant General Donald Bennett. He asked them all to meet with Huston to work out a coördinated plan for dealing with internal threats. At the first meeting, Huston informed the group of a decision by President Nixon that in facing the domestic threat, "everything is valid, everything is possible." After several meetings, the group agreed on a plan. A secret corps made up of representatives of the four intelligence agencies; the counter-intelligence agencies of the Departments of the Army, the Navy, and the Air Force; and—if the Interagency Group on Domestic Intelligence and Internal Security, as this new corps was to be called, thought it necessary—the State Department, the Treasury Department, the Justice Department, "and such other agencies which may have investigative or law-enforcement responsibilities touching on domestic intelligence or internal security matters," and overseen by the White House, would be, in effect, empowered to commit a wide variety of crimes against the members of any group that it suspected of being subversive. The Interagency Group would be empowered to open mail, to tap telephones without warrants, and to break into people's houses and offices. Huston knew that these activities were criminal: he wrote that surreptitious entry was "clearly illegal" and "could result in great embarrassment if exposed." Of course, the C.I.A. and the F.B.I. had been doing all of these things for years *without* written instructions from the White House; yet the Nixon Administration, in proposing its new plan, was attempting to do much more than ratify an existing state of affairs. For one thing, the White House envisioned a broadened scale of operation, and one objective of the Interagency Group was to be "maximum use of all special investigative techniques, including increased agent and informant penetration by both the F.B.I. and the C.I.A." For another thing, whereas in earlier days, the unlawful spying upon and harassment of American citizens had had to be secret to some extent from the highest officers of the government, now an instruction had gone out from a President ordering the agencies to break the law. In other words, all restraints internal to the executive branch were to be lifted. The proposed coördination of the agencies into a single force would be an important step, too. The citizen who ran afoul of the F.B.I.'s Cointelpro program or the I.R.S.'s Special Service Group might suffer serious interference in his life, but the person whose name got onto the computers of an organization that commanded the combined resources of the F.B.I., the C.I.A., the N.S.A., the D.I.A., and the I.R.S., not to mention the State Department, the Treasury Department, and the other agencies and departments of the government, would be up against a virtually irresistible foe. He would be up against a secret police organization that could reach into his life in countless ways—into his personal life, into his financial affairs, into his work, into his public life. Even more dangerous, however, than the links of the agencies to each other would be their link to the White House. By placing the Interagency Group under White House guidance, the Administration would be able to direct it towards targets of its own choosing; and since the President was inclined to believe that his political adversaries were also adversaries of the nation—for no number of C.I.A. reports could shake his conviction that the disorders at home were planned abroad—the new group could become a powerful political instrument in his hands.

Huston was pleased with the first phase of his work. In reference to the assembled chiefs of the intelligence agencies, he wrote in a memo to Haldeman, "Unlike most of the bureaucracy, the intelligence community welcomes direction and leadership from the White House." Huston went on to give the intelligence chiefs high marks for their performance at his meetings. "The discussions were frank and the quality of work first-rate," he wrote. "All were delighted that an opportunity was finally at hand to address themselves jointly to the serious internal security threat which exists." In fact, he was so well pleased with the chiefs that he recommended a little reward for them. The President, he said, should "present each with an autographed copy of the photo of the first meeting which Ollie took." The reference was to Oliver Atkins, a White House photographer. Of course, they wouldn't be able to hang the award on the wall, because the entire operation was secret.

Huston was particularly eager to use the Internal Revenue Service to harass radical groups. He got in touch with the I.R.S. to inquire about the Special Service Group, which he had set up in July of 1969. "What we cannot do in a courtroom via criminal prosecutions to curtail the activities of some of these groups, I.R.S. could do by administrative action," Huston wrote, and he added, "Moreover, valuable intelligence-type information could be turned up by I.R.S. as a result of their field audits." In Huston's eyes, government agencies were interchangeable. The Justice Department, the nation's chief law-enforcement agency, was to be used to "curtail the activities" of "groups," and whenever this failed, the I.R.S., a tax-collecting agency, was to be used to punish them. And if the C.I.A., which in any case was barred by its charter from collecting information at home, could not get the facts that the White House wanted about some of the "groups," the I.R.S. could do that, too.

Huston had expected trouble from Richard Helms, the Director of the C.I.A., who was a holdover from the Johnson Administration, but Helms seemed to agree fully to the White House plan, and he won a commendatory "Most coöperative" in his young overlord's review of the situation to Haldeman. Then the plan ran into unexpected trouble from another holdover—J. Edgar Hoover, the Director of the F.B.I. Earlier, Hoover, on his own initiative, had claimed as the province of the F.B.I. the responsibility for disrupting the left, and he did not care to have other agencies—or the White House—muscling in on his territory. Now, finding himself in a minority of one, the Director had recourse to "footnotes." At the bottom of Huston's final report to the President, his objections were typed in. Hoover said he was afraid—as Huston paraphrased it in a memo to Haldeman—that "the risks are too great," and that "these folks are going to get the President into trouble," because " 'the jackals of the press' and the A.C.L.U. will find out." Huston, a dedicated soldier of the reorganizational wars, was scandalized. "For eighteen months, we have watched people in this government ignore the President's orders, take actions to embarrass him, promote themselves at his expense, and generally make his job more difficult," he wrote in his memo to Haldeman. "It makes me fighting mad, and what Hoover is doing here is putting himself above the President." Given the way the President and his top aides felt about the "guerrillas" in the bureaucracies, these were no doubt the kind of words they liked to hear from their subordinates. Unfortunately for Tom Huston and his plan, Director Hoover was no ordinary holdover. Hoover had more than footnotes to use in his fight. For instance, he knew all about the President's warrantless-wiretapping program, and he knew that if the jackals of the press and the A.C.L.U. found out that the President had been wiretapping members of his own staff and newsmen such as Joseph Kraft, the President would truly be in trouble. In mid-July, the President approved the Huston plan. But the plan was never put into effect. Employing a check that the Founding Fathers had not envisioned—sheer bureaucratic clout and secret-police power—Director Hoover indeed put himself above the President, and overruled him; and the liberties of the people, to some small extent, were protected.

The A.C.L.U., if it had got wind of the White House intelligence plan, would certainly have considered it repressive, as Hoover guessed. But Huston did not think of it that way. He saw it as a means of *heading off* repression. As he expressed it much later, "the first problem from the intelligence point of view was to try to identify these people [violently inclined radicals] as quickly as possible to get the damned thing stopped before there was real repression." Vice-President Agnew had used a similar logic in many of his speeches. On one occasion in the fall of 1969, he had said, "Right now we must decide whether we will take the trouble to stave off a totalitarian state. Will we stop the wildness now before it is too late, before the witchhunting and repression that are all too inevitable begin?" Henry Kissinger was another who was afraid of right-wing repression, and he told journalists on occasion that the United States must leave Vietnam without suffering a defeat in order to avert a dangerous right-wing backlash, such as occurred after the "fall" of China in 1949. Speaking to a group of editors in Hartford, Connecticut, about the Administration's policy during the Cambodian crisis, he said, "It has been our conviction that if political decisions were to be made in the streets the victors would not be upper-middle-class college kids, but some real tough guys. . . . The society which makes its decisions in this manner will sooner or later be driven towards some form of Caesarism in which the most brutal forces in the society take over. Therefore, we believe that what really was at stake here was not this President. What was at stake here was the problem of authority in this society altogether." Outside the Administration, too, this argument carried considerable weight. In a widely read speech in the spring of 1970, Senator Margaret Chase Smith, Republican of Maine, had argued that the disruption caused by the left was dangerous because it could provoke a repressive reaction. And the *Times,* in its editorials, had often made the point that if the left continued to disrupt the universities, repressive government action might be taken which would destroy the universities' traditional independence. Even within the left itself, strong pressure was put on demonstrators and others to wear conventional clothes and behave in a dignified manner, so as not to provoke an angry reaction among people on their right—

115

which in this case meant almost everyone. In 1970, then, almost the whole of America, from Huston on left, was looking in fear over its right shoulder.

As the tempo of reorganization increased throughout the executive branch, Constitutional offices became misshapen. Some offices were expanding beyond their normal limits; other offices were dying from neglect. Power was ebbing from many of the old positions, whose duties and authority were defined by history and by law, and was flowing into newly invented positions, whose duties and authority were left all but undefined. For example, the office of the Secretary of State, a post formally established by an act of the Congress almost two hundred years ago, was shrivelling into insignificance, while the recently established ad-hoc office of Assistant to the President for National Security Affairs was swelling with newly grasped power. Many offices had sprung into existence at the President's behest, emerging without public discussion from the secret deliberations of the Advisory Council. The duties of nine Cabinet Secretaries concerned with domestic affairs had been superseded by an institution newly created by executive fiat—the Domestic Council—but its duties, and also those of the Office of Management and Budget, had hardly been specified at all. A message to Congress stated hazily that two functions, "policy determination and executive management, closely connected but basically separate," were centered in the President's office, and went on to explain that, corresponding to these functions, the two new entities would "involve (1) what government should do, and (2) how it goes about doing it." When an aide in the Budget Bureau—shortly to be absorbed by the new Office of Management and Budget—was asked to clarify what the roles of the two organizations would be he replied, vaguely, "Most probably the relationships cannot be defined yet and will have to work themselves out in time." In the executive order establishing the Domestic Council, the section titled "Functions of the Council" was even less specific. It stated, in full, "The

116

Council shall perform such functions as the President may from time to time delegate or assign thereto."

Posts that are clearly articulated by law and tradition are essential in a system of public accountability, because they render the officeholders visible, and therefore accountable, to the public. If a post is fairly stable, the performance of a particular holder can be measured against clear, well-known obligations, and his performance can be compared with the performances of his predecessors. But in the Nixon system of rapidly fluctuating posts with no fixed responsibilities the frame of reference was lost, and the public was faced with a blur of unknown, uninvestigated men shifting back and forth between unfamiliar posts whose duties were in any case unclear. Another reason that stable, duly authorized positions are important is that they have a reassuring effect on the men who hold them. They are fixed points that men can cling to in the rapid flux of political affairs. The government official whose duties are clearly defined possesses a mandate that derives from someone other than the man who appointed him, and, if he wishes, he may invoke that mandate to resist illegitimate pressures. Moreover, certain limits are set on his own ambitions—at least, until he is appointed to some new post. But the men holding the new, amorphous, malleable, evanescent positions in the Nixon Administration knew that not only they but their posts could be promoted or demoted. They knew that their superiors were responsible for creating the ground they stood on as well as for the fact that they were the particular men standing on it. They knew that, depending on their performance, or even on pure chance, they might suddenly find themselves holding sway over Cabinet members or agency heads, as Tom Huston did in June and July of 1970—or, just as suddenly, they might find themselves without any authority at all, as Huston did some months later.

A Constitutional government is a structure of fixed forms, but the men of the Nixon Administration were acting as though it were up to them to decide the shape of the United States government, and under their stewardship the fixed forms of the American gov-

ernment were dissolving. In the Nixon Administration, just as certain images were created and then discarded when their usefulness
was over, institutions and organizations rose and fell with dizzying
rapidity. Indeed, it was in part the insubstantiality and the transience of the Administration's aims—so many of which were geared
to the demands of public relations—that underlay the transience of
its institutional arrangements. The American system was losing the
harmony, proportion, and balance conferred upon it by its founders
in the eighteenth century. A spirit of reckless innovation had gained
the upper hand. The three branches had become unevenly weighted.
The Congress was surrendering one power after another to the
executive branch. An apparent attempt to degrade the third coequal
branch of government—the judicial, represented by the Supreme
Court—was under way. The Cabinet had been humbled. In wide
areas, Constitutionally delegated authority was yielding to grants
of discretionary power. The rights of assembly and free speech were
under heavy assault. Military campaigns were being waged in
secret. The lines that had from the beginning divided one governmental power from another and divided governmental power from
personal power were fading and disappearing. The American Constitutional polity was caught up in a process of rank, patternless
change. An Administration had seemed to decide that it could govern without reference to the Constitution or to any other given blue-
print of government, and the country, by its reaction—or lack of
one—seemed, for the moment, to acquiesce.

Immediately after the invasion of Cambodia and the shootings at
Kent State University, a strong feeling had developed in Washington and in the press—and, to all appearances, in the Administration
itself—that the Presidential Offensive against the Administration's
adversaries had run into a dead end. The President, as though
acknowledging that the strain had become too great, had abruptly
changed his course. At his press conference shortly after the Kent
State killings, he had said that he would now be governed by the
rule "When the action is hot, keep the rhetoric cool." In the months

that followed, while Tom Huston, John Ehrlichman, and others were getting on with reorganization, he reverted in his public utterances to his inspirational style. He reiterated his promise to run an "open" Administration, and professed solidarity with the aspirations of the young. At the end of May, he told a rally assembled in Knoxville, Tennessee, to hear the evangelist Billy Graham, "I want to tell you that I'm very proud that on our White House staff we have the largest proportion of staff members in responsible positions below the age of thirty of any White House staff in history." And he said, "Government can provide, as I've indicated, peace, clean water, clean air, clean streets, and all the rest," but most important of all, he went on, was "that quality of the spirit that each one of us needs" and that Billy Graham could supply. A month later, in a speech in St. Louis before a convention of the Jaycees, formerly the United States Junior Chamber of Commerce, he said, "I have seen, as you have seen, those deeply troubled people, and I understand why they feel as they do, carrying their signs and shouting their slogans, 'Peace, Now.'" Only then did he go on to defend his policy of staying in the war until the right kind of peace could be arranged. The mood of doubt—and certainly the mood of outrage—that swept the country in the spring had seemed to evaporate shortly after the Cambodian episode ended. While the crisis lasted, it had shaken many observers more deeply than anything in recent memory, but once it was over, people had appeared to push it out of their minds. Not for the first time, the nation had convinced itself that a return to "the known and familiar" was at hand. Once again, the prevailing opinion was that the war was "no longer an issue." As for the students who had protested in the spring, one student seemed to reflect the general feeling when he said, "Everything sizzled out in May, leaving a bad taste in everybody's mouth."

On September 10th, some two months before the congressional election of 1970, Vice-President Agnew set off on a tour of the country, in the company of several White House aides, including the speechwriters Patrick Buchanan and William Safire, and began to sound the opening themes of the approaching campaign. A member of Agnew's campaign entourage said to a reporter, "The tactic of this whole campaign is not to let those on the left get back to the center." On the second day of the tour, in an address to a Republican State Convention in San Diego, the Vice-President declared, "The great question for all of us this fall is becoming clearer and clearer," and he went on to ask, "Will America be led by a President elected by a majority of the American people, or will we be intimidated and blackmailed into following the path dictated by a disruptive, radical, and militant minority—the pampered prodigies of the radical liberals in the United States Senate?"

The next week, the President, in a speech at Kansas State University, seemed to embroider the Vice-President's theme. No longer did he want what the demonstrators against his policies wanted. Citing the hijacking of airplanes as a recent manifestation of a new global wave of "violence and terror," he told the students, "That same cancerous disease has been spreading over the world and here in the United States. . . . We have seen it in other bombings and burnings on our campuses, and [in] our cities, in the wanton shootings of policemen." The President drew a connection between these episodes and large international events, as he had done in his speech announcing the invasion of Cambodia. "A nation that condones blackmail and terror at home," he said, "can hardly stand as the example in putting an end to international piracies or tensions that could explode into war abroad." Therefore, he went on, something that was still worse than the violence itself was "the passive acquiescence or even fawning approval [of violence such as bombing, hijacking, and the shooting of policemen] that in some fashionable circles has become the mark of being 'with it.'" The President, far from growing more tolerant of "the Establishment" (in his view "fashionable circles" and "the Establishment" were evidently allied), as many observers expected him to do after the hard lessons of the Cambodian invasion, had come to believe that large numbers of "the Establishment" delighted in the murder of police officers and the bombing of university buildings. In an earlier expression of the drift of his thinking, he had mused on this subject in early August, at an informal press conference. He had just seen the Western film *Chisum*, and it had got him wondering why Western movies were so popular. "One of the reasons is, perhaps—and this may be a square observation—the good guys come out ahead in the Westerns, the bad guys lose," he suggested. That was right and proper. But in the President's opinion there were now significant numbers of Americans whose morality was completely inverted— who actually wanted to see the bad guys win. "As we look at the situation today," he said, "I think the main concern that I have is the attitudes that are created among many of our younger people and also perhaps older people as well in which they tend to glorify and to make heroes out of those who engage in criminal activities." An example, he pointed out, was a man named Charles Manson. The California newspapers, he had noticed, were devoting a good deal of space to news of the mass murder of a film star and some of her friends by a cultist group led by Manson. Apparently, this affair, and the coverage it got, had merged in the President's mind with thoughts about the political system in the United States and about international affairs, and he went on to remark that Americans all had to respect "the system of law and order and justice which we have inherited from over hundreds of years." He warned, "It is that system that is now under attack in so many areas. . . . We must come to its defense." The Presidential Offensive, it seemed, had taken a new lease on life.

In the August press conference and then in the September speech, the President had reverted—perhaps in anticipation of the fall congressional campaign—to the vision of the world he revealed in the Cambodia speech. In private, it seems, he had never lost that vision. If anything, it had grown more horrific. His picture of the way things were moving at home, in particular, was more alarming than before. Now the American system was threatened not only by anarchists systematically destroying universities but by glorifiers of criminal violence, lovers of mass murder, and fawners upon the murderers of policemen: outright advocates of the most hideous forms of evil. And from the Vice-President's remarks it appeared that some of these clearly sick and dangerous people were in the

United States Senate. These were not the "cool" words that the President had recommended after the Kent State shootings. Much less did they have anything to do with his advice to "lower our voices." (That phrase, which the President used in his Inaugural Address, had long been forgotten.)

For a brief period in September, Jeb Magruder found himself out of step with the prevailing White House thinking. He feared that the image that the White House was now promoting might be the wrong one for the congressional campaign of 1970. In fact, he was still dreaming of promoting the "image quite different than that of the Vice President, the Attorney General, and Judge Carswell" that he had favored in the spring—the image that would show the White House to be filled with "young, well-educated men who *care*." On September 11th, he wrote in a memo to Haldeman, "We won't take a back seat to anyone on progress—and we haven't. . . . Let's tangle with them [the Democrats] on a *philosophy* of government. The Establishment Democrats and opposition want a government that *tells* people what to do. RN wants a government that is responsive to all people, not just special interests." Magruder hoped that the new image he was proposing might prove acceptable. But Haldeman wrote back, "The attached still doesn't do it. Read the Scammon memo again [Richard Scammon was the author, with Ben Wattenberg, of a book titled *The Real Majority*] and then listen to a few of the Vice President's speeches and see if you don't get a better fix on what our theme is." Magruder quickly revised his ideas, and wrote to Haldeman, "The Democrats should be portrayed as being on the fringes: radical liberals who bus children, excuse disorders, tolerate crime, apologize for our wealth, and undercut the President's foreign policy."

The ideas of Scammon and Wattenberg, which were proving so influential in the White House, revolved around what they called "the social issue." The social issue was a cluster of fears that were said to afflict the average American voter as he went about his daily life, and included fear of drug addicts and rising crime rates, fear of school busing and of black people who might move into white neighborhoods, and fear of radical demonstrators. These fears, even more than economic worries, Scammon and Wattenberg thought, would determine how Americans voted in the future. Among many Americans, a feeling had been growing for some time that what were often called "old values" were collapsing, and that the society was in a state of disintegration. The old values were, among other things, thrift, a high regard for hard work, and respect for traditional inhibitions in personal matters. A number of theories as to the causes of the malaise were put forward. Some said that a general relaxation of discipline in all spheres of life—a spreading "permissiveness"—and a decline of respect for authority were the causes. And a few of these analysts thought that the very manhood of the authorities was open to question. For instance, the Vice-President had declared that many Americans, including Americans in positions of authority, were "snivelling" and "effete," and that some were in fact "eunuchs." Other analysts traced the problem not to a lack of discipline or manliness but to a lack of candor and integrity generally in the conduct of public affairs. These observers pointed out that truthfulness, tolerance, and a sense of justice, too, were "old values," and that the authorities had shown little respect for them in recent years. In the Presidential campaign of 1968, Nixon had seemed to favor this interpretation, but then he had changed. While he was in office, he had come to see the malaise from a special perspective. He drew a connection between the crisis of Presidential authority in foreign affairs which disturbed him so deeply and a broader crisis of authority in the society as a whole. In the citizen's helplessness in the face of crime, busing, and the like he saw a reflection of his own threatened helplessness in the world in the face of domestic opposition against the war, which, in his view, was threatening to cripple the power of the executive branch of the government. He hoped that the public's fear that the authorities were becoming impotent on the local level would encourage it to grant him increased authority on the global level. And to judge by his publicly expressed enthusiasm for the hard-hats, he was willing to resort to the most extreme measures in seeking the sort of support he wanted.

To the men in the White House, the time seemed ripe for an "offensive" against the opposition which would outdo in uncontrolled vehemence and intensity anything they had attempted so far. Attorney General Mitchell said to a reporter, "This country is going so far right you are not even going to recognize it." They believed that, as one White House aide put it, they "had the liberal Establishment in total rout." They had been encouraged by the unresisting response to their earlier attacks from both the Democratic Party and the press. And now the anti-war movement seemed to have collapsed, too. The moment had come, they thought, to reap the political rewards of their year of combat. They saw a rich harvest of votes and a compliant Senate in the offing. Since the fall of 1969, when the Administration had scrapped its controlling image of itself as a great conciliator and reconstituted itself as the scourge of its enemies and rivals, almost every political institution of significance in the country, from the Supreme Court to the Harris poll, had come under some form of attack. The Congress, as it happened, had thus far been spared a frontal assault. To be sure, the Senate had been exposed to attacks of the "shotgun" variety. Like television and the press, some senators had been showered with rigged mail; the President, improving on the start made by his predecessors, had taken over the formation and conduct of all foreign policy, including the launching and waging of war; and he had scolded the Senate severely on several occasions, particularly in connection with its rejection of two of his Supreme Court nominations. But there had been no organized, systematic assault on the legislative branch as a whole. Now the President seemed determined to take advantage of the congressional campaign to rectify the omission.

The White House intervention in the congressional campaign had a secondary purpose as well. It could serve as a rehearsal for the Presidential campaign of 1972. One aide expressed the wish that the Presidential election could be held then and there. "We'd run the Democrats off the map," he told a reporter. Indeed, planning for 1972 had already begun. The White House had become convinced that Senator Edward Kennedy was the most likely Democratic candidate for 1972, and in 1969, after Kennedy told the nation he had driven off a bridge on Chappaquiddick Island in Massachusetts, killing a young woman in the car with him, John Ehrlichman had sent Anthony Ulasewicz to the scene of the accident to spy on his personal life. Ulasewicz, a retired New York City policeman who had been interviewed by John Ehrlichman at La Guardia Airport in May of 1969, only a few months after the President's Inauguration, and hired shortly thereafter, at Ehrlichman's direction, to carry out sensitive political investigations into the personal lives of potential candidates of the opposition party, was not on the government payroll. Instead, he received a salary of twenty-two thousand dollars per year, plus expenses, from secret funds left over from the 1968 Presidential campaign, and the money was paid to him by the President's personal attorney, Herbert Kalmbach. Then, in 1970, the White House encouraged the candidacy of a right-wing Republican, John McCarthy, in the senatorial primary in Massachusetts. John McCarthy had no chance of winning either the primary or the election, but Charles Colson, the White House aide who encouraged him to run, wanted him to attack Kennedy on the issue of the car accident, among other things, and thus tarnish Kennedy's reputation in preparation for 1972. Another problem that the White House men anticipated in 1972 was the possible candidacy of former Governor George Wallace, of Alabama, on a third-party ticket. Wallace, they believed, would tend to draw votes away from President Nixon. In 1970, Wallace was involved in a close primary race for the Democratic gubernatorial nomination in Alabama. Accordingly, the White House funnelled four hundred thousand dollars—part of those secret funds left over from the 1968 Presidential campaign—to the campaign of his rival, Governor Albert Brewer, who had succeeded to the governorship in 1968, after the death of Wallace's wife, Governor Lurleen Wallace. This transaction, like many other secret White House financial transactions, was handled by Kalmbach, who had in his keeping some two and a half million dollars in surplus campaign funds, of which about two million was in cash. He made the contribution to the Brewer campaign by handing a hundred thousand dollars to an anonymous man in a hotel lobby in New York, a hundred thousand dollars to an anonymous man in the lobby of a Los Angeles bank, and directing that the remaining two hundred thousand dollars be handed over, in the lobby of the same New York hotel, by France Raine, H. R. Haldeman's brother-in-law.

Toward the end of September, as the campaign got going in earnest, the Administration decided to frighten the television networks anew. Charles Colson, who had no official responsibilities connected with television, and whose chief duties at the White House were purely political, initiated a series of off-the-record meetings with the chief executives of the three major networks: William Paley, the board chairman of CBS; Frank Stanton, the president of CBS; Julian Goodman, the president of NBC; James Hagerty, a vice-president of ABC; and Leonard Goldenson, the president of ABC. The meetings were held at the headquarters of the networks in New York on September 23rd, and none of those taking part in them revealed the fact to the public. On September 25th, Colson reported on the meetings in a memo to Haldeman (with a copy to Herbert Klein, the President's Director of Communications). Colson had openly mentioned the possibility of government intervention in television news, he noted, and he was delighted with the results. "The networks are terribly nervous over the uncertain state of the law—i.e., the recent F.C.C. decisions and the pressures to grant Congress access to TV," he wrote. (The decisions concerned, among other things, the balancing of competing claims to television time of the President, the Democratic National Committee, and the Republican National Committee.) "They are also apprehensive about us. Although they tried to disguise this, it was obvious. The harder I pressed them (CBS and NBC) the more accommodating, cordial, and almost apologetic they became." He went on, "They were startled by how thoroughly we were doing our homework . . . [by] the way in which we have so thoroughly monitored their coverage and our analysis of it." The President's unfettered access to prime-time television had proved immensely valuable in the past year, and Colson reported, "There was unanimous agreement that the President's right of access to TV should in no way be restrained." He wrote, "They are terribly concerned with being able to work out their own policies with respect to balanced coverage and not to have policies imposed on them by either the [Federal Communications] Commission or the Congress. ABC and CBS said that they felt we could, however, through the F.C.C., make any policies we wanted to. (This is worrying them all.)" Colson had gone on to discuss specific news stories with the executives: "They told me anytime we had a complaint about slanted coverage for me to call them directly. Paley said that he would like to come down to Washington and spend time with me anytime that I wanted. In short, they are very much afraid of us and are trying hard to prove they are 'good guys.'" In conclusion, he wrote, "This all adds up to the fact that they are damned nervous and scared and we should continue to take a very tough line, face to face, and in other ways."

In mid-October, the President plunged directly into the congressional campaign, visiting ten states in four days. Inviting the citizenry to vote for men who would "stand with the President," he did to the congressional campaign what he had done to so many other contests: he made himself and his prestige the central issue. The President worked from a basic speech, repeating it at each campaign stop with minor variations. On one occasion, he described some of the people he opposed. There were the demonstrators: "You hear them night after night on television, people shouting obscenities about America and what we stand for. You hear those who shout against the speakers and shout them down, who will not listen." (Actually, of course, obscenities were never permitted to be broadcast on television.) There were the murderers: "And then you hear those who engage in violence. You hear those, and see them, who, without reason, kill policemen and injure them and the rest." He went on to make the point that, fortunately, the people shouting obscenities and killing policemen for no reason were not a majority of the American people. "You wonder," he said, "is that the voice of America. I say to you it is not!" And there was a recourse for those of the electorate who opposed the shouting of obscenities and the killing of policemen. In one version of the speech, he said, "All over this country today, we see a rising tide of terrorism, of crime, and on the campuses of our universities we have seen those who, instead of engaging in peaceful dissent, engage in violence. . . . It's time to draw the line and say we're not going to stand for that! . . . It is time for the great silent majority of Americans to stand up and be counted—on November 3rd, in the quiet of the polling booth. If a candidate has condoned violence, lawlessness, and permissiveness, then you know what to do." He said, "The four-letter word that is the most powerful of any in the world is 'vote,'" and asserted on several occasions that "one vote is worth a hundred obscene slogans."

If the basic tactic of the campaign was not to let candidates on the left move into the center, the President had carried it out to the full. He had pushed the opposition so far to the left that it was off the edge of the scale of electoral politics. On the opposition's side, by his account, there were the demonstrators and the murderers; all they could do was shout foul words and kill policemen. The voting types were on his side. The campaign was not a contest between candidates looking for votes—it was a contest between criminals, on the one hand, and the voters, on the other.

At the very first stop on the President's tour—a snowy airport in Burlington, Vermont, where he went to give support to the candidacy of Winston Prouty in his race for the Senate—an incident occurred that seemed to illustrate, in a small way, some of the points he was making. A single small chip of concrete flew out of the crowd and landed about twenty-five yards away from the President's plane. Charles Colson thereupon turned to a reporter and said, "Those rocks will mean ten thousand votes for Prouty." Colson believed that opposition of this sort to the President actually helped the President. The White House had now entered into a new relationship with the far left, and soon began to exploit it. At each of the

President's stops, reporters noted, the President's men would let a certain number of demonstrators into the area where he was speaking—not enough to seriously disrupt the proceedings but enough to supply a dramatic illustration of the President's remarks concerning "those who shout against the speakers and shout them down, who will not listen." The Nixon Administration had an affinity with the far left in that both wanted to tear down "the Establishment." Now the affinity blossomed into an alliance, albeit an unknowing one on the part of the young demonstrators: they dutifully trooped in to shout at the President, thereby playing an essential role in the President's scenario for the congressional elections.

But was it true that a rock thrown at the President was worth ten thousand votes? In a subsequent campaign appearance that same day, and in other speeches during the campaign, the President sought to make political use of the incident. Yet the polls were not encouraging. Mr. Nixon's intervention in the campaign had apparently had a negative impact: a national survey of the voters' party preferences showed the Republicans running even farther behind the Democrats than they had two years earlier. Besides, the public did not seem to be responding to the campaign in the right spirit. The President's remarks were of a kind meant to evoke excitement and wrath. Certainly there was no excitement *in favor* of demonstrators against the President. But reporters were finding that voters were not taking sides at all. Instead, they appeared to be growing tired of all politicians. Remarks like that of a man in Grand Forks, North Dakota, who told a reporter, "One's like the next— they all promise everything and they don't do anything," were being heard all over the country. The theme of "division" was wearing thin. Its career had been long. First emerging in the Johnson years, it had led the country to vote for peace abroad and calm at home in 1968, but, instead, the country had got "positive polarization" the next fall. Then once again the yearned-for calm began to show itself, but it was soon disrupted by the invasion of Cambodia. Now the President, angrier than ever, had made division the theme of another campaign. The country seemed to have been dragged into a quarrel for which it no longer had any heart. Even the opposition lay dormant—so dormant, in fact, that the White House men had to take special steps to make sure that signs of the supposed "rising tide of terrorism" would actually be visible "night after night on television."

For the time being, in the increasing excitement of the campaign, the President and the Vice-President appeared oblivious of these signs of fatigue and lack of interest. The President was campaigning in twenty-three states in seventeen days, and as the tour proceeded his words seemed, if anything, to become more torrid. Five days before the election, when he was to speak in an auditorium in San Jose, California, reporters received advance word that there might be some sort of trouble that night; they noticed, too, that police barricades to hold back demonstrators outside the auditorium were unusually close to the motorcade route. After the President's speech, a crowd of demonstrators was on hand when he left the auditorium. Spotting them, the President jumped up on the hood of his limousine and, raising both hands in a V sign, exclaimed, "That's what they hate to see!" He was answered by a hail of thrown objects. Later that night, his aides, far from being distressed that the President had been physically attacked, were—according to the columnists Rowland Evans and Robert Novak—"jubilant." (When the President's press secretary, Ronald Ziegler, was asked to explain the President's behavior, he said that the President had spotted "a friendly face" among the demonstrators and had wanted to wave to him.) Immediately, the episode was made into the principal feature of the remainder of the campaign. Two days earlier, the Vice-President had announced, "It's time to take my gloves off. No more of this Mr. Nice Guy." The day after the San Jose episode, he called the domestic rebels "misfits" and "garbage," and said, "It's time to sweep that kind of garbage out of our society." The President, too, seemed to throw off whatever restraint he had preserved. Just three days before the election, he gave a speech calling the San Jose demonstrators "a thousand haters," and said that the reason they had "gained such prominence in our national life" and were able to "increasingly terrorize decent citizens" could be "summed up in a single word: appeasement." Of course, one reason these particular demonstrators had gained prominence was that he had, to all appearances, provoked them into attacking him, and then had made them the central theme of his speeches. He went on to say, "For far too long the strength of freedom in our society has been eroded by creeping permissiveness —in our legislatures, in our courts, in our family life, in our universities. For far too long we have appeased aggression here at home." And then he shifted his ground, arriving at the point where every issue he dealt with seemed to wind up—the question of his own authority. "The terrorists of the far left," he said, with angry gestures, "would like nothing better than to make the President of the United States a prisoner in the White House. Let me set them straight: as long as I am President no band of violent thugs is going to keep me from going out and speaking with the American people." The speech was filmed, and excerpts of it were shown on Election Eve. When it was over, a voice was heard saying, "Support men who will vote for the President, not against him. Bring an end to the wave of violence in America."

At some point in his first two years in office, the President had apparently had one of the most irresistible and irreversible experiences that the human mind can undergo. He had been struck by a vision of the world that seemed to bring it all together, into a single pattern. He had concluded that a wide array of apparently disparate evils were branches of one large evil—that a hundred enemies of his country, of his beliefs, of his office, and of his political survival were in fact part of a single network of enemies. There were the thugs, the hoodlums, the hijackers, the muggers, and the killers of policemen, and, barely distinguishable from them, the anarchists and terrorists shouting down speakers and burning university buildings. In the background were the sheeplike, "permissive" parents, professors, legislators, and judges. Abroad, marching in perfect step with the domestic enemies, were the Vietnamese guerrillas, and the Russians and the Chinese accompanying them as guides.

On the sidelines were the "with-it," "fashionable" people, cheering on the whole rabble. But most repulsive of all were people who were not themselves violent but, rather, weirdly passive: "effete." They came "snivelling" and "hand-wringing" and "fawning." They were the "élitists" or "radical-liberals," who, cloaked in respectability, actually "condoned" the outrages of the mob—gave them the "green light." They were living examples of what could happen if the structure of authority gave way to the challenge from the rebels, and allowed itself to be rendered impotent. For, diverse as these many evils might seem, their genesis was the same. It was we ourselves who brought them into being, by our softness, our permissiveness, our appeasement. The thugs and the anarchists and revolutionaries were the physical embodiment of our moral failures. Like the rebellious children they were, they had, at root, only one aim. It was to weaken our authority, the authority of our country, and, above all, the authority of the embodiment of authority in our country, our President. The solution, too, rested with us. We must toughen ourselves and *punish them:* punish them with strict laws, punish them with the Justice Department and the Internal Revenue Service and the Federal Communications Commission, punish them by taking away their government handouts, punish them with harsh words, and punish them with napalm and phosphorus and B-52s.

On one level, President Nixon's anxiety that the Presidency was in danger of declining into impotency was apparently instinctive. He seemed to lash out with spontaneous, visceral anger at any move he perceived as a challenge to his authority, whether it might come from a Senate supposedly out to substitute its "subjective judgment" for his, from emboldened criminals to whom "soft" judges had given the "green light," from the "band of violent thugs" that was trying to prevent him from giving speeches, from "holdovers" conducting "guerrilla warfare" against Presidential policy in the federal bureaucracy, or from North Vietnamese forces who, in the name of international Communism (and with the help of their allies here at home), were threatening the United States with humiliation and defeat. But on another level all these responses conformed to strategic theories. It was an unprecedented characteristic of international affairs in the nuclear age that no military resolution of a large, "real" crisis was possible. The most hotly contested issues in international affairs, if they were to be worked out at all, would have to be resolved by symbolic action in small, unreal crises—or so a succession of Presidents had come to believe. The crises that characterized the Presidency of Richard Nixon, at home as well as abroad, were nothing if they were not unreal. The Vietnamese rebels did not pose a real threat of defeat to the United States. The Senate did not threaten any power of appointment actually given to the President by the Constitution. The domestic rebels, although they were numerous, did not pose any real threat to the sovereignty of the federal government. And the "holdovers" did not have the power, ultimately, to thwart a lawful Presidential directive. What all these challengers did pose was a symbolic threat. They posed a threat on the level of images: threatened to create the impression that the President was crippled and could not have his way in the world—that he was in truth a pitiful, helpless giant. They posed a threat, that is, to the credibility of American power and, more particularly, the credibility of Presidential power. The threat to credibility underlay the crisis of authority that so greatly worried President Nixon and Mr. Kissinger—requiring them, in their view, to adopt an unrelentingly militant posture when they were confronted with even the slightest threat to their authority. It was the doctrine of credibility, too, that molded the disparate elements of policy into a unity. For an image of weakness could crop up anywhere. The appearance of "softness" in any realm could give rise—in President Nixon's thinking—to the imputation that the whole structure of American authority was "soft." The appearance of "softness" at home could serve to undermine American power abroad. As President Nixon had put it to the students at Kansas State, "a nation that condones blackmail and terror at home can hardly stand as the example in putting an end to international piracies or tensions that could explode into war abroad." "Appeasement" had to be resisted everywhere or it could be resisted nowhere. A "fawning approval" of rowdy demonstrators at home was inseparable from a fawning approval of the Vietnamese rebels abroad, and even of Moscow and Peking. In fact, it was preferable to make the demonstrations of strength in minor matters rather than to let things deteriorate to the point where a demonstration might have to be made at the brink of nuclear war with the Soviet Union.

On Election Night, it turned out that the Republicans had a net gain of two seats in the Senate, a net loss of nine seats in the House, and a net loss of eleven governorships. Despite the Nixon Big Charge, the political complexion of the Senate remained about the same.

III.
MAN
OF
PEACE

O<small>N DECEMBER</small> 10, 1970, some five weeks after the congressional elections, President Nixon was asked at a press conference about the "divisions" in American life. "Well . . . it is, of course, a problem, but I should emphasize that divisions in this country are never going to end—there's always going to be a generation gap and there's always going to be differences between the races and between the religions," he answered. "The problem is trying to mute those differences, to mitigate them to the greatest extent possible, and to develop a dialogue. I think we've made some progress in that respect. Not as much as I would like." A few weeks later, he was asked what had become of the "lift of a driving dream" he had promised in his State of the Union message in January, and he answered, "Well . . . before we can really get the lift of a driving dream, we have to get rid of some of the nightmares we inherited. One of the

137

nightmares is a war without end. We're ending that war. . . .
Second, we've got to quiet this country down at home." On neither
of these occasions did the President make any mention of the rising
tide of violence and crime which had disturbed him so deeply just a
few months back. The anarchists, the totalitarians, the thugs, the
hoodlums, the haters, and the snivelling, fawning "Establishment"
that glorified criminals had all vanished from his public pronouncements. The "age of anarchy" that he had announced just eight
months before, as the Cambodian invasion was getting under way,
was apparently over. Earlier still, in the fall of 1969, the President's
mood had reversed itself so that a controlling image of national
division had replaced a controlling image of national unity. Now
the President's mood seemed to have reversed itself again, and
national division, too, had disappeared. The Nixon Big Charge had
served well to intimidate other politicians, the television networks,
and the press, but it had failed to take hold with the public. It was
not that the public had rejected the Administration's outlook in favor
of some other; rather, in a change unforeseen by either of the "sides"
of the divided political realm, the public had been distancing itself
from all politicians and all political views. A new kind of division
had been opening up: a gap between the people in or around public
life, whose interest in politics was undiminished, and the broad mass
of ordinary people, who had come to the conclusion that nothing
worthwhile ever happened in the political realm.

The White House began to cast about for a new controlling
image for itself and for national politics as a whole. One White House
staff man told a reporter of a plan to bury the President's image as a
mere politician and have him reëlected in 1972 as a "statesman." For
the moment, the President reverted to the old "bring-us-together"
image he had produced before his Inauguration and had then
abandoned. In January of 1971, he gave a speech at the University of
Nebraska that took as its theme "We Need an Alliance of Generations." Once again, there was no mention of the rising tide of
violence and crime which in his speeches of three months before had
been about to finish off the Republic. Nor was there any mention
of the tide's having receded. Like its predecessor, the controlling

image of unity, the controlling image of division had dissolved without leaving a trace. Now the nation's first order of business was not putting a stop to terrorism but dealing with the old, forgotten issues of 1968—what the President defined in his speech as "the problems of our cities," "the problems of our environment," and the concluding of the war, along with a few others. "We must face them together," the President told the students and faculty of the University of Nebraska. "There can be no generation gap in America." Continuing in this vein, he said, "And I believe that . . . as we put our hands together, your generation and mine, in the alliance we forge we can discover a new understanding, a community of wisdom, a capacity for action with which we can truly renew both the spirit and the promise of this great and good land."

On January 22nd, in the State of the Union message for 1971, the President picked up the abandoned themes of his Inaugural Address of 1969. Borrowing a phrase or two outright from that speech, and from his first State of the Union message, he told the senators and representatives assembled in joint session, "In these troubled years just past, America has been going through a long nightmare of war and division, of crime and inflation. Even more deeply, we have gone through a long dark night of the American spirit. But now that night is ending. Now we must let our spirits soar again. Now we are ready for the lift of a driving dream." This was the third time the curtain had gone down on the long night of war and division, and the third time it had gone up on the lift of a driving dream. It almost seemed that the two personae of the President's public self were engaged in a debate. Mr. Outside, back in charge now, almost seemed to be delivering a rebuke to Mr. Inside. The nightmare of war and division of the "troubled years just past," when Mr. Inside had been in charge, had turned into the nightmare of failure in the congressional elections of 1970. Now it was time to try the lift of a driving dream again. Now it was time for Mr. Outside.

Two weeks later, Vice-President Agnew praised the "youth-libera-tion movement," with no mention of any vultures, misfits, eunuchs, or garbage.

Patrick Buchanan, who was responsible for a great deal of the Mr. Inside material, was unhappy with the latest turn of events. "We suffer," he wrote to the President, "from the widely held belief that the President has no Grand Vision that inspires him, no deeply held political philosophy that girds, guides and explains his words, de-cisions and deeds. The President is viewed as the quintessential political pragmatist, standing before an ideological buffet, picking some from this tray and some from that. On both sides he is seen as the textbook political transient, here today, gone tomorrow, shuttling back and forth, as weather permits, between liberal programs and conservative rhetoric. As someone put it, 'the bubble in the car-penter's level.'" The President, Haldeman wrote to another aide, found the memo "very interesting."

In the 1971 State of the Union message, and in subsequent mes-sages to Congress that winter, the President called for a "New American Revolution"—one that would be "as exciting as that first revolution almost two hundred years ago." The two principal features of the new revolution were to be "revenue sharing"—a program for returning federal money to state and local govern-ments—and yet another round of executive-branch reorganization. As for the principal feature of the reorganization—the third he had undertaken in three years—it was to be a reduction in the number of Cabinet departments from twelve to eight. His main aim, he told Congress, would be to return "power to the people."

Upon assuming office, the President had promised to be truth-ful and speak calmly, to give his Cabinet Secretaries full inde-pendence (and, in particular, to have a strong Secretary of State), to prevent his staff from growing overpowerful, to run an "open" Administration, to do more for black people than any President in history, and to end the war. Now, at the start of his second two years in office, his promise was to reduce his own power and that of the Congress. "Giving up power is hard," he told the assembled houses of Congress. "But I would urge all of you, as leaders of this country, to remember that the truly revered leaders in world history are those who gave power to the people, not those who took it away."

Though Mr. Inside might not be required as a speechwriter for the moment, there was covert work for him to do. His message and his style were banished from the President's public utterances, but they found ample expression in Presidential messages that the President did not acknowledge. The Presidential Offensive was reined in in public, but it was going forward in secrecy. After the President's December 10th press conference, for instance, the "standard" campaign (as Gordon Strachan, a White House aide, put it in a memo) of fraudulent phone calls and rigged letters and rigged telegrams was set in motion to provide the press with a "public response" to the President's performance on that occasion. It included a dozen telegrams-to-the-editor drafted by Patrick Buchanan and his assistant Kenneth Khachigian, and sent to *Time* and *Newsweek* by "twenty names around the country from our letter-writing system" (as Jeb Magruder described it in a memo to H. R. Haldeman). The telegrams praised the President and attacked the press for treating him roughly. One telegram began, "Thank goodness this country has President Nixon." Another began, "Last Thursday night, the President of the United States handled that pack of wolves gathered in the White House with a great deal more gentility and generosity than their conduct deserved." Another referred to the press conference as though it had been an athletic match, and read, in its entirety, "With regard to the President's news conference, score it: President Nixon, 100—Media, 0."

Another hidden aspect of the Presidential Offensive was going forward, too. F.B.I. Director Hoover's veto of the plan for the Interagency Group on Domestic Intelligence and Internal Security in the summer of 1970 had by no means put an end to the Administration's hopes for coördinating into a single force the government's resources for spying on and harassing the protest movement. On September 17, 1970, Attorney General Mitchell had had lunch at the headquarters of the C.I.A. with Director Helms, the Chief of Counter-Intelligence, the Deputy Director for Plans, and the Chief of Operation CHAOS, and the group had talked over the idea of setting up an interagency intelligence unit under cover of the Justice Department. The new unit, the luncheon group decided, would "provide evaluated intelligence from all sources" and would "allow preventive action." Shortly, an "Intelligence Evaluation Committee," which included representatives from the Justice Department, the F.B.I., the C.I.A., the Department of Defense, the Secret Service, and the National Security Agency, was set up. The C.I.A. representatives on the Committee were the Chief of Counter-Intelligence and Richard Ober of Operation CHAOS; the Justice Department representative was Assistant Attorney General for the Internal Security Division Robert Mardian; and the White House Representative was the legal counsel to the President, John Dean—a young lawyer who had worked for Attorney General Mitchell in the Justice Department until the summer of 1970, when he had moved to the White House.

During the first days of February, the headlines brought news from outer space. On February 5th, the third manned mission to the moon made a successful landing. Far down the page from the huge black letters announcing the moon news was news from earth of feverish military activity of an undefined sort in the northwesternmost corner of South Vietnam. Military trucks, armored personnel carriers, transport planes, and helicopters roared toward the Laotian border, without any official explanation of what they were up to. Rumors of something that was happening or was about to happen in Laos were spreading but could not be confirmed. American officials both in Washington and in Saigon refused to comment. South Vietnamese officials refused to comment. Then word came that a news blackout

—a "news embargo," it was called—had been imposed, for the first time in the war, by the American command in South Vietnam.

On February 6th, spokesmen for the Pathet Lao, the Communist-led rebel movement within Laos, announced that the South Vietnamese Army had invaded Laos, and was receiving American air support, including B-52 strikes. Washington refused to comment. The next day, President Nguyen Van Thieu, of South Vietnam, acknowledged that an invasion was under way. Washington still remained silent. The day after President Thieu's announcement, President Nixon made an announcement, but it was not about the war—it was about the environment. " 'Clean the air, clean the sky, wash the wind,' " he said, quoting T. S. Eliot, and he added, "'I have proposed to Congress a sweeping and comprehensive program to do just that and more—to end the plunder of America's natural heritage." But by then reporters in Indo-China were managing to get through to the battlefield, and were sending home photographs and films of the fighting. In the fall of 1969 and through most of 1970, the President had spoken of the war as though the freedom and safety of the entire world were at stake in Indo-China. Now he made a show of disregarding the war: while the films on television and the pictures in the press were of soldiers dying, the words from the White House were of the air, the sky, and the wind.

On February 17th, the President held a news conference. His answers to questions about the military activity in Indo-China were ambiguous but menacing. "I won't speculate on what South Vietnam may decide to do with regard to a possible incursion into North Vietnam in order to defend their national security," he said. Concerning the American bombing, he said, "I am not going to place any limitations upon the use of air power except of course . . . the use of tactical nuclear weapons." This was the first time since President Johnson's bombing halt in March, 1968, that the United States had threatened unlimited bombing of North Vietnam. Asked why the United States and South Vietnam had invaded Laos, he would say only, "Laos would not have been possible had it not been for Cambodia."

By mid-March, the invasion had turned into a rout of the South

Vietnamese. American helicopters had flown them in but could not get them out again. Hundreds of helicopters were lost or damaged trying. Now the pictures that the country saw were of South Vietnamese soldiers clinging to the skids of the helicopters as B-52s continued to blanket the territory around them with bombs.

For the third consecutive spring, the President had suddenly launched a major military action in Indo-China. Each action had been carried out in a manner that suited the controlling image of the moment. The bombing of Cambodia in 1969 had been carried out in complete secrecy, as it had to be if the American people were to go on believing that the President meant to fulfill his promise of bringing peace and uniting the country. The invasion of Cambodia on the ground a year later had been announced on national television and portrayed as a measure that would help check a spread of anarchy at home and abroad—a portrayal designed to dramatize the controlling image of national division. Now, in the day of the New American Revolution and the Alliance of the Generations, the invasion of Laos was being carried out almost without explanation. Just as there were loud, overt attacks on the political opposition and quiet, covert attacks on the political opposition, there were loud invasions and quiet invasions. The invasion of Laos was one of the quiet ones. The war aim was suitably understated. No longer was it to protect institutions that had been created by free civilizations in the last five hundred years, as it had been just nine months before, when Cambodia was invaded. Now the chief aim (as the State Department put it after the invasion was under way) was to "promote the security and safety of American and allied forces," or—an even more modest one—to protect "the withdrawal of American forces." The war aims, as they were publicly stated, had lost their grandiose importance. The war had shrunk into itself: American forces had to stay in Vietnam so that they might leave; the war had to continue so that it might end; the men had to die to save their lives. Every detail of the invasion reflected the new White House line. Nine months before, the President had compared himself to Churchill and Roosevelt—great wartime leaders. A few weeks after the invasion of Laos, he said, in an interview, "I rate myself as a deeply committed pacifist, perhaps because of my Quaker heritage from my mother." Nine months before, he had spoken of his decision to "go to the heart of the trouble" with his military moves into Cambodia. Now he said nothing about military moves. One "senior official" told a newsman, "If we learned anything at all from Cambodia, it was how *not* to break the news of a major development in the war." The thing to do, it appeared, was simply never to break the news.

The press, the Congress, and the anti-war movement, seemingly following the President's cue, reacted mildly to the new escalation. The campuses remained calm, the Congress remained unaroused. In the earlier Nixon years, the Administration's theme of national division had always had an anachronistic quality, and behind it had lurked a national yawn. The White House campaign in the congressional races had been swallowed up by the yawn. Indifference had won out over demagoguery and hysteria. The new line, it seemed, was better attuned to the mood of an apathetic public. Instead of troops, the President used planes, and instead of theatrical exaggeration there was a news embargo. Instead of talking about an "age of anarchy," the President talked about the elements.

By the early spring of 1971, the Presidential election of 1972—still some twenty months away—was beginning to exert a powerful influence on every phase of White House operations. In fact, the abrupt change in the Administration's image following the 1970 congressional elections had been part of a strategy for the 1972 Presidential campaign. In March, detailed planning for 1972 began in earnest. All of it was covert.

In the spring of 1971, most observers believed that Senator Edmund Muskie, of Maine, was the man most likely to be the Democratic candidate for President in 1972. On March 24th, Patrick Buchanan, who had been asked to work out a political strategy for the Presidential election campaign, recommended in a memo to the President that a "Muskie Watch" be set up in the White House. The best strategy, he believed, would be to force Muskie to take positions on what he called in his memo "divisive issues." The idea was to prevent Muskie from unifying the Democratic Party. Therefore, Buchanan wrote, "we ought to go down to the kennels and turn all the dogs loose on Ecology Ed." All the dogs, that is, but one. "The President is the only one who should stand clear, while everybody else gets chewed up," Buchanan wrote, and he went on, "The rest of us are expendable commodities; but if the President goes, we all go, and maybe the country with us. My view." The strategy was to damage Muskie even before he entered the Democratic Presidential primaries, still a year away. For "if Mr. Muskie is not cut and bleeding before he goes into New Hampshire, he will very likely do massively well there," Buchanan noted, concluding, "This scenario is not in our interest."

An election effort required an organization as well as a strategy, and an organization required money. By March, extensive contacts had been made with the political arm of the dairy industry, and it had pledged contributions to the President's 1972 reëlection-campaign fund. The industry wanted increased government price support for milk. On March 23rd, President Nixon, after meeting in the morning with representatives of the dairymen, directed that the price support for milk be increased, reversing a decision of the Secretary of Agriculture that the President had concurred in just two weeks earlier. In the months that followed, dairy groups contributed about two hundred and fifty thousand dollars to the President's reëlection effort. Some of the money was channelled through committees with names such as Americans Dedicated to Better Public Administration, Volunteers Against Citizen Apathy, and Americans United for Objective Reporting, and it was used to finance a campaign committee. This committee's existence remained unknown to the public for some months.

Looking back on the events surrounding the contribution, William Powell, the president of a lobbying organization called Mid-America Dairymen, Incorporated, wrote in a letter to a member of his organization, "The facts of life are that the economic welfare of dairymen does depend a great deal on political action. If dairymen are to receive their fair share of the Governmental financial pie

146

that we all pay for, we must have friends in government." And he wrote, "Whether we like it or not, this is the way the system works."

In February, 1971, the Secret Service, acting at the request of President Nixon, installed microphones in the White House which would record all conversations in the Oval Office and in the Cabinet room. About two months later, the Secret Service installed microphones in the President's office in the Executive Office Building, and it also tapped the President's phones in the Oval Office, in the Lincoln Room, and in the Executive Office Building. At the same time, it installed equipment to record phone calls in a cottage at Camp David, the President's Maryland retreat.

In the spring of 1971, the Vietnam war penetrated to the courts of the United States, in four highly publicized legal encounters.

The first was the case of First Lieutenant William Calley, who had been a platoon leader when, on March 16, 1968, American soldiers entered the hamlet of My Lai, in the northern part of South Vietnam, and massacred more than three hundred people. On March 29 of 1971, a jury made up of Calley's peers found him guilty of murder. A large part of the public soon made known its unhappiness over the verdict, but judges and juries are not meant to weigh public opinion, and this judge and this jury had not done so.

One person who did weigh public opinion was President Nixon. A few days after the verdict, as the storm of public protest was rising, he made calls to a few Republicans in the Congress to ask what the political reaction would be if he were to pardon Calley. The feeling was that it would be favorable. On April 3rd, the President announced that he would personally review Calley's final sentence. Since the case was still under judicial review, and the hint of Presidential pardon or leniency tended to undercut any decisions that the courts might make, the President's intervention was criticized as legally improper. The prosecutor in the case, Captain Aubrey Daniel, wrote the President a letter in protest. "The greatest

147

tragedy of all will be if political expediency dictates the compromise of such a fundamental moral principle as the inherent unlawfulness of the murder of innocent persons," he wrote. "You have subjected a judicial system of this country to the criticism that it is subject to political influence." An issue growing out of the war had, for the first time, grown into a full-blown crisis of American justice, directly involving the President of the United States.

The second legal encounter over a war issue occurred when, on April 18th, a group of veterans calling themselves the Vietnam Veterans Against the War arrived in Washington to hold a demonstration. They had come to testify willingly to war crimes that they themselves had committed. In their persons, they united the extremes of the nation's war experience. There were many cases in which the war hero, the war criminal, and the war protester were embodied in one individual. They were the "bums" the President had denounced immediately after his speech making known the Cambodian invasion, and they were the soldiers he had praised. Their ragged uniforms, decked out with combat medals and peace emblems, mingled the styles of two Americas. They, virtually alone among Americans, had had to resolve within themselves the full dilemma posed by the Indo-China war—to travel the entire measureless distance between William Calley's Vietnam and the Washington of April, 1971. Now they encamped on the Capitol Mall, midway between Capitol Hill and the White House—at the geographic midpoint of political America. And for a few days, owing to extensive television coverage, they were also encamped somewhere near the center of the country's attention. From the Mall, they went out in small units to the various branches of government to tell their stories. (On the Mall one morning, the words "Will all war criminals please assemble across the street" were heard over a public-address system.)

The President had nothing to say publicly about the veterans' protest. But privately his interest in it was intense, and he received hourly reports from security agencies on the progress of the demonstration. On April 16th, the Justice Department went into Federal District Court and obtained, from Judge George Hart, an injunction against the veterans' sleeping on the Mall. The veterans, whose legal representative was former Attorney General Ramsey Clark, appealed the injunction to the Court of Appeals, which modified the injunction to permit sleeping under certain conditions. But the Supreme Court reversed the Court of Appeals' decision and reinstated the District Court's decision. The veterans then voted to defy the court order and remain. They argued that they had a right to sleep on the earth that they had been told they were fighting to protect. Some had been wounded in the war, and of these some were in wheelchairs. The political wisdom of sending in the police to remove them forcibly was doubtful. The veterans prepared to occupy the Mall for the night and waited to be carried away, but the Justice Department never ordered the police in.

The government's failure to enforce the court order it had urgently requested enraged Judge Hart. "One equal, coördinate branch of government—the judiciary—has been dangerously and improperly used by one equal, coördinate branch of government—the executive—represented by the Department of Justice in this case," he stated from the bench. For a second time that spring, the Administration had intervened in a legal case growing out of the war and had been rebuked by an officer of the court.

The third of that spring's legal encounters over a war issue grew out of another demonstration. In early May, the Mayday Tribe, an amorphous group of young people who were coming together for this one action, announced its intention of "stopping the government" if the government didn't stop the war. Its prospects for success seemed poor. The government employed some three million people, not counting the military, and it had a near-monopoly of the instruments of force at the nation's disposal. The Mayday Tribe, when it arrived in Washington and had a chance to look at itself, turned out to number some thirty thousand young men and women. Their plan of action was to sit down in Washington's streets, thus stopping traffic and, they hoped, the government. The job of keeping Washington traffic moving was ordinarily the responsibility of Chief Jerry Wilson, of the Washington Police Department. But once again the Administration involved itself. The first job of the Administration's new Intelligence Evaluation Committee had been to prepare for the May Day protest. As in the demonstrations of 1969, the C.I.A. and the Washington police set up a joint command. The C.I.A. sent out agents to penetrate the groups organizing the May Day events, and the Washington Police Department supplied the C.I.A. men with some twenty police badges so they could be on hand when the protesters arrived. A threat to "stop the government," however implausible, was the sort of threat that aroused one of the President's deepest fears—the fear that the authorities in the United States, including, above all, its President, were menaced with a loss of will and were in danger of being rendered impotent. The President vowed that the government would not be stopped for even an hour.

During the next two days, in an action with no precedent in the long history of demonstrations in the United States, the Washington police seized almost ten thousand people in the streets of the capital without bothering to charge them with any offenses, and threw them in jail. One problem that arose immediately was how to present the cases in court. The Police Department, at the prompting of the Justice Department, hit upon the solution of falsifying the arrest forms. On the line asking for "Location of the Arrest" they wrote (truthfully but vaguely) "D.C." Under "Specification" they wrote (again truthfully but vaguely) "Arrested during demonstrations in D.C. on May 3, 1971." Under "Arresting Officer" they wrote (falsely) the name and badge number of a policeman taken from a rotating list of seven policemen which had been supplied for the occasion. The Intelligence Evaluation Committee had been put together by the Administration in part to arrange for "preventive action" in case of civil disturbances, and the mass suspension of legal procedure now under way in Washington was apparently the first example of its work. The public, of course, had no knowledge of the existence of an Intelligence Evaluation Committee, or of any of the Administration's previous attempts to weld local and federal law enforcement and intelligence agencies into a single force that would be empowered to suspend or to break the law.

While the policemen were improvising procedures to handle the situation, the Administration was improvising law—or, at least, legal-sounding phrases—to account for it. Assistant Attorney General William Rehnquist described the proceedings as an instance of "qualified martial law," although there is no such thing. A few days later, an Administration spokesman announced that President Nixon was "totally satisfied" with the results of the episode. And Attorney General Mitchell said he hoped that "Washington's decisive opposition to mob force" would "set an example for other communities."

The judges, meanwhile, had to decide what to do with the illegally jailed thousands, many of whom had been incarcerated in dangerous and insanitary makeshift prisons. During the next months, the "cases" arrived in court for disposition. In the first two thousand cases, one defendant was found guilty. The charges against nearly twenty-five hundred additional defendants were dropped, because the evidence against them was inadequate. And among a third group of several thousand defendants just sixty-one were found guilty—all on minor charges. The government had not been stopped (there had never been any chance that it would be), nor had the war been stopped (that, too, had been unlikely). What had been stopped, for a period of days, was the working of the law. Once again, an incident growing out of the war had turned into a judicial crisis.

The fourth legal encounter over a war issue arose when, on June 13th, the *Times* began to run excerpts from a top-secret, multi-volume study of the conduct of the Vietnam war, beginning with events involving the French forces in Indo-China just after the Second World War, and ending with the Johnson years—a study that had been ordered by Secretary of Defense Robert McNamara in 1967 and had eventually been passed along to the *Times* by

Daniel Ellsberg, who had worked under McNamara in the Pentagon and had later grown disillusioned with the war. Here was still more war news out of the past, and this time it was a deluge. The lead time for news from Indo-China, it now seemed, was years.

The Pentagon Papers—as the study soon came to be known—showed in voluminous detail that both before and after the election of 1964 the Johnson Administration had misled the public about its intentions in Vietnam. They did not show that the Administration had consistently lied outright—although outright lying had apparently occurred. Rather, they revealed that in the world of its public statements and in the world of its private memoranda the Johnson Administration had been moving in opposite directions—away from the war in public, deeper into the war in private. The Pentagon Papers thus chronicled a major breakdown of democratic government, for the over-all effect of the Johnson war policy had been deception of the public on the most important issue facing the country at the moment when it was choosing its President. Also, the Pentagon Papers seemed to pinpoint the period of American history when an Administration went beyond the occasional lie and began to treat what it said and what it did as two separate matters. Whether it was because this separation had become a rule of thumb in the framing of virtually all policy in the Nixon Administration, and the Administration therefore had a stake in suppressing all news of governmental duplicity, or because there was a constant fear of leaks in the Nixon White House, or for some other reason, the men around Nixon once again intervened. The Justice Department sought, and received, a temporary injunction in Federal District Court in New York ordering the *Times* to cease publication of the Pentagon Papers. In the days that followed, newspapers in Washington, Boston, and St. Louis also received copies of the Pentagon Papers, began to publish them, and were enjoined by Federal Courts in their areas from continuing. All over the country, the printing presses were being held up. For the first time in the nation's history, the government had prevented the press from bringing news before the public.

On June 30th, the Supreme Court ruled against the government in the Pentagon Papers case, by a margin of six to three. One of the dissenting opinions incorporated the Administration's view of its war efforts. The government had argued that it possessed an "inherent" power to prevent the publication of documents when such public exposure would constitute a grave threat to the national security. The vital matter of national security cited was withdrawal from the war. "The heart of our case," Solicitor General Erwin Griswold had argued, "is that the publication of the materials . . . will . . . materially affect . . . the process of the termination of the war. It will affect the process of recovering prisoners of war." And Justice Harry Blackmun (who had been nominated and confirmed shortly after Carswell had been rejected) wrote in his dissent that if because of publication of the papers there was "prolongation of the war and . . . further delay in the freeing of United States prisoners, then the nation's people will know where the responsibility for these sad consequences rests"; namely, with the newspapers and with the Court majority. Griswold's argument and Blackmun's dissenting opinion reflected the change in the rationale of the war which had taken place after the 1970 congressional elections. In 1969 and 1970, the President had castigated his critics for lacking the patience to accept a prolongation of the war. Now his Solicitor General was in court arguing that the opposition, by publishing the Pentagon Papers, was preventing him from ending the war as quickly as he would like to end it. He was trying to end it, but Daniel Ellsberg, the *Times*, the Washington *Post*, and a few other newspapers were standing in his way. Of course, Ellsberg and many of the newspaper editors believed that by publishing the papers they might be *speeding* the end of the war. In other words, all the actors in the legal drama were, by their own account, falling over each other in their eagerness to get the United States out of the war. And yet the United States stayed in the war, as though held there by an invisible force. The situation was a historical novelty. The nation had had Presidents who took emergency actions in the name of winning a war, but it had never before had one who took emergency action in the name of leaving a war. If in this President's laborious, protracted, belligerent extrication of the

United States from the war another goal—victory—was concealed, he did not acknowledge it to the Supreme Court or to the country. In 1970, the dying war had precipitated a national political crisis. Now, in 1971, the same war, still dying its long-drawn-out death, had provoked a legal crisis.

Ever since Richard Nixon took office, the war had been "coming home." Many Americans had hoped that as the United States withdrew its forces from Vietnam the nation would be able to leave the war's bitterness behind in Southeast Asia. Now it seemed they would have no such luck. From the start, the American war effort had had the quality of an American obsession imposed upon a people that was trying to work out its own destiny, through a civil war of its own. It was as though the United States had ignored what the Vietnamese were actually doing and had cast them in roles on opposite sides of a struggle that was troubling the American, not the Vietnamese, soul. And there were in fact two wars going in Vietnam. One was the war that the Vietnamese were fighting among themselves for control over their country, and the other was the public-relations war that the United States was fighting against the Russians, or the Chinese—the war that the government was prepared to fight against all comers in order to favorably resolve the crisis of Presidential authority and to maintain American credibility. Under the Nixon Administration, the United States was gradually leaving the first war (the Vietnamese civil struggle) behind it in Vietnam but was bringing the second war (the war for Presidential authority and American credibility) home along with the troops. The governmental anger and fear that had been vented outward on the Vietnamese for about a decade were now being vented inward on Americans. In a way, the Vietnamese had never been more than incidental victims. As President Nixon pointed out in November, 1969, it had never been within their power to "defeat or humiliate" the United States. In a war to uphold American credibility, only Americans could do that, as he also pointed out. While the skirmish in Vietnam had been "winding down," the battle of the main forces in the United States had been gearing up. The forms of the war's homecoming had been various. Almost at the start of the Nixon Administration, official anxiety that the expansion of the bombing into Cambodia in March of 1969 woud be made known had given rise to a program of warrantless wiretaps. Then, in his speech of November 3, 1969, the President, disappointed by the domestic response to his war policies, had identified groups of Americans as the real threat. And when the press and television-network reaction to that speech proved less enthusiastic than he had hoped, he had sent out the Vice-President to inaugurate the overt half of a campaign to intimidate the press and the networks. Then he had broadened his assault into a Presidential Offensive against many of the other institutions of American life—institutions that he had come to see as the elements of a treacherous "Establishment." Now, in the spring of 1971, the war was coming home in a new way, and the systemic crisis that had grown out of the war—and out of the strategic doctrines that had given rise to the war—was deepening and changing character. Lieutenant Calley was bringing the war home. Daniel Ellsberg was bringing the war home. The Vietnam veterans were bringing the war home. The Mayday Tribe was bringing the war home. And the Administration, in its responses to Calley, Ellsberg, the veterans, and the Mayday Tribe, was bringing the war home. But the new actors, instead of bringing the war home to the streets, or to the voting booths, or to the front page or the television screen, were bringing the war home to the courtroom. The courts had managed for many years to stay out of the systemic crisis that the war had precipitated, but now they were being drawn in. The courts might ignore the question of the legality of the war itself, but in the Calley case, the veterans' case, the Mayday case, and the Pentagon Papers case the war issue had taken forms that the courts were not free to ignore: murder, the right of assembly, the right of criminal suspects to due process, and censorship of the press. It was as though the systemic crisis, seeking resolution, were trying out each branch of the government in turn. In mid-1971, the war issue was becoming adjudicable.

As the issue was being joined in the courts, there were growing signs that the men in the executive branch of the government were ignorant of the spirit of the law in general and ignorant of the substance of American law in particular. The spirit of the law is conservative; it follows precedents and throws a thousand yokes from the past over the present. But the bent of the Nixon Administration was for ad-hoc, experimental action. The spirit of the law is sensitive to roles and prescribes channels through which political power must flow. But the Nixon Administration was impatient with roles and impatient with the differences between one institution and another, and sent its orders down through whatever channels it pleased. The law is concerned with facts and substance. But the Nixon Administration was concerned with appearances—with images. The spirit of the law is impartial. But the Nixon men were partisan to the marrow of their bones. In the United States, the role of the law in defining the shape of political life is of particular importance. For in the United States, where the national government and the nation itself were brought formally into existence when the states ratified the Constitution, the very being of the government is founded in law. The Founding Fathers' act of creation was a legal act, and the institutions they framed were defined and empowered by law. In the American system, the law is more than a set of restrictions, and more, even, than a universal code of justice; it is to the nation's institutions the breath of the creator. The people decide in elections who will man the institutions, but the law continues to define what the institutions are. It binds them together into a whole that can be seen, understood, and brought to account, and that works. And since, in the United States, customs, communities, and even buildings tend to be rubbed out almost as soon as they appear, there is very little in the way of tradition for the nation to fall back on if legal forms break down. If the controlling, molding influence of the law declines, then the outlines of the political system itself blur and eventually disappear. Institutions, no longer able to grasp firmly what is expected of them and what they are, grow slovenly and misshapen, and wander away from their appointed tasks in the Constitutional scheme. Roles and jurisdictions clash and become confused, power goes to whoever grabs it, and the system warps and sags and heads toward collapse.

The men of the Nixon Administration were intolerant of the shaping, restraining influence of American law. Instead of responding to the imperatives of the Constitutional system, they responded to the imperatives of another system, whose requirements and form were determined, in large measure, by national security. And since the Nixon Administration had become persuaded that the struggle on the home front against rebellious Americans was more important to the national defense than the war effort in Vietnam, the methods it used at home, even in legal encounters, were, increasingly, the methods of war.

The Administration's misunderstanding of the American system of government revolved around the question of power, but it ran deeper than its misconceptions about the distribution of power among the three branches of the federal government. The Administration was confused about the nature of powers, on the one hand, and rights, on the other. The Constitution grants government officers specific, limited powers. Rights are granted to the people, to protect them against abuse of the government powers. One does not speak, for example, of the President's "right" to command the armed forces, or of his "right" to veto legislation. These are powers. And one does not speak of the "power" of due process, or of the "power" to speak and assemble freely. These are rights. But the officers of the Nixon Administration had fallen into the habit of defending their "right" to take this or that governmental action, as though they were put-upon citizens, not powerful figures in the government. The President referred, for example, to his "right" to appoint Supreme Court Justices. And the Vice-President defended his "right of free speech" when he was criticized for attacking the integrity of the national press. At the same time, the President had become worried about the "powers" of the citizens and of the press. The most powerful men in the country—men armed not only with the great, unimpaired Constitutional powers of their offices but with an awesome array of new powers—had, in their own minds, maneuvered themselves into the position of victims, whose rights were menaced by usurpers in television studios, rambunctious citizens in the streets, upstart congressmen, and saboteurs in the federal bureaucracy. They had developed a fear that the President might be made impotent—that he might be turned into a pitiful, helpless giant. The fear had been born out of foreign affairs, but, because the dividing line between the foreign area and the domestic area had been erased in the Administration's thinking and the Administration had discovered enemies at home that were even more dangerous than the ones abroad, the President felt obliged to work to increase his power in domestic affairs as well. The dangers to the American system that he now foresaw were the exact reverse of the dangers that the Founding Fathers had foreseen when they wrote the Constitution. The Founding Fathers had been afraid that the people would be overwhelmed by the power of government. President Nixon, who served in a time when the government was more powerful than it had ever been before, was afraid that the government would be paralyzed by powers arisen among the people.

The same cast of mind was revealed in the President's thinking on the question of criminal justice. In this area, too, he feared that the authorities were menaced with impotence by the people's exercise of their rights. He was afraid that, just as the public might "tie the hands" of the President in foreign policy, the courts might tie the hands of the police in their efforts to cope with crime. For example, he referred on occasion to the citizens' "right" to be free of crime. This might have been taken merely as a figure of speech, comparable to the "right" to good housing, the "right" to a certain income, and so on. However, the President wished to balance this "right" to be free of crime against the rights of criminal suspects in court. He balanced society's need to prevent crime—a very desirable end but not, strictly speaking, a right—against the right of criminal suspects to due process, which was in fact a right spelled out in the Constitution. And if the no-knock provision and the preventive-detention provision of the D.C. crime bill were any indication, the new "right" weighed more heavily in the balance than the Constitutional right. The President's disposition to regard domestic matters in military terms was also revealed in his thinking on the question of criminal justice. He often said that "the peace forces" should be strengthened in relation to "the criminal forces." The police, of course, truly were a force, which could be strengthened or weakened. But the President usually concentrated his fire on the courts, which were not part of any force. In fact, the courts' obligations were as much to criminal suspects as they were to the government.

The consolidation into a single structure of a militarized system for enforcing the law, of the President's campaign against his political enemies, and of the enormous machinery of national security threatened to replace the traditional legal system, in which all citizens, including those in positions of privilege and power, are meant to be equal before the law, with a new, two-tiered system, made up of a lower realm, which is inhabited by ordinary people, and in which a thousand harsh restrictions are in force, and a higher realm, which is inhabited by the powerful, and in which those restrictions are invented but do not apply. By mid-1971, the theoretical underpinnings of such a higher realm were being laid. The realm was that of "inherent powers"; that is, of powers beyond any check except the exerciser's own discretion. It was the realm in which "self-discipline on the part of the executive branch will provide an answer to virtually all of the legitimate complaints against excesses of information gathering," as Assistant Attorney General William Rehnquist put it at a hearing on wiretapping which was held by the Senate Subcommittee on Constitutional Rights. It was the realm in which the President's Advisory Council on Executive Organization worked in secrecy to produce new, experimental institutions of government whose duties were to "perform such functions as the President may from time to time delegate or assign thereto." It was the realm in which, in the words of Chief Justice Burger in his dissent in the case of the Pentagon Papers, the requirements of the First Amendment were weighed against the "imperative" of the "effective functioning of a complex, modern government." (In Burger's legal thinking, there apparently existed a process of gov-

ernmental "functioning" which rose, to some extent, above Constitutional requirements.) It was, in sum, the realm—centered on the
imperative of national security but including other imperatives—in
which power flowed from hidden or mysterious sources and cancelled the visible, established, slowly evolving rights and powers
spelled out in the law.

In the aftermath of the 1970 congressional elections, the President
had jettisoned the controlling image of national division, but he had
not yet settled on a new image. For a while, he had reverted to
warmed-over Mr. Outside material—"the lift of a driving dream,"
the end of the "nightmare of war and division," the aim of bringing
the nation together. In January of 1971, he had announced with
great fanfare a New American Revolution. But no sooner was the
New American Revolution born than it was forgotten. It dominated
the nation's attention for about three days and then virtually disappeared. Thinking about this period, Jeb Magruder later wrote, "In
particular, we kept looking for the slogan that would capture the
essence of the Nixon Administration. We had been seeking our
'New Frontier' for two years and never found it. Various slogans
came and went—The New Federation, The New American Revolution . . . but none ever caught on." In early July, in a speech in
Kansas City, Missouri, the President adopted a pensive, melancholic
pessimism about the future of American civilization. Referring to
the columns of the National Archives Building, in Washington, he
reflected aloud, "Sometimes when I see those columns I think of
seeing them in Greece and in Rome. And I think of what happened
to Greece and Rome, and you see only what is left of great civilizations of the past—as they became wealthy, as they lost their will
to live, to improve, they became subject to the decadence that de-
stroys the civilization. The United States is reaching that period."
But if the long-term prospects were for doom, America could still
look forward to a few good years. "I honestly believe that the
United States has in its hands the future of the world for the next
twenty-five years," he said in the same speech. Then, whether be-

cause the view-from-the-ruins failed to strike a responsive chord with the Missourians or merely because the President felt uncomfortable with his new material, the collapse of American civilization swiftly joined the New American Revolution and other recent ideas in oblivion. By August, the nation had pulled out of its decline and was heading toward a rebirth. "The time has come for us to speak up for America," the President now urged, in a speech to the Knights of Columbus in New York. "Tonight, I can feel in this audience and I can feel in this land of ours a new birth of faith in ourselves. I feel a willingness to face reality, a revival of moral courage, a fresh determination to succeed."

Once the idea of bringing the country together was discarded, the first two years of the Nixon Administration had become a strident, lurid, exhibitionistic time, marked by exaggerated, theatrical posturing in high places as well as by real turmoil and real bloodshed. The opening months of 1971, by contrast, were a muted—almost a drowsy—time. The surface explosions of 1969 and 1970 had given way to muffled explosions beneath the surface. Even bloody or dramatic events that were in the public eye, such as the calamitous invasion of Laos or the seizure of ten thousand people in the nation's capital, went by almost unnoticed. For the covert operators and planners in the White House, however, the period was a busy one. With the President letting his "spirits soar" and trying to "quiet this country down," the job of attacking the press and of working up Buchanan's "divisive issues" fell upon the undercover group. Its activities were banned from the Administration's public image for the moment but were going forward on a large scale anyway. Indeed, the entire burden of the campaign strategy—or pre-campaign strategy, as it happened to be—fell on it, because part of the strategy was that while the President was secretly scheming to divide the country he would publicly appear to abjure politics, and would pose as a "statesman."

For the White House undercover operators, the Pentagon Papers episode marked a momentous turning point. On June 28th,

Daniel Ellsberg was indicted for violating the Espionage Act and for theft of government property. But this move was only one small part of a much broader campaign, involving overt and covert moves, to destroy him politically. To accomplish this aim, the undercover group was expanded greatly. The group's financing would come from the clandestine financial arm of the White House, which had already obtained the milk money and was now engaged in negotiations with the International Telephone & Telegraph Corporation for another secret contribution, and its role would be to commit crimes against the political opposition. The Pentagon Papers episode was the gateway through which the lawbreaking of the war entered American society at its very highest level and became lawbreaking at home. It was the war-coming-home in its most virulent form.

In early July, Charles Colson, who was now one of four men in policymaking roles in the White House who enjoyed direct and constant access to the President (the three others were H. R. Haldeman, John Ehrlichman, and Henry Kissinger), called an old friend of his, E. Howard Hunt, to sound him out on an "Ellsberg project." Hunt had an unusual combination of talents. He had worked as a C.I.A. man, he had had experience as a public-relations man, and he was a writer of spy novels. (His most recent book had been about a cult of Devil worshippers which was controlled by left-wingers.) In his C.I.A. days, one of his special fields of expertise had been the overthrow of Latin-American governments. He had been closely involved with the C.I.A.'s successful connivance in the overthrow of the left-wing regime of President Jacobo Arbenz of Guatemala in 1954, and he had played an important role in the C.I.A.'s attempt to overthrow Fidel Castro in 1961. Hunt had advocated Castro's assassination, and the C.I.A. had, in fact, attempted to arrange the assassination of Castro, once with the help of American gangland figures. Now Colson, unbeknownst to Hunt, was tape-recording their phone conversation, in order to be able to transcribe it for Haldeman. "I want to see the guy hung if it can be done to the advantage of the Administration," Hunt said to Colson, speaking of Ellsberg. Hunt agreed with a suggestion by

Colson that the White House "should go down the line to nail the guy cold," but he wanted to know if the "proper resources" would be available. Colson assured him that they would. However, when Hunt went on to suggest that the case "has to be made on criminal grounds," Colson disagreed. "This case won't be tried in the court, it will be tried in the newspapers," he said. Earlier in the conversation, he had described what he meant. "This thing could go one of two ways," he said. "Ellsberg could be turned into a martyr of the New Left . . . or it could be another Alger Hiss case, where the guy is exposed. . . . We might be able to put this bastard into a hell of a situation and discredit the New Left." And, making his point still clearer, he described "the profit to us in nailing any son of a bitch who would steal a secret document." Later in July, in an apparent attempt to make clear just what sort of profit this would be, President Nixon asked the operational head of the Ellsberg investigation, Egil Krogh, to read the chapter of the President's book *Six Crises* which dealt with the Hiss case. In that chapter, Nixon had written that the profit—and the loss—of the Hiss case had been great. "Had it not been for the Hiss case, I might have been President of the United States," he had written, after losing the Presidential election of 1960. "But equally: had it not been for the Hiss case, I might never have been Vice-President of the United States and thus a candidate for President." If the Ellsberg case was another Hiss case, then it could make or break the President in 1972. The profit could be his reëlection. Hunt accepted Colson's offer, and a few days later a second man from outside the White House, G. Gordon Liddy, was hired to be Hunt's partner. Liddy was a former F.B.I. agent who had run unsuccessfully for the Republican nomination for a congressional seat in upstate New York. He had promised the voters strong law enforcement, and had carried—and often displayed—a pistol as he campaigned. "He knows the answer is law and order, not weak-kneed sociology," his campaign literature had declared.

Hunt and Liddy became part of a secret unit in the White House whose mission was to find the sources of leaks. The unit included Egil Krogh, who came from the staff of John Ehrlichman, and David Young, who came from the staff of Henry Kissinger. For the Ellsberg project, though, a special group, made up of representatives lent by all the agencies of government which might be able to help out, was assembled. The project was organized on a scale commensurate with the presumed high electoral stakes. From the State Department came Deputy Under-Secretary of State William Macomber; from the Defense Department came its General Counsel, J. Fred Buzhardt; and from the Justice Department came Assistant Attorney General Mardian. (Mardian, of course, was in charge of the Interdivisional Information Unit, which had been formed to coördinate the gathering of information on domestic dissidents after the Huston plan had been dropped.) This group, in turn, hoped to make use of the Congress, the courts, and the press. In short, almost every major institution of the Republic was to be brought to bear in some way on the anti-Ellsberg campaign.

Given the tremendous governmental power assembled on the team, the aim of the project was curiously insubstantial. It was to "develop . . . [an] image," as David Young put it in a memo to Ehrlichman. It was to "destroy his [Ellsberg's] public image and credibility," as E. Howard Hunt put it in a memo to Colson. The first step would be to "slowly develop a very negative picture around the whole Pentagon Study affair," Young wrote, and the second step would be to "identify Ellsberg's associates and supporters on the New Left with this negative image." Hunt, adapting the language of assassination to public relations, later referred to the effort as one aimed at the "neutralization of Ellsberg." To this end, Deputy Under-Secretary of State Macomber and General Counsel Buzhardt were to "set the format . . . and develop the scenario" for an investigation of "questions of security clearance, classification and declassification" by the House Armed Services Committee—an investigation that would start "in a low key" and then "move into the more specific case of the Pentagon study." Young noted in his memo that he was hoping to widen the case against Ellsberg to include former high officials of the Democratic Party. He believed that he could develop information implicating men such as Morton Halperin, a "holdover" who had worked for Henry Kissinger after serving in the Johnson Administration, and who was now working for Senator Muskie; and Leslie Gelb, who had been in charge of assembling the Pentagon Papers. Even the former Secretary of Defense, Clark Clifford, was under suspicion and was to be interviewed. And beyond these men Young thought he could see "still another and even larger network," which might include William Bundy, who had been a State Department official in the Administrations of Presidents Kennedy and Johnson. The technique was fundamentally the same as the one used in the 1970 congressional campaign—attack radicals and then draw connections between them and liberal and moderate Democrats—the only difference being that whereas the congressional campaign of 1970 had been loud and open, the campaign against Ellsberg and, by extension, against high-ranking Democrats was quiet and clandestine, in conformity with the Administration's new, unprovocative public image. A portrait of the Democrats as treacherous and disloyal would gradually emerge, but this time no one would know who the artists had been.

Young, like Huston before him, was open-minded about which government agencies to use in getting the job done. "Do we want to prosecute, or do we want to bring such material out through the congressional investigation?" he asked Ehrlichman in his memo. Since the underlying aim was to tear down Ellsberg's image rather than to bring Ellsberg to justice, it hardly mattered to them whether they threw him in jail for life or merely smeared him with damaging publicity. The press, too, would be an important tool. Patrick Buchanan, like Charles Colson, wanted to destroy Ellsberg's image by using the press, and had contributed a memorandum on how to go about it. And Young, too, was careful to note, "If there is to be any damage of Ellsberg's image and those associated with him, it will . . . be necessary to fold in the press planting with the congressional investigation."

Young was also looking forward to the fruits of "Hunt-Liddy Project No. 1." This was a plan to procure still more damaging material on Ellsberg by burglarizing his psychiatrist's office, in Los

165

Angeles, for Ellsberg's psychiatric records. In the meantime, Young and Krogh had applied to the C.I.A. for a "psychological profile" of Ellsberg. One was produced, and it read, in part, "There is no suggestion that Subject saw anything treasonous in his act. Rather he seemed to be responding to what he deemed a higher order of patriotism." Krogh and Young wrote Ehrlichman that they had found the C.I.A. study "superficial" and meant to meet with its author to "impress upon him the detail and depth we expect." Hunt now procured from the C.I.A. some equipment for the burglary, including a camouflaged camera and a red wig. (In September, the burglary was carried out, but it provided little of value to the project.)

All these plans were only half of the "scenario" for defaming the Democratic opposition through the use of the Pentagon Papers. While the White House was hoping to bring public disgrace upon high-ranking Democrats for supposedly having been involved in the release of the papers, it was planning to carry disgrace even higher in the Democratic ranks by making political use of the information whose release it was ostensibly trying to block. Young wrote to Ehrlichman, "I am sending you a separate Hunt-to-Colson memorandum which attempts to select the politically damaging material involving the Democratic hierarchy. I personally believe a good deal more material could be developed along these lines." Young was quite aware that the Administration had embarked on two clashing courses—to destroy politically whoever had contributed to or released the documents and at the same time to use the information in the documents to discredit the opposition—and he made a note of some of the contradictions that might arise. If the White House was too successful in defaming "the objectivity and the intent of the participants in the Pentagon study," he wrote, then it would be difficult to use the papers to defame the Democratic hierarchy. If, on the other hand, the White House was too successful in defaming the Democratic hierarchy, a different problem arose: there might be some "credibility fallout on us."

With Colson and Hunt, the latter consideration carried no weight at all. As far as they were concerned, the Pentagon Papers did not go anywhere near far enough in defaming the Democrats. The two men turned to forgery. Hunt, with a razor blade, a typewriter, and a Xerox machine, and using stacks of cables supplied to him by Deputy Under-Secretary of State Macomber, set about forging false Pentagon Papers, even more shaming to the Democrats—and to the United States—than the real ones. In particular, he forged two cables that framed a former President, John F. Kennedy, for murder. He constructed cables showing that Kennedy had, in effect, ordered the death of President Ngo Dinh Diem, of South Vietnam, in 1963. Colson's thinking was that since Diem had been a Catholic, news that Kennedy, a Democrat and himself a Catholic, had had him murdered would help President Nixon win Catholic votes in the next Presidential election. On September 16th, President Nixon made a reference to the non-fact in public. "I would remind all concerned that the way we got into Vietnam was through overthrowing Diem, and the complicity in the murder of Diem," he said at a news conference. A few days later, Colson attempted, unsuccessfully, to leak Hunt's false cables to a reporter from *Life*.

When Ellsberg was indicted, there were many people in the country who regarded the move as an act of repression. But there were few—perhaps none—who dreamed that it had anything to do with the 1972 Presidential election or with a plot to defame the Democratic Party. And much less did anyone suspect that when the President insinuated that one of his predecessors was implicated in murder, he might be trying to win Catholic votes. Political planning in the White House had become deeper and stranger than anyone in the outside world could imagine. Yet if the country had been able to follow the evolution of the White House undercover operations since President Nixon ordered the secret bombing of Cambodia and hired a former New York policeman to harass Senator Edward Kennedy after the Chappaquiddick episode it would have recognized the style of the Ellsberg project, in all its unlikely strangeness, as pure Nixon White House. It was planned and executed in secrecy. It sought to portray the political opposition as traitorous and disloyal. It was directed by an ad-hoc group with no legal authorization. It used agencies of government interchangeably, and for purely political ends. But most characteristic of all was the fact that the whole aim of the Ellsberg project was not to accomplish any tangible end but to create an image.

Sometime in late June or early July of 1971, the President's legal counsel, John Dean, met Assistant Attorney General Mardian on a flight to San Clemente, California, where the President was staying. Each man was travelling on White House business, but neither man told the other what his business was. In those months, more and more Administration business was being conducted in secret. Dean, as it happened, was on his way to try to stop a White House fire-bombing of a research institute. A short while back, a White House undercover man, John Caulfield, had come to see Dean. Charles Colson, he said, had asked him to firebomb the Brookings Institution. Colson wanted the White House men to steal some documents concerning the Vietnam war which, Colson speculated, might be in the possession of Brookings, and he thought that a good way of doing it would be to change the fire regulations in the District of Columbia to provide that the F.B.I. would respond to fire calls, and then firebomb the place, so that the F.B.I. could rush in and re-trieve the documents. Caulfield told Dean he thought that Colson's plan was "asinine," and asked if Dean could do something about getting it called off. Dean was now on his way to see John Ehrlich-man and ask him to countermand Colson's instructions. (His mission was successful; the firebombing was never carried out.) Mardian's business that day was to get orders from the President about how to head off blackmail of the White House by J. Edgar Hoover. Mardian had been approached by Assistant Director of the F.B.I. William C. Sullivan. Sullivan held in his office safe the summaries of the wiretapped conversations of newsmen and White House staff men. He believed that Hoover "might use these . . . for the purpose of preserving his position as Director of the F.B.I.," as Mardian later described his understanding of the situation. (What-ever the source of the Director's extraordinary power, he had already used it against the Administration once, in blocking the White House plan—the so-called Huston plan—to turn the foreign-intelligence-gathering agencies loose at home.) Sullivan was afraid that Hoover might fire him and take the tapes into his own hands. Now Mardian was on his way to ask the President how to prevent this potential disaster. (The President ordered him to get the summaries and hand them over to the White House, and also to make sure that all copies of the summaries, which had been sent to Haldeman, Kissinger, and Kissinger's assistant Alexander Haig, were still in loyal hands, and Mardian immediately did so.)

The secret missions of the two men on their way to San Clemente were characteristic of the way a growing amount of White House business was being carried out. Lawful procedures had been breaking down steadily since the Inauguration. The President's irregular order to bomb Cambodia secretly had thrown the military into confusion. Now it was turning out that, in an only slightly more indirect way, it had spread confusion within the White House, too. It had led, in part, to the warrantless-wiretapping program. That program, in turn, had generated material that the Director of the F.B.I. might use to blackmail the President. And now the President, in his fear of blackmail, was once again acting irregularly himself. Instead of simply asking Hoover for the summaries, and firing him if he refused to hand them over, he was sending his own secret agent to the Director's subordinate to make off with them secretly.

While the White House undercover group was getting ready to create a political extravaganza on the basis of its project for defaming Daniel Ellsberg, and the President was scheming to get the tape recordings of illegally wiretapped phone conversations from the Assistant Director of the F.B.I., the financial arm of the White House undercover operation was going forward with its fund-raising. After discussions during the spring with Administration officials, an officer, or officers, of I.T.T. promised to contribute four hundred thousand dollars to the President's reëlection campaign. At that time, the Anti-Trust Division of the Justice Department, which was under the direction of Richard McLaren, was bringing major anti-trust actions against I.T.T. Company officials began to engage in extensive lobbying of high officials of the Nixon Administration. At one point, President Nixon intervened directly, ordering Richard Kleindienst, who had succeeded John Mitchell as Attorney General, to drop the cases. Kleindienst, however, would agree only to a postponement, and the lobbying and maneuvering continued. On June 25th, one I.T.T. lobbyist, Mrs. Dita Beard, wrote to her superior, Vice-President William Merriam, that everything was going well. "Other than permitting John Mitchell, Ed Reinecke [the lieutenant governor of California], Bob Haldeman, and Nixon, no one has known from whom that $400,000 had come," she wrote. "I am convinced . . . our noble commitment has gone a long way toward our negotiations on the mergers coming out as Hal [Harold Geneen, I.T.T.'s chief executive officer] wants them. Certainly the President has told Mitchell to see that things are worked out fairly. It is still only McLaren's Mickey Mouse we are suffering. . . . Please destroy this, huh?" A month later, on July 31st, the cases were settled. I.T.T. divested itself of two of the smaller companies it had acquired, the Canteen Corporation and the Grinnell Corporation, but was allowed to keep its major acquisition, the Hartford Fire Insurance Company, which was the sixth-largest property-and-casualty-insurance company in the country.

In the first two years of the Administration, it had become clear that the public record was now a blackboard that only the President, among all the actors on the political scene, had the power to write on and to erase. In late 1968, he had inscribed "National Unity" as the text for the time. In late 1969, he had erased it and put up "National Division" in its place. In late 1970, he had erased that, and now the nation waited for him to write something else on the blackboard. All other political actors had been reduced to graffitists. They could only scribble in the corners. They could only—in the

President's words—"criticize" and "complain" and "doubt" and "tear down." And even then they were indirectly controlled by the President, for it was he whom they must criticize and his wisdom that they were obliged to doubt. Indeed, in his world they became simply "the critics" or "the doubters"—"skeptics" who had "lost the vision indispensable to great leadership." They may or may not have lost their vision, but they had certainly lost the power and the will to make themselves heard in Richard Nixon's America. The position they occupied in the world arranged by him condemned them to be the ones who spread anxiety and unease while he was busy building up and reassuring. They had lost the power to initiate and to define, which is to say that they had lost the power to act. The President acted. "The critics" reacted. And sometimes they didn't even do that. The President had observed in his news conference after the invasion of Cambodia, "The only difference is that of all these people—and I refer particularly to some of my lively critics in the House and Senate—they have the luxury of criticism. . . . They have the luxury of criticism because they can criticize and if it doesn't work out, they can gloat over it, or, if it does work out, the criticism will be forgotten. I don't have that luxury. As Commander-in-Chief, I alone am responsible for the lives of four hundred and twenty-five or thirty thousand Americans in Vietnam." In Richard Nixon's America, his role was to act and to take responsibility, theirs to criticize, to gloat, and to forget.

But in the first months of his second two years the President had not acted boldly. (Neither, to be sure, had his opposition.) In some respects, these months had been like the first months of his first two years. Now, as then, most of the important work was clandestine, and what was written on the public record was wobbly and indecisive and a bit sparse. The President had erased the image of national division, but he had not replaced it with a new image. His standing in the polls was the lowest it had been so far, and one poll had shown Senator Muskie leading by forty-seven per cent to thirty-nine in a trial heat of the election. But while the domestic staff of the White House had been planning Daniel Ellsberg's ordeal and arranging things with I.T.T. and the dairy producers, Henry Kissinger, in an operation that was no less secret than these, had made a trip to China. In early July, while pretending to be laid up with a stomach ailment in Pakistan, he had gone to meet with Chou En-lai in Peking. The President, having erased his blackboard after the 1970 congressional elections, now began to write again. On July 15th, he went on national television and, in a statement that lasted only three minutes, informed the country that he planned to make a trip to China.

The news was as much of a surprise to his American listeners as it must have been to the Chinese. The Chinese, of course, had been taught for decades that the American government was the incarnation of everything evil in the world. American leaders had been called gangsters, monsters, hyenas, mad dogs—no abuse had been too rough. Now the Chinese learned that the worst imperialist, the head gangster—the President of the United States himself—was about to visit their shores. To the Americans the gesture was in some ways even more startling. America had paid in blood for its supposed enmity with "Asian Communism," whose headquarters was presumably in Peking. Just twenty months before, the President had spoken of nations whose dreams of "world conquest" were still alive, and more recently than that he had warned the country of rampant worldwide totalitarianism and anarchy. But by July of 1971 all these spectres had apparently gone down the same capacious memory hole that had swallowed up the domestic terrorists, vultures, hoodlums, eunuchs, and assorted other menaces.

Certainly the announcement was the greatest surprise that had been sprung on the nation from the White House since the announcement of the invasion of Cambodia. But this time, although bewilderment was again universal, the shock was accompanied by approval—indeed, by delight—in almost all quarters. (The trip violated the most deeply held principles of the American right wing, yet only a few mutterings of protest were heard even from there.) The White House offered no reasons whatever for the trip. In fact, Ronald Ziegler, the President's press secretary, asked that the nation not do too much thinking along those lines: when a reporter inquired what influence the trip might have on the war in Vietnam, Ziegler answered that he would not speculate on "the effect of these discussions [in China] on any other matters," and he added that "general speculation on this matter would not be helpful." (Officials in the Administration often refused to "speculate" on what the Administration itself was doing or was about to do, as though they were third parties to their own actions and had to engage in guesswork about their own intentions.)

The China trip and the scheme to "nail" Ellsberg, both of which had been planned in the White House in the early summer, might have seemed to an outsider like the actions of two totally dissimilar Administrations. For one thing, the decision to mount the Ellsberg operation seemed to assume a greatly intensified concern about America's enemies in the world and at home, but the decision to make the trip to China seemed to assume that tensions were relaxing to some extent. Yet in some of the thinking around the White House the two projects were not contradictory but complementary. Of course, both would be helpful at election time, but beyond that—or intermingled with it—was a conviction that both were necessary to an indivisible, all-encompassing structure of national security. In fact, as the White House men saw things, it was precisely the importance of the President's efforts to improve relations with the nation's foreign adversaries which made the assaults on its domestic adversaries necessary. As John Ehrlichman put it later, all foreign-policy matters were "completely interrelated." And, as the President put it later, "leaks of secret information about any one [policy] could endanger all." That is, the Pentagon Papers "leak" threatened the trip to China and the peace of the world. If this ship of state sprang just one leak, the whole vessel and everything it was carrying would go down.

In August, the President imposed wage and price controls on the American economy and severed the dollar from the gold standard. The announcement of the two moves was as sudden and unexpected as the announcement of the trip to China, and constituted as sharp a reversal in the President's thinking. In July, he had declared that wage and price controls would "snuff out" the country's economic "dynamism."

In October, the President announced that he was planning to make a trip to the Soviet Union in the spring. The announcement of the Russia trip, like the announcement of the China trip, was as empty of detailed explanation as it was full of evident high significance. For a third time, he had stunned the world with an unanticipated announcement of tremendous import. In the United States, the announcements were known simply as the President's "surprises." The Japanese, upon whose national life they had had severe dislocating effects, called them "Nixon shocks." Nations abroad had begun to join the circle of those who complained that they were not consulted in advance about decisions by the President.

In four months, the President had seemed to turn the world upside down. He had placed the full array of his powers on display: his absolute command over the nation's diplomatic and warmaking machinery, which included the machinery that could incinerate the earth; his power to transform the economic life of the country with a few orders; and his power utterly to dominate the air waves and the news columns with his words, his deeds, and his image of himself, of the country, and of the world. The vacuum that had developed when the President suddenly abandoned the image of national division following the 1970 congressional elections had now been filled. The experimentation with a New American Revolution and other transient notions was over, and the background for a strong new image had been established. The President would deliver the world from the threat of nuclear annihilation. He would be a man of peace.

This latest broad change in Administration policy, like the sudden changes that preceded it, had not been prepared for by any public announcements. Its genesis had been in the hidden deliberation of just two men—the President and his national-security adviser

Henry Kissinger—and the foundation for it had been laid in deeper secrecy than had ever prevailed before in American policy. Even the Joint Chiefs of Staff had been excluded from knowledge of the plans, and they, in one of the many breakdowns of orderly procedure in the White House during this period, had attempted to set up a system for spying on Kissinger and the President. They had been "reorganized" out of their traditional role in advising Presidents, and were far from happy about it. After the announcements of the two trips had been issued, the President and Kissinger, instead of revealing the thinking that had gone into the two decisions, regaled the country with details of how secrecy had been maintained. Henry Kissinger told the story of his pretended stomach ailment in Pakistan. A White House staff member revealed that the President had never worked on the China trip in the Oval Office, for fear someone might learn something about it by glancing at papers lying on his desk.

Over three years, the character—or, at least, the public image—of the Nixon Administration had changed several times with jarring abruptness. But the manner in which change itself occurred in the Nixon Administration had remained unchanged. Continuity in all its forms had been dispensed with. The productions of the Nixon Administration emerged from nowhere, and sank back into nowhere when their usefulness was at an end. Policy that shook the country and the world sprang full-grown from the brains of a handful of men. New law, lacking in any precedent, emerged from the bottomless well of power—the "inherent" power to defend the Constitution in whatever manner the Administration pleased. New, formless institutions were brought into being through the secret, unrecorded labors of the Advisory Council. And if any Nixon policies were anticipated by public statements, these were usually virtual antiguides to what was about to occur. When the President was on the verge of dividing the country in a way that it had never been divided before, for example, and was about to enclose himself in the deepest isolation ever experienced by an American President, he announced his wish to bring America together and to run an "open'" Administration. (Oddly, there is no evidence that in this instance the President

175

was aware of the about-face he was soon to perform.) When he was about to exclude the Secretary of State almost completely from the major decisions on foreign policy, he announced, "I intend to have a very strong Secretary of State." When he was about to launch a drive to further centralize power in his own hands, he promised to return power to the people. Once a policy had emerged, discussion of it was often discouraged. Sometimes—after the trip to China and the trip to Russia had been announced, for example—the information released about the policy was insufficient for informed debate. At other times, it was suggested that debate would ruin the policy and would therefore be unpatriotic. Finally, when a policy or a new institution was discarded—to be replaced, often, by its apparent opposite—it vanished absolutely; no trace remained of its ever having existed. A few weeks after the President attempted, in public addresses in a succession of cities and states, to incite the nation against its rebellious young people, for example, he had referred to his efforts "to quiet this country down." Policy became a series of unconnected episodes. Memory and anticipation were both sheared away, leaving the public enclosed in a supercharged, claustrophobic present—a present in which the rule was to keep your eye riveted on the prestidigitator's surprise of the moment, and never look back.

As the President stepped up his activities in foreign affairs, he also stepped up his efforts to use government information to discredit the activities in foreign affairs of his Democratic predecessors in office. Colson and Hunt were already searching the Pentagon Papers for material that would be useful "in demonstrating the collective bad judgement of the Kennedy Administration and/or a number of its high level appointees," as Colson put it in a memo to Hunt; and these two had already gone as far as to fabricate information that would serve the same purpose. Now the President cast his net wider. Awakened to the possibilities of blackening the reputations of former Presidents by releasing state secrets—and thus of indirectly enhancing his own reputation by contrast—the President sought information on other key episodes in the nation's recent history. On September 22, Ehrlichman met with C.I.A. Director Helms and announced that the President wished to declassify documents having to do with the Bay of Pigs incident, the Cuban missile crisis, and some other matters. Colson spelled out the reason for the declassifications in a memo to Ehrlichman a few days later in a memo titled "Rekindling the Pentagon Papers Issue." Mentioning the desirability of "each day hopefully creating some minor embarrassment for the Democrats," he advised, "we should very soon release declassified documents relating to the Lebanon crisis, the Cuban missile crisis and perhaps one or two others. Releasing of declassified documents will keep press interest alive in the whole issue. We should start doing it soon to avoid the charge of election year politicking." On October 1, Director Helms gave all of the files but the Vietnam file to Ehrlichman. On October 10, in a meeting with Ehrlichman and the President, Helms handed that file over, too.

In early October, a few days before the announcement of the Russian trip, the affair of Richard Nixon, William C. Sullivan, J. Edgar Hoover, and the summaries of the warrantless telephone taps reached a temporary climax. A power struggle between Nixon and Hoover which was of a sort never seen before in the United States between a President and one of his appointees broke out. Hoover forced the retirement of Sullivan and changed the locks on his door. Sullivan, however, had already handed the summaries over to Assistant Attorney General Mardian, and they were now in John Ehrlichman's office in the White House. Sullivan's forced retirement was the signal for the White House to initiate a covert public-relations offensive against Hoover. The list of grievances against him was long. He had blocked the Huston plan single-handed. The White House was afraid that he might reveal the warrantless taps. He had not coöperated with the campaign to tear down Ellsberg's image in order to get at the Democrats. (In the summer, David Young had written in a memo to Ehrlichman that "only the F.B.I." thought Ellsberg had been "the sole prime mover" in the release of the Pentagon Papers. This opinion threw cold water on the enticing theory of the "even larger network" of conspirators which Young was developing.) And in August Hoover had seemed to deliberately misconstrue an instruction from H. R. Haldeman in a way that caused the Administration serious embarrassment. Haldeman had ordered a discreet investigation of the CBS newsman Daniel Schorr. Hoover, instead of conducting a discreet inquiry, conducted a full investigation, including interviews with Schorr's friends and acquaintances, who naturally told Schorr what was happening. The incident was soon in the news, and the Administration had to invent a story to the effect that Schorr was under consideration for an Administration job having to do with environmental affairs.

Now the White House set out to tear down Hoover's image. The techniques were some of the usual ones: the leaking of distorted information to the press, the hidden orchestration of an "offensive" against the man who was to be "discredited." On October 10th, the campaign opened with an article in the *Times*, citing "high officials of the intelligence community," about Hoover's conduct of his office. The gist of the information was that Hoover was doddering and had become a menace to national security. "Leading members of the intelligence community" were so alarmed by his behavior, the article said, that they were breaking their customary rule of silence in order to recommend that he be "deposed." The article went on to report that "several prominent members of the Administration" were said to favor his retirement, but not Nixon himself. One of the complaints against Hoover was that "the F.B.I. broke off direct liaison with the C.I.A. a year and a half ago." That was around the time the White House had been pushing the Huston plan. A second complaint was against the forced retirement of Sullivan, who was described in the article as enjoying "a reputation as a scholarly researcher on Communist philosophy and tactics." A third complaint was that Hoover was reluctant to run the "risks of counter-espionage work." He supposedly feared the "sullying of his reputation" if he should bungle a job. "As an example of such risks," the article said, "the officials point out that an F.B.I. man might find himself apprehended by the police when he does a 'bag job'—a surreptitious piece of counter-espionage sometimes involving illegal activity." The article implied that the proposed "bag jobs" were against foreign enemy agents. A "Justice Department official" commented that "the agents are basically trained in criminal procedures . . . and the subtleties of intelligence work seem to elude them." Hoover's political foes were many, particularly among the people he was said to have described as "the 'jackals of the press' and the A.C.L.U." They had wanted him removed for many years, and they were not choosy about the grounds for his removal. He would not maintain liaison with the C.I.A.? He had forced the retirement of a "scholarly researcher on Communist philosophy"? He would not perform "bag jobs"? Then he must go. But Hoover endured.

On October 14th, H. R. Haldeman received a memo from an advance man informing him that in the course of a scheduled trip to Charlotte, North Carolina, to attend a rally with Billy Graham the President could expect demonstrations that were "violent" and would find the demonstrators carrying signs that were "obscene." Haldeman wrote the word "Good" next to the two adjectives, and when the memo went on to report that the demonstrations would be against Billy Graham, too, he wrote the comment "Great!" The memo continued, "The Charlotte Police Department is extremely tough and will probably use force," and Haldeman wrote "Good" once again. The memo went on to say that arrangements had, however, been made to keep demonstrators out of the rally itself. The formula devised for the 1970 congressional campaign was still in effect: use the demonstrators as a foil to win popularity for the President—and if some are beaten up by the police, all the better—but don't let them get too close. The difference was that now the President, in accordance with the rules imposed by his new image, would remain aloof rather than jump into the fray.

All through the spring, summer, and the early fall, Patrick Buchanan and his "planning group" for the 1972 Presidential campaign had been pondering strategy and sending memos to Haldeman, Mitchell, and the President. By October, the strategy had jelled. Buchanan outlined it in a memo to Haldeman and Mitchell dated October 5th and titled "Dividing the Democrats." The theme had been emerging gradually during the year. Back in March, in his memo on the "Muskie Watch," Buchanan had recommended to the President that the Republican "attack" should "focus on those issues that divide the Democrats, not those that unite Republicans," and had gone on to explain, "It should exacerbate and elevate those issues on which Democrats are divided—forcing Muskie to either straddle, or come down on one side or the other." Then, in July, he had advised, "Maintain as guiding political principle that our great hope for 1972 lies in maintaining or exacerbating the deep Democratic rift." As Buchanan saw it, a united Democratic Party was the greatest danger that the President faced in the coming election, and therefore everything possible should be done to make Democrats angry at one another and destroy their unity. Indirect as this strategy might be, it was not to be a peripheral effort; it was to be the "guiding political principle" for the election year. One question, though, was how the Republicans in the White House could exercise remote control over the behavior of the Democratic Party. How could the central plank of the Republican platform be something that the Democrats would do; namely, destroy themselves? The planning group had many techniques to suggest. Almost all of them involved covert action, action taken under false pretenses, or action taken for a hidden purpose. Together, the planning group's proposals added up to the first plan for a wholly subterranean Presidential campaign strategy ever to be devised.

One technique was secretly to promote extreme elements on both the far right and the far left of the Democratic Party. On the right, the candidacy of George Wallace would be promoted. Not long before, the White House, far from trying to promote Wallace's candidacy, had wished to eliminate him altogether from Presidential politics, and had secretly funnelled four hundred thousand dollars left over from the 1968 Presidential campaign to his rival in the Democratic gubernatorial primary in Alabama in 1970. But now the White House had found a use for Wallace. If he ran in the Democratic Presidential primaries, this would be "an excellent vehicle for surfacing and hardening the divisions within the Democratic Party," Buchanan wrote in his October 5th memo. On the left, Buchanan wanted the White House to promote a fourth-party movement. "Top level consideration should be given to ways and means to promote, assist, and fund a Fourth Party candidacy of the Left Democrats and/or the Black Democrats," he wrote. "There is nothing that can so advance the President's chances for reëlection—not a trip to China, not four and a half per cent unemployment—as a realistic black . . . campaign." At this point in his memo, Buchanan, shifting to an alternate strategy, began to sound like a chairman of the Democratic National Committee. "We should continue to champion the cause of the blacks within the Democratic Party," he wrote, the point being that a party identified with black people would be less appealing to white people. The policy of promoting extremism while pretending to oppose it was born in 1969 and 1970, during the Presidential Offensive. In those years, the President had systematically exaggerated the threat posed to him by the far left. Now his men were yearning once again for violence, and the President's chief aide, H. R. Haldeman, was noting on memos that violent and obscene demonstrations against the President were "good."

A second technique for dividing the Democrats was to make public statements whose sole purpose was to start quarrels between the right and the left wings of the Party. There was, for instance, the strategy of "Republican Praise for Any Democratic Support on Vietnam." If the White House praised, say, Senator Humphrey or Senator Muskie for supporting the President on Vietnam, it would go "far toward making them 'Establishment' and driving a wedge between them and the ideological hard core of their party," the planning group wrote. The complementary strategy was for the White House to "take the side of the Far Left" whenever possible— for instance, by "saying we disagree with them, but that they have a just cause, and the Power Elite within the Party is denying them effective participation." The planning group was indifferent about whether to promote the far right more or the far left more. As long as a move increased national division, it was acceptable. Muskie was the prime target during this period, and in the July memo Buchanan and his planning group had recommended that "any stick should be used to beat him"—that "he can and should be attacked from Right and Left."

The whole gamut of covert operations would also be brought into play. The rigged letters-to-the-editor would, of course, continue to flow. And Buchanan thought that an "outside direct mail group"— a front group, that is—would be useful in sending things to "columnists, editorial writers, and political writers in order to get all our negative propaganda into their hands." Another suggestion was to "get a poll" showing Humphrey as the leading candidate, since this would frighten the left wing of the Party. Also, "we should have several divisive questions worked up and distributed at major press conferences of the leading Democrats." Turning to the "Governors/ Cabinet officers/Hill people," Buchanan wanted a decision on "how these types are to be used"; for instance, a decision on "Dole's use" —Senator Robert Dole of Kansas, the chairman of the Republican National Committee. Buchanan and the planning group even gave momentary consideration to a "straight" operation: "We ought to consider how to set this [a 'Mailing Operation to Democrats'] up, with perhaps the least possible 'Republican' credentials; or perhaps if that cannot be avoided, set up some 'Kremlinologist' operation for the Democratic Party, acknowledge it, and play it straight." He meant that in this case the White House might consider acknowledging its sponsorship of one of its anti-Democrat operations. It was the planning group's sole recommendation of a "straight" operation. The group's operations were all designed in the White House, and were therefore the responsibility of the President (it was he, not Patrick Buchanan, whom the people had elected), but, as far as the public was to know, the President would be taking no part in any of them. Not after 1970. He was a "statesman" now. He was to be "used to the absolute minimum." For "the President and the Presidency" were the "quintessential political assets" and should be "used" only *"in extremis."*

But all these techniques—clandestine support for far-right and far-left groups, public statements slyly designed to set one Democrat against another, and covert propaganda of various kinds—were only incidental to a far more important technique: to divide the Democrats by exploiting the full range of policy decisions available to the President. Though the exploitation of policy to win votes for oneself or one's own party was far from unfamiliar in American politics, the White House strategy for 1972 was different. The aim was not to make the President an appealing candidate but to arrange circumstances so that the Democratic candidate would be forced to make himself unappealing. By no means the least strange thing about adopting "dividing the Democrats" as the principal aim of the election effort was the fact that virtually no one outside the White House was to know that that was the strategy. For example, when, during the summer, in a speech before a Catholic fraternal organization, the President promised aid to Catholic schools, there were many people who interpreted his move as a crude attempt to win Catholic votes, but there were few or none who guessed that he might be doing it because, as Patrick Buchanan put it, "clearly this divides the Democrats who run the New York *Times* from the Democrats who run for office in Queens and the North Bronx." The public's mind was prepared for a less highly developed strain of cynicism than the one that the White House was concentrating on. No one guessed that Nixon's purpose was not so much to draw votes to himself as to "elevate" the issue so that it became an irritant in the body politic which would prevent Democratic unity.

Supposedly, one good issue for dividing the Democrats, in the opinion of the planning group, was the war. At times, however, the White House seemed to be stymied as to how to keep the issue alive. In his memo in March on the "Muskie Watch," Buchanan had written, "Less and less is this an issue dividing Democrats; more and more is it a unifying issue as conservative Democrats begin to adopt a 'let's get the hell out' stance." A few months later, he said that the issue should be exacerbated, but he made no specific suggestions about how to do it. (The experience of the two previous years had shown that an escalation of the war would bring about all the division you could ever want, yet it had also shown that such division did not necessarily pay off at the polls.)

Another good action to take for the purpose of embittering Democrats against each other was "a cutback in welfare," Buchanan believed. Cutting off aid to the poor "might well be considered philistine or worse by the media, but would seem to be good politics," he wrote in his October memo. And he noted, "Like other proposals, the above calls for what the Vice-President termed 'positive polarization.'" "Positive polarization," then, had been the steady policy of the Administration since the fall of 1969. In the first two years, it had been partly out in the open. Now it was concealed.

Still another division that Buchanan thought it would be a good idea to exacerbate by framing provocative policy was "South versus North." "Here the dividing line is essentially that of the race issue," he pointed out. Therefore, the issue of race was the one to dwell on. But to do that "we need more than just rhetoric and mailings," he wrote. "Actions taken by the President and Administration are decisive here." One action that offered high promise for dividing the Democrats along racial lines, Buchanan thought, was the nomination of certain kinds of Supreme Court Justices. The nomination of a "Southern Strict Constructionist will force Democratic Northern Liberals and major candidates to anger either the South with a veto vote or the blacks and the labor movement and the northern liberals," he explained. The struggle over the nominations of Haynsworth and Carswell had already shown just how much division you could get if you were to choose Justices for their capacity for stirring up the opposition. At that time, the President had assailed the Senate for its "act of regional discrimination" in refusing to confirm Haynsworth and Carswell. Now Buchanan was apparently hoping for a repeat performance.

But although the nomination of a certain kind of Supreme Court Justice was one means of proved effectiveness for promoting

hostility between the North and the South, a still greater opportunity lay in the President's power to provoke a Constitutional
crisis. Buchanan reported that the voters tended to blame the
busing of schoolchildren on the Administration in power, regardless
of any statements against busing which it might put out. The public,
he thought, did not understand that the integration of schools took
place by order of the judicial branch and was therefore a matter
of law. Mere statements were not enough to get on the politically
advantageous side of this issue. Instead, "this requires the kind of
historic decision, bringing a Constitutional end to the national
pressure to integrate races in housing and schooling—which requires a decision on the part of the President," he wrote in October.
"This would really tear up the pea patch; and our current policy is
one of accommodation with the courts not confrontation." The President is sworn to faithfully execute the laws of the United States,
and it is the duty of the courts to decide what these laws are, but
Patrick Buchanan and his planning group wanted the President to
engage in a "confrontation" with the courts. Once again, the affinity
of the right-wing strategists in the White House with the left-wing
fringe in the streets was showing itself. And once again the difference was that when a few disorderly defendants defied a judge a
commotion of manageable proportions would occur, but when the
President engaged in a "confrontation" with the courts the foundation of the law, and of the courts, could be destroyed. For if the
executive branch defied the law, then who would enforce it? The
benefits in terms of national turmoil could be great, Buchanan
thought. "In conclusion, this is a potential throw of the dice that
could bring the media on our heads, and cut the Democratic Party
and country in half; my view is that we would have far the larger
half," he wrote. "But that is not my decision." Whether or not it had
been White House strategy in the first two years of the Administration intentionally to embitter American life and destroy national
unity in the hope of consolidating itself in power, that was the
strategy now. It was to "throw . . . the dice," "cut . . . the country
in half," and pick up "far the larger half" of the shattered remains.

On October 13th—the day after the President announced his trip to
Russia, and a week after his planning group had sent him its recommendations on how to divide the Democrats—the President submitted six names to the American Bar Association as possible
nominees for two new vacancies that had opened up on the Supreme Court. The names were those of Sylvia Bacon, a trial judge
on the Superior Court of the District of Columbia, who had been
a lawyer in the Nixon Justice Department and had worked on the
District of Columbia crime bill; Robert Byrd, a Democratic senator
from West Virginia, who had been to law school but had not been
admitted to the bar and had never practiced law, and who had
once been a member of the Ku Klux Klan (an affiliation he had
since repudiated); Charles Clark, of Mississippi, a judge on the
United States Court of Appeals for the Fifth Circuit, who had first
come to prominence when, as a lawyer, he defended Governor Ross
Barnett of Mississippi against contempt charges after Barnett tried
to block James Meredith from enrolling at the University of Mississippi; Paul Roney, also a judge on the United States Court of Appeals for the Fifth Circuit, whom President Nixon had appointed to
Judge Carswell's seat when Carswell made an abortive run for the
Senate in 1970; Mildred Lillie, a judge on the California Court of
Appeals, about whom very little was known; and Herschel Friday, a
municipal-bond lawyer from Little Rock, Arkansas, who was an
acquaintance of Attorney General Mitchell (Mitchell had been a
municipal-bond lawyer before joining the Nixon Administration),
and who had done considerable work in an effort to prevent the
integration of public schools in Little Rock. None of the President's
choices enjoyed a national reputation as a jurist. Only Senator Byrd
and Mr. Friday, for example, were listed in *Who's Who in America*,
to which newsmen and people in the legal profession turned in bewilderment when they learned the potential nominees' names. In
legal circles, there was dismay, and in some political circles there
was anger. In a statement issued two days after the names were
made known, Senator Edward Kennedy said, "Surely, the compila-

tion and submission of this list will rank as one of the great insults to the Supreme Court in its history." And he charged that President Nixon was "a radical in the true sense of the word . . . a man who seeks to undermine one of the basic and vital institutions of our nation—the Supreme Court as an equal partner of government." By October 20th, the President had narrowed the list before the American Bar Association to two—Judge Lillie and Mr. Friday. That night, the Association, which had approved both Haynsworth and Carswell, refused to approve either Lillie or Friday. But instead of making its decision public it informed President Nixon of it privately. The next day, he went on national television to announce the nomination of two men who had not been on the list of six. They were Assistant Attorney General Rehnquist, who had announced the state of "qualified martial law" during the May Day demonstration, and Lewis Powell, a conservative lawyer from Virginia and a former president of the American Bar Association.

The President's potential nominees may have been unqualified as Justices of the Supreme Court, but, just as Buchanan had predicted, they were perfectly qualified to "divide the Democrats." The suggestion of Senator Byrd was particularly well suited to this work, since it forced Democrats who supported civil-rights legislation (which Byrd had strongly opposed in the Senate) to repudiate either their convictions or their colleague from the South. And the planning group in the White House couldn't have hoped for better results from the President's move than the statement by Senator Kennedy in which he called the list "one of the great insults" to the Supreme Court. Another man to fall into the trap was Senator McGovern, who first praised the trial nomination of Byrd and then, a day later, in a move that must have been especially annoying to Senator Byrd, withdrew his praise, saying that it would be intolerable to have a "racist" on the Court.

Within a few months, the Senate confirmed Powell and Rehnquist.

The last half of 1971—from the time when the Pentagon Papers were published through the final months of the year—was a period of clandestine preparation for the Presidential campaign of 1972. Funds had secretly been raised. An election strategy had secretly been settled upon. A team of underground operators had secretly been recruited and had carried out its first crime—the break-in at Ellsberg's psychiatrist's office. A plan to stage a political show trial—Ellsberg's—that would drag in members of the opposition party was forming. The Ellsberg project, however, was only part of a much larger plan to use government agencies to punish people who White House staff men decided were "enemies." Their idea of enemies was sweeping. In its first two years, the Administration had engaged in "combat" with what it perceived to be a network of foes including, among others, supposed anarchists and murderers, whom it merged with demonstrators against the war and the Democratic Party. Now the field of enemies had expanded, and the men in the White House had come to look upon many Americans in all walks of life—businessmen, professional people, actors, athletes, professors —as enemies. In its early stages, the Enemies Project was an informal, ad-hoc undertaking. Any high White House official who wanted to get someone in trouble could put that person's name down on the list. Hundreds of names poured in. They were taken from lists of Democratic contributors, and lifted from political advertisements, and culled from newspaper articles. In August, it fell to John Dean to systematize the effort. In a memo prepared for Haldeman and Ehrlichman, he recommended steps to "maximize the fact of our incumbency in dealing with persons known to be active in their opposition to our Administration." He thought that the Administration should explore ways to "use the available federal machinery to screw our political enemies"—ways, that is, to find out "who . . . we should be giving a hard time," and to "screw them (e.g., grant availability, federal contracts, litigation, prosecution, etc.)." In September, Charles Colson sent John Dean an "Opponent Priority Activity" list of twenty enemies, which had been prepared the previous June by a member of Colson's staff, and is believed to be the first of a series of formal enemies lists. Other lists were much longer. One composite list had seven categories—"Politicos," "Media," "Organizations," "Labor," "Celebrities," "Business," and "Academics"—and included people barely connected with politics, such as Joe Namath, the football player, and Barbra Streisand, the actress. Many of the Democratic officials whom Young had hoped to entangle in his "larger network" of Pentagon Papers conspirators —Morton Halperin, Leslie Gelb, Clark Clifford, and Robert Mc-Namara—were on the lists.

The twenty people on Colson's September list were classified as being on "go status." The separate names were followed by comments and, in most cases, by recommendations. Daniel Schorr was on the list and was described as a "real media enemy." The columnist Mary McGrory was on the list and was described as having written "daily hate-Nixon articles." Sidney Davidoff, an aide to Mayor John V. Lindsay of New York, was included and was described as "a first class S.O.B., wheeler-dealer, and suspected bag-man." And it was noted that "positive results would really shake the Lindsay camp and Lindsay's plan to capture youth vote." S. Stanley Munro, Jr., who was Senator Henry Jackson's administrative assistant, was on the list, and the notation was "We should give him a try. Positive results would stick a pin in Jackson's white hat." And after the name of Morton Halperin was the comment "A scandal would be most helpful here." The Enemies Project, like so many of the Nixon Administration's undertakings, was aimed largely at manipulating images. In its aims, the project was no different from the project to smear Ellsberg or to smear the late President Kennedy. The Ellsberg prosecution was only a means of putting on a show; throwing Ellsberg in prison for life was only one method of getting at the really important thing—his image. The cable forgery, too, was only a means of destroying the image of a highly regarded Democrat—albeit a deceased one. For this public-relations campaign did not stop at the grave's edge. Not content to defame the living, the men in the White House had gone to work on the images of the dead.

The punitive spirit of the Enemies Project carried over into the rest of the Administration's work, and began to permeate the business of the White House in its small details as well as in its broad philosophy. At the pettiest level, White House social life came to be regulated by a system of punishments and rewards. During the summer, an aide named Frederic Malek, who kept an eye on this aspect of White House affairs, told a reporter, "We've corralled all the goodies that are available." Cabinet aides who were "deserving" or who needed à boost "from a morale standpoint" would be rewarded with an engraved invitation to a White House black-tie function. Under the old, disorganized system of socializing at the White House, Malek pointed out, the President "could be inviting someone we want to get rid of." Now anyone of that kind would be left out in the cold. Malek was also empowered to impose more serious punishment. One of his principal jobs, he told the reporter, was to ferret out "bad guys" and to fire them. Almost from the start, Malek had been an important figure in the reorganizational struggles. For example, in 1970, two days after Interior Secretary Walter Hickel left his post, Malek had installed himself in the Interior Department and ordered six high Interior officials to clear out their desks and get out of the building by five o'clock that afternoon.

One organization that the White House was particularly eager to get under control was the Internal Revenue Service. Randolph Thrower, the head of the I.R.S., was removed, and a new man, Johnnie Walters, was appointed. John Dean, in a "talking paper" to Haldeman briefing him for a meeting with Walters, wrote, "Walters *must* be more responsive in two key areas: personnel and political actions." He added that "Walters should understand that when a request comes to him, it is his responsibility to accomplish it— without the White House having to tell him how to do it." The whole agency should be reorganized, Dean thought: "Walters should be told to make the changes in personnel and policy which will give the Administration semblance of control over the hostile bureaucracy of I.R.S." Dean looked forward to the same level of coöperation throughout the government. The Enemies Project, he wrote, "should have access to and the full support of the top officials of the agency or department in proceeding to deal with the individual."

The Administration was also laying plans for corralling "the goodies" on a government-wide scale. It had begun to divide up the federal budget to reward friends and punish enemies. A "responsiveness program" was set up, under Malek's guidance, which channelled federal money to groups that gave the President political support, and cut off federal money from groups that opposed the President. In March of 1972, after planning had been under way for some months, Malek submitted a master design of the responsiveness program to Haldeman which warned of the danger of "adverse publicity" and of the need to "keep the President and the White House disassociated" from the program. To accomplish these ends, "written communications would be kept to a minimum. . . . Information about the program would be transmitted verbally." As for the few documents that would have to be prepared, they "would not indicate White House involvement in any way." But, whether oral or written, "communications concerning the program . . . would be structured to give the impression that the program was initiated by the [Cabinet] Department head without the knowledge of the White House." Patrick Buchanan, in one of his memos on "Dividing the Democrats," had written, "Since taking office, the President has increased by five hundred per cent . . . the food-stamp and food-assistance funds, and he still gets it in the neck for 'starving the poor.' Methinks there would have been more gratitude and greater rewards if those funds had been directed to the President's potential friends in the working class and their interests." (What's more, such a move would, Buchanan wrote, "force a division within the Democratic Party.") The law was already well on its way to being restyled as an instrument for punishing political enemies. Now federal funding was being diverted to the same purpose. By late 1971, in other words, the federal government was being transformed into a machine for punishing and rewarding the whole American people.

Throughout the President's tenure, the press had repeatedly developed the notion that the "open," trusting Administration so many people had looked forward to eagerly in 1968 was at hand. The fall of 1971, when the Enemies Project was getting under way, was another such period, and one news magazine informed its readers that "the political paranoia of the first years, when the entire Administration from the President down behaved as if all of Washington was booby-trapped, is fading."

Early in December, a full-scale war broke out between India and Pakistan, both of which received military aid from the United States. At issue was the fate of East Pakistan, a region that was separated from the seat of government in West Pakistan by the full breadth of India. In the winter of 1970 and 1971, elections had been held in East Pakistan, and a party in opposition to the ruling party in West Pakistan had won a heavy majority of the votes. The government's initial response was to suspend the newly elected government and to jail its leader, Sheikh Mujibur Rahman. Then, in the months that followed, government forces began to massacre hundreds of thousands of people in East Pakistan. At the same time, millions of refugees flooded across East Pakistan's western border into India. The United States government made no comment on the massacres, and it continued to ship arms to West Pakistan. In the summer of 1971, India, a nation that had a long history of bitter and bloody relations with Pakistan and an equally long history of good relations with the United States, signed a friendship treaty with the Soviet Union—in part because of the apparently close relationship between the United States and Pakistan.

The area was one that the government had not been greatly concerned about in recent years, and the crisis seemed to offer opportunities for fresh thinking; before long, however, certain familiar patterns, well-known to observers of government policy in regard to Indo-China, began to assert themselves. When the war broke out, the officially stated United States policy was one of neutrality. Washington announced that arms shipments to both sides were being suspended. The President, in a seemingly off-the-cuff remark, described India as "a clear-cut aggressor." At about the same time, information that the United States was continuing to send military supplies to Pakistan surfaced in the press. Because the President's remark seemed to undercut the official policy of neutrality, Henry Kissinger called a "background" news conference, at which he told reporters that there had been "some comments that the Administration is anti-India," but that these were "totally inaccurate." He also made reference to a "love affair" between India and the United States. However, in a meeting of a high-ranking White House committee called the Washington Special Action Group, whose function is to deal with crises, Kissinger described the President as "furious," and told the members, "I am getting hell every half hour from the President that we are not being tough enough on India. He has just called me again. He does not believe we are carrying out his wishes. He wants to tilt in favor of Pakistan. He feels everything we do comes out otherwise." And the following day he informed them that "whoever is doing the backgrounding at State is invoking the President's wrath." Through the Action Group, Kissinger ordered that steps be taken against India. One was financial: A.I.D. programs to India were to be cut off. Another had to do with demeanor: American officials were to show "a certain coolness" toward Indian officials. The Indian Ambassador was to get the treatment prescribed by Frederic Malek for "bad guys" in the federal bureaucracy—he was "not to be treated at too high a level." Not for the first time, the Administration was pursuing one policy in public and pursuing an opposite policy in private.

Very shortly after the war began, it became evident to most observers that India would win and East Pakistan would become an independent nation. Nevertheless, the President's wrath continued unabated, and he took two more steps, which briefly transformed what had been a local war into a global crisis. The President began to look upon the war on the subcontinent as the doing not of India or Pakistan but of the Soviet Union. Accordingly, the Administration began making gestures of warning to the Russians. First, the President ordered the aircraft carrier *Enterprise* into the Indian Ocean. Second, Henry Kissinger let it be known, in another "background" press conference, that if the Soviet Union did not show restraint in the crisis, the President might be obliged to reconsider his plans for a trip to Moscow. Apparently, the Administration had come to believe that Moscow was in control of the course of events on the subcontinent. Outside the White House, however, there were very few observers who believed that the Russians had enough influence with India to call her back from the greatest—indeed, the only—military victory in her history as an independent nation. Shortly thereafter, India did win the war, and eventually the *Enterprise* retired, unused, from the field.

The war had come at a time when the Administration was sorting out its friends from its enemies. Plainly, someone had put India on the enemies list, and it seemed to have been the President. The distinguishing features of an enemies operation were all present: the conflict with the bureaucracies (in this case, the State Department), the use of the available federal agencies to punish the offender, and the strenuous attempts to keep the policy concealed from the public. What was new was that the target for retribution in this case was not Joe Namath or Barbra Streisand but a nation of five hundred million people.

The Administration's actions in the India-Pakistan crisis and its actions at home in preparation for the 1972 election showed once more the unity of the Administration's preoccupations; as early as 1969 the President had come to regard the various crises he faced at home and abroad as parts of a single crisis of Presidential authority. John Dean spoke of "screwing" those whom the President considered his domestic enemies. Henry Kissinger spoke of "tilting" against a country that the President considered the nation's foreign enemy. Dean's word was spiteful and vindictive. Kissinger's was cold and neutral. Yet they referred to government actions that were strikingly alike. The technique of "tilting" against a nation—a sort of across-the-board churlishness, in which military policy, aid policy,

diplomacy, and even personal demeanor were all focussed on providing unpleasant experiences for the target nation—grew naturally
out of a tendency in foreign affairs which had been strengthening
at least since the beginning of the Vietnam war. This was the tendency to frame American policy in terms of "inducements" and
"sanctions," which were merely discreet terms for rewards and
punishments. There was nothing new or complicated in the idea.
But it was new as a guiding principle for American policy; and in
the hands of foreign-policy analysts of the nineteen-sixties who devised such policies as that of "graduated pressure," or "escalation,"
in which a carefully measured level of punishment was combined
with carefully calculated threats of more punishment, the strategy
reached a high degree of apparent sophistication. It developed a
specialized vocabulary, and seemed capable of endless elaboration.
For instance, in the new thinking the two main possibilities—punishment and reward—were not mutually exclusive. The United States
might bomb a country and at the same time offer it large amounts
of foreign aid. And if this policy was emotionally and morally confusing to the recipient country, it was a point of pride with the
policy's practitioners that *they* kept *their* emotions out of it. The
sanctions and the inducements were to be applied dispassionately,
and the softening influence of compassion and the hardening influence of belligerent anger were to be banished equally. The technique for harassing the Administration's enemies, on the other hand,
was born of passion and nurtured on pique, and was carried forward in a spirit of vengeance and hope of partisan political gain.
While foreign policy was becoming colder and colder, domestic
policy was heating up. It was Americans, not Russians or Vietnamese, who aroused the bitterest hatred in the Administration.
The special epithets were reserved for their countrymen. There
might be foes abroad, but the "vultures" and "eunuchs" were all at
home. Still, the domestic technique, too, was part of a system of
punishments and rewards. It could be said that one important
strategy in the President's reëlection effort was to "tilt" the whole
federal government against the Democrats and their natural con-

stituencies. Equally, it could be said that foreign policy was becoming, in one of its aspects, a matter of "screwing" the enemies of the United States.

The two techniques overlapped in more than one way. A cardinal tenet of United States global strategy was the notion of "linkage." The doctrine of linkage dictated that conflicts in different parts of the world had to be considered primarily in the context of the overarching struggle between the great powers of the world, and only secondarily in terms of local significance, so that a setback for South Vietnam was to be seen primarily as a setback for the United States, and a setback for North Vietnam was to be seen as a setback for Russia, or perhaps for China (depending on which of the two powers preoccupied the United States more at a given moment in the war). It was by a sudden extension of the linkage theory to affairs on the Indian subcontinent that President Nixon had been able to interpret the Indian campaign in East Pakistan as a menace to the United States. Again, the permutations were endless, since defeat on the subcontinent might jeopardize the American position in Indo-China, and defeat in Indo-China might threaten the American position in the Middle East. In the system for punishing the domestic enemies, the notion of linkage had its counterpart in the blurring of all the domestic enemies into one big enemy. Just as India was construed as an agent of the Soviet Union, Daniel Ellsberg—or Charles Manson, for that matter—was construed as somehow in league with the Democratic Party.

There was another way, too, in which the two techniques overlapped. The Nixon Administration's foreign-policy strategists had long been convinced that each series of events in each crisis around the world was far more important for the appearance—or image—it created than for any tangible results. The strategists' preoccupation with images was in one sense an elaboration of the theory of linkage, for they assumed that the power of the United States and that of its Communist adversaries were linked on the level of appearances. This combination of the doctrine of linkage and the interest in appearances was, of course, nothing other than the doctrine of credibility, which had been guiding ever-wider areas of American foreign policy for more than a decade. And President Nixon and his men, by instinct and emotion, had arrived at a similar doctrine to guide their conduct of domestic affairs.

The tendency to transform policy into a system of punishments and rewards, the tendency to link all events into a single global scheme, and the tendency to value the images, or symbolism, of events more highly than the substance were the elements of a pattern of behavior which now seemed to determine the actions of the Nixon Administration in every political area, both foreign and domestic. The pattern apparently had its source in the doctrine of credibility, particularly in connection with the war in Indo-China, but now it had spread to encompass events as disparate as United States policy toward India and Pakistan and the attempt to make a show trial out of the case of Daniel Ellsberg. Credibility was an image of power. Punishments and rewards were the weapons with which to battle for credibility. And since the President's image was at stake wherever he chose to intervene with those weapons, the world of Presidential action became a totally "linked" battleground on which the prime issue was always the issue of the President's credibility. The struggle, therefore, was carried forward on a single, boundaryless field of action, against a single, undifferentiated foe. And since, in this far-ranging, often abstract and symbolic combat, the foe abroad was indistinguishable from the foe at home, and the President's political foes were indistinguishable from the nation's foes, what was the coming election but one more front, to be held at any cost, and by any means, in the struggle to protect the nation from its enemies?

IV.
FOR THE
RE-ELECTION
OF
THE PRESIDENT

A GOVERNMENT POLICY ordinarily consists of actions together with explanations of the actions, but during the summer and fall of 1971 President Nixon had developed policies in which he made bold moves on the world stage without offering any explanations. Some of the moves, such as the announcement of his trips to China and Russia, were widely acclaimed, and others, such as the American intervention in the India-Pakistan war, were widely condemned, but all of them were presented to the public as *faits accomplis*. Then, in early 1972, the President made a move of exactly the opposite kind: it was all explanation and no action. On January 25th, he appeared on national television to reveal that Henry Kissinger, while the formal Vietnam peace talks were going on in Paris, had been engaged for more than a year in secret talks with the North Vietnamese, but that these talks had failed. He said that the Administration had been offering terms in private which were more

201

generous than the ones it had been offering in public, and implied that since the North Vietnamese had refused to accept those lenient terms, the fault for the continuation of the war was theirs. Disclosure of this diplomatic failure naturally had no effect on the war, but it had a dramatic effect on domestic politics. The Democrats had been scoring political points off the Administration by condemning the President for not offering the North Vietnamese a withdrawal of American troops from South Vietnam in exchange for the return of American prisoners of war. Now the President was saying that he had been doing just that, but in secret. The Democrats were generally considered to have been badly undercut; the President, it was said, had taken away one of their most promising issues—the war in Indo-China. The Administration pressed its advantage in a public-relations offensive on the war issue. H. R. Haldeman made a rare appearance on television to assert that Democrats who continued to oppose the President's war policy were "consciously aiding and abetting the enemy of the U.S."—language that was close to the Constitutional definition of treason. Secretary of State Rogers attacked Senator Muskie—saying that his criticism of the war policy was damaging the chances for peace.

The President had previously been criticized for using the tool of concealment for domestic political purposes. Now his opposition was learning that disclosure, too, could be a powerful political weapon. The President had stunned the opposition twice by disclosing successes: the arrangements for the China trip and the Russia trip. Now he stunned them by disclosing a failure. In much the same way that in 1969 he had won credit with Southern voters for trying, but failing, to undermine court-ordered integration, he now won credit with the whole public for trying, but failing, to negotiate a peace. He had mastered the public relations of failure. But whether he was concealing or disclosing, succeeding or failing, he was, through the deft manipulation of information, keeping the opposition off balance. It wandered in a world of fact and non-fact which he had constructed and could manipulate to his own advantage. In other words, as the election year was beginning, the factual world on which all the candidates for the Presidency relied as the foundation for the planning of their strategy was under the control of the candidate who was the incumbent. He gave them the factual ground on which they stood and then he took it away. In this instance, he opened up a supposed piece of the public record—the American negotiating position on the war—like a trapdoor beneath their feet, and swallowed them up.

Between Christmas of 1971 and New Year's Day of 1972, the United States sent some three hundred and fifty planes each day to bomb North Vietnam. No explanation was offered. The official announcement from the American command in South Vietnam read, in its entirety, "For a limited duration, protective-reaction air strikes against military targets in North Vietnam are being conducted by United States Air Force and United States Navy aircraft. The air strikes are in reaction to enemy activity which imperils the diminishing United States forces currently in South Vietnam. When these limited-duration air strikes, which are being conducted to protect the safety and security of our remaining American forces in South Vietnam, are completed, additional details will be provided. Until that time, for reasons of military security and safety of our pilots, we will have nothing further to say." A "senior Pentagon official," speaking off the record, added, "We don't intend to allow Hanoi to take advantage of our troop drawdown to threaten a rout against those who remain. Every once in a while, we feel we have to remind Hanoi of this."

On January 4th, Senator Muskie formally announced his candidacy. "I am seeking the Presidency not merely to change Presidents but to change the country," he stated. And he said, "For a generation what we have done has not been good enough." A week later, Senator Humphrey entered the race. He promised to "get our country moving again," and he also promised to "put our house in order." One of his remarks had to do with what he might have done. "Had I been elected in 1968, we would now be out of that war," he said.

Senator George McGovern had announced his candidacy almost a year before, and had promised, before all else, to end the war. From the White House point of view, the principal "enemies" were in the field.

In these months of summit plans, secret negotiations, and early election maneuverings, the country developed a fascination with the techniques whereby the President and Henry Kissinger brought forth their surprises: now peace, now war; now "anarchy," now "the lift of a driving dream." A virtual cult of Henry Kissinger grew up in the press. Reporters followed him in packs. His facial expressions made news. He was given sobriquets like Mr. Nixon's Secret Agent and the Superstar of the Nixon Administration. Articles were titled "The Clandestine Life of Dr. Henry Kissinger" and "I Wonder Where's Kissinger Now." He was seen in the company of beautiful women, and he jokingly suggested that they were merely a cover for his secret negotiations. On one occasion, he revealed to fascinated newsmen that at a time when "a few hundred of you were chasing me around Paris rather intensely," he had managed nevertheless to hold several secret meetings with the North Vietnamese.

As these episodes were made known, tales of secrecy and intrigue became a vogue. When the public was not reading about Kissinger's secret trips and gorgeous dinner partners, it could read the story of Clifford Irving, a writer who pretended to have been co-author of an autobiography of the multimillionaire recluse Howard Hughes. This story, pitting a con man against an incalculably wealthy mystery man, involved such goings on as a young woman making secret trips under an alias to deposit money in a Swiss bank account, and a phone call to an entire group of newsmen, said to be from Mr. Hughes, denouncing Mr. Irving. The public might have been even more taken with the constantly shifting and dissolving story if it had known that Hughes was also involved with the President: that a figure with not only an alias but a disguise —Howard Hunt—was on the scene at the behest of the White House, plotting a burglary of materials having to do with Hughes from a publisher's safe in Nevada; that the C.I.A., Hunt's former employer, had gone into partnership with Hughes to raise a sunken Soviet submarine from the bottom of the Pacific; that a brother of the President's also had connections with Hughes; and that the President had ordered the Secret Service to place a wiretap on that brother. As it was, the public, knowing the little it did know, had become entranced, in politics as in entertainment, with the processes of its own deception.

By mid-December of 1971, Hunt's partner in the White House undercover group, G. Gordon Liddy, had a new title. He was chief legal counsel to the recently established Committee for the Re-Election of the President. That is, he was the man to whom the men of the Committee for the Re-Election of the President now turned when they wanted advice concerning the law. (In the White House, it was to John Dean, the President's legal counsellor, that the President's men turned.) But part of Liddy's job was still the same—to commit crimes against the political opposition. If his title was hardly in keeping with the work he would be doing, it was perfect as a cover. On January 27th, he met with Attorney General Mitchell, John Dean, and Jeb Magruder, who, like Liddy, had moved over from the White House to the reëlection committee. Liddy had brought a set of charts to the meeting, and displayed them on an easel to elucidate the points he was making. On the charts were words and diagrams, but the other men could not grasp what some of them meant. Liddy explained why: they were in code. The cryptic charts, Liddy continued, outlined an extensive plan of sabotage and surveillance of the opposition. Mugging squads would be mustered to beat up demonstrators at the Republican Convention. Teams would be formed to kidnap the leaders of demonstrations. Electronic surveillance would be employed against the Democrats both in their Washington headquarters and at their Convention. At the Convention, too, prostitutes ("high-class" ones, "the best in the business," Liddy is reported to have said) would be sent out to lure Democrats to a yacht rigged with secret cameras and recording equipment. The cost would be about a million dollars. Mitchell found the plan too expensive, and rejected it.

In early February, Liddy returned to Mitchell's office with a reduced plan, costing half a million dollars. Mitchell found even half a million dollars too high, and rejected that plan, too. Liddy, undiscouraged, returned to his drawing board.

In late February, on the eve of the Presidential primaries, the President made his journey to China. The coverage alone was dazzling. For the first time in history, a summit meeting was broadcast live, by satellite, back to the United States, and to other parts of the world as well. In America, it was night when the nation settled down before its television sets to await the arrival of Air Force One at the Peking Airport, but it was morning on the television sets. The broadcast of the daytime hemisphere into the nighttime hemisphere made the earth's oneness palpable. The whole globe seemed to have been wired for picture and sound. All America looked on as a camera took in an eventless hour in a public square in Peking. Network commentators, waiting, like the rest of the world, for the President's arrival, spoke in reverential, lowered voices, as though afraid of disrupting a respectful global silence. They had nothing to say, for they had been told nothing. ("Is there a mood of anticipation in Peking, Roger?" "No, there isn't, Walter.") But the newsmen's humble ignorance of what, if anything, was to be transacted only enhanced the grandeur of the occasion. The information that emerged in the course of the President's visit was no more substantial. There were banquets, toasts of friendship, a visit to the Great Wall of China one frosty morning (evening here), and a handshake and an exchange of jokes with Chairman Mao.

A few thousand miles to the south, in Indo-China, a war still raged in which United States troops were engaged—according to recent explanations to the American people—in "containing" China. No explanations had been offered of how the President could be drinking toasts of friendship with the Chinese at the very time he was sending men to die in a war directed against them. And yet this split, instead of detracting from the spectacle, seemed only to add to its mystery and awesomeness. As we in America watched the President and Henry Kissinger and Chairman Mao shake hands and burst into gales of silent, unrecorded laughter, we were made aware that we were watching men of authority so tremendous and of designs so esoteric that they could laugh and shake hands while in other parts of the globe men died and nations burned in their names.

On the last full day of the President's visit, the two nations affixed their official stamps of approval to a paradoxical document that affirmed the spirit of agreement while evading the substance by recourse to the device of having two main nations write down their clashing views on each issue side by side. The nation had been introduced to a new world—a world in which benevolent televised beings seemed to cradle the fate of the earth in their hands as the country looked on. We had been allowed a glimpse, it seemed, of that "office of the command" where, in Franz Kafka's words, "one may be certain that all human thoughts and desires revolved in a circle and all human aims and fulfillments in a countercircle," and where "through the window, the reflected splendors of divine worlds fell on the hands of the leaders as they traced their plans."

The White House was now fully prepared for the election. While barely a word concerning the Presidential contest of 1972 had been heard from the Administration, the fourteen months between the Republicans' failure in the congressional races in 1970 and the President's trip to Peking had been a time of vast hidden preparations. Everything that had been done in that period had been done with one eye—and often with both eyes—on the political test ahead. The fruit of these efforts was a campaign strategy coextensive with the full range of United States policy, and a campaign machine coextensive with the machinery of the executive branch of the federal government. The immense whole was divided, as in a cosmology, into three distinct but related realms.

The uppermost realm was the empyrean of the summit, where radiant figures, bathed in publicity, seemed to personify the aspirations of a humanity anxious to escape its own extinction. In the electoral scheme, the President's public place was there—floating above politics (so the phrase went) as he attended to matters of state. By his side was Kissinger, Administration superstar and diplomatic magician. He alone among the men in the President's official family was allowed to reside above the electoral fray, with the President. All the rest were Buchanan's "dogs," to be turned loose from their "kennels" upon the opposition. The summit realm was the abode of the President's new image. He had discovered the political potential inherent in the perilous situation of mankind in the nuclear age. The new image had been long in the making, but now, after several false starts, it had emerged in its full effulgence. As far back as 1970, the President's advisers had wanted to have him reëlected as a "statesman," and now he was a statesman: the man of peace. A week before his departure for China, Mr. Nixon sent to the Congress his third annual State of the World report, titled "United States Foreign Policy for the 1970's: The Emerging Structure of Peace." Although his tone—and the tone associated with the new image generally—was not the high-pitched tone of alarm about the "age of anarchy" which had worked out so poorly in the recent congressional elections, neither was it the euphoric, almost delirious tone of the Mr. Outside speeches. The new tone was majestic and serene. "The United States is once again acting with assurance and purpose on the world stage," the President said. "We know where we are going. We are moving with history and moving history." "History" seemed to be more than ever on the President's mind. In December, for example, he had described a new monetary agreement—one in which the United States had a prominent role—as "the most significant monetary agreement in the history of the world." Vietnam was read out of the picture containing the new image. "Vietnam no longer distracts our attention from the fundamental issues of global diplomacy," the President declared. (The country had already had an example of Vietnam's not distracting its attention: the unannounced invasion of Laos early in 1971 by the South Vietnamese with American support.) The official picture of life at home, too, had been brought into line with the new image.

The league of terrors that had supposedly menaced the nation during the first two years of the Administration had vanished. In the fall of 1971, Attorney General Mitchell had taken the first step in putting an end, oratorically, to the "wave of crime" that had been a key element of the "age of anarchy" in its domestic manifestations. "Fear is being swept from the streets of some—though not all—American cities," the Attorney General had said, with a touch of modesty, in an address before a conference of law-enforcement officials. The President was now speaking of national division and turmoil of all kinds as things of the remote past. In his State of the Union address for 1972, he told the joint session of Congress, "When I took the oath of office on the steps of this building just three years ago today, the nation was ending one of the most tortured decades in its history. The nineteen-sixties were a time of great progress in many areas. But, as we all know, they were also times of great agony—the agonies of war, of inflation, of rapidly rising crime . . . and of anger and frustration that led finally to violence and to the worst civil disorder in a century." The image of 1972 was being made retroactive to 1969. The national "violence" and "disorder," which had in fact reached their peak in the first two years of his Administration, were being pushed back into the Johnson Administration. The new image had no room for Vice-President Agnew's tirades, and for some time he had been held in check. The restriction evidently did not please him, for in the fall of 1971 he had said upon excusing himself from a meeting, "The President needs me at the White House. It's autumn, you know, and the leaves need raking."

The middle realm of the election effort was the domain of the White House election "planning group." The aim there—"dividing the Democrats"—fell off considerably from the high purpose of the summit realm, and the publicity was correspondingly dimmed. The policies designed by the planning group with this ulterior aim in mind naturally unfolded in public view, but their divisive intent was veiled. In this realm, also, the poison-pen letters were streaming out to editors of publications; the semi-concealed attempts to intimidate the press into giving more favorable coverage of the Administration were going ahead; and the shadowy Nixon campaign

209

apparatus was busy raising funds. The Committee for the Re-Election of the President was turning out to be a characteristic offspring of the Nixon Administration. It brought the well-tested principles of reorganization to the election effort. Like the Domestic Council, the Office of Management and Budget, and any number of other organizations created by the Administration, the Committee for the Re-Election of the President, as well as the offshoot Finance Committee for the Re-Election of the President, had duties that ran parallel to those of a traditional organization—in this case, the Republican Party, and, more specifically, the Republican National Committee. Like the other creations of reorganization, the campaign committee had been set up in secrecy and staffed by men from the White House whose personal loyalty to the President was beyond question. In other words, the campaign committee was to the Republican Party what the reorganized White House staff was to the Cabinet system: its replacement.

The lowest realm of the election effort—its hellish netherworld—was the realm of the White House spies, burglars, forgers, and bagmen, all of them burrowing out of sight in their efforts to undermine and "discredit" the opposition. Here the high purposes of the summit realm were entirely eclipsed, and there was, of course, no publicity at all. In this netherworld, federal agencies were being converted into instruments for punishing and rewarding the political friends and enemies of the Administration, public servants were massing to "nail'" Daniel Ellsberg, and White House staff men were at work trying to frame President Kennedy for the murder of President Ngo Dinh Diem. Of course, everything that was done in every realm of the election effort was a product of one White House, and in that White House, regardless of how large its staff might grow, there was one elected authority. He had fixed the size of the staff, fixed its members' positions and ranks, and put them to work at whatever it was they were doing.

For the fund-raising side of the President's reëlection campaign, March was a special month. Shortly after the middle of January, the

Congress completed action on a new Federal Elections Campaign Act, which tightened the disclosure requirements for contributions to political campaigns but which contained a clause delaying the effective date of the act until sixty days after it was signed. In early February, the President signed the act, and said, "By giving the American public full access to the facts of political financing, this legislation will guard against campaign abuses and will work to build public confidence in the integrity of the electoral process." It did not, however, guard against abuses committed by his finance committee in the sixty-day gap. Maurice Stans, the former Secretary of Commerce, who had become chairman of the Finance Committee for the Re-Election of the President, wrote a letter urging donors to contribute before the new law became effective, on April 7th, in order to avoid the requirement of disclosure. The Finance Committee organized a system of fund-raising that was, in effect, a political tithe on wealthy corporations and persons having dealings with or seeking posts in the federal government. The dealings might involve a federal regulation of one sort or another, a federal prosecution, a petition for parole, an investigation by a commission (such as the Securities and Exchange Commission), or an application for a federal grant; among the posts sought, ambassadorships were popular. Sometimes the quid pro quo was spelled out precisely, and sometimes it was left implicit. And sometimes a corporation would pay up simply to stay in the good graces of the Administration, in case there might be some trouble with the government in the future. As one corporation executive later put it, not to give was to stray into *"terra incognita,"* where unguessable dangers lurked. For the companies on one list, the tithe was a hundred thousand dollars. For others, which were apparently in a different class, Stans is reported to have said that the obligation amounted to one per cent of corporate profits. For wealthy individuals in California, the "standard of giving," according to a letter sent out by a co-chairman of the state fund-raising committee, was "one-half per cent, more or less, of net worth," and he reminded prospective contributors of the April 7th disclosure deadline, "which we all naturally want to avoid." Very often, the funds from companies were extracted illegally from corporate coffers, and that was no simple matter. The money had to be raised outside normal accounting procedures, and since accounting procedures are to a company what the chain of command is to the military, the companies had to work out elaborate irregular procedures to come up with the money, just as the military had had to set up virtually a second, secret command system to deal with the secret bombing of Cambodia ordered by the President in 1969. Corporation records were falsified. Money was sent abroad to be "laundered" and then was brought back. Top corporation executives rushed about the nation and the world carrying huge sums of cash in their attaché cases. By the cutoff date, some twenty million dollars had been secretly raised. At least six million of it had been collected in the two days before the cutoff. Five and a half million was disbursed by the finance committee before April 7th in "pre-payments" for various campaign services, in order to avoid full disclosure of disbursements, which the new law also required.

In respect to the whole White House campaign strategy, March was turning out to be perhaps the most crucial month not just of the spring but of the entire election year. For March was the month of the first Presidential primaries, and it was there—not in the general election—that the basic White House strategy for 1972 was to unfold. "Our great hope for 1972," as the White House saw it, lay in "exacerbating the deep Democratic rift," and the best place to exacerbate the rift was in the Democratic Presidential primaries. Since the strategy was not one of defeating the strongest candidate that the Democrats might put forward but one of seeing to it that they chose a weak candidate, the Republican strategy for the election would have succeeded or failed just as the Presidential campaign was getting under way.

The strategy of dividing the Democrats was necessarily a strategy for defeating Senator Muskie, since Muskie was, by all accounts, the man with the best chance of uniting the Democratic Party. His public image—an image as carefully tended as the President's, in its way, though with only a tiny fraction of the President's resources—was of a calm, patient, conciliatory man. His public statements tended toward the blurry and evasive, and seemed designed not to offend any important element in the Party. By most political observers, his nomination was seen as all but inevitable. His showing in the polls was the highest of any Democrat. The press, in a nearly unanimous exercise of its predictive powers, had anointed him the "front-runner" in the Democratic race. And, as he entered the primaries, virtually the full weight of Democratic officialdom—at any rate, among those who spoke up at all—was behind him. Muskie's staff estimated his strengths in much the same way the White House staff did: both sides saw his strengths as his potential for appealing to a wide variety of voters and the fact that he already held a commanding position in the field. In an internal memo written in the summer of 1971, and later described by Muskie's campaign manager as "the most vital document we had put together" up to that time and as a document "reflective of our entire political strategy," a staff member wrote to the Senator, "Only a broad base of support will support your position as front-runner and your image as a winner. And the only way to develop this broad base is to identify you with as many different groups of people, their hopes and their needs, as possible." One section of the memo was titled "General Assumptions of the Muskie Candidacy" and ran to four pages, and in that entire section there was not a single mention of any issue before the country. Just as Patrick Buchanan's chief strategy was to try to break Muskie's momentum, the chief strategy of Muskie's aides was to try to maintain it; in neither camp did issues seem to enter into the basic strategy for their own sake. To a high degree, Senator Muskie's candidacy was a tautology in action: he was the front-runner because he was the front-runner. His candidacy was also, to a large extent, something fabricated to fill a special need: it was the product of an effort by the Democratic Party to draw together behind one man without actually resolving the deep rift within it. Muskie's aides, like the White House aides, understood this. The difference was that whereas the President possessed the power to break up Muskie's desired broad base by breaking up the whole country—by framing policy that would "really tear up the pea patch," as the President's political planning group had put it in their memo—the Muskie people had only the slender resources of their campaign with which to attempt to hold the Democratic Party together.

In the New Hampshire primary—the first of the season— Muskie's candidacy suffered a serious blow. He won the primary by a margin of forty-six per cent, but Senator McGovern got thirty-seven per cent, and, according to the wisdom of the day, a "front-runner" running in a state next door to his own had to win by a huge margin to do himself any good. Though Muskie had won, his "image as a winner" had been tarnished, and the "news" in New Hampshire was Senator McGovern's thirty-seven per cent. Senator McGovern's principal issue was the war. The issue of the war was not like other issues. To a significant part of the electorate, the war was a passion, and opposing it had become something like a way of life. It had defined the politics of a generation. And now the war had been going on so long that to passion was added memory. To the Vietnam generation, it was not only a candidate's current position on the war that counted but his position on the war at every moment in the war's long history. To them, a man's record on the war was an index to his character, and Senator McGovern's opposition had been strong and consistent from an early date. In the primaries, as opposed to the general election, a solid core of impassioned support can carry tremendous weight. And so in New Hampshire the war did its divisive work, and Senator Muskie, the candidate of unity, was deprived of a triumph he badly needed.

The next primary was in Florida, and Senator Muskie, if he was to prove that he was plausible as a unifier of the Party, had to do well there. Senator McGovern, however, who at the moment had no pretensions to being a unifier, had written off Florida in advance. One of the peculiarities of the Democratic Presidential primaries of 1972 was that each man's performance was measured against a separate standard—the standard of what he himself had proclaimed that he would accomplish. That was part of the reason Senator Muskie's standing declined when he won in New Hampshire and Senator McGovern's standing rose when he lost there. It also explained why Senator McGovern could afford to lose in

Florida and Senator Muskie could not. In Florida, Muskie's candidacy received a second, probably fatal blow. Governor George Wallace won, with forty-one per cent of the vote, and Senator Muskie came in fourth, with only nine per cent. (Second and third places went to Senator Humphrey and Senator Henry Jackson.) In the North, the issue had been the war, and the rival candidate had been McGovern. In the South, the issue had been busing, and the rival candidate Wallace. (The White House planning group, of course, had been eager to have Governor Wallace run in the Democratic Presidential primaries precisely in order to raise this issue.)

In a straw vote that was also taken in the Florida primary, seventy-four per cent of the voters had registered disapproval of the court-ordered busing of schoolchildren. Two days afterward, on March 16th, the President took the action that Buchanan had recommended to him as one that would "cut the Democratic Party and country in half," and enable him to pick up "far the larger half." In a televised address, the President asked the Congress to enact a "moratorium" on the court-ordered busing of schoolchildren. (By this time, the President had established his power to preëmpt television time to speak to the nation on any subject whatever.) He had already sent legislation to Congress which would curtail the government's efforts to integrate American society, and he had attempted to alter the complexion of the Supreme Court to achieve that end, among others—or so it appeared. Now he sought to do nothing less than alter the Constitutional balance between the Congress and the Court, so as to bring about what Buchanan had called a "Constitutional end" to integration in the United States. Since the Supreme Court's 1954 ruling that the segregation of the public schools on racial lines by municipal and state law was un-Constitutional, nearly two decades of legal precedent had grown up around the civil-rights issue. And more than a century and a half of legal precedent had grown up around the Supreme Court decision, made in the 1803 case of Marbury v. Madison, that the Supreme Court was in fact supreme when it came to interpretation of the law—even if the Court nullified an act of Congress in reaching its interpretation of the Constitution. But now the President seemed to suggest

215

that the Congress should take over the prerogative of defining the Constitution. "The Congress," he said in commending his anti-busing legislative proposals to it the following day, "has both the Constitutional authority and a special capability to debate and define new methods for implementing Constitutional principles." At one point in the televised address, he spoke of court-ordered busing almost as though it were a spreading crime wave. "What we need now is not just speaking out against more busing, we need action to stop it," he said. (His words mirrored the phrasing used the previous fall by Buchanan: "We need more than just rhetoric. . . . Actions taken by the President and Administration are decisive here.") The President said that while a Constitutional amendment to prohibit school busing should not be ruled out, he had reservations about an amendment. The reservations had nothing to do with a conservative's horror of tampering with the fundamental law of the land to achieve a transitory objective; rather, as he explained them, "the Constitutional-amendment approach has a fatal flaw—it takes too long." For the Congress simply to defy the Supreme Court would be much faster—and, of course, the issue would be joined in plenty of time to divide the Democrats before their Convention, scheduled for July.

So dominant was the policy of dividing the Democrats that every White House action, whether immense or minute or in between, was examined from the point of view of its possible use as an irritant to the Democratic Party. National issues were regarded as so much sand for clogging the Democrats' gears. With respect to some issues, the formula was simple: the more division the better. Race was one of these, and the President seemed quite willing to precipitate a Constitutional crisis in order to divide the nation sufficiently. But with respect to other issues the formula was complex, and a precise calibration of the most politically advantageous amount of division was necessary. The war, for example, was useful for dividing Democrats, as the planning group had pointed out, but it was useful only up to a certain point. The continuation of the war assured that the left wing of the Democratic Party would remain strong. However, if the war loomed too large in the nation's awareness it would mar the President's new image as a man of peace. So the war, useful though it was in promoting left-wing incursions into Senator Muskie's strength, such as had occurred in New Hampshire, would be harmful in the general election. Similarly, the candidacy of George Wallace was useful in the Democratic primaries but—since he appealed to many of the same voters as Nixon—would be damaging in the general election. In fact, even while the White House was hoping that Wallace would disrupt the Democratic primaries in the spring it was taking steps to block his candidacy in the fall. In late 1971, John Mitchell had budgeted ten thousand dollars to be used in an effort to keep Wallace's name from appearing on the ballot in California in the 1972 general election. Most of the money went, in cash, to Robert Walters, a California businessman who was a disillusioned Wallace supporter. In early 1971, Walters had conceived a scheme in which voters who had registered as members of Wallace's American Independent Party would be encouraged to re-register as Republicans or Democrats, in the hope of driving the registration of Wallace's party below the minimum required by California law to qualify for a line on the ballot. Walters mailed registration literature to members of the American Independent Party, using as a front the Committee Against Forced Busing. He also hired the regional head and several members of the American Nazi Party to go from door to door in the fall of 1971 and, without identifying themselves, urge Wallace voters to re-register. The Nazis' leader received some twelve hundred dollars from the ten thousand budgeted for the re-registration project. Their efforts were unsuccessful in keeping Wallace off the ballot. (Also, the California Republicans were helping to finance the left-wing Peace and Freedom Party, in the hope of drawing votes away from the Democrats. In California, at least, the Republican Party was following to the letter Patrick Buchanan's strategy of promoting extremes.) Ideally, the war in Vietnam and the Presidential candidacy of George Wallace would be two irritants that would do their divisive work during the primaries but would disappear before the general election. Even

217

during the primaries, however, the amount of division had to be held within bounds: there had to be enough so that the President could point to the Democrats as the party of the "nightmare of war and division" he had so often mentioned but not so much that he would be unable to portray himself as the man who had calmed the country down.

Large national issues—race and the war—were being employed as political irritants to the Democratic Party. Indeed, the whole divided nation was being employed as a political irritant. But irritants on a small scale were planned, too. A program of sabotage against the Democrats, and against Senator Muskie in particular, was organized by the White House in conjunction with the Committee for the Re-Election of the President. If a divided nation was one irritant to the Democrats, stink bombs, heckling, forged press releases, forged campaign literature, forged letters, disrupted schedules, and fouled-up telephone lines would be others. Herbert Kalmbach, the President's personal attorney, with the approval of H. R. Haldeman, hired a young lawyer named Donald Segretti to organize one wing of the program, and Segretti, in turn, hired operatives in each state that held a major primary. Dwight Chapin, the President's appointments secretary, oversaw Segretti's work by mail and phone, both men using aliases in their communications. The program marked a major expansion of the White House undercover operations. (A smaller group was put together by the Committee for the Re-Election of the President, under the direction of a "scheduling director" named Herbert Porter.) The principal aim of the sabotage, like the principal aim of the divisive policies, was not to win votes away from the Democrats directly by damaging their campaigns (although that would be a welcome side effect); it was to embitter the Democrats against one another and thus destroy Party unity. One Segretti operative who had worked in Florida, Martin Kelly, later explained to the Ervin committee, "These things . . . were not done to influence votes, necessarily, at all. . . . You are not going to affect the primary by sending fifty letters out. [The reference was to forged letters on the stationery of one candidate denouncing others unfairly.] They were expected to

218

be brought to the notice of the candidates . . . and for him to be upset about it and for him to blame possibly another candidate. . . . The idea was to get the candidates backbiting each other and possibly starting doing it to each other outside of our activities." Of course, almost any sabotage would seem to one Democrat to be the work of some other Democrat, since virtually no one outside the White House knew that the White House had any active strategy at all for the Democratic primaries, or that its "great hope for 1972" was, in effect, to choose the Democratic candidate.

In the New Hampshire primary, several incidents of sabotage came to the attention of Muskie campaign workers. They learned that a number of white voters had received calls late at night from what was said to be a "Harlem for Muskie Committee," informing them that Muskie had promised to do his best to help black people if he was elected. Campaign schedules and other campaign documents disappeared. Most telling of all, however, was a letter to the Manchester *Union Leader,* a New Hampshire newspaper, that accused Senator Muskie of laughing at, rather than repudiating, a disparaging remark made by an aide of his about Americans of French-Canadian descent, who are numerous in New Hampshire. (The signature was that of a supposed ordinary citizen—a Paul Morrison, who was never found—and later a White House aide first admitted authorship of the letter and then denied it.) The letter was one of many attacks on Muskie in the *Union Leader*—attacks that included, for example, a reprint of an unflattering article about his wife in *Newsweek*. The accumulation angered the Senator, and ten days before the primary he assailed the editor of the newspaper in a speech one snowy day from the back of a flatbed truck and, in the process, appeared to shed tears. The public evidently did not like to see any displays of emotion on the part of would-be Presidents, and many observers dated the decline of Muskie's fortunes from that moment.

In the Florida primary, which followed New Hampshire's by only a week, the level of sabotage was stepped up. The aim was still to "derail" the "bandwagon" of the unity candidate—as the operative Kelly later put it—by embittering the atmosphere of the primaries.

About a thousand four-by-six-inch cards were distributed at a Wallace rally in Tampa reading, "If you liked Hitler, you'll just love Wallace," and urging a vote for Muskie. The idea was to arouse Wallace supporters, and perhaps Wallace himself, against Senator Muskie. About three hundred posters that read, "Help Muskie in Busing More Children Now," were put on display around the state. Ads supposedly placed by the Muskie campaign and stating, in Spanish, "Muskie was born in Maine and is a good American" were broadcast over a radio station serving the Spanish-speaking community and appeared in a Spanish-language newspaper. The aim of these was to insult the many people in Florida who were Cuban-born. Political gatherings that were not in fact planned were announced by the Nixon operatives, and gatherings and appointments that *were* planned were "cancelled" by them. And then calls were made to the disrupted organization suggesting that a rival Democratic organization had caused the disruption. A press release issued on Muskie stationery attacked Senator Hubert Humphrey for his position on Israel—a move aimed at discrediting Muskie with Jewish voters. (The Nixon operatives had a penchant for sabotage that involved racial, religious, or ethnic minorities in one way or another.) A letter sent out on Muskie stationery read, "We on the Senator Ed Muskie staff sincerely hope you have decided upon Senator Muskie as your choice. . . . However, if you have not made your decision, you should be aware of several facts." The "facts" were false charges of sexual impropriety against Senator Humphrey and Senator Henry Jackson. Like almost all the fraudulent campaign literature put out by the White House undercover group, this letter embittered the atmosphere in two ways: it made the senators who had been attacked tend to believe that Senator Muskie was playing dirty politics, and it made Senator Muskie believe that either some misguided supporter of his was playing dirty politics or someone else—perhaps even Senator Humphrey or Senator Jackson—was playing dirty politics.

The program of sabotage was supplemented by a program of espionage. A wiretapping project designed by G. Gordon Liddy and code-named Gemstone was moving forward. Also, in Washington, a taxi-driver was hired by the Nixon reëlection committee to join the Muskie campaign. He was taken on as a volunteer, and was eventually assigned the task of carrying the Senator's mail between his Senate office and his campaign headquarters. On the way, he would give the Senator's campaign documents, including internal memoranda and drafts of speeches and position papers, to a Republican operative whose code name was Fat Jack and who held a post in the Office of Economic Opportunity. Fat Jack would photograph the papers in a downtown office rented for that purpose, and would pass the film along; for the first few months, he passed it to Kenneth Rietz, director of the youth division of the Committee for the Re-Election of the President, and then, after Rietz withdrew, he handed it to E. Howard Hunt on a Washington street corner. As was the case in more and more of the White House undercover transactions, the two men used special aliases for this special job. Hunt called himself Ed Warren, and Fat Jack, whose real name was John Buckley, used the second alias of Jack Kent. The code name of the project was Ruby I. The code name Ruby II was in use, too; it referred to a college student hired by Hunt who had joined the Muskie campaign and was passing information along. Also, Donald Segretti hired people to act as spies in several primary states. In Tampa, Florida, for example, a man named Robert Benz was hired; and he, in turn, hired two more people to act as spies. Two agents independent of the Segretti operation had the code names Sedan Chair I and Sedan Chair II. Sedan Chair I carried out sabotage in New Hampshire and California. Sedan Chair II began by joining Senator Muskie's Wisconsin primary campaign, in March of 1972, and then, over the next few months, he successively joined Senator Humphrey's campaign in Pennsylvania, the McGovern and Humphrey campaigns in California, and McGovern's national headquarters, in Washington, and served on the security staff at McGovern's headquarters in the Doral Hotel, in Miami Beach, during the Democratic Convention. At each point in the course of his months-long infiltration, the agent relayed intelligence reports to the Nixon campaign headquarters, and the reports were sent up through the chain of command to Haldeman, in the White

221

House. Finally, in a project for espionage titled Chapman's Friend, Murray Chotiner, a former aide to President Nixon, hired two reporters to travel with the Democratic campaigners under false pretenses and report back to the Nixon campaign headquarters through him.

While the information was pouring in from Gemstone, Ruby I and Ruby II, Sedan Chair I and Sedan Chair II, and Chapman's Friend, and from the whole broad array of spies hired by Donald Segretti, still more information was being obtained by the continued use of the federal government as a huge vacuum cleaner for the collection of damaging information about the opposition. One White House aide caught the spirit of this operation perfectly when, in a memo to John Dean (these efforts were in fact a part of what the White House called its Enemies Project) concerning an attempt to find damaging material on Senator McGovern's chief fund-raiser, Henry Kimelman, he wrote, "As Colson says, there must be something that we can use some place in this government, and he wonders if we are still pushing to try to locate this information."

The Florida primary dealt the final blow to the strategy that Senator Muskie had been pursuing all year. His campaign foundered on the issues most divisive of Democrats: in the North, the war; in the South, race. The attraction of the extreme positions had been too great, and the broad middle of the Party, which he had hoped to lay claim to, disintegrated, just as the White House had hoped. And since the central strength of Senator Muskie's campaign had been his "image as a winner," two defeats, one in the North and one in the South, were enough to make his campaign collapse. Suddenly, there was talk, inside and outside the Muskie camp, of a "new Muskie." Both the style and the content of his campaign changed abruptly. He lurched leftward. Two days after the Florida vote, he attacked George Wallace, calling him a representative of everything that was worst in American life. A reporter in the *Times* described the "new Muskie": "His voice was louder, harsher, almost rasping. His eyes looked intense and angry. . . . The pedagogical style was gone. There was fire in his words, too." The speech could not have fitted in more neatly with White House plans if it had been written there. Wallace was proving to be exactly the divisive force in the Democratic ranks that the White House wanted him to be, and, what was even more important, Muskie, too, was now behaving in the manner planned for him in the scenario for dividing the Democrats. Ironically, it may be that the "new Muskie'" was closer to the real Muskie than the old one had been. According to many reports, he is a man of strong feelings and strong convictions, who tends to be headstrong. But the emergence of the real Muskie —if that is what it was—did not attract the voters, and his candidacy continued downhill. In March, he won a primary victory in Illinois, but Illinois had been virtually uncontested; and then he came in fourth in Wisconsin, fourth in Pennsylvania, and second in Massachusetts. At the end of April, he withdrew from further primaries, and, although he did not declare himself out of the race, his candidacy was dead.

As early as the latter part of 1969, President Nixon had succeeded in subordinating the full range of policymaking to the requirements of public-relations scenarios. The practice had got its start when the President and his men began to frame policy not to solve real problems but only to appear to solve them, and had gained considerably in refinement as the Administration discovered the techniques of presenting conservative policy as liberal policy, of presenting liberal policy as conservative policy, and of framing policies that would predictably fail but in failing would make a political point. And the practice had been further elaborated during the early stages of the Nixon Big Charge, when the resources of the whole Administration were mobilized behind a public-relations assault on the opposition. Now, in the spring of 1972, the President extended the reach of his scenarios still farther. Not only did he seek to guide the actions of his own executive branch with the scenarios but he sought to guide the actions of his political rivals. To accomplish this ambitious task, he turned to the techniques known in the intelligence trade as "black" techniques. In black techniques, one actor on the political stage arranges circumstances so that certain actions and words seem to be emanating from another. In black propaganda, for instance, one actor releases propaganda in such a way as to make it seem like someone else's work. Using this technique, an actor may step outside his own identity and assume a multiplicity of identities. For example, after the Second World War the C.I.A. propagated anti-Stalinist material that was made to look like the work of moderate Communists in Eastern Europe. The aim of the exercise was intricate and indirect, as it usually is with black operations. It was to goad Stalin into killing off the moderates, in the hope that the moderate center would be destroyed, the result being to strengthen the extremists, encourage civil war, and hasten the collapse of Communist rule. At one time, in the United States, the F.B.I. employed similar tactics in its Cointelpro campaign against the radical left: it wrote letters to American gangland figures which seemed to be from the leftists and criticized the gangsters for labor practices in companies under their control—the aim being to precipitate action by the gangsters against the leftists. All the letters written by the Nixon operatives on the stationery of one Democratic candidate scurrilously attacking other Democratic candidates were in the category of black propaganda. By making Senator Muskie appear to attack Senator Humphrey for sexual misconduct, or by making Senator Muskie appear to take a politically unwise position on the issue of the Middle East, the men of the Nixon Administration climbed right inside Muskie's image and effectually deprived him of his right to appear before the public or his fellow-candidates as himself. The Administration's main purpose was not unlike that of the C.I.A. in its Eastern European operation. It was to harm the political center in the hope of strengthening the extremes. The Nixon Administration's rigged letters to the editor also fell into the category of black propaganda. In that case, the actor upon whom words were being foisted was the American public. The cables forged by Hunt to implicate President Kennedy in the murder of Diem were likewise designed according to the principles of black propaganda. This time, the aim was simply to discredit a much-loved figure who had belonged to the opposition party. The most time-honored of the black techniques, however, is probably that of provocation. The aim of a policy of secret provocation is, of course, to stage incidents (the Reichstag Fire is the prototype) that will discredit the opposition in the eyes of the public, or to create pretexts for extreme actions by the authorities against the opposition. Haldeman caught the spirit of such a policy perfectly when he wrote that violent and obscene demonstrations against the President would be "good," and that such demonstrations against Billy Graham would be "great." Whether the method employed was forgery, impersonation, or provocation, the aim of the black operations was to load the public record with false information that would be politically useful to the Administration. For this purpose, the techniques of black propaganda were greatly superior to the usual, open techniques of propaganda. The open propagandists went to work after the fact and attempted to rewrite history. The black propagandists had no need to engage in any rewriting. They plunged into the thick of things right at the start, and wrote false chapters into the history books even as events unfolded.

But of far greater importance than the techniques of black propaganda were national policies designed to attain the same end —dividing the Democrats. Just as the black propaganda was aimed at loading the public record with spurious information that would serve to divide the Democrats, the policies recommended by the White House political-planning group loaded the world itself with real events that would induce the Democrats to turn against one another. Policies framed with this aim had a dual character. On the one hand, they were real, publicly announced policies, with large consequences in the lives of millions of people—policies altering the complexion of the Supreme Court, determining the size of programs for the benefit of the poor, influencing the conduct of the Vietnam war. In their own right, they enjoyed some popularity with the public. On the other hand, the policies were subterfuges aimed at setting the nation against itself, and were designed to provide a tumultuous atmosphere in which the President could pick up "far the larger half" of the electorate. The use of government policy in this dual fashion put the opposition in a quandary. If it responded to the programs straightforwardly—for instance, by opposing the President's Supreme Court nominations, or opposing the President's proposals on busing—it ran the risk of casting itself as an actor in a White House scenario whose hidden last act was the opposition's political demise, for the opposition's cry of protest might be just the thing that the White House scenario called for. But if the members of the opposition remained silent in order to frustrate the scenario, they betrayed their principles. Almost everyone who attempted to oppose White House policy in the Nixon years was caught in this bind at one time or another. The experience was one of walking into a waiting stereotype—of finding oneself caricatured as, for example, a "radical-liberal," who reflexively denounced anything the government might undertake. Just as the President would condemn violence while secretly working to promote it, he would condemn the opposition for its perpetual criticism while taking actions secretly designed to provoke just such criticism and "really tear up the pea patch." The press was one victim of this dilemma. The Administration would accuse the press of systematic prejudice against the Administration, and then would take actions that any independent press was bound to criticize. Thus it would become true that the press was heavily critical of the Administration, and the Administration would proceed to attack the press further for "unfairness." The choice for the press was to mute its reporting and editorializing in order to show a spurious objectivity or to go ahead with its work at the cost of being caricatured as "irresponsible." (A strong temptation for newsmen in this period was to take a position halfway between the one demanded of them by the President and the one demanded of them by the opposition, if any, and to call that position objectivity.) The new way of framing policy posed difficulties for the public, too. It cast all politics into a limbo of ambiguity. The meaning of every action in the public realm became obscure. In 1970, when President Nixon sent American troops into Cambodia, for example, his decision was debated around the country on its military merits. People asked themselves whether or not the invasion would hurt the enemy, and whether or not it would help to end the war. A few months later, however, it turned out that the President regarded the national division engendered by the invasion as his most invaluable political asset in the congressional elections of 1970. A sophisticated citizen, therefore, would have had to ask himself not only whether the invasion had been wise or unwise as military policy but whether it had been directed to the military situation at all or had been just one more attempt to exacerbate a divisive issue. But the sophisticated citizen, even if he had thought to ask such questions, would not have been able to answer them, for the memos that might reveal the truth were not available to him. Moreover, the truth might not appear in any memos but might simply lie in the mind of the President. The sophisticated citizen would probably have had to do what millions of citizens did do: stop trying to figure out what the government's intentions were. The public's revulsion against politics as a whole was one more feature of an orchestrated political life. Bewildered and exhausted by the repeated experience of responding with real emotions to illusory or false policies that would reverse themselves or disappear the minute their public-relations usefulness was finished, the public was withdrawing from political life altogether.

By the spring of 1972, President Nixon was setting himself up as the scriptwriter of the whole of American political life. He looked upon America as his predecessors in the White House had looked upon Vietnam: as a great theatre for a sweeping dramatic production, in which a real nation was used as the stage, real public figures were used as unwilling actors, and the history of the nation was used as the plot. Unsatisfied with playing just one part in the national life, even though it was by far the greatest part, the President secretly planned to play all the parts, and to provide the lighting and the sound effects, too. Using his untrammelled access to the system of modern communications, he fixed the themes of national politics; through his techniques of staging and black propaganda, he fixed the roles of the other characters; and through government policy, he furnished the world with events suitable to his themes. One man, the President, had made himself larger than the political nation of which he was supposed to be only a part. He sought to substitute for the normal evolution of American history, with its countless spontaneous impulses, a false, planned evolution, manufactured in the White House. In some ways, the role to which he aspired was godlike. In his world he was the author of all that happened. He was the author even of harm to himself. Rebels against him were necessary at times, and when demonstrators threw rocks at him, his staff rejoiced, for the incident meant that the scenario was proceeding according to plan. Crises, too, were required, and the President was the author of many of these. They, too, were important to the scenarios, for how could the "great decisions" be made without great matters to decide? And a high level of national discord was also important, for if the President did not first divide the nation, how could he pose as a unifier and pick up "far the larger half" of the country in the next election? In President Nixon's America, no one was without his predetermined role. In President Nixon's vision, American life would unfold according to a script written by him and his men; and, long after any real opposition had been silenced, hired actors would go on playing the part of an opposition on the public stage.

In the second week of April, when the results of the Wisconsin primary had made it clear that even if Senator Muskie should somehow be nominated it would not be as a unity candidate, Patrick Buchanan wrote, in one of his memos to Mitchell and Haldeman, "Our primary objective, to prevent Senator Muskie from sweeping the early primaries, locking up the Convention in April, and uniting the Democratic Party behind him for the fall has been achieved. The likelihood—great three months ago—that the Democratic Convention could become a dignified coronation ceremony for a centrist candidate who could lead a united party into the election is now remote." It was a bold boast. Had it really been the White House, staging its secret scenarios, that had "achieved" the downfall of Senator Muskie, the Democratic "front-runner," and, in the process, denied the Democrats the chance to unite their party at the Convention? The answer depends on the answers to several other questions, and those are probably unanswerable. Possibly the campaign of sabotage alone would not have accomplished so much. But there had also been the program to use the policies of the federal government to divide the Democrats. To what extent had the President been following his planning group's recommendations when he framed policy, and to what extent had he been following his own ideas of what was best for the nation? What, for instance, were his real views on the racial issue? Did he have any? To what extent did the policies that were framed—the policy on busing, say— actually divide the Democrats, and to what extent was the division their own work? How successful was the campaign of sabotage in embittering the candidates against one another and in stopping the candidacy of Senator Muskie? No definitive answers to such questions can be given. What is known is that the White House did carry out a program of sabotage, and that the President did make his decisions on national policies—including his decisions on race, on the war, on the nomination of Supreme Court Justices, and on observance of the provisions of the Constitution—while at least keeping the aim of dividing the opposition in mind. (There is no evidence that he ever reprimanded his chief political strategists for making the recommendations they made, or that any other group was put to work devising an alternative political strategy for him to pursue.) It is also known that the President did—for whatever reasons—adopt virtually every one of the policies that were recommended to him for the purpose of dividing the opposition by dividing the country. And it is known that the candidacy of Senator Muskie did in fact founder upon exactly those divisions which the White House planning group wanted the President to exacerbate by taking the actions that he did in fact take. Of course, it is known, as well, that the Democrats seemed to make mistakes of their own, quite independent of the White House—for example, attempting to create an impression of unity of purpose by joining together, in advance of the primaries, behind a man whose stand on many issues was deliberately vague. Theirs was a party more than usually open to an effort to divide it, and quite possibly Senator Muskie's strength preceding the primaries, based, as it was, on the support of the press and the political professionals, was more apparent than real. Yet right from the outset—beginning as early as 1970—the Democrats were carrying on their activities in an America that was secretly mined to tear them apart. Both within their campaign, where the spies and saboteurs were at work, and outside it, where a shifting world was arranged by the President to confound their hopes, they felt the hidden hand of the White House. The fusion of politics and policy in the White House was complete. The boundary lines had blurred until they disappeared. To an extent theretofore unknown in American politics, the White House had, in the year leading up to the beginning of the Presidential election campaign, made uninhibited use of federal agencies to smear the opposition, to raise money for its own campaign, and to commit a wide variety of crimes against the opposition, and had also manipulated the full range of public policy, sometimes according to deep strategies unguessed at by the public, to create what was not only a rigged campaign but a rigged America and a rigged world for the campaign to take place in.

At the end of March, as Senator Muskie's campaign was sinking, the North Vietnamese Army invaded South Vietnam in force. For the Administration, the attack precipitated a crisis that mingled the war, the campaign, and prospective summit talks in Moscow, which were scheduled for sometime in May. The attack was embarrassing politically, because an expanded war could disrupt the President's new campaign image, in which the war was not to "distract our attention" from the President's "global diplomacy." On the other hand, to leave the war and permit the North Vietnamese to take over South Vietnam would discredit the policy that the President had now been pursuing for more than three years. The Administration's initial response was to begin a quiet, unannounced buildup of American air forces in and around Indo-China. Even before this buildup began, the American war effort in Vietnam was being carried on largely in the air. The move from the ground, where casualties were heavy, to the air, where they were light, had all along suited the strategy of keeping the war going but keeping it out of the public eye, and the move proved especially useful now. By the

For the Re-Election of the President

time the buildup was complete, the largest and the most powerful air force ever assembled in history was, behind a curtain of silence, bombing Indo-China. The air force was also the most technically elaborate ever to fly. One innovation was the use of what came to be known as "smart bombs," which were bombs guided by television cameras in their noses or by laser beams projected from nearby aircraft.

The Administration at first seemed at a loss to know how to explain the expanded warfare to the public. For a while, it played down the new events in Indo-China. The war aims that had been offered to the public in the early months of the year were the most minuscule ones available on the entire sliding scale of war aims, the largest being, of course, the protection of American credibility. The most frequently mentioned aim had been an even less ambitious one than that of "protecting our withdrawal"; it had been that of protecting the American prisoners of war held by the North Vietnamese. At the beginning of the year, the President had said in a television interview, "Can the President of the United States sitting in this office with the responsibility for four hundred P.O.W.s . . . withdraw all of our forces as long as the enemy holds one American as a prisoner of war? And the answer is no." Around that time, with the encouragement of the White House, a remarkable movement began to grow up around the issue of the prisoners of war. Although the public in wartime has traditionally felt great sympathy for the nation's prisoners of war, it has usually reserved its main sympathy for the men fighting and dying on the front, but now this state of affairs was turned upside down. The wounded, the dying, and the dead went virtually unnoticed as attention was focussed on the prisoners of war. They became the objects of a virtual cult, and many people were persuaded that the United States was fighting in Vietnam in order to get its prisoners back—even though prisoners have traditionally been returned as a matter of course at the end of hostilities between nations. Following the President's lead, people began to speak as though the North Vietnamese had kidnapped four hundred Americans and the United States had gone to war to retrieve them.

231

The newly intensified fighting and the new air buildup put a strain on the prisoner-of-war justification. The aim was too slight to justify the dangerous expanding effort. The North Vietnamese opened new fronts. The American air attacks grew constantly heavier. Expanded war aims were plainly required, but what could they be, in the new "generation of peace"? And what was the meaning of summit trips if not to help end wars? After all, the true foe in Vietnam, in the official telling, had never been little North Vietnam. It had been China or Russia, or both—"Communism." If these great powers were not, after all, the true foe in Indo-China, then the Indo-China war really *was* a civil war in a small country, as its opponents had always said, and the United States had no business taking part in it. As the fighting spread, the Administration publicly began to espy the hand of the Soviet Union behind the new offensive. On April 10th, in a veiled but unmistakable reference to the Soviet Union, the President warned that great powers must not "directly or indirectly" encourage "other nations to use force or armed aggression against neighbors." And a few days earlier Secretary of Defense Melvin Laird had criticized the Russians openly for placing "no restraints" on the North Vietnamese Army's use of Russian military equipment. There had not been any evidence up to that point in the war that the Russians had ever either restrained the North Vietnamese or set the timing or the objectives of North Vietnamese military offensives; those matters, as far as anyone can know, had been decided by the North Vietnamese themselves. The Administration's appeal to the Soviet Union to restrain North Vietnam therefore seemed to assume a degree of Russian influence over North Vietnam which did not necessarily exist. Just a few months earlier, the Administration had seemed to make a similar mis-estimation of Soviet influence over the Indians. On both occasions, the Nixon Administration was displaying its determination to treat regional crises as global events. In the case of the India-Pakistan war, there had simply been no way for the Russians to exercise the influence that the Administration adjured them to. Vietnam was somewhat different. Though the Russians might not already exercise control over the North Vietnamese, it would perhaps be possible for them to *establish* some measure of control. The Nixon Administration seemed to be saying to the Russians that, whether or not they had instigated or approved the North Vietnamese offensive, the United States would hold them accountable for it. The Administration seemed, in effect, to be appealing to the Soviet Union to intervene with the North Vietnamese in behalf of the United States.

The point that had thus been reached in Soviet-American relations was a crucial one for many nations of the world. In the period of the Cold War, which was now purportedly ending, the United States had intervened in disputes between nations all over the globe, on the theory that almost all nations were "linked" either with the United States or with Communism. Now, in what was purportedly a period of "détente," the United States, assuming the same linkage, was hoping to deal with the same disputes by urging the Soviet Union to exercise restraint in unleashing its proxy warriors. Just as the government had earlier seen the rivalry of the Cold War as a global struggle by virtue of linkage, the government now expected coöperation between the superpowers to be global by virtue of linkage; that is, it considered linkage as much the precondition for coöperation as it was for Cold War. The word "détente" (although there was, perhaps, no better) was not, with its connotations of relaxation and disengagement, precisely suited to the new relationship envisaged by the United States government. The process that the Nixon Administration had in mind seemed to be closer to partial fusion. The Soviet Union and the United States, instead of disengaging from one another, were becoming more heavily involved with one another than ever before. It was not so much that the traditional rivalry was diminishing as that it was being overlaid with areas of recognized common interest. The main interest, which gave détente its principal impetus, was, of course, the avoidance of mutual extinction in a nuclear war. The enmity that had grown up between the two nations became, in the nuclear age, the prime factor impelling them toward what the statesmen sometimes called their nascent "friendship." But there were other areas of common interest, too, including areas of economic interest. The two behemoths were fusing at the head while continuing to kick one another with their feet. And since their relationship, even if it had taken on a coöperative aspect as well as a hostile one, was, after all, a single relationship, involving the same governments, the war in Indo-China and other points of conflict were bound to be influenced, insofar as the superpowers could influence such things, by the negotiations on the points of common interest. The affairs of little countries would now be discussed at a Russian-American bargaining table at which such matters as nuclear-arms control, trade deals between the great powers, and simultaneous troop reductions were also discussed. At this table, the North Vietnamese aim of uniting their country—pursued for more than a quarter of a century—might be balanced in Russian minds against some advantage in a wholly unrelated transaction with the United States.

On April 19th, Henry Kissinger secretly arrived in Moscow to make preparations for the summit conference. On the 20th, he delivered a speech in private to Soviet Communist Party Secretary Leonid Brezhnev. Later, the fourth, and final, draft of the speech was made public. (On one occasion, Kissinger is reported to have told the Nixon speechwriter William Safire that the draft accurately reflected what he had said to the Russians, but later he wrote in a letter to *Harper's* that he had taken "quite a different line" with the Soviet leaders.) In one passage, the draft had him speaking not in the manner of a man speaking on behalf of the President but in the manner of a man standing back and objectively describing the President. Through the use of this device, he was apparently to establish the President's credibility with Brezhnev. At the beginning of a description of the President's "attitudes, orientation, and predictability," the draft depicted the President as eager for coöperation between "interacting major powers, competitive but respectful of each other's interests," and then pointed out that the President "can be tough and even ruthless in dealing with specific problems." The draft was spelling out the lesson that the Administration's whole conduct of the Vietnam war was meant to teach: it affirmed the

President's "will" to use the military power of the United States in world affairs. Then it turned to the relation between the war and President Nixon's personal political future. "You probably recognize that the President is bound to see the present situation in Vietnam not only in its local context but as a renewed effort by outside powers to intervene in our domestic political processes," the draft read. "Moreover, as President he is bound to be keenly sensitive to the fact that our last President was forced to vacate his office because of the effects of the Vietnam war. President Nixon will not permit three Presidents in a row to leave office under abnormal circumstances. It may seem that what he is doing to prevent this from occurring is 'unpredictable'; it is in fact quite consistent with his fighting instincts when issues of principle and vital interest are at stake. His reaction should have been expected." The draft had Kissinger inviting the First Secretary of the Communist Party of the Union of Soviet Socialist Republics to join in President Nixon's campaign for reëlection. When it said, "President Nixon will not permit three Presidents in a row to leave office under abnormal circumstances," it seemed to be saying that the President wished to remain in office for a second term. The structure of peace, it seemed to say, was also a structure for the reëlection of the President. In the course of his first term, President Nixon placed the full power of the executive branch of the United States government at the disposal of political strategists. Now, having apparently found these resources insufficient, the President seemed to entertain the hope that the resources of the government of the world's other superpower could be enlisted in the reëlection effort. This strategy bore a marked resemblance to Patrick Buchanan's recommendation that the President use his power to provoke a Constitutional crisis and thus divide "the Democratic Party and country." Both Kissinger and Buchanan were merging government policy with electoral strategy in an unprecedented fashion. Kissinger's policy could be regarded in either of two ways. If, on the one hand, one looked at the draft of Kissinger's speech in the context of the reëlection effort, it could be seen as a frank admission that President Nixon was fighting the war in Vietnam primarily to preserve himself in office, and as an astoundingly improper invitation to a foreign enemy of the United States to ally itself with the President's faction in domestic politics. If, on the other hand, one looked at the draft in the context of the doctrine of credibility, it could be seen as an astute move that would enhance national security. For at the heart of the question of credibility was the question of will. As President Nixon put it a few months later in a talk with a group of congressmen about the events that were then unfolding, "strength means nothing unless there is a will to use it." Kissinger, by apparently associating the survival of South Vietnam with President Nixon's political survival, would be making a strong "demonstration" of Nixon's will to save South Vietnam. The Russians might doubt Nixon's will to save half of a small, remote country in the face of domestic opposition, but they could hardly doubt his will to be reëlected. It could be argued, therefore, that by associating the two goals in the Russians' minds Kissinger would be strengthening the negotiating position of the United States on the issue of Vietnam.

Having affirmed the President's credibility in this remarkable fashion, the draft listed some of the advantages that the Soviet Union might win by coöperating with the United States. After citing "bilateral relations and trade," it read, "Both of us stand to gain." Then came a warning: "But we must be realistic: a lasting and productive set of relationships, with perhaps hundreds or thousands of our people working with each other and perhaps billions of dollars of business activity, can only be achieved in a healthy political environment. The past history of our relations has clearly shown the connection between the political aspects and others, like the economic." And it had Kissinger going on to state, "I say this not because we want you to 'pay a price' for economic and other relations with us or because we expect you to sacrifice important political and security interests for the sake of trade relations. I say it as an objective fact of political life." In other words, according to the draft, Kissinger didn't *want* the Russians to help the President get reëlected by paying a price in Vietnam; it was just an objective fact of political life that if they wanted the "billions of dollars of business activity" to go forward they would have to pay that price.

But the war went on, and the North Vietnamese continued to advance. The Soviet Union either would not or could not call them back from their mission, the peril to the President's reëlection notwithstanding. The American bombing therefore continued to expand. Four Russian ships were damaged in Haiphong Harbor. And as the war grew the war aims continued to grow, too. The expanded aims turned out to be the familiar ones, well known to the nation from the President's speeches of 1969 and from the speech announcing the invasion of Cambodia—and, indeed, from the pronouncements of past Administrations. In late April, the President went on national television and once again spelled out the familiar doctrine of credibility. "If one country armed with the most modern weapons by major powers can invade another nation and succeed in conquering it," he said, "other countries will be encouraged to do exactly the same thing—in the Mid-East, in Europe, and in other international danger spots." In other words, if America lost credibility anywhere, it would have lost it everywhere. As usual, he saw the authority of his office, and therefore his own authority, as the ultimate issue. "Any man who sits here in this office feels a profound sense of obligation to future generations," he said. "No man who sits here has the right to take any action which would abdicate America's great tradition of world leadership or weaken respect for the office of President of the United States." And he said, "All that we have risked and all that we have gained over the years now hangs in the balance." The President's words and the thought behind them were not new. ("Respect for the office of President of the United States" was merely one more term for credibility.) But the context in which he was speaking them was new. In the time of the Cold War, the words had one meaning, but in the time of the President's "generation of peace" and "structure of peace" they had a quite different meaning. Since the great powers that the President was visiting on what he liked to call his "journeys for peace" were, under the doctrine of credibility he had temporarily revived, the very ones that were threatening "all that we have risked and all that we have gained," he seemed to have put forward simultaneously two clashing conceptions of the world and the American role in it—one growing out of the structure of peace, and the other borrowed from the past to explain the sudden flare-up in the Vietnam war. In one conception, the Cold War was waning, the President was arranging world peace with the leaders of Communist nations, and the Soviet Union might even be aiding the United States in bringing about a satisfactory end to the war in Southeast Asia. In the other conception, the Cold War was intensifying, armed minions of the Soviet Union all over the world were working to undermine respect for the United States, and the Soviet Union was encouraging the North Vietnamese to defeat the United States. The atmospheres of peace and war had become mingled and confused in the President's public statements. In this speech in late April, the President went on to attempt an amalgam of the two conceptions. "Earlier this year," he said, "I travelled to Peking on an historic journey for peace and next month I shall travel to Moscow on what I hope will also be a journey for peace." He continued, "In the eighteen countries I have visited as President, I have found great respect for the office of the President of the United States and I have reason to expect, based on Dr. Kissinger's report [Kissinger had recently returned from his trip to the Soviet Union, which had been revealed only the previous day], that I shall find that same respect for the office I hold when I visit Moscow." But, he added, "if the United States betrays the millions of people who have relied on us in Vietnam, the President of the United States, whoever he is, will not deserve nor receive the respect which is essential if the United States is to continue to play the great role we are destined to play of helping to build a new structure of peace in the world." Earlier in the year, in his State of the World message, the President had seemed to recognize the incompatibility between détente and an extended war in Vietnam, and had said, "Vietnam no longer distracts our attention from the fundamental issues of global diplomacy." But the words he spoke now seemed to mean that the Vietnam war and the structure of peace were the same thing. The journeys for peace, instead of leading to an end to the war, as had been widely hoped, were leading in a circle right back to expanded war.

The President's feat of putting forward two apparently clashing conceptions of the world at the same time and of propagating two contrary global atmospheres at the same time marked a new stage in the growth of his power. In his years in office, he had often advanced policies and then revoked them suddenly and without explanation. His three "shocks" of 1971—the announcement of the trip to China, the announcement of wage-price controls, and the announcement of the Moscow summit—had brought the technique to a high level of refinement: they had enlarged his freedom of action by establishing his right to defy himself. And now, in 1972, he was putting on a still more awesome performance. The carefully constructed image of the President as the man of peace had been badly disrupted by a sudden intensification of the war. But this time, instead of revoking one explanation of things and unexpectedly putting forward another, he put forward the original explanation and its apparent opposite simultaneously. The citizen listening to him describe how it was necessary to defy the Soviet regime in Vietnam so that he could drink toasts with the Soviet regime in Moscow had no way of guessing whether the world was heading toward expanded war or toward peace. The President seemed to point the country in both directions at once. Like the pronouncements of an oracle, his statements had become susceptible of infinite varieties of interpretation. To most politicians, self-contradiction is politically harmful. President Nixon had turned self-contradiction to his advantage. The power to defy common sense, like the power to erase his own past actions and statements from memory, had apparently become one more of the multiplying privileges of his office.

On May 1st, the northern defenses of South Vietnam cracked. The top officers and American advisers of the division holding the northern city of Quang Tri abandoned their troops in helicopters, and the troops threw down their weapons and ran south to the city of Hué, which they proceeded to loot and terrorize. In their wake came American B-52s, atomizing the landscape. Refugees were streaming along highways through much of the country. A complete collapse of the South Vietnamese Army seemed possible.

The next day, F.B.I. Director J. Edgar Hoover died. The days that followed were a complex period in the history of the White House undercover group. In a press release on the day of Hoover's death, the President had said, "Mr. Hoover was never a man to run away from a fight." Having fought a fierce, hidden war with Hoover over the so-called Huston plan and the summaries of the Administration's warrantless wiretaps, among other things, he had good reason to know. Two days after Hoover's death, the President stood near the flag-draped coffin of his former adversary in the National Presbyterian Church, in Washington. His manner was strangely defiant and his words strangely harsh for a eulogy. He used the occasion to assail the supposed philosophy of his opposition. "The trend of permissiveness in this country, a trend which Edgar Hoover fought against all of his life, a trend which has dangerously eroded our national heritage as a law-abiding people, is now being reversed," he said. And he said, "The American people today are tired of disorder, disruption, and disrespect for law. America wants to come back to the law as a way of life."

The day before the President delivered his eulogy, a White House mugging squad arrived at the foot of the Capitol steps, where Daniel Ellsberg was speaking to a group of anti-war demonstrators. The new squad was made up of members of the team that had been put together by E. Howard Hunt to burglarize the office of Ellsberg's psychiatrist. Its task this time was to beat up Ellsberg. The squad's leader, Bernard Barker, told his men, "Our mission is to hit him—to call him a traitor and punch him in the nose. Hit him and run." In the event, members of the squad attacked some of the people listening to Ellsberg but were stopped by the police before they could reach Ellsberg himself. It had, of course, been in part Hoover's reluctance to "nail" Ellsberg in the manner desired by the Administration that had led the President to set up the ad-hoc team to destroy Ellsberg. Now a truculent President was standing over the Director's coffin urging a return to "the law as a way of life."

For a week, the world awaited the President's next moves in the war. " 'What will he do?' they ask from one end of the country to the other," Max Frankel wrote in the *Times* on May 7th, in an article titled "No One Knows What He Might Do." Frankel continued, "The President who wanted to be respected for his calculated fury in the face of adversity has indeed inspired that kind of respect—and a good measure of fear as well—at least among his own people. The fear was so intense that even the regular voices of protest were muted." The next day—May 8th—the President revealed, in a televised address to the nation, what he would do. He would mine the entrances to the ports of North Vietnam against all shipping, including Russian and Chinese shipping, and would also bomb the railroad lines that connected North Vietnam and China. The mines, he said, were being seeded in North Vietnamese waters even as he spoke. The structure of peace seemed to have disappeared. The President-as-peacemaker was hiding his face, and the President-as-wartime-leader was before the nation. His speech was in the mold of his address on the invasion of Cambodia. The words were filled with anger. He said he was taking "decisive military action." He called the North Vietnamese "international outlaws." He accused them of having shelled South Vietnamese cities in "wanton disregard of human life." They had met peace overtures from the United States "with insolence and insult," he said.

The mining was the first frontal challenge of one nuclear power by another since the Cuban missile crisis. The war, which only a few months earlier was supposed not to "distract us" any longer from the President's "global diplomacy," had now expanded—for the first time in its long history—to a point where it threatened to escalate into world war. At the time of the invasion of Cambodia, the President had wondered aloud whether history would give him the opportunity to make a "great decision" in the Oval Office. Now he seemed to have concluded that the opportunity had come. At the time of the invasion, he had said that the nation was undergoing a testing that would be crucial in the event of a "real" crisis—apparently meaning a crisis at the brink of nuclear war with another great power. Now the real crisis seemed to be here. In the spring of 1970, the dying war had been parlayed into a national political convulsion. In the spring of 1971, when war issues had penetrated to the courts in the Calley case, the Mayday case, the case of the Vietnam Veterans Against the War, and the Pentagon Papers case, it had precipitated a legal crisis, and had given birth to, among other things, the White House undercover group. Now, in the spring of 1972, the war, still dying its long-drawn-out death, had been parlayed into an international convulsion.

A hush fell as the shadow of nuclear war passed over the world. In the United States, the voices of public opinion were, for the most part, stilled. From Moscow there was no decisive word for several days. In one quarter, however, a loud clamor arose, all of it in support of the President's action. The White House undercover group was temporarily diverted from its efforts to undermine the Presidential election and directed to get to work fabricating public approval of the mining. Just before the President's speech, E. Howard Hunt alerted the chief of his undercover squad and told him to collect signatures for telegrams of support to the White House. Charles Colson, using a White House apparatus for placing spurious advertisements in the press, ran an ad in the *Times* titled "The People vs. the New York *Times*" and taking the *Times* to task for an editorial critical of the mining. The advertisement did not say so, but "The People" in this case were the people in the White House. Over at the Committee for the Re-Election of the President, part of the staff was put to work sending in thousands of fraudulent "votes" to an informal television poll of public reaction to the mining. Donald Segretti got in touch with a number of his saboteurs in Florida and ordered them to stop harassing the Democrats long enough to send in messages of support. When all the instructions had gone out, just about every spy, saboteur, con man, extortionist, forger, impostor, informer, burglar, mugger, and bagman—for that, astonishingly, is what they were—in the employ of the White House was at work manufacturing the appearance of public support for the President.

Three days after the President's speech, there was a signal that the Soviet Union would not challenge the mining of the ports, and that the global aspect of the crisis was passing: in Moscow, on May 11th, a denunciation of the mining was issued, but the same day two Soviet officials in Washington visited President Nixon at the White House, and the three men, together with Kissinger, Secretary of Commerce Peter Peterson, and a Presidential aide, Peter Flanigan, were photographed smiling broadly. One of the Soviet officials was Anatoly Dobrynin, the Russian Ambassador to the United States, and the other was Nikolai Patolichev, the Soviet Minister of Foreign Trade. The President had an excellent reason for smiling, which the public could easily deduce: the White House meeting seemed to mean that the Russians not only would acquiesce in the mining but would go ahead with the summit while the mining was still on. The smiles on the faces of the Soviet officials were harder to understand, since their country had just suffered what much of the world might interpret as an international humiliation. (The public, naturally, had no knowledge of the speech that Kissinger had made to the Russians, in which he apparently linked trade agreements with a favorable outcome in Vietnam and linked a favorable outcome in Vietnam with the President's reëlection.) But the Ambassador and the Foreign Trade Minister had their reasons for smiling. In recent months, the Soviet Union had experienced widespread crop failures and now faced the prospect of food shortages, but now the Foreign Trade Minister was in the midst of arranging to buy fully one-quarter of the American wheat crop, at favorable prices; and he was also arranging to buy a wide variety of Western manufactured goods, including tractors, that were unavailable in Russia.

In Vietnam, American pilots were killing and being killed to prevent Soviet supplies from getting through to the North Vietnamese, but in Washington the government was arranging the sale of tremendous amounts of American goods to the Soviet Union. The draft of Kissinger's speech had had him telling the Russians that he was not asking them to "pay a price" for trade agreements but that it was "an objective fact" that some accommodation would have to be reached. The Russians now were acting as though they were willing to recognize this "objective fact." The shape of détente was such that while the troops were dying in the field the generals were striking deals in the conference room. The Soviet Union and the United States had become enemies and partners at the same time. While it cannot be known to what extent the Russians may have been induced to overlook the events in Indo-China by the hope of trade advantages, a "confrontation" unquestionably appears in a different light when the principals are engaging in large trade deals on the side. For to whatever extent the Soviet Union softened its response to the mining in the hope of obtaining tractors and wheat, it can be said that to that extent the Soviet Union was a party to the American mining of Vietnam, rather than its victim. To that extent, the Russians allowed President Nixon his mining, and allowed him to work his will in Vietnam with the B-52s, in exchange for advantages to themselves. And since the President's public posture was one of belligerent defiance, it can be said that to that extent, too, the mining was a piece of theatre played before the world—including, of course, the American electorate. The drama was meant to show the President protecting the authority of his office, and no less an actor than the Soviet Union had been engaged, at no mean cost, to play a supporting role. Of all the scenarios to be put together by the White House, this one was the broadest: it encompassed the world. In another scene in the same drama, the White House secret operatives had been engaged to play the role of the American public. In other words, the crisis, dangerous as it was, was not, after all, *quite* the "real" crisis that the President had spoken of in his speech announcing the invasion of Cambodia. It was a little bit unreal.

The advantages won by each side in the crucial first weeks of May, in which détente and confrontation seemed to be gathering momentum with equal velocity, showed something about the differences between the two major powers. The United States, a democracy, in which power is won through public approval, was willing to pay in solid goods to protect appearances—to protect its credibility. The Soviet Union, a totalitarian dictatorship, was willing to pay in credibility to get goods. We wanted "respect." The Russians wanted tractors and wheat. Here was the basis for a deal.

A new field of political action, more spacious than any known to the world before, had opened up before the Nixon Administration: the bargaining table of détente. At this table, the question of human survival in the nuclear age, the question of the survival of nations around the world which might be linked in some way to either of the two superpowers, the question of economic relations between the superpowers, and the question of the political survival of the participating regimes were placed on a single agenda. No longer could any one of these questions be considered separately. All were now to be weighed in a single balance. Here was linkage of unprecedented breadth. In the thinking on the American side of the bargaining table, at least, the survival of man was linked with the survival of South Vietnam, and the survival of both was linked with the political survival of President Nixon. In this thinking, too, North Vietnam, the Soviet Union, and President Nixon's domestic "enemies" were all linked in an opposing network, with the astonishing consequence that in the Administration's view an intervention by North Vietnam in the affairs of South Vietnam was to be read as an intervention by the Soviet Union in an American election. Surprising as such a conclusion might seem, it flowed naturally from the thinking that had prevailed in the highest circles of the Nixon Administration from its first days. The Administration had concluded long since that the domestic opposition it faced was as great a menace to national security as any foreign foe. In fact, in the matter of the Vietnam war President Nixon had stated that the domestic opposition was an even more dangerous foe than the foreign one. (Only Americans could "defeat or humiliate" the United

States, he had said.) It was just a small step from this view to the view that the foreign foe represented a domestic threat. In the Nixonian scheme, political self-interest and the national interest were melded at the summit no less than anywhere else. Formerly, an aura of selflessness and virtue had surrounded most schemes of "international coöperation," as though when it came to setting up an international order only the most high-minded aspirations could be expected to enter in. In practice, however, when any two regimes met under conditions of near-perfect secrecy they did not leave their ruthlessness, self-interest, and greed behind; the association held opportunities not only for mankind but for the domestic political interests of each regime. The international order, like any political order, was no more high-minded than the regimes participating in it. In these early, tentative, groping moments of détente, it was difficult to judge just what the implications would be over the long run for American domestic affairs, but from the first it was plain that new burdens would be placed on the American Constitutional system. For one thing, the new field of action gave President Nixon new opportunities for the arbitrary exercise of his swollen powers. No Presidential powers were greater than the ones exercised at the bargaining table of détente, none required a higher degree of centralized control, and none were wielded in deeper secrecy. For another thing, no objective was more compelling than the one that provided détente with its overriding justification—human survival. Already, President Nixon had put his undercover operators to work defending the "structure of peace" against various supposed challenges on the home front, and already his aides were convinced that even the slightest interference with any aspect of that structure by the domestic opposition might bring the whole structure tumbling down. And in the Soviet Union, where domestic political opposition was well under control, the regime was beginning to say that the few dissidents who did dare to speak up were guilty of harming détente.

None of this is to say that President Nixon had made a decision to subordinate the cause of human survival to the cause of his personal political survival. Rather, he appeared to have decided that the two causes were one. To an outsider, it might seem baffling and contradictory that the President should make peace with the Russians at the same time he was stepping up the struggle against the Vietnamese and his own countrymen, but in the full context of his global strategy these apparently clashing policies were reconciled. Moreover, they were continuous with the policy that had prevailed before the period of détente. In Administration thinking, they converged upon a strategy for national and human survival which was of long standing. The strategy of limited war, which had given rise to the war in Vietnam, had grown out of an early attempt by Kissinger and other theorists to come to grips with the problem of nuclear weapons. The thought had been that since the United States could not fight the Soviet Union directly at the brink, it would carry the war to the enemy in indirect ways and on lower levels of violence by fighting limited wars. The policy involved an exchange. The imperative of preserving world peace in the nuclear age would find expression in a policy of coexistence in the nation's direct relations with the Soviet Union, while the imperative of battling Communism would be given free scope on the level of limited war. One might say that the plan was to pay for nuclear peace with limited war. President Nixon's present policy of combining a strategy of détente at the summit level with a strategy of confrontation in Vietnam was only an extension of this earlier policy. Once again, a move toward peace at the brink was compensated for by an intensification of hostilities in the fringe areas of relations between the two powers. To an outsider, it might seem that a time of improved relations with the Soviet Union would be the logical moment to reduce the American commitment in Vietnam. In Administration thinking, the case was just the opposite. A relaxation of tension at the summit required, if anything, increased militancy in other parts of the world. Otherwise, the Soviet Union might place the wrong construction on détente: Soviet leaders might construe America's willingness to negotiate at the summit as weakness. Thus, the crucial appearance of toughness would be diminished, and credibility would be lost. The Russians would decide that the United States was truly a pitiful, helpless giant, and would decide that, as President Nixon put it to some congressmen a few months later in defending the mining, the United States wasn't "worth talking to." The President wouldn't get "respect," or even "deserve" it. The same logic applied to hostilities in the domestic sphere. In their way, the domestic wars were also limited wars. Within the United States, too, as President Nixon had tirelessly pointed out, Presidential credibility was at stake. And if the President could not allow appearances of weakness to develop in Vietnam, nine thousand miles away, still less could he allow them to develop at home.

On May 15th, as the nation waited to hear whether the summit talks would definitely take place, Governor Wallace was shot by an assassin, and was left paralyzed. Startling and horrifying events were piling up too fast for many people. "It's getting so that you don't know what's going to happen in our country anymore in politics," Hubert Humphrey remarked when he heard the news about Wallace. In the White House undercover group, there were immediate stirrings. The morning after the assault, Charles Colson suggested to Hunt that he go to Milwaukee, Wisconsin, the home of the assassin—a young man named Arthur Bremer—to see what he could find out; then he withdrew the suggestion.

Before long, it became clear that the summit talks would go forward despite the mining of the North Vietnam ports, and on May 22nd the President arrived in Moscow. In the course of the talks, an array of agreements was signed, including an agreement to establish a commission to encourage trade between the two countries. (In July, the United States agreed to sell the Soviet Union at least seven hundred and fifty million dollars' worth of American wheat and other grains over a three-year period.) But the most important were the Strategic Arms Limitation agreements. They were the fruit of five full years of negotiations, which had been started by President Johnson and carried forward under President Nixon. They fixed a limit on the quantity, although not on the quality, of some of the nuclear-weapons delivery systems which each side would be allowed to possess. The agreements were the first of their kind. They were the cement binding the two great powers together at the most fundamental level, and, as such, constituted the most substantial justification for the claim the President was making that the new structure he was building at home and abroad was in fact a structure of peace.

New miracles of television coverage were performed, still more wonderful than the ones in Peking. On May 28th, the President addressed the Russian people and the American people simultaneously. In some of his remarks, he seemed to imply that the entire world was at peace. Yet during the President's visit to Russia the obstruction of Russian ships in North Vietnam continued. The United States and the Soviet Union remained at the brink in Vietnam. The world had been brought simultaneously to the brink and to the summit. The logic of the Cold War and the logic of détente had been carried to their extremes at the same time. However, if in announcing the mining the President had relied on the language of the Cold War, now that he was in Moscow he reverted to the language of détente. The wartime President asking his people for support in the battle against a ruthless and determined foe had given way once more to the peacetime President engaged in friendly negotiations with that same foe. "America's flag flies high over the ancient Kremlin fortress," he said. In the vision of world affairs put forward by the President in Moscow, the Vietnam war had again disappeared altogether. He told a story about a little Russian girl named Tanya, whose family had been killed, one by one, in the course of the siege of Leningrad during the Second World War. "As we work toward a more peaceful world," the President said, "let us do all that we can to insure that no other children will have to endure what Tanya did, and that your children and ours—and all the children of the world—can live their full lives together in friendship and in peace." While he spoke, of course, the heaviest bombing campaign in the history of warfare was being carried on by American planes in Vietnam.

On the night of the President's speech in Moscow, members of the White House burglary squad broke into the headquarters of the Democratic National Committee, in the Watergate office building, in Washington. They photographed documents and installed two wiretaps. They were carrying out the first stage of G. Gordon Liddy's Gemstone plan. That night, they reconnoitred the head-quarters of the McGovern campaign, hoping to install wiretaps there, too, but there was activity in the offices, and they were deterred. This was one of several such visits that the burglary squad made to the McGovern headquarters, and on one of those missions Gordon Liddy, who was armed, shot out a street light for no particular reason.

On June 1st, the President made a triumphal return to the United States. He arrived at Andrews Air Force Base, near Washington, during prime television time. From the airport he proceeded by helicopter to Capitol Hill. Television cameras were waiting to catch the first glimpses of the Presidential helicopter in the night gloom, and to watch it settle, roaring, beside the porches of the Capitol, and to follow the President's progress as he alighted and walked up the brilliantly illumined Capitol steps. Within, the assembled Houses of Congress—and more television cameras— awaited him. As he entered the House Chamber, the members rose, and the tumult of their applause resounded throughout the nation.

In the spring of 1972, the President had placed the staggering mani-fold powers of the modern Presidency on lavish display. The em-blems of his newfound authority were the television eye and the hydrogen bomb. On a moment's notice, he could make himself visible to the whole world or he could blow up the whole world. At his bidding, immense, clamorous events—wars abroad, "anarchy" at home—would appear before the public's view or suddenly disappear. When he gave an order, cities were shattered on the other side of the globe. The vagaries of his moods were translated into global atmospheric conditions. His activities were mysterious: half he held in total secrecy, the other half he explained in paradoxes and conundrums. Under his guidance, the world could be brought simultaneously to the threshold of a "generation of peace" and to the brink of annihilation.

Meanwhile, Senator Muskie, Senator Humphrey, Senator McGovern, Senator Jackson, Governor Wallace, Mayor John Lindsay, Mayor Sam Yorty, Representative Shirley Chisholm, and Representative Wilbur Mills, among the Democratic Presidential candidates, competed for votes, and for coverage on local news programs, in Manchester, New Hampshire; Tampa, Florida; and Racine, Wisconsin. While the President resided in the near-transcendental realm of the summits in Peking and Moscow, and under the very eye of world television, the Democrats were racing around in the trivialized realm of domestic politics, which the President had carefully sown with division. Measured against the awe-inspiring figure in Peking, the Democrats were tiny, frantic, all but inaudible figures. Their voices did not carry in the atmosphere created by the President. Natural campaign issues fell into their laps, but they were unable or unwilling to make good use of them. In May, the war that was supposed to have ended four years earlier had brought the country to the edge of a nuclear war, but even Senator McGovern, whose candidacy had been founded on his opposition to the war in Vietnam, found little to say about this. Instead, his followers' indignation at the war gave the impression of having been carried over from some event in the distant past. The Democratic Presidential campaigns had an air of remoteness from the wider national scene. No candidate seemed to possess whatever it is that enables a leader to fire men with fresh enthusiasm. Each seemed to be involved in a private dialogue with his own small band of adherents.

Senator McGovern evoked passionate support from the anti-war movement. Senator Humphrey retained the loyalty of many black people and the leaders of organized labor. Governor Wallace attracted a constituency that was, in some undefined way, fearful, and angry at events of recent years. Each campaign was, in its own fashion, backward-looking. Even as the candidates travelled about the country, in the midst of crowds of people, each of them seemed to have sealed himself off from his surroundings, as though in preparation for solitary confinement in the White House. The campaign as a whole attracted minimal interest. The press often ran the campaign news on a separate page, or under a separate heading—"The 1972 Campaign," or some such—as though the campaign were not the national business but a subject of narrowly specialized interest, on the order of auto racing or stamp collecting. Reporters found the public mood to be one that combined boredom and revulsion, much like the mood during the congressional elections of 1970. But it was stronger now. Talk of "the lesser of two evils" and of politicians' all being "the same" was on everyone's lips. The polls showed that the public held almost all politicians and public institutions, including the press, in low repute. The public's self-seclusion from politics appeared to be deepening.

Nor was the ineffectuality of the Democratic challengers something anomalous on the national scene. If there was one thing in American politics as striking as the swelling power of the executive branch, it was the enervation of the democracy's other institutions. Congress was showing all the signs of a serious decline: loss of vigor, slowed reactions, impaired vision, paralysis, decomposition. The executive onslaught appeared not only to have cut back congressional powers but to have induced a loss of nerve throughout Congress. The perceived loss of nerve invited further executive depredations, and it also invited public contempt, for although the public often sympathizes with an underdog, it wants to see him fight back, and generally despises a display of will-lessness. And loss of public support, of course, opened the way to still more executive depredation. Moreover, since each of the beset institutions depended to some degree on the strength of the others for its own strength (the Congress, for example, depended on a strong press to transmit its point of view to the public), whereas the executive branch stood alone, the weakening of one of the institutions tended to weaken all. Thus, weakness became endemic, and a contagion of worthlessness seemed to spread through the country's institutions.

The arena of democratic politics is a place for the free expression of ideas, but it must be more than that—it must also be the nation's place of decision. Under President Nixon, the public could plainly see that, express itself as it might, the fact was that the nation's fundamental decisions were being made far from that arena. They were being made in secret councils where the mysteries of national security and human survival in the nuclear age were guarded, and then they were being presented as *faits accomplis* by the President speaking on national television. Nor had the power of the vote proved an adequate recourse. For when the public elected a man to do one thing, he felt no hesitation, it seemed, in doing the exact opposite the moment he was elected. By 1972, the public realm as a whole had been robbed of its functions and degraded in the eyes of the people. The country was forgetting the uses of its institutions. The ties that bound them into an effective whole were breaking down. Each element of the system was left in isolation. The Democratic Presidential candidates were enclosed in little worlds where they heard only the applause of their supporters. The Presidential campaign as a whole had been cut off from the mainstream of national life. The President was making his "great decisions" and then sending himself telegrams of support. The public was retreating into the world of personal pleasures and griefs. And as the public realm fragmented, the words and actions of the people in it lost their meaning. In the White House briefing room, the President's press secretary was speaking empty words. In the Oval Office, the President was talking to his tape recorder. In Indo-China, bombs were falling. In the country at large, Democratic Presidential candidates were flying about in airplanes. The political world had become like an asylum where each person lives in a private reality. Here, someone talks to the air. There, someone mutters to himself. One person is in an incomprehensible rage. Another quietly weeps. Someone else laughs loudly. Still another is attacking a stranger. Outside, the public averts its gaze and quickens its step as it passes by.

V.
THE SCRIPT
AND
THE PLAYERS

I N MID-1972, as President Nixon's reëlection campaign was getting under way, the crisis of Constitutional government in the United States was deepening rapidly. The crisis had apparently had its beginnings in the war in Vietnam. Certainly the lines connecting the crisis to the war were numerous and direct. The war had been the principal issue in the struggle between the President and his political opposition—a struggle that had provoked the Presidential Offensive, which was aimed at destroying independent centers of authority in the nation. In more specific ways, too, the evolution of the Administration's usurpations of authority had been bound up with the war. Almost as soon as the President took office, he had ordered the secret bombing campaign against Cambodia, and when details of the campaign leaked out, he had placed the warrantless wiretaps on the phones of newsmen and White House aides. And when the Director of the Federal Bureau of Investigation seemed to be on the verge of getting hold of summaries of those tapped conversations, the President, in his efforts to prevent this, had entered into his venomous hidden struggle with the Director. The White House attempt to "nail" Daniel Ellsberg was another improper action to grow out of the war. And it had been operatives first hired to carry out this project who had gone on to carry out some of the most serious crimes in the plan to spy on and disrupt the Democrats. The evolution of the warrantless-wiretap incident and of the Pentagon Papers incident illustrated one of the ways in which the crisis of the Constitutional system was deepening. Large quantities of secret information were building up in the White House, first in connection with the war policy and then in connection with the President's plans to insure his reëlection. Every day, as the White House operatives went on committing their crimes, the reservoir of secrets grew. And the very presence of so many secrets compelled still more improper maneuverings, and thus the creation of still more secrets, for to prevent any hint of all that information from reaching the public was an arduous business. There had to be ever-spreading programs of surveillance and increasing efforts to control government agencies. Only agencies that unquestioningly obeyed White House orders could be relied upon to protect the White House secrets, and since in normal times it was the specific obligation of some of the agencies to uncover wrongdoing, wherever it might occur, and bring the wrongdoers to justice, some agencies had to be disabled completely. In effect, investigative agencies such as the F.B.I. and the Central Intelligence Agency had to be enlisted in the obstruction of justice.

At some point back at the beginning of the Vietnam war, long before Richard Nixon became President, American history had split into two streams. One flowed aboveground, the other underground. At first, the underground stream was only a trickle of events. But during the nineteen-sixties—the period mainly described in the Pentagon Papers—the trickle grew to a torrent, and a significant part of the record of foreign affairs disappeared from public view. In the Nixon years, the torrent flowing underground began to include events in the domestic sphere, and soon a large part of the domestic record, too, had plunged out of sight. By 1972, an elaborate preëlection strategy—the Administration strategy of dividing the Democrats—was unfolding in deep secrecy. And this strategy of dividing the Democrats governed not only a program of secret sabotage and espionage but the formation of Administration policy on the most important issues facing the nation. Indeed, hidden strategies for consolidating Presidential authority had been governing expanding areas of Administration policy since 1969, when it first occurred to the President to frame policy not to solve what one aide called "real problems" but to satisfy the needs of public relations. As more and more events occurred out of sight, the aboveground, public record of the period became impoverished and misleading. It became a carefully smoothed surface beneath which many of the most significant events of the period were being concealed. In fact, the split between the Administration's real actions and policies and its pretended actions and policies was largely responsible for the new form of government that had arisen in the Nixon White House, in which images consistently took precedence over substance, and affairs of state were ruled by scenarios. The methods of secrecy and the techniques of public relations were necessary to one another, for the people, lacking access to the truth, had to be told something, and it was the public-relations experts who decided what that something would be.

When the President made his trip to Russia, some students of government who had been worried about the crisis of the American Constitutional system allowed themselves to hope that the relaxation of tensions in the international sphere would spread to the domestic sphere. Since the tensions at home had grown out of events in the international sphere in the first place, it seemed reasonable to assume that an improvement in the mood abroad would give some relief in the United States, too. These hopes were soon disappointed. In fact, the President's drive to expand his authority at home was accelerated; although the nation didn't know it, this was the period in which White House operatives advanced from crimes whose purpose was the discovery of national-security leaks to crimes against the domestic political opposition. The Presidential Offensive had not been called off; it had merely been routed underground. The President spoke incessantly of peace, and had arranged for his public-relations men to portray him as a man of peace, but there was to be no peace—not in Indo-China, and not with a constantly growing list of people he saw as his domestic "enemies." Détente, far from relaxing tensions at home, was seen in the White House as one more justification for its campaign to crush the opposition and seize absolute power.

On Sunday, June 18, 1972, readers of the front page of the *Times* learned, among other things, that heavy American air strikes were continuing over North Vietnam, that the chairman of President Nixon's Council of Economic Advisers, Herbert Stein, had attacked the economic proposals of Senator McGovern, who in less than a month was to become the Presidential nominee of the Democratic Party, and that the musical *Fiddler on the Roof* had just had its three-thousand-two-hundred-and-twenty-fifth performance on Broadway. Readers of page 30 learned, in a story not listed in the "News Summary and Index," that five men had been arrested in the headquarters of the Democratic National Committee, in the Watergate office building, with burglary tools, cameras, and equipment for electronic surveillance in their possession. In rooms that the men had rented, under aliases, in the adjacent Watergate Hotel, thirty-two hundred-dollar bills were found, along with a notebook containing the notation "E. Hunt" (for E. Howard Hunt, as it turned out) and, next to that, the notation "W. H." (for the White House). The men were members of the Gemstone team.

Most of the high command of the Nixon Administration and the Nixon reëlection committee were out of town when the arrests were made. The President and H. R. Haldeman were on the President's estate in Key Biscayne, Florida. John Dean was in Manila, giving a lecture on drug abuse. John Mitchell, who was then director of the Committee for the Re-Election of the President, and Jeb Magruder, who had become the committee's assistant director, were in California. In the hours and days immediately following the arrests, there was a flurry of activity at the headquarters of the committee, in a Washington office building; in California; and at the White House. Magruder called his assistant in Washington and had him remove certain papers—what later came to be publicly known as Gemstone materials—from his files. Gordon Liddy, by then the chief counsel of the Finance Committee to Re-Elect the President, went into the headquarters himself, removed from his files other materials having to do with the break-in, including other hundred-dollar bills, and shredded them. At the White House, Gordon Strachan, an aide to Haldeman, shredded a number of papers having to do with the setting up of the reëlection committee's undercover operation, of which the break-in at the headquarters of the Democratic National Committee was an important part. Liddy, having destroyed all the evidence in his possession, offered up another piece of potential evidence for destruction: himself. He informed Dean that if the White House wished to have him assassinated he would stand at a given street corner at an appointed time to make things easy. E. Howard Hunt went to his office in the Executive Office Building, took from a safe ten thousand dollars in cash he had there for emergencies, and used it to hire an attorney for the burglars. In the days following, Hunt's name was expunged from the White House telephone directory. On order from John Ehrlichman, his safe was opened and his papers were removed. At one point, Dean—also said to have been acting under instructions from Ehrlichman—gave an order for Hunt to leave the country, but then the order was rescinded. Hunt's payment to an attorney for the burglars was the first of many. Herbert Kalmbach was instructed by Dean and, later, by Ehrlichman, Haldeman, and Mitchell to keep on making payments, and he, in turn, delegated the task to Anthony Ulasewicz. Theirs was a hastily improvised operation. Kalmbach and Ulasewicz spoke to each other from phone booths. (Phone booths apparently had a strong attraction for Ulasewicz. He attached a change-maker to his belt to be sure to have enough coins for his calls, and he chose to make several of his "drops" of the payoff money in them.) He and Kalmbach used aliases and code language in their conversations. Kalmbach became Mr. Novak and Ulasewicz became Mr. Rivers—

names that seem to have been chosen for no specific reason. Hunt, who had had some forty mystery stories published, was referred to as "the writer," and Haldeman, who wore a crewcut, as "the brush." The payoff money became "the laundry," because when Ulasewicz arrived at Kalmbach's hotel room to pick up the first installment he put it in a laundry bag. The burglars were "the players," and the payoff scheme was "the script." Apparently, the reason the White House conspirators spoke to one another from phone booths was that they thought the Democrats might be wiretapping them, just as they had wiretapped the Democrats. In late June, the President himself said to Haldeman, of the Democrats, "When they start bugging us, which they have, our little boys will not know how to handle it. I hope they will, though." Considerations like these led Kalmbach, Ulasewicz, and others working for the White House to spend many unnecessary hours in phone booths that summer.

All these actions were of the sort that any powerful group of conspirators might take upon the arrest of some of their number. Soon, however, the White House was taking actions that were possible only because the conspirators occupied high positions in the government, including the highest position of all—the Presidency. For almost four years, the President had been "reorganizing" the executive branch of the government with a view to getting the Cabinet departments and the agencies under his personal control, and now he undertook to use several of these agencies to cover up crimes committed by his subordinates. In the early stages of the coverup, his efforts were directed toward removing a single evidentiary link: the fact that the Watergate burglars had been paid with funds from his campaign committee. There was a vast amount of other information that needed to be concealed—information concerning not just the Watergate break-in but the whole four-year record of the improper and illegal activities of the White House undercover operators, which stretched from mid-1969, when the warrantless wiretaps were placed, to the months in 1972 when the secret program for dividing the Democrats was being carried out— but if this one fact could somehow be suppressed, then the chain of evidence would be broken, and the rest of it might go undetected.

On June 23rd, the President met with Haldeman and ordered him to have the C.I.A. request that the F.B.I. halt its investigation into the origin of the Watergate burglars' funds, on the pretext that C.I.A. secrets might come to light if the investigation went forward. The problem, Haldeman told the President, was that "the F.B.I. is not under control, because Gray doesn't exactly know how to control it." Patrick Gray was Acting Director of the F.B.I. "The way to handle this now," he went on, "is for us to have Walters call Pat Gray and just say, 'Stay to hell out of this.'" The reference was to Vernon Walters, Deputy Director of the C.I.A. A moment later, Haldeman asked the President, concerning the F.B.I., "And you seem to think the thing to do is get them to stop?" "Right, fine," the President answered. But he wanted Haldeman to issue the instructions. "I'm not going to get that involved," he said. About two hours later, Haldeman and Ehrlichman met with C.I.A. Director Richard Helms and Deputy Director Walters, and issued the order.

The maneuver gave the White House only a temporary advantage. Six days later, on June 29th, Gray did cancel interviews with two people who could shed light on the origin of the burglars' funds. (On the twenty-eighth, Ehrlichman and Dean had handed him all the materials taken from Hunt's safe, and Dean had told him that they were never to "see the light of day." Gray had taken them home, and later he burned them.) But soon a small rebellion broke out among officials of the F.B.I. and the C.I.A. Meetings were held, and at one point Gray and Walters told each other they would rather resign than submit to the White House pressure and compromise their agencies. Several weeks after the request was made, the F.B.I. held the interviews after all. The rebellion in the ranks of the federal bureaucracy was not the first to break out against the Nixon White House. As early as 1969, some members of the Justice Department had fought Administration attempts to thwart the civil-rights laws. In 1970, members of the State Department and members of the Office of Education, in the Department of Health, Education, and Welfare, had protested the invasion of Cambodia. In 1970, too, J. Edgar Hoover had refused to go along with the Huston plan. The executive bureaucracy was one source of the President's great power, but it was also acting as a check on his power. In some ways, it served this function more effectively than the checks provided by the Constitution, for, unlike the other institutions of government, it at least had some idea of what was going on. But ultimately it was no replacement for the Constitutional checks. A President who hired and fired enough people could in time bring the bureaucracy to heel. And although a Gray, a Walters, or a Helms might offer some resistance to becoming deeply involved in White House crimes, they would do nothing to expose the crimes. Moreover, the bureaucracy had no public voice, and was therefore powerless to sway public opinion. Politicians of all persuasions could—and did—heap abuse on "faceless," "briefcase-toting" bureaucrats and their "red tape," and the bureaucracy had no way to reply to this abuse. It had only its silent rebellions, waged with the passive weapons of obfuscation, concealment, and general foot-dragging. Decisive opposition, if there was to be any, had to come from without.

With respect to the prosecutorial arm of the Justice Department, the White House had aims that were less ambitious than its aims with respect to the F.B.I. and the C.I.A., but it was more successful in achieving them. Here, on the whole, the White House men wished merely to keep abreast of developments in the grand-jury room of the U.S. District Court, where officials of the Committee for the Re-Election of the President were testifying on Watergate, and this they accomplished through the obliging coöperation of Henry Petersen, the chief of the Criminal Division, who reported regularly to John Dean and later to the President himself. Dean subsequently described the coöperation to the President by saying, "Petersen is a soldier. He played—he kept me informed. He told me when we had problems, where we had problems, and the like. Uh, he believes in, in, in you. He believes in this Administration. This Administration has made him." What happened in the Grand Jury room was further controlled by the coördinating of perjured testimony from White House aides and men working for the campaign committee. As for the prosecutors, a sort of dim-wittedness— a failure to draw obvious conclusions, a failure to follow up leads, a seeming willingness to construe the Watergate case narrowly—

appeared to be enough to keep them from running afoul of the White House.

While all these moves were being made, the public was treated to a steady stream of categorical denials that the White House or the President's campaign committee had had anything to do with the break-in or with efforts to cover up the origins of the crime. The day after the break-in, Mitchell, in California, described James McCord, one of the burglars, as "the proprietor of a private security agency who was employed by our Committee months ago to assist with the installation of our security system." Actually, McCord was the committee's chief of security at the moment when he was arrested. Mitchell added, "We want to emphasize that this man and the other people involved were not operating either in our behalf or with our consent. . . . There is no place in our campaign or in the electoral process for this type of activity, and we will not permit nor condone it." On June 19th, two days after the break-in, Press Secretary Ziegler contemptuously dismissed press reports of White House involvement. "I'm not going to comment from the White House on a third-rate burglary attempt," he said. On June 20th, when Lawrence O'Brien, the chairman of the Democratic Party, revealed that the Party had brought a one-million-dollar civil-damages suit against the Committee for the Re-Election of the President and the five burglary suspects, charging invasion of privacy and violation of the civil rights of the Democrats, Mitchell stated that the action represented "another example of sheer demagoguery on the part of Mr. O'Brien." Mitchell said, "I reiterate that this committee did not authorize and does not condone the alleged actions of the five men apprehended there."

Among the nation's major newspapers, only one, the Washington *Post*, consistently gave the Watergate story prominent headlines on the front page. Most papers, when they dealt with the story at all, tended to treat it as something of a joke. All in all, the tone of the coverage was not unlike the coverage of the Clifford Irving affair the previous winter, and the volume of the coverage was, if anything, less. "Caper" was the word that most of the press settled upon to describe the incident. A week after the break-in, for instance, the

Times headlined its Watergate story WATERGATE CAPER. When another week had passed, and Howard Hunt's connection with the break-in had been made known, *Time* stated that the story was "fast stretching into the most provocative caper of 1972, an extraordinary bit of bungling of great potential advantage to the Democrats and damage to the Republicans in this election year." In early August, the *Times* was still running headlines like THE PLOT THICKENS IN WATERGATE WHODUNIT over accounts of the repercussions of the burglary. "Above all, the purpose of the break-in seemed obscure," the *Times* said. "But these details are never explained until the last chapter." The President held a news conference six weeks after the break-in, and by then the story was of such small interest to newsmen that not one question was asked concerning it.

Disavowals such as those made by Mitchell and Ziegler carried great weight in the absence of incontrovertible evidence refuting them. The public had grown accustomed to deception and evasion in high places, but not yet to repeated, consistent, barefaced lying at all levels. The very boldness of the lies raised the cost of contradicting them, for to do so would be to call high officials outright liars. Another effective White House technique was to induce semi-informed or wholly uninformed spokesmen to deny charges. One of these spokesmen was Clark MacGregor, a former member of Congress from Minnesota, who became reëlection-campaign director early in July, when John Mitchell resigned, pleading family difficulties. A few weeks later, when Senator McGovern described the break-in as "the kind of thing you expect under a person like Hitler," MacGregor called McGovern's remark "character assassination." The practice of using as spokesmen officials who were more or less innocent of the facts was one more refinement of the technique of dissociating "what we say" from "what we do." In this manner, honest men could be made to lend the weight of their integrity to untruths. They spoke words without knowing whether the words were true or false. Such spokesmen lent their vocal cords to the campaign but left their brains behind, and confused the public with words spoken by nobody.

The apprehension of the Watergate burglars marked a watershed in the progress of the systemic crisis that had been developing ever since President Nixon assumed office. It marked the moment when the expanding sphere of executive lawbreaking encountered law enforcement. In the spring of 1971, legal cases arising out of the Vietnam war and out of the habits of executive lawlessness that grew up during the war years had finally arrived in the courts in forms that the courts could not escape dealing with; and when that happened—in the Pentagon Papers case, in the case of William Calley, in the case of the demonstrations in Washington by the Vietnam Veterans Against the War, and in the case of the seizure of thousands of young people during the Washington Mayday demonstration—aspects of the crisis became adjudicable. Now things had gone one stage further. The White House undercover group that had been formed to "nail" Daniel Ellsberg had gone on to commit their other crimes, and the President had sought to cover up these crimes, and the lawbreaking within the executive branch had become indictable. Some of the President's men were in court as criminal defendants, and others, perhaps including the President, might soon be in court, too, if the criminal-justice system was allowed to work. Now the war, which had been coming home for years in countless forms, was all the way home. The body of secret information which had begun to build up in the White House as far back as the Kennedy years had grown to a size that was unmanageable within the framework of a Constitutional democracy. The underground history of the United States was threatening to burst into the open. The situation was beyond limited repair jobs; the coverup that was now required extended to all branches of the government. Already, a huge quantity of secret information having to do with the actions of past Administrations—the Pentagon Papers —had poured out (the objections of the Nixon Administration had been strenuous), and since the end of the period covered in the Pentagon Papers a new mass of secret information had accumulated.

At some point in the Nixon years, the importance of this underground history had superseded that of the aboveground history; that is, the underground stream had swollen to the point where if it should come to light in its entirety it might alter the future of the United States more radically than any or all of the events that were being reported in the newspapers. Revelation of the full story of the White House undercover operations might, for instance, decide the outcome of the forthcoming Presidential election. And just such a revelation threatened, for each figure in the Watergate story, if he were ever to talk freely to investigators, could disclose large bodies of hidden information. The undercover operative John Caulfield could disclose the tapping and bugging of newsmen—information that might lead, in turn, to full publication of the circumstances surrounding the secret bombing of Cambodia. And Caulfield, together with Ulasewicz, could disclose the complete story of the clandestine White House surveillance of rival political figures, including the shadowing of Senator Edward Kennedy, and also disclose such schemes as the aborted plan to firebomb the Brookings Institution. And they could disclose Herbert Kalmbach's involvement in making secret payoffs. Kalmbach could tell about the secret Administration funds and all the uses they had been put to: among other things, supporting George Wallace's opponent for governor in the 1970 Alabama primary, and establishing the special undercover network headed by Donald Segretti. Then the connection with Segretti might lead to information on the entire program of sabotage waged against the Democrats in the Presidential primaries. Kalmbach could also alert investigators to the millions of dollars that were raised for the President's reëlection campaign through extortion and the sale of government favors. And he could tell of how he took over from Hunt the job of paying attorneys for the Watergate burglars. If Hunt and Liddy should ever speak freely, they, too, would have quite a bit to tell. They could describe the attempted break-ins at Senator McGovern's campaign headquarters; the shadowy scheme to break into a publisher's safe in Las Vegas to obtain documents having to do with Howard Hughes; the plan to destroy Ellsberg, both by attacking his image and by attacking him physically on the Capitol steps; the power struggle with Hoover over possession of the summaries of the warrantless taps; the attempt to destroy Hoover's image; and the forgery of State Department cables implicating President Kennedy in the murder of President Ngo Dinh Diem. John Dean, who in time passed on from Hunt to the President requests for more defense money which were tantamount to blackmail, was the key to still another world of White House misdeeds: the manipulation of government agencies to punish opponents and reward supporters; the use of the F.B.I. to harass newsmen and other "enemies"; and the short-circuiting of investigations into the White House in the Watergate case. And knowledge of these matters could easily lead investigators back to the attempts to subvert the intelligence agencies and employ them to harass and commit crimes against domestic political groups that the Administration disapproved of. No *limited* coverup could contain indefinitely as much information as this. No free press could live alongside as much information as this without sooner or later tripping over some of it. No Congress could conduct even its ordinary business without finding out something sooner or later. No judicial system could overlook as much crime as this and go on operating to uphold the law. And yet if the information did come out, the survival of the Administration was in peril. Thus, a total coverup, which would mean the irrecoverable collapse of the press, the Congress, and the courts, was now the only way to save the Administration itself from debacle.

During the summer and early fall, a good deal of information about the origins of the break-in was made public. It became known (through interviews given to the press by Alfred Baldwin, a former F.B.I. agent and the member of the Watergate break-in team who had been in charge of the monitoring equipment) that transcripts of phone conversations tapped by the Watergate bugging team had been delivered to someone at the Committee for the Re-Election of the President. It became known (through White House and campaign-committee responses to the inquiries of reporters) that G. Gordon Liddy and E. Howard Hunt had once worked for the White House. And it became known (through the investigative reporting of the Washington *Post*) that twenty-five thousand dollars that had been given as a contribution to the Nixon campaign had been deposited in a Florida bank to the account of Bernard Barker, who was one of the Watergate burglars. These facts seemed to point to certain inescapable conclusions, but somehow the public's interest was not awakened. A poll taken in October showed that only half of the public had even heard of the break-in. Stories pertaining to the aboveground history of the country dominated the news. As the Democrats headed toward their National Convention, an intraparty struggle broke out over the candidates' claims on the votes of several state delegations. Hubert Humphrey, having lost the whole California delegation to Senator McGovern in an all-or-nothing primary vote, now argued that the rules under which the primary had been conducted should not be binding on the Convention, and that he and the other primary candidates should receive the numbers of delegates proportionate to their shares of the vote. In early July, the Convention was held, in Miami Beach, and Senator McGovern won the nomination. Shortly after that, it was revealed that the running mate he had chosen, Senator Thomas Eagleton, of Missouri, had twice undergone shock treatment for mental depression, and Eagleton was forced off the ticket. These stories filled the headlines in the summer and fall of 1972. They were stories natural for a campaign season, yet they were not the pivotal stories in the political life of the time. The pivotal stories were the ones having to do with the hidden encounter between the Nixon Administration and the law. The *Times* noted in an editorial that the campaign had an "unreal" quality, and the writer's intuition was more soundly based than anyone could have guessed at the time. The public had come to live in a world of unreality. Usually, the main events of current history are to be found in the headlines of each day's papers, but now the nation had, in a sense, been temporarily separated from its current history. The footnotes of current American history were in the headlines, and the chapter headings were buried in the back pages or were absent altogether.

On June 30th, Vice-President Agnew described Senator McGovern as "one of the greatest frauds ever to be considered a Presidential candidate by a major American party." When Senator Muskie's campaign faltered in the spring, the White House had adopted a policy of clandestinely supporting Senator McGovern's candidacy. Patrick Buchanan had written in an April memo, "McGovern's The One." And later that month he had written, "The temptations will be high in many quarters to go after McGovern, but word ought to go out to lay off. . . . We have plenty of time to attach labels later." Buchanan would allow one exception to this rule: McGovern should be attacked on the war issue. The purpose, however, was not to hurt McGovern's candidacy but to help it: "He can be hit hard on this subject—a point which not only elevates his candidacy but also gets the President's position restated while reinforcing the strong anti-war sentiment behind McGovern." Buchanan also recommended helping out candidates to the left of McGovern. He recommended that the White House secretly channel whatever help it could to the candidacy of Dr. Benjamin Spock, the renowned pediatrician and anti-war activist, who was also running for President that year. Votes for Spock, Buchanan observed in his memo, would come "one for one" out of "the hide of George McGovern." Now, in June, the time for applying labels had arrived. The strategy would be to "tar McGovern as an extremist," Buchanan wrote. A lot of thought had gone into just which label to apply. "There is a strong feeling on our part that the term 'radical' was overused in 1970, that it has lost much of its electric charge, that the term 'extremist' is a far more difficult one to defend against," Buchanan went on. The strategy for the next five months, then, was to secretly promote extremism within the Democratic Party and then publicly denounce extremism in the Democratic Party.

Buchanan had also given some thought to a special problem. How, Buchanan asked in an "Assault Book" he had put together,

271

could the President, who was now running as the man who quieted the country down and made peace, "recapture the anti-Establishment tradition or theme in American politics"? Buchanan looked back fondly to 1969, the heyday of "positive polarization," when the campaign to divide the country had been right out in the open, instead of being the furtive business it was now. But how could a President, apparently the leading figure in "the Establishment," also be "anti-Establishment"? "Incumbent Presidents *can* do this," Buchanan insisted. "RN did it in November, 1969, when, as President of U.S., he called on the common man to stand with him against the élitist-backed mobs in the streets. That, coupled with the Vice-President's standing up to the Establishment media and slugging it out, raised RN to the highest point of his Presidency—69 per-cent approval. . . . RN led both the Presidency position and the anti-Establishment position." Alert observers of the Nixon Presidency had often noted the "anti-Establishment" streak in the President. Some of these observers, seeking answers to their questions in psychological analyses of his character, thought that his rage against "the Establishment" and his need to destroy it arose from an irremediable inability ever to fully believe that he had actually been given the highest honor in the gift of the American people, and thought that his additions to the pomp of his office—such as the use of trumpeters to herald his entrance on state occasions—were part of a strenuous but losing effort to convince himself that he was indeed the President. But none of these observers suspected that the President and his advisers were themselves aware of his ambivalence and were deliberately exploiting it for political gain.

The Republican Convention was held toward the end of August. In the days leading up to it, the Resolutions Committee went through the motions of preparing to write a platform. It heard witnesses. (In a break with tradition, a number of Cabinet officers—including William Rogers, the Secretary of State; Melvin Laird, the Secretary of Defense; and Elliot Richardson, the Secretary of Health, Education, and Welfare—came to praise the President and attack his political opposition.) It held closed meetings. It discussed the issues. But it did not write a platform. That had already been done, at the White House. The White House document—whose very existence was supposed to be a secret, since the Resolutions Committee was so elaborately pretending to write the platform—was protected by means usually reserved for state secrets. When secretaries typed copies of it, guards were posted behind them to stop them from making any extra copies. The platform was carefully kept out of the hands of the Resolutions Committee. Not only did the members not write the platform but they were not allowed to read it. Instead, there came a night when the committee broke up into closed meetings of its subcommittees, and at each meeting an emissary from the White House appeared bearing a copy of the platform in a red binder and read out the section having to do with that subcommittee's business. No subcommittee was allowed to lay eyes on the document or to hear what was in other parts of it. At least one committee member was displeased. "We only heard seventeen pages of the platform read," he said to a reporter, and he added, "I am a lawyer, and I like to see something in print." Only one witness likely to give testimony questioning the platform—Senator Jacob Javits, of New York—was allowed before the full committee. Representative Donald Riegle, of Michigan, a strong critic of the President's policies, was barred from speaking before it; the committee chairman, Representative John Rhodes, of Arizona, was reported to have told him, "You're crazy if you think anyone is going to appear before the full committee that would say anything to embarrass the President." Many of the state caucuses, when they got going, were closed to reporters and the public. The chairman of the New York State delegation explained why his caucus was closed. "We want to discuss . . . very important questions without the impediment at this stage of outside influences on our thinking process," he said.

The White House took over the entire Doral Hotel, in Miami Beach, as its headquarters, and large signs reading "Closed to the Public" were put up in front of the hotel. Guards equipped with walkie-talkies were posted in the driveway to keep unauthorized people out. Each of the hotel employees, including the life guards at its pools, was obliged to wear a card around his neck bearing his name and his photograph. Plastic badges of different colors were issued to Republicans of different rank—white for the more important Republicans, red for the working staff, and blue for volunteer and professional workers. Badges were required for getting out of the hotel as well as for getting in. (A former member of Congress from Georgia who was also an official of the Republican National Committee was prevented from leaving until he could produce his badge.) In the hotel, the badges had to be worn at all times. A memo to badgeholders marked "Confidential" warned them emphatically, "If you plan to swim, walk, sunbathe, etc., *bring your credential*." Men were seen around the pools wearing their credentials on their bathing trunks. The same memo described several special facilities that had been installed at the hotel for the Republicans' use. "While at the hotel," the memo read, "you are requested to put all sensitive paper in the 'confidential burn' bags found in every office. These are not general trash bags but for sensitive memos, papers, etc. only. At approximately 9 P.M. each day, a security officer will pick up these bags. A paper shredder is available in the security office." And the memo went on to say, "The hotel will be totally secured and considered a restricted area." Special regulations were in force for interviews with reporters. All interviews were to be set up through a central desk. The memo to the Republicans advised, "You will be notified when your appointment has arrived. A temporary badge or ID will be issued, and your appointment will be escorted to the location you request. Following the appointment, please escort your guests back to the reception desk in the hotel lobby so that they may be checked out and their ID returned. Guests with a temporary badge must be escorted at all times." There were no plans for the President to stay at the Doral. The lavish security had nothing to do with his safety; it had to do with Party business.

Until James McCord was arrested in the headquarters of the Democratic National Committee in Washington, he had been in charge of planning "security" for the Republican Convention. Now his successors had planned the Republican Convention as though the

Democrats were going to do to the Republicans what James McCord and his colleagues and Donald Segretti and his agents had been doing to the Democrats. However, the Democrats were not doing these things, and the entire "security" operation was pointless. The thinking of President Nixon and his aides seemed to run in a circle. They seemed to form their impression of how the opposition was behaving by studying the pattern of their own behavior while at the same time patterning their own behavior on their misimpression of how badly the opposition was behaving; and in the process they gave themselves a license to misbehave.

At the Convention Hall, a towering, many-tiered cream-colored rostrum had been put up, so that speakers addressing the Convention looked down upon the audience as though from the ramparts of a castle. In back of the rostrum were three giant movie screens. As the Convention began, instructions such as DELEGATES AND ALTERNATES PLEASE BE SEATED flashed on these screens. On the floor of the Convention, passes given to the press read "Limited Access." A group called Young Voters for the President was stationed in one section of the galleries. They had been organized by the White House and brought to the Convention from around the country, and were divided into three battalions, each a thousand strong and each supplied with identification badges of a separate color. The battalions were divided, in turn, into units of a hundred, identified by letters of the alphabet. Throughout the Convention, the Young Voters for the President were bused from event to event on a tight schedule, and everywhere they went they shouted, "Four more years! Four more years!"—the President's campaign slogan of that election season. Stephen Nostrand, the staff director of Young Voters for the President, explained the system to a reporter. "If the President calls and says, 'I need five hundred kids at a press conference,' we can get them there in twenty minutes," he said.

As the Convention got under way, Senator Goldwater set the tone for the proceedings by describing the opposition as an alien force whose aim in the election was to destroy the United States. "I would like to call attention to what happened last month when the shattered remnants of a once great party met in this city, and

275

what I listened to and saw on my television set made me question whether I was sitting in the United States or someplace else," he said, speaking of the Democratic Convention. At that Convention, relatively large numbers of young people, women, and black people had attended as delegates, partly because of a quota system insuring their representation at the Convention in numbers roughly equal to their representation in the population, and Senator Goldwater had apparently been horrified by what he had seen. He went on to say of Senator McGovern and his supporters, "They just wait, like the old coyotes, until they can tear something down or destroy a part of America." Shortly after Senator Goldwater's speech, a film titled *Richard Nixon—Portrait of a President* was shown. (A film about the President's wife, *Pat—Tribute to a First Lady*, had been shown earlier.) In *Portrait of a President*, President Nixon's subordinates in the White House were heard praising him. Among them was Henry Kissinger, who said, "There's a certain—you know, it's a big word—but it's a certain heroic quality about how he conducts his business. . . . Of course, I can only judge foreign policy, and I believe that his impact on foreign policy will be historic, no matter what happens." The film showed scenes of President Nixon with Chairman Mao Tse-tung and Chairman Leonid Brezhnev. Many of the delegates and speakers at the Convention were ardent anti-Communists and had not been pleased with the President's trips to China and Russia, but none objected to seeing images of Chairman Mao and Chairman Brezhnev at their Convention. Nor were dissenting voices heard on the left. President Nixon had had only one challenger on the left in the primaries, Representative Paul McCloskey, of California, and he had won a single delegate. However, the rules committee, faced with this threat to the smooth operation of the proceedings, decided at the last minute that no candidate could be placed in nomination unless he had the backing of a majority of the delegates of three states. John Ehrlichman explained to a reporter that allowing McCloskey's name to be placed in nomination would be "a time-waster."

The day before the Convention opened, the platform was at last released. "The contest," it read, "is not between the two great parties Americans have known in previous years. For in this year 1972 the national Democratic Party has been seized by a radical clique which scorns our nation's past and would blight her future." Then, having drawn a distinction between the "great" traditional Democratic Party and the radical clique that had "seized" it, the platform went on to deride the Democratic record in its "great" days under President Johnson. "The choice," the platform asserted, "is between going forward from dramatic achievements to predictable new achievements, or turning back toward a nightmarish time in which the torch of free America was virtually snuffed out in a storm of violence and protest." The platform gave a description of life in those days: "It is so easy to forget how frightful it was. There was Vietnam —so bloody, so costly, so bitterly divisive. At home our horrified people watched our cities burn, crime burgeon, campuses dissolve into chaos . . . and yet, as our eyes were fixed on the carnage in Asia, in Europe our alliance had weakened. The Western will was dividing and ebbing. The isolation of the People's Republic of China, with one-fourth of the world's population, went endlessly on. . . . To millions of Americans it seemed we had lost our way. . . . So it was when our Republican Party came to power." Then, making use of the "great helmsman" image that President Nixon's recent hosts the Chinese favored in describing their leader, the platform presented a picture of life in Richard Nixon's America: "Now, four years later, a new leadership with new policies and new programs has restored reason and order and hope. No longer buffeted by internal violence and division, we are on course in calmer seas with a sure, steady hand at the helm. A new spirit, buoyant and confident, is on the rise in our land, nourished by the changes we have made. It is a saga of exhilarating progress. . . . Looking to tomorrow, to President Nixon's second term and on into the third century of this Republic, we of the Republican Party see a quarter-billion Americans, peaceful and prosperous as never before, humane as never before, their nation strong and just as never before." The platform gave the President's new campaign image, which had by then been in the making for close to two years, its fullest expression so far. "Positive polarization" had gone down the memory hole. All that—the demonstrations of 1969, the uproar following the invasion of Cambodia, the killings at Kent State University, the "age of anarchy" that the voters had been invited to oppose by voting for the President's men in the congressional elections of 1970—had been expunged from the record. The present was revised as well. The mining of the harbors of North Vietnam and the nation's recent trip to the brink of nuclear war were cut out of the record, leaving only the trips to China and Russia and the structure of peace as the official events of the period. The war in Vietnam had been excised from the President's image once and for all, and was now mentioned only in the past tense. ("It is so easy to forget how frightful it was. There was Vietnam.") Nevertheless, the war went on existing in the image that had been arranged for Senator McGovern—as it did, indeed, in the real world —and he was portrayed as being "bemused with surrender," and ready to perform an "act of betrayal" by withdrawing American forces.

The Convention moved ahead, and new voices rose in praise of the President. The White House staff had been heard from, and now many of the President's former political rivals and antagonists were brought in. Governor Nelson Rockefeller, who had opposed Nixon for the Republican nomination four years earlier, placed his name in nomination. Former Secretary of the Interior Walter Hickel seconded the nomination. Then ten more people seconded the nomination, including a Spanish-American leader, a Vietnam veteran, a former astronaut, the wife of a Democratic mayor, and a Polish-American member of Congress. When the vote was held, the President was renominated by a margin of one thousand three hundred and forty-seven to one.

On the day of the President's nomination, however, a document fell into the hands of the press which showed the atmosphere of enthusiasm for the President in a new light. It was a script for the Convention, and it had been written in the White House. Impromptu remarks, places for applause, and even gestures for the speakers to make were written out in the script. For example, the script instructed one speaker, a former football quarterback, to "nod" to a group of young people at a certain moment. It allotted the amounts of time, calculated to the minute, for screams of enthusiasm and shouts of "Four more years" from the Young Voters for the President. It was not only the platform, therefore, but the whole Convention that had been secretly written at the White House. In a memo dealing with the Convention, Buchanan had advised, "The attack speeches should be orchestrated and advanced, with an audience cheering at the right lines, the way the President did it himself in 1968, in his acceptance speech." (This appears to be the sole reference on record to the President's having staged the response to his acceptance speech of 1968.) And Buchanan recommended that the White House "help draft the speeches for the attacks on the Democrats." (Indeed, some of the President's supporters had in effect renounced their intention of speaking for themselves, and had allowed the White House to designate them publicly as "surrogates" of the President. The President, of course, was alleged to be too busy with affairs of state to occupy himself very much with mere campaigning.) Needless to say, there was no mention in the Convention script of that other, far more crucial White House "script" for the 1972 campaign—the one that Anthony Ulasewicz was promoting in conversations in phone booths, and that the Watergate defendants and their lawyers were supposed to act out. One woman at the Convention, Mrs. Nora Hussey, a National Committeewoman-elect from South Dakota, found the atmosphere puzzling. She said to a reporter, "When you get a group of people this large together, it's bound to be exciting. But maybe it isn't exciting. I can't really tell."

The events surrounding the President's nomination, in particular, had been a tour de force of orchestration. The script specified that when the vote was announced, the Convention chairman, Representative Gerald Ford, would try to restrain the delegates' enthusiasm but would be unsuccessful. After the nomination was voted upon, he would read out, "Would the delegates please come to order. The vote of all the delegates has been recorded. I am informed that . . ." And then his voice would be drowned out by screams of delight, launching a demonstration for which the script allotted exactly twelve minutes. In the event, Ford made his remark, and the demonstration went off as planned. As the demonstration ended, the President unexpectedly appeared on the Convention's giant screens. He was about to speak to a rally of young people in a stadium some ten miles away. The President's screen appearance had been carefully stage-managed. A White House aide had been stationed outside the Convention Hall in a communications van that allowed for simultaneous contact with the proceedings on the floor of the Convention and the President's motorcade making its way to the youth rally. After the roll call, as the delegates took to the Convention floor to engage in their twelve-minute display of enthusiasm for the renominated President, the aide in the van directed the motorcade to slow down and the officials on the floor of the Convention to get the delegates back to their seats. Once the delegates had settled down, the motorcade was directed to pick up speed. The President, when he reached the youth rally, paused briefly, and then, on a signal from the van, with the cameras at the rally now relaying the episode to the Convention's screens, he jumped up and embraced the master of ceremonies.

The following evening, a helicopter bore the President to the site of the Convention to make his acceptance speech. Two other helicopters, each emblazoned with the Presidential Seal and the numeral "1," flew alongside, the idea being to confuse any possible attackers. The President's role in the Convention script was, of course, special. He was the object of the praise that had been pouring out during the whole Convention. On such an occasion, the usual thing for the nominee to do is to acknowledge the praise he has heard and to make a few gracious remarks that might be appropriate to an object of praise. And since President Nixon was not only running for the Presidency but *was* the President, and was then running some thirty percentage points ahead of his rival in the polls, there seemed no need for anything more aggressive. Moreover, the strategy of the campaign had been to let the lesser people—the surrogates—wrangle with the Democrats and to "use" the President only *"in extremis,"* as Patrick Buchanan had put it in his memo on "Dividing the Democrats." Indeed, the entire strategy of the campaign, starting as far back as 1970, had been to embroil the Democrats in unseemly partisan squabbling while elevating the President "above" politics, in a realm of statesmanlike calm. The President began his acceptance speech in the apparently inevitable vein. "I shall not dwell on the record of our Administration, which has been praised, perhaps too generously, by others at this Convention," he said. In saying this, he seemed to acknowledge his special position in the proceedings as the object of the delegates' praise. But the next moment, ignoring his announcement that he would not dwell on the record of his Administration, he seemed to forget that special position. "It can truly be said that we have changed America and that America has changed the world," he said, the tone of his words indistinguishable from that of the Party platform. Then he moved into a bitter attack on the opposition. "The critics," the President said, "contend it [the American system] is so unfair, so corrupt, so unjust that we should tear it down." (Actually, Senator McGovern had never suggested tearing down the American system.) And the President went on, "Let us reject, therefore, the policies of those who whine and whimper about our frustrations and call on us to turn inward. Let us not turn away from greatness."

Observers groped for words to describe the speech. *Time* called it "curiously flat." James Reston called it a "slashing partisan attack that was a jumble of distortions, misleading half-truths, and downright lies." Senator McGovern called it "the strangest Presidential acceptance speech in American history." Somewhere, it had been decided that the President, too, must praise the President. The President had become one more idolater of the Presidential image. But in doing so he had deprived the image of its object: the calm helmsman—the President. In his memo on "Dividing the Democrats," Patrick Buchanan had described the President and the Presidency as "the quintessential political assets," to be employed only in an emergency. But someone, even in the absence of an emergency, had not been able to resist putting the assets to use. And so the President, instead of exemplifying the qualities of great statesmanship which had been described all week, abused the opposition and praised the leadership of the last several years as though he, too, were waiting for "the President" to arrive. *He* had become a surrogate. The image had eclipsed its object. The script had swallowed up its author.

The Republican Convention brought to perfection in microcosm a Nixonian style of action which had been developing since he first assumed office. For years, the President's speechwriters and public-relations advisers had been engaged in a novel enterprise. Most Presidential speechwriters have restricted themselves to writing what the President employing them is to say, but President Nixon's speechwriters also involved themselves in writing what was said about the President by others. They wrote the plays, and they wrote the reviews, too. The White House writers wrote speeches for Administration officials and friendly members of Congress to deliver about the President. (At the Convention, they even wrote the cues for the applause to those speeches.) They wrote rigged letters-to-the-editor and telegrams-to-the-editor with messages like "Thank goodness this country has President Nixon." They had organized campaigns of telegrams of support to be sent to the White House, tried to arrange for newspaper columns to be written supporting the President. And, since the President's speechwriters are, probably to a greater degree than any other employees of the government, creatures of his power —are, in fact, his alter egos, or "ghosts"—it could be said that the praise for the President which they arranged was in fact praise of the President for himself. The true author of the statement "Thank goodness this country has President Nixon" was President Nixon. The scorekeeper who in a "telegram" to a news organization scored the President's press conference "President Nixon, 100—Media, o" was none other than the President. And yet in the country at large, no matter how many telegrams of support the President sent to himself, and no matter how many letters-to-the-editor were dispatched, and no matter how many surrogates were appointed to read the President's opinion of himself to the public, and no matter how severely the President and his aides assailed the press, the result, although impressive, was in his view imperfect. Discordant voices were still heard. "Unfair" comments still reached the President's ear. The President found that the sound of his own voice streaming back to him from a chorus of a thousand surrogates was spoiled by murmurs that were off-key. Other voices, other wills interfered.

The world of the Convention was different. In the Republican Party, it turned out, the White House had a perfectly malleable material. Here was a group wholly "responsive" to the President's wishes. No one here, it seemed, had the ability or the will to substitute his own "subjective judgment" for that of the President—as the President had accused the Senate of doing when it was rejecting the second of his nominees for a Supreme Court vacancy, in 1970. There were no Democratic "holdovers" here to carry on "internal guerrilla warfare" against the President's policies, no "critics" to make unfair comments on them. No "reorganization" was needed. In the Convention world, the imperfections of the wider world were ironed out, and one will reigned absolute. The Republicans at the Convention had not even insisted on praising the President with their own voices. They had almost certainly been willing to praise the President spontaneously and to applaud with genuine enthusiasm the speeches of others praising him, but the White House preferred the manufactured article to the real thing. It preferred the script. The delegates' impulses had been replaced by White House impulses, their words had been pushed aside by White House words, their gestures had been suppressed in favor of White House gestures. A political Convention is often seen as a glimpse of the party's vision of the America which would take shape under its stewardship. Certainly the Republicans had chosen to interpret the Democratic Conventions of 1968 and 1972 in this way. At the Republican Convention of 1972, the proceedings were made to seem spontaneous and joyful but were in reality minutely regimented and carefully staged; the press had "Limited Access"; no "outside influences" were allowed to disrupt the "thinking processes" of the decision-makers; and the public business was "Closed to the Public."

The day after the Convention ended, Vice-President Agnew held a press conference. He announced that he was changing his public image. He had been left out of the last change in the White House image—perhaps because he was indelibly engraved in the public's mind as a proponent of the earlier, supposedly discarded image of "positive polarization." When it was thrown away, after the 1970 congressional elections, as the dominant image in the White House propaganda, he was, in effect, thrown away, too. In truth, he had never been highly respected by those who programmed him at the White House. To some there, he had been known as "the clown." For a while, it seemed that he might be dumped from the ticket; in fact, Haldeman and Nixon had talked over the possibility of replacing Agnew on the 1972 ticket with Secretary of the Treasury John Connally. Still, as a White House staff member put it to a reporter, "Agnew is a monster, but he's Nixon's monster," so Agnew was kept on. The Vice-President's acceptance speech at the Convention had heralded the change in image. Some parts of his speech had sounded like a brief against his own role in the first term. "At this time," he said, "when some people seem determined to fasten group labels on people and in the process to turn American against American, it would be well to remember that this kind of behavior is not progressive but regressive." While Buchanan was writing long memos pondering which labels to apply to McGovern, the Vice-President was accusing McGovern of being the man who had a penchant for attaching labels. (In one respect, the Vice-President had not changed: he still liked to use unusual words. Speaking of any attempt that might be made to divide the nation, he added, "It is not reform but recidivism.") At his press conference, he explained that in his divisive days he had played the role of the "cutting edge" of the Republican Party, because he had been a "team player" and had been "the President's man." As for the present, he said, "If I seem conciliatory, I am."

As President Nixon's scenarios for national and world politics multiplied and expanded, scenarios on a much smaller scale came to rule the day-to-day routine of life in the White House—even its tiniest details. In these minute matters, as in the large ones, President Nixon was preoccupied above all with the appearance of things.

Alexander Butterfield, whose office adjoined President Nixon's, later told a congressional committee, "Social functions were always reviewed with him, the scenario, after they came to me from Mrs. Nixon." Butterfield also said, "The President often, of course, was concerned whether or not the curtains were closed or open; the arrangement of state gifts; whether they should be on that side of the room or this side of the room; displayed on a weekly basis or on a monthly basis. . . . He was deeply involved in the entertainment business—whom we should get, for what kind of group, small band, big band, black band, white band, jazz band, whatever. He was very interested in meals and how they were served and the time of the waiters. . . . He wanted to see the plan, see the scenarios; he wanted to view the musical selections himself. He was very interested in whether or not salad should be served and decided that at small dinners of eight or less the salad course should not be served." The President, Butterfield went on, took a detailed interest in the pageantry of White House occasions. When a ceremony of some kind was to be held at the White House, the President wanted to know "whether or not [it] should be public on the South Grounds or whether we should have only administrative personnel; the details of the drive up the walkway; whether the military would be to the right or left; which uniforms would be worn by the White House police; whether or not the Secret Service would salute during 'The Star-Spangled Banner' and sing; where the photographer would be." At least as great as the President's passion for meticulously prearranging events was his passion for recording the meticulously arranged events as they occurred. The President placed himself under the scrutiny of several overlapping systems of surveillance. Secret Service agents, White House "ushers," military aides to the President, and White House switchboard operators were required to note down every meeting he held, every phone call he initiated or received, and, generally speaking, every move he made. At the end of each day, the notes were turned in to a central office, where a Presidential "diary" was put together. Also, aides who sat in on any of the President's meetings were required to take rough notes. These were then collected—"for the President's file," as Butterfield put it.

Butterfield recalled that "he was wholly taken up with history." Any notes that the President himself might take for any purpose were collected by his personal secretary, Rose Mary Woods. The President sometimes transformed himself from political actor into political reporter, and gave an account of the day's events to a Dictaphone. In addition, there was, of course, the automatic taping system. And if some nuance of the President's utterances should happen to escape this small army of scribes and collection of machines, it might be captured by aides who had been asked to serve as "anecdotists," or "color reporters," as Butterfield put it, and who were to record "vignettes of human interest." These vignettes, too, were to go in a file "for history." So thorough was the President's reporting system that even the reactions of guests to each of several paintings that had been hung in the West Lobby of the White House were to be written down, Butterfield recalled, in order "to see how popular" each painting "might be to guests who were awaiting appointments in the West Lobby."

The President's preoccupation with "history" seemed to deepen as his second term progressed. According to Butterfield, "He would write little notes on precisely what time he finished handwriting a portion of a speech—3:14 A.M. He made it known to me in various ways that he wanted to be sure that that 3:14 got someplace, was logged." The President seemed to have developed a habit of looking back on himself as if from a thousand years in the future, and to have developed a nagging anxiety that some of his actions and words might be lost. (As far as is known, it was this anxiety, more than anything else, that inspired the President to install the automatic taping system.) In the President's thinking, a ceremony could be historic even in its planning stages, and the President was evidently determined, through the use of scenarios, to plan every detail of every event. What he most disliked, it seemed, was anything that might happen of itself, unauthorized by him, and even unforeseen by him, since that, when it was recorded, might provide unwanted details in the "historical" account that he was assembling. Historians write history after the event; President Nixon was attempting to write "history" before the event. The attempt to determine the content of historical accounts that would one day be written was in keeping with the President's concern with images, for the historical image was, of course, the final image of his Administration.

On September 15th, the five men who had been caught in the Democratic National Committee headquarters were indicted—together with E. Howard Hunt and G. Gordon Liddy, who were elsewhere in the Watergate complex at the time of the break-in—for the felonies of burglary, conspiracy, and wiretapping. A few days later, the seven defendants pleaded not guilty. As the case stood at that moment, their crimes were officially motiveless. The prosecutors had not been able to suggest who might have asked employees of the Committee for the Re-Election of the President to wiretap the Democratic headquarters, or why a check belonging to that committee should have found its way into the bank account of Bernard Barker. That afternoon, the President met with Haldeman and Dean, and congratulated Dean on his work. "Well," he said, "the whole thing is a can of worms. . . . But the, but the way you, you've handled it, it seems to me, has been very skillful, because you—putting your fingers in the dikes every time that leaks have sprung here and sprung there." Representative Wright Patman, the chairman of the House Banking and Currency Committee, was planning to hold hearings on the Watergate break-in, and the President, Dean, and Haldeman went on to discuss ways of "turning that off," as Dean put it. Dean reported to the two others that he was studying the possibility of blackmailing members of the Patman committee with damaging information about their own campaigns, and then the President suggested that Representative Ford, who was the minority leader of the House, would be the man to pressure Patman into dropping the hearings. Ford should be told that "he's got to get at this and screw this thing up while he can," the President said. Two and a half weeks later, a majority of the members of the committee voted to deny Patman the power to subpoena witnesses. But Patman made the gesture of carrying on anyway for a while, and asked questions of an empty chair.

At the end of September—more than a month before the election—
the Washington *Post* reported that John Mitchell had had control of
a secret fund for spying on the Democrats. Throughout October,
denials continued to pour out from the Administration. As before,
some were outright lies by men who knew the facts, and others were
untruths spoken by men who were simply repeating what they had
been told. On October 2nd, Acting Director Gray of the F.B.I. said
that it was unreasonable to believe that the President had deceived
the nation about Watergate. "Even if some of us [in federal law
enforcement agencies] are crooked, there aren't that many that are.
I don't believe everyone is a Sir Galahad, but there's not been one
single bit of pressure put on me or any of my special agents." In
reality, of course, Gray had once considered resigning because the
pressure from the White House to help with the coverup had been
so intense, and even as he spoke he was keeping the contents of
E. Howard Hunt's safe in a drawer of a dresser at his home in
Connecticut. Gray went on to say, "It strains the credulity that the
President of the United States—if he had a mind to—could have done
a con job on the whole American people." Gray added, "He would
have to control the United States."

On October 5th, the President, speaking at a news conference,
attempted to make a campaign issue out of a charge by Senator
McGovern that he was "the most deceitful President in history" and
that his Administration was "the most corrupt in history." Nixon
predicted that Democrats would be put off by such charges. The
following day, the Republican campaign chairman, Clark Mac-
Gregor, charged McGovern with having used "gutter tactics," and
asked rhetorically, "What will next week's slander be?" Two days
later, Republican congressional leaders filed a formal complaint
with the Fair Campaign Practices Committee, charging that Senator
McGovern and his staff were using "smear" techniques, which were
"an affront to every American and a disgrace to the political process."

The complaint cited, among other things, a statement that was alleged to have been made by the political director of McGovern's campaign, Frank Mankiewicz: "Richard Nixon is a shifty politician and he always has been."

On October 10th, the Washington *Post* ran a story revealing the White House sabotage of the Democratic Presidential primaries by Donald Segretti and his team, and Press Secretary Ziegler, after a careful rehearsal in the White House, said that the *Post* story was "based on hearsay, innuendo, and guilt by association."

In a speech on October 13th, the "new Agnew" unveiled his definition of "the American philosophy." It was a belief in the primacy of reason in public affairs, the acceptance of the need for a just order based on law, and "acknowledgment of a transcendent moral order."

On October 15th, the President said in a radio address, "I will work unceasingly to halt the erosion of moral fibre in American life, and the denial of individual accountability for individual action. Government must never become so preoccupied with catering to the way-out wants of those who reject all respect for moral and legal values that it forgets the citizen's first civil right—the right to be free from domestic violence."

On October 21st, the President derided what he said was the philosophy of his "critics." "To them, the will of the people is 'the prejudice of the masses,'" he said. "They deride anyone who wants to respond to that will of the people as 'pandering to the crowd.' A decent respect for the practice of majority rule is automatically denounced as 'political expedience.'" He added, "I totally reject this philosophy." He took his stand with the majority. "It is time that good, decent people stop letting themselves be bulldozed by anybody who presumes to be the self-righteous moral judge of our society," he said. He assured the majority that "there is no reason to feel guilty about wanting to enjoy what you get and get what you earn, about wanting your children in good schools close to home or about wanting to be judged fairly on your ability." The President offered to protect the people against the self-righteous moral judges who made them feel guilty. Describing as "values" the people's wants he had just mentioned, he said, "Those are values to be proud of; those are values that I shall always stand up for when they come under attack."

On October 26th, twelve days before the election, Henry Kissinger told a relieved and grateful nation that peace was "at hand" in Vietnam.

Four days before the election, Senator McGovern charged that peace was not at hand. "What we are seeing in this campaign is the manipulation of our hope by men who know how to get power and want to keep it, but do not know what it is for," he said, and he added, "In politics, there are some things more precious than victory. One of them is truth. But these men will say anything to win."

The press, on the whole, accepted President Nixon's assertions that McGovern's charges against him derived from self-righteousness, and, of all the words it used to describe McGovern in this period, "righteous" and "self-righteous" were perhaps the most common. (Indeed, the White House was so pleased with the press coverage of McGovern that it made a decision to let up on its attacks on the press for the duration of the campaign.) The preëlection issue of *Newsweek* was characteristic. In an article titled "McGovern's Politics of Righteousness," it stated, disapprovingly, "The issue, in his campaign, is no longer merely peace against war, or the people against the interests; it is 'a coalition of conscience and decency' against 'the most corrupt and immoral Administration in history.' " The article closed by noting, "To argue that the society is unjust is to demand further changes of a people grown weary of change. The failure of George McGovern's evangelism, if that is the final outcome next week, may not be that his manner is too cool but that what he is trying to tell America is too hot." In the same issue, Stewart Alsop wrote that McGovern thinks "he is running . . . against Satan," and after dismissing McGovern's charges against Nixon as exaggerated he concluded, "And thus what seems to McGovern self-evident truth seems to a lot of voters colossal self-righteousness." In the article on the Nixon campaign and the Nixon Presidency that week, *Newsweek* described the President as lacking in personal magnetism but as being businesslike and efficient. The Nixon currently on display before the nation is "not, in any very important sense, another New Nixon," *Newsweek* wrote. "For of all the constants of character that hold steady throughout the President's supposed metamorphosis, perhaps the most important is a steady, sobersided bent for running the government, if not for inspiring the nation."

As the election approached, a Gallup poll showed President Nixon ahead of Senator McGovern by a margin of almost two to one. (An earlier Gallup poll had shown that people of voting age found President Nixon "more sincere and believable" than Senator McGovern by a margin of three to one, and that voters under the age of twenty-nine found the President more sincere and believable by a margin of fifty-seven per cent to twenty-eight per cent.) According to a poll taken by *Editor & Publisher*, seven hundred and fifty-three daily newspapers had endorsed the President, and fifty-six daily newspapers had endorsed Senator McGovern. Still another poll showed that ninety-one per cent of the nation's businessmen planned to vote for Nixon and seven per cent planned to vote for McGovern. The Soviet government let it be known informally that it preferred President Nixon. A Soviet newsman was reported to have said, "We've already picked our man, so we'll stick with him."

On Election Day, President Nixon was reëlected by a margin of sixty-one per cent to thirty-eight per cent.

During the last weeks of the campaign, as it became clear that President Nixon would win the election, observers had pondered what his second term would be like. According to one school of thought, now that he had his last Presidential election behind him, he would drop his defiant, punitive approach to his adversaries and become more generous and open. There was speculation that he might be planning a program for helping the poor, perhaps along the lines of the Family Assistance Plan. These were the perennial hopes, which had sprung up after each crisis in the President's career, only to be quickly dashed each time. With the President's encouragement, they had blossomed after the 1968 election; they had been stirred again in the spring of 1970, when, after the invasion of Cambodia, the President said that he wanted just what the demonstrators against the war wanted; and they had been revived after the congressional elections of 1970, when the President announced his "New American Revolution."

Observers at the time of the 1972 election naturally took their bearings from the public record—from, that is, the aboveground facts of the period. To anyone judging from these, there did appear to be compelling reasons for believing that a time of relative calm was ahead. The temper of the nation seemed more relaxed than it had been since the beginning of the war in Vietnam, almost ten years earlier. In fact, the nation had been determined at least since 1968 to put the war and the rancorous mood of the war years behind it, and had elected Nixon on a platform of peace, lowered voices, and national unity. Now peace was "at hand," and it hardly seemed possible that the division over the war could outlast the war for very long. And there had apparently been a further calming of the nation's anxieties when the President—one of the most consistent anti-Communists the country had ever known—went to China and Russia and drank his toasts of friendship with Communist leaders. After the election results were in, observers also speculated that if the President had been harboring any residual feelings of hatred for his opposition, his anger had most likely been assuaged by his land-slide victory. And the fact that the President was barred by the Twenty-second Amendment from seeking a third term made it seem all the more possible that he would turn his attention away from destroying political adversaries with Presidential Offensives and the like, and turn it toward establishing the "place in history" that now appeared to be so much in his thoughts.

The President, however, who lived in the world of the secret facts and was striving to cope with powerful and dangerous currents in the underground stream of events that flowed through his Adminis-tration, was preparing the biggest Presidential Offensive yet. Not for the first time, his mood, his perception of his situation, and his plans were precisely the opposite of those commonly attributed to him. The public believed that he was more powerful than ever, and his opposition weaker than ever. But he knew that he faced the most terrible threat that he or any other President had ever faced, and he was laying his plans accordingly. What threatened him, of course, was not any renewed vigor on the part of his political opposition— there was none—but exposure of the covert activities of his Adminis-tration during its first term, including his own criminal involvement in the effort to conceal the origins of the Watergate break-in. In other words, his greatest enemies were his own hidden actions over the past few years. If these actions were made known, the revelation would touch off an explosion of unguessable dimensions. But if the actions remained hidden, no amount of opposition from his "enemies" could touch him. The exigencies of this predicament had been uppermost in his mind ever since the break-in. In conversations with Dean, both before and after the election, he revealed some of his plans. The Watergate struggle, he told Dean, was to be "the last

293

gasp of . . . our partisan opponents." Far from looking forward to a truce, he was looking forward to the final destruction of his foes. "They are, they're, they're going to Watergate around in this town, not so much our opponents, but basically, it's the media, uh, I mean it's the Establishment," he said. "The Establishment is dying, and so they've got to show that after some rather significant successes we've had in foreign policy and in the election, they've got to show, 'Well, it just is wrong because this is—because of this.' In other words, they're trying to use this to smear the whole thing." If "the Establishment" should happen not to die of its own accord, he would kill it. "This is war," he told Dean on one occasion, and he talked over the progress of the coverup, and outlined his plans for the Justice Department and the F.B.I. for repression of his political opposition. "We haven't used the Bureau and we haven't used the Justice Department, but things are going to change now," he said to Dean. "For us to come into this election campaign and not do anything with regard to the Democratic senators who are running, and so forth . . . that'd be ridiculous. Absolutely ridiculous. It's not going, going to be that way anymore." Speaking of Edward Bennett Williams, a lawyer working for the Democrats, Haldeman, who was also present, said, "That is a guy we've got to ruin." The President added, "We are going to fix the son of a bitch." And the Washington *Post* would have "damnable, damnable problems," the President said. "They have a television station." On another occasion, he wanted to know whether Dean was getting enough material from the I.R.S. for the Enemies Project, and recommended ways of getting more. As for the Congress, the President believed it to be "irrelevant." "They become irrelevant because they're so damned irresponsible," he told Dean. The posthumous destruction of the images of enemies would go forward, too. "The person who could, would destroy Hoover's image is going to be this man Bill Sullivan," Dean told an approving President in March—a reference to William C. Sullivan, the former F.B.I. official who had helped the White House prevent the summaries of the warrantless White House taps from falling into Hoover's custody.

Never had the gap between the President's thinking and the public's perception of his thinking been wider. The nation was tranquil—even exhausted—but at the center of that tranquillity was a President who was planning to lash out with all the power at his disposal to protect his political survival and to destroy his opposition once and for all.

On November 12th, Charles Colson attacked the Washington *Post* and CBS news in a speech at a convention of newspaper editors. He charged them with "McCarthyism." He called the *Post*'s executive editor, Benjamin Bradlee, "the self-appointed leader of a tiny fringe of arrogant élitists," and he denounced Eric Sevareid, the CBS correspondent, for "rehashing all of the old charges, coming up with no new information and noting only a selective few denials." Colson was clearly referring to recent coverage of the Watergate affair. A few days later, Aram Bakshian, a speechwriter for the President, attacked the recently defeated Senator McGovern in an article on the Op-Ed page of the *Times*. "The people," Bakshian wrote, "looked at the philosophic and programmatic menu offered by the McGovern movement and they rated it unfit for American consumption." And, writing as though the campaign were still on, he continued, "The various campaign blunders of the McGovern staff, the unhappy Eagleton affair, and the candidate's constant waffling on the issues were not the seeds of the defeat. They merely confirmed the public's suspicion that unacceptable fare is usually served up by inept chefs." On November 24th, Patrick Buchanan charged, also in an article on the Op-Ed page, that Senator McGovern and his "frenetic accomplices" had run "just about the dirtiest, meanest campaign in this nation's history." These attacks were so out of keeping with the national mood that they were, by and large, merely baffling to observers. In fact, they were so far out of keeping with the general conviction that American politics was finally entering the long-awaited period of calm and good feeling that they were, in effect, inaudible. And the few people who did pay any attention to them merely assumed that a few hotheaded speechwriters had been unable to cool off after the election. In actuality, these attacks were the beginning of the Watergate offensive.

Some other signs of the vengeful mood in the White House received more attention. Almost as soon as the election was over, the President asked for letters of resignation from the top two thousand officers in the executive branch and announced his intention of accepting the resignations of those whose jobs he thought unnecessary. The request was the opening move in a plan for "reorganization" which would dwarf all the President's previous efforts at reorganization, and would, in fact, place the President in complete control of the Cabinet departments and the agencies of the federal government. This time, reorganization was to be total. The President removed himself to his mountain retreat at Camp David, Maryland. There he received the members of his Cabinet, one by one. According to the *Times,* they "trooped" in "like so many schoolboys visiting the principal to learn whether they had passed or failed." Then the President began to rain down orders on a frightened capital. Each Cabinet Secretary had been instructed to make a report on how best to reorganize his department. In the middle of the period of hiring and firing, the President related at a press conference that when he had asked the Cabinet Secretaries whether his idea of having them all write such reports was a good one, "each member of the Cabinet, virtually to a man, has said that having that opportunity—as a matter of fact being directed to take that opportunity—proved to be valuable." Those who didn't find the opportunity valuable, it may be presumed, were not invited to stay around very long to tell the President of their reservations. As the weeks went by, men in Washington who were known to have preserved at least some small measure of independence during Nixon's first term began to disappear from the government. They included Secretary of Defense Melvin Laird, Secretary of Commerce Peter Peterson, Solicitor General Erwin Griswold, and Secretary of Housing and Urban Development George Romney. A new system to assure White House control over the Cabinet departments and the agencies was to be put into effect. Frederic Malek, the man in charge of sorting out "good guys" from "bad guys," and doling out "the goodies" to politically deserving people and organizations through the political "responsiveness program," set up in the Cabinet departments a network of men loyal to the White House, one of them often holding the crucial post of Assistant Secretary for Administration, which has the responsibility for personnel. Other White House men of proved loyalty were sent into the Cabinet departments and the agencies as under-secretaries and other key administrative officers. The network, according to one knowledgeable observer, would provide "an instant bush telegraph into the jungle." The first stage of reorganization had been to turn the White House into an autonomous bureaucracy that duplicated the functions of the established bureaucracy. The second stage, taken now that total reorganization was under way, was to disperse the loyalists in the White House into the old bureaucracy and to assume control over it directly. Firings were carried out on a grand scale throughout the government. At the Department of the Interior, eight top officials were removed. At the F.B.I., Patrick Gray was bringing his own men in, much to the dismay of the old guard there. At the C.I.A., the largest purge in the history of the agency was launched.

In addition, the White House was further reorganized. When commending an earlier White House reorganization plan to the Congress, the President had said, "I expect to follow with other reorganization plans, quite possibly involving ones that will affect other activities of the Executive Office of the President. Our studies are continuing." Now he was doing what he had said he might do. In December, Roy Ash, who, as head of the President's Advisory Council on Executive Organization, was Mr. Reorganization himself, was brought directly into the White House to fill the position of director of the Office of Management and Budget—an office that his council had helped to set up, and that the President defined, with characteristic ambiguity, as having the power to reëxamine "all government programs now in existence to determine whether they are actually meeting the purpose for which they were designed." Ash was quoted as having once said, "Reorganization is the permanent condition of a vigorous organization." In January, a "super-Cabinet" was set up, consisting of three Cabinet officers who assumed posts at the White House in addition to carrying out their regular duties, and divided up a large part of domestic policy among them. Above them was a "super-super-Cabinet," consisting of Secretary of the Treasury George Schultz, who was to coördinate economic policy; Henry Kissinger, who was to oversee foreign policy; and Mr. Ash. And above *them*, of course, were Haldeman and Ehrlichman, who watched over everything. In 1971, President Nixon had told a reporter that the Cabinet system, which had served the country for almost two hundred years, was "totally obsolete." Now he was abolishing it by executive fiat in favor of something else. As the latest reorganization unfolded, some observers began to take note of an odd atmosphere in the White House. In January, Mel Elfin, of *Newsweek*, reported a "sour mood" in Washington, and wrote, "If the recent past is any guide to the political future, then the nation faces four more years of an increasingly reclusive, sometimes vindictive, and disturbingly uncommunicative Chief Executive."

As soon as the election was over, it became clear that any hope that the President planned to revive the Family Assistance Plan, or to do anything else for the poor, had been drastically misguided. In an interview given just before the election but published afterward, the President spelled out his thinking on the subject. Most of the Great Society programs of the nineteen-sixties, he said, were "massive failures"—a point he had not mentioned during the campaign. He said, "We are going to have to shuck off those programs and trim down those programs that have proved simply to be failures." And he said, "H.U.D., H.E.W., Transportation are all too fat, too bloated." As he saw it, in the nineteen-sixties there had been "a breakdown in . . . the leadership class of this country." By "breakdown" he meant a trend toward "permissiveness" in law enforcement and in welfare programs—the tendency to give people things for nothing and not to punish them enough. The "average American" was "just like the child in the family," he told the interviewer. "You give him some responsibility, and he is going to amount to something."

Throughout his first term, President Nixon had been convinced that a crisis of authority was hobbling the executive branch in its conduct of foreign affairs. Now he seemed to apply the same thinking to questions of domestic spending. Throughout his first term, he had vacillated between trying to establish expanded programs of social spending, such as the Family Assistance Plan, and trying to cut back on social spending. Now he seemed to have finally decided that an attitude of "toughness" was as necessary here as it was in every other sphere of government. In foreign affairs, the President had defied the "permissive" people who were in the "leadership class." Now he would defy the "permissive" members of the "leadership class" in domestic affairs, and stop them from continuing their "soft" practices of coddling criminals and handing out money to the spoiled children who he thought made up the American family. A new propaganda campaign was launched from the White House. A public-relations kit was put together called "The Battle of the Budget, 1973," and a new phrase was suddenly on the lips of the surrogates: "the big spenders." The big spenders were congressmen who supported programs that the President wanted to kill. Now the combined power of the White House public-relations machine and the White House reorganizational machine were brought to bear on the Congress, in an attack on its one major power that remained intact—the power of the purse. By cutting back social spending, the President could claim that he was reducing "big government," and thus give the appearance of voluntarily relinquishing a part of his own power. Actually, the cutback was part of the President's drive to concentrate the powers of the government in the White House, for only by cutting back on spending could the President make inroads into the Congress's spending power. A President who seeks to increase spending is at the mercy of Congress; in order to accomplish his aim he must secure the support of a majority in both houses. A President who wishes to cut back on spending, however, more often than not has Congress at his mercy, for the veto power enables the President to have his way if he can secure the support of just one-third of the members of one house— enough to sustain a veto. And even if Congress should override a veto of a money bill, the President could impound the funds voted— although the practice was of doubtful legality. (Three weeks after the election, the President did impound six billion dollars that the Congress had appropriated for projects to improve the environment.) By not spending money that Congress had authorized, the President would, it is true, shrink the spending power of the federal government; but he would hold all its shrunken power in his own hands. The technique of impoundment was one method of exercising an unreviewable Presidential veto. Another was the pocket veto—a veto that takes effect when, as frequently happens, legislation is passed within ten working days of a congressional adjournment and the President fails to act on the bill before Congress adjourns; the bill is then dead. (After Congress adjourned in October of 1972, the President employed the pocket veto on eleven bills that authorized or appropriated money.) The White House was proposing that the Congress grant the President a third form of unreviewable veto. It proposed that the Congress adopt a budget ceiling and then empower the President to cut the budget wherever he pleased, to bring it down to that ceiling in the event that Congress should exceed the ceiling in its appropriations. In the early fall, the House of Representatives passed such a bill. And the Senate, clearly demonstrating the power of the White House to define issues, responded to the proposal not by rejecting it outright as a violation of the Senate's own Constitutional appropriating power but by coupling a rejection of the Presidentially enforced budget ceiling with a proposal for another sort of budget ceiling, to be enforced by the Senate itself; that way, the Senate could not be included among those to whom the new tag "the big spenders" was being applied. Many senators were prepared to vote away their appropriating power if this alternative budget ceiling, which would protect the Senate against the White House propaganda campaign, was part of the bill. The President also resorted to still another form of unreviewable veto: sheer unilateral executive action in defiance of the will of Congress. In January, the President appointed a young administrator named Howard Phillips acting director of the Office of Economic Opportunity. Phillips' job, however, was not to run the O.E.O. but to liquidate it. In ordering the destruction of the O.E.O., the President defied the law by misusing the power he had been granted to execute the law: he used his power of appointment, granted him so that he could execute what Congress legislated, to terminate a program that Congress had authorized.

On December 16th, a month after the Ninety-second Congress had adjourned, Henry Kissinger announced that the negotiations with the North Vietnamese were ninety-nine per cent complete—only one per cent of disagreement remained. That day, too, John Ehrlichman and Communications Director Herbert Klein released an assessment of the White House by the White House. "In the past four years, a new sense of calm and confidence has begun to grow up in America," it read, in part. "A nation that had grown skeptical, accustomed to promises which outran reality, has been learning to trust its institutions again. A nation that had fallen into shouting and posturing has started to lower its voices."

Two days later, Hanoi radio reported that "waves" of American planes were bombing the city and other parts of North Vietnam. (The bombing of North Vietnam had been halted when Kissinger announced that peace was "at hand.") The United States command in Vietnam refused to comment. In a press conference, Ronald Ziegler responded to questions about the bombing by saying that the raids "will continue until such time as a settlement is arrived at," but he would offer no explanation of why the bombing had been resumed. News filtering out of Hanoi told of B-52s in the hundreds "carpet-bombing" populated areas. It was the most intense bombing of the war. Around the world, the nearly unanimous reaction was amazement and outrage. Willy Brandt was reported to have called the bombing "disgusting and unfathomable." Prime Minister Olof Palme, of Sweden, said, "One should call things by their proper name. What is happening today in Vietnam is a form of torture."

That same day, the United States told Sweden not to send a replacement for its departing ambassador, and directed the chargé d'affaires of the American Embassy in Stockholm, who was on vacation in the United States, not to return to his post. Sweden, it appeared, had been put on the enemies list. In France, *Le Monde* likened the attacks on North Vietnam to the bombing of Guernica by the Germans in 1937. In much of Europe, there were demonstrations and drives to raise relief funds for North Vietnam. The Canadian House of Commons voted unanimously to censure the bombing. Here and abroad, the raids were commonly referred to as "the terror-bombing." Soon it became clear that the bombing was not only the most intense of the war but also the most costly for the United States. Each day, one or two B-52s were shot down. At that rate of loss, the entire United States fleet of B-52s would be eliminated within a few months. The morale of the B-52 pilots was reported to have deteriorated badly and fast.

On December 30th, the bombing was halted above the twentieth parallel, which ran through the central part of North Vietnam. Some two thousand bombing runs had been flown. Ninety-three airmen were missing or dead. And still there was no explanation from the White House.

On the first day of the bombing, the Administration resumed its attack on the press. In fact, action on all fronts of the first-term Presidential Offensive was apparently being stepped up. A man named Clay Whitehead, who operated the White House Office of Telecommunications Policy—an organization with vague duties which had been set up in 1970, during an earlier period of reorganization—assailed television news coverage in the most menacing language that anyone in the Administration had used thus far. He announced that the Administration intended to propose legislation under which local stations affiliated with the networks would be held responsible at license-renewal time for the content of the network news and all other network-supplied programming they broadcast—or about sixty per cent of their broadcast material. The

Federal Communications Commission, he said, should impose requirements with "teeth" for the renewal of the license of a network-affiliated television station. The kind of thing that the affiliated stations would be held accountable for accepting from the networks, Whitehead said, was "ideological plugola" and "élitist gossip in the guise of news analysis." By implication, Whitehead was proposing direct government interference in the news. In the same speech, he advocated legislation that would strengthen the local stations' hold on their licenses. His basic idea was apparently to use the threat of government interference in the licensing of affiliates to induce the affiliates to pressure the networks into revising their news policies.

By early January, when the Ninety-third Congress convened, virtually every power that Congress held under the Constitution was being subjected to heavy executive assault. There was brave talk of resistance as the Congress opened. The House Speaker, Carl Albert, declared that a revival of Congress's powers was the first order of business. *Time* organized a series of symposia around the country to inquire into the reasons that Congress had suffered such a drastic decline. *Newsweek* titled an article on the new Congress "Congress Throws the Gauntlet." "The battle was joined," the article asserted, in reference to a Senate vote requiring that the President's appointment of Roy Ash as director of the Office of Management and Budget be submitted to it for confirmation. "At bottom it was a Constitutional struggle to stop the steady erosion of power from Congress to the White House—and while Congress has huffed and puffed threats in the past, there were strong signs last week that determination and muscle had finally been found as well." The challenge that the members had before them was a curious one. The powers of Congress were fixed in the Constitution, and, since the congressmen were legislators, the remedy for the loss of their powers which came most naturally to their minds was legislation. In other words, they were gathering their strength to spell out in legislation what was already spelled out in the fundamental law of the land.

They were intent on *re-legislating* the Constitution. The fact that the battle with the executive branch was joined on this ground gave the White House a nearly insuperable advantage. The President could go ahead and break the law, and then simply veto any bills designed to bring him back into line. In other words, as long as he retained the support of one-third of either house of Congress, he not only could veto federal spending but could veto the Constitution itself. What was worse, the Congress, by setting out to legislate its powers back into existence, ran the risk of lending legitimacy to the President's lawlessness, since if it failed to muster the two-thirds vote of both houses needed to override his vetoes, it would be adding the authority of the legislative process to his usurpations. Therefore, it was dangerous for the Congress even to address itself to these matters through legislation. A perhaps sounder course was the one that some senators and representatives followed in seeking to release impounded funds: they filed a suit in the federal courts.

As Congress set about trying to recover its powers in the wake of total reorganization and the bombing of North Vietnam, the trial of the seven Watergate defendants got under way in U.S. District Court. In the months since the election, the issue of Watergate had faded, and the papers had devoted their front pages to other news. Shortly after the trial began, however, the front-page news was that all the defendants but two had pleaded guilty. In the courtroom, Judge John Sirica, who presided, found himself dissatisfied with the questioning of witnesses by the government prosecutors. The prosecutors now had a suggestion as to the burglars' motive. They suggested that it might be blackmail. They did not say of whom or over what. At the trial, the key prosecution witness, the former F.B.I. agent Alfred Baldwin, related that on one occasion he had taken the logs of the Watergate wiretaps to the headquarters of the Committee for the Re-Election of the President. But this suggested nothing to the Justice Department, one of whose spokesmen had maintained when the indictment was handed up in September that there was "no evidence" showing that anyone except the defendants was involved. Sirica demurred. "I want to know where the money comes from," he said to the defendant Bernard Barker. "There were hundred-dollar bills floating around like coupons." When Barker replied that he had simply received the money in the mail in a blank envelope and had no idea who might have sent it, Sirica commented, "I'm sorry, but I don't believe you." When the defense lawyers protested Sirica's questioning, he said, "I don't think we should sit up here like nincompoops. The function of a trial is to search for the truth."

All the Watergate defendants but one were following the White House scenario to the letter. The exception was James Mc-Cord. He was seething with scenarios of his own. He hoped to have the charges against him dismissed, and, besides, he had been angered by what he understood as a suggestion from one of his lawyers that the blame for the Watergate break-in be assigned to the C.I.A., his old outfit, to which he retained an intense loyalty. There was some irony in the fact that McCord's anger had been aroused by an Administration plan to involve the C.I.A. in its crimes. McCord believed that Nixon's removal of C.I.A. director Richard Helms, in December of 1972—at the very time that McCord himself was being urged to lay the blame for Watergate at the door of the C.I.A.—was designed to pave the way for an attempt by the Administration itself to blame the break-in on the agency and for a takeover of the agency by the White House. He had worked for the White House, but he did not see the reorganizational wars from the White House point of view. He saw them from the bureaucrats' point of view; in his opinion, President Nixon was attempting to take over the C.I.A. in a manner reminiscent of attempts by Hitler to take control of German intelligence agencies before the Second World War. The White House, that is, belatedly discovered that it had a disgruntled "holdover" on its hands. And this particular holdover really was prepared to perform sabotage; he was prepared, indeed, to sabotage not just the President's policies but the President himself, and, what was more, he had the means to do it. McCord was putting together a scenario that could destroy the Nixon Administration. In a letter delivered in December, to his White House contact, the undercover operative John Caulfield, McCord pronounced a dread warning: If the White House continued to try to have the C.I.A. take responsibility for the Watergate burglary, "every tree in the forest will fall," and "it will be a scorched desert." Piling on yet another metaphor of catastrophe, he wrote, "Pass the message that if they want it to blow, they are on exactly the right course. I am sorry that you will get hurt in the fallout." McCord was the first person in the Watergate conspiracy to put in writing exactly what the magnitude of the Watergate scandal was. Many observers had been amazed at the extreme hard line that the President had taken since his landslide reëlection—the firings in the bureaucracies, the incomprehensible continuation of the attacks on Senator McGovern, the renewed attacks on the press, the attacks on Congress's power of the purse, the bombing of Hanoi. They could not know that at the exact moment when President Nixon was wreaking devastation on North Vietnam, James McCord was threatening to wreak devastation on him.

On January 20th, in his second Inaugural Address, the President said, "When we met here four years ago, America was bleak in spirit. . . . As we meet here today, we stand on the threshold of a new era of peace in the world," and, continuing in the accents of self-praise that had become habitual with him, he gave a "historical" evaluation of his accomplishments. "Because of America's bold initiatives," he said, "1972 will be long remembered as the year of the greatest progress since the end of World War II toward a lasting peace in the world."

Three days after the Inauguration, a peace agreement with the North Vietnamese was announced. Its main provisions were for the withdrawal of American forces from South Vietnam and the return of the American prisoners of war from Hanoi. There were also provisions for a political settlement in Vietnam, for a cease-fire, and for international supervision, but these were in truth only wistful

hopes, or window dressing, since neither of the Vietnamese governments showed any signs of having the will to carry them out. The
North Vietnamese forces would remain in the South, which is to
say that the United States was withdrawing its forces unilaterally.
In 1971, the President had said, "The policy of this government is
for a total withdrawal, provided there is a withdrawal by the other
side." Now our policy was withdrawal while they stayed in place.
In 1965, when the United States first entered South Vietnam in
force, a State Department White Paper had said that some twenty
thousand North Vietnamese soldiers were operating in South
Vietnam. In 1973, as the United States left, some one hundred and
forty-five thousand were operating there. Along with the announced
terms of the settlement, there were, as usual, terms that had not
been announced. Both before and at the height of the Christmas
bombing, President Nixon had sent President Nguyen Van Thieu,
of South Vietnam, written assurance that the United States would
"respond with full force" if the North Vietnamese should break the
agreement.

The President's new strategy in Vietnam amounted to one of
the purest applications of the American doctrine of credibility which
had ever been attempted. The purpose of building credibility,
whether in the nuclear sphere or in the sphere of limited war, was to
deter foes from attacking the United States and its allies. In other
words, by building a formidable image of power and of willingness
to use it the government hoped to achieve ends that might otherwise
have to be achieved through a large-scale use of force. For nearly a
decade, the United States had battled to achieve its ends in Vietnam
by using force in limited amounts. President Nixon, during his years
in office, had, under severe public pressure, withdrawn American
forces from Vietnam, but as he did so he had tried to build up
American credibility, so that the diminution of forces would be
compensated for by an increase in credibility. The invasion of Cambodia in 1970, the invasion of Laos in 1971, the mining of the ports
of North Vietnam in mid-1972, and, finally, the terror-bombing of

Hanoi in December of 1972 had all served to strengthen America's reputation as a nation still willing and able to launch sudden and unpredictable military attacks. The President apparently hoped that now that American forces were out of Vietnam the North Vietnamese would refrain from taking over the South for fear of other such spasms of military action by the United States. The bombing of Hanoi in the Christmas season of 1972, in particular, had been crucial to the effort to build up credibility. For by launching a savage military attack in the face of nearly unanimous political opposition at home and without consulting anyone in Congress, at a moment when his disagreement with the foe amounted to only one per cent, the President declared his freedom to do what he would in Indo-China, whether public opinion supported him or not. The message to the North Vietnamese was that in military affairs his will reigned absolute and it would be no use for them to try to rely on American public opinion for their safety. Nor was the President's message an implausible one in the winter of 1972, for if he should succeed in his total reorganization of the executive branch, in his drive to frighten the press into submission, and in his subjugation of the Congress, then he would indeed have an absolutely free hand in Indo-China—or anywhere else, for that matter. Then he would have broken free once and for all from the restraints on his power which had so deeply frustrated him in his first term; he would, in fact, have secured the power of a dictator.

On January 27, 1973, the peace agreement was signed, and that evening the President attended a nationally televised religious service in Key Biscayne, at which a minister was seen and heard praising the President and his policies. "Thank God! We thank God that we have a President that realizes that peace does not come at any price!" the minister, who happened to bear a striking physical resemblance to the President, said to his congregation, which included the President. The President, in fact, was being publicly praised to his face by a clergyman for the third time since his reëlection. On a visit he made to New York in late November, his friend the Reverend Norman Vincent Peale had praised him at a Sunday-morning church service as "one of the great peacemakers," and at a White House prayer service in January, again, a rabbi had praised him as a "beautiful human being."

As the peace agreement was signed and the church bells were ringing in Key Biscayne, the order went out for American planes to cease their bombing runs over Vietnam and to begin runs over Cambodia.

Less than a week after the signing of the peace agreement, Charles Colson, who had just left the White House to enter private law practice in Washington, wrote an Op-Ed piece in the *Times* attacking the "sell-out brigades" who, he said, had wanted to get out of Vietnam at any cost. "For four agonizing years, Richard Nixon has stood virtually alone in the nation's capital while little, petty men flayed him over American involvement in Indo-China," he said. And an assessment distributed that same week by Senator Goldwater, and reported to have been written at the White House, said, "No President has been under more constant and unremitting harassment." The war in Indo-China was, for the moment, over. The war at home continued.

On February 7th, the Senate, by a vote of seventy-seven to none, established a Select Committee on Presidential Campaign Activities, to look into abuses in the Presidential campaign of 1972, including the Watergate break-in; and the Democratic leadership appointed Senator Sam Ervin, of North Carolina, the author of the resolution to establish the Select Committee, to be its chairman. Three days later, the Administration secretly convened a Watergate committee of its own, in California—at the La Costa Resort Hotel and Spa, not far from the President's estate in San Clemente, with John Dean, H. R. Haldeman, John Ehrlichman, and Richard Moore, a White

House aide, in attendance. The meeting lasted for two days. Its work was to devise ways of hampering, discrediting, and ultimately blocking the Ervin committee's investigation.

On February 17th, the President sent to the Senate the nomination of Patrick Gray—Acting Director of the F.B.I.—as its Permanent Director. On March 2nd, faced with a request to allow John Dean to testify at Senate Judiciary Committee hearings on Gray's nomination, the President refused by invoking the doctrine of "executive privilege," and a few days later, in a formal policy statement, Nixon asserted that executive privilege permitted a President to forbid any of his past or present aides to give testimony before the Congress. But, the President added, "executive privilege will not be used as a shield to prevent embarrassing information from being made available but will be exercised only in those particular instances in which disclosure would harm the public interest." Two days later, Dean refused to appear before the Judiciary Committee and cited the President's policy statement to justify his refusal. In the second week of April, Attorney General Richard Kleindienst expanded the executive-privilege claim. He told three Senate committees then jointly considering the issue of executive privilege that the President had the authority to prevent any or all of some three million civilian employees of the executive branch from giving testimony before the Congress. If the senators wanted some testimony that the President would not allow, Kleindienst said, then the Congress could impeach the President. The senators were amazed to hear such talk. The very sound of the word "impeach" seemed to shock them. Another White House move to impede the flow of information from the executive branch was to be found in the fine print of a Justice Department proposal for a bill revising the criminal code—a bill then pending in Congress. The Justice Department bill would make it a crime for a government employee to pass out "classified" information or for a reporter to receive it. Any government employee prosecuted under the provisions of the bill would also be prevented from challenging the reasonableness of the "classified" designation of any unauthorized release. And any government employee who only knew about an unauthorized release of classified information and failed to report it would be indictable. The penalties ranged up to seven years in jail and fifty thousand dollars in fines.

On January 21st, Senator McGovern, speaking at Oxford University, warned that the United States was "closer to one-man rule than at any time in our history." He added, "We have experienced an exhaustion of important institutions in America. Today only the Presidency is activist and strong, while other traditional centers of power are timid and depleted." A few of his colleagues in the Senate were similarly apprehensive. But their concern was not widely shared, for the public, insofar as it still took any interest in politics at all, was preoccupied with two other matters: a precipitous rise in food prices—especially the price of meat—and the return of the prisoners of war from Hanoi. Housewives, in a burst of consumer activism, had organized a nationwide one-week boycott of meat. The return of the prisoners of war turned out to be a highly organized affair. They were flown from Hanoi to Clark Air Base, in the Philippines. There each released prisoner was joined by an "escort officer," who accompanied his charge back to the United States. Upon the arrival of a planeload at the airport in the United States, many of the debarking prisoners expressed their gratitude to President Nixon. None of the prisoners were allowed to meet with the press or the public, or, for the first few days, to stay with their families. Instead, they were whisked away to hospitals.

The President had won a landslide reëlection victory, and his popularity stood high in the polls; in February, a Gallup poll showed the President to be popular with sixty-eight per cent of the public—a rating equal to the best he had received during his first term. His power had never been greater. His rivals were in disarray. The war, it seemed, was at last over for the United States. To an outsider's eye, these looked like propitious circumstances for the beginning of the President's second term. In actuality, the nation's exhausted calm posed a terrible danger to the President. Those on the inside could see that his popularity rating of sixty-eight per cent was based on public ignorance of the Administration's true record, and that if that record were to be made known the popularity could evaporate. The nation's calm was perilous to the President because it was a poor atmosphere for the progress of the coverup: the next stage of the coverup called for large amounts of that old stock in trade among the President's political strategies—national division. The President, in his actions since his reëlection, had given his political opposition plenty of cause to protest his policies, and so to divide the country. He had launched his attempt to take over the federal bureaucracy and to fashion it into an instrument of personal political power; he had begun his attacks on the remaining powers of Congress; his spokesman had openly recommended government management of television news; and he had carried out the terror-bombing of North Vietnam. Yet these moves had encountered virtually no opposition. In a meeting in February, John Dean warned the President that any congressional investigation into the Watergate affair would be very "partisan," as though that were something to be feared, but the President replied, "I frankly would say that I perhaps rather that they be partisan." He realized that only in a highly charged, contentious atmosphere could the men who might uncover the damning facts about his Administration be portrayed as irresponsible characters out to fabricate charges against him. The atmosphere of 1973, however, simply did not offer any opportunity for these tactics. The old targets of Presidential wrath had all disappeared from the scene. The Communists had been neutralized as such a target by the President's own visits to Russia and China. As for the hippies, demonstrators, and anarchists, they had been dropped from the official history of the Nixon years at the time of the Republican Convention; and, of course, by 1973 the days of demonstrations against the war were actually over, once and for all. Referring to these various supposed menaces, the Republican platform had read, "It is so easy to forget how frightful it was." The President's speechwriters might attempt to prop up the fallen McGovern and his "frenetic accomplices" in order to trample them once again, and Charles Colson might lash out at the "sell-out brigades" one more time, but these were bogies of the past. How could the President exacerbate "divisive issues," as he had done in preparation for the campaign of 1972, when he himself had laid all the divisive issues to rest? In the sedated mood of 1973, the Presidential Offensive came across merely as an oddity.

In the second week of March, the President said that he would veto a string of bills, and that if his vetoes were overridden he would impound the funds appropriated in the bills. The brave talk about how Congress had thrown down the gauntlet was at an end. At the beginning of April, the Senate had failed to override a veto of an aid-to-the-handicapped bill, and the failure to override was interpreted by congressional leaders to mean that the President would be able to do with the budget what he wished. Senator Mike Mansfield, of Montana, the Democratic majority leader, remarked, "The President's in the driver's seat." What was more important, the failure to override meant that the attempt of the Congress to relegislate its Constitutional powers would most probably fail.

The President's drive to take over the federal government was going well. By the end of March, those legislators who were worried about the possibility of a collapse of the Constitutional system were in a state of near-hopelessness. It seemed that the President would have his will, and Congress could not stop him; as for the public, it was uninterested in Constitutional matters. Senator Muskie had now joined Senator McGovern in warning against the dangers of "one-man rule," and he said that the Administration's proposal for preventing the release of "classified" information, no matter how arbitrarily the "classified" designation had been applied, could impose "the silence of democracy's graveyard." Senator William Fulbright, of Arkansas, had expressed fear that the United States might "pass on, as most of the world has passed on, to a totalitarian system." In the press, a new feeling seemed to be crystallizing that Congress had had its day as an institution of American life. Commentators of all political persuasions were talking about Congress as though it were moribund. Kevin Phillips, a political writer who had played an important role in formulating "the Southern strategy," and who had once worked in John Mitchell's Justice Department, wrote, in an article in *Newsweek* called "Our Obsolete System," that "Congress's separate power is an obstacle to modern policymaking." He proposed a "fusion of powers" to replace the Constitution's separation of powers. "In sum," he wrote, "we may have reached a point where separation of powers is doing more harm than good by distorting the logical evolution of technology-era government." In *The New Republic,* the columnist TRB, who, like Senator McGovern and Senator Muskie, was worried that "one-man rule" was in prospect, wrote, "President Nixon treats Congress with contempt which, it has to be admitted, is richly deserved. We have a lot of problems—the economy, inflation, the unfinished war, Watergate—but in the long run the biggest problem is whether Congress can be salvaged, because if it can't, our peculiar 18th-century form of government, with separation of powers, can't be salvaged." And he wrote, "A vacuum has to be filled. The authority of Congress has decayed till it is overripe and rotten. Mr. Nixon has merely proclaimed it." At the Justice Department, Donald Santarelli, who was shortly to become head of the Law Enforcement Assistance Administration, told a reporter, "Today, the whole Constitution is up for grabs." These observers took the undeniable fact that the Congress was impotent as a sign that the Congress was obsolete. And the executive branch, having helped reduce the Congress to helplessness, could now point to that helplessness as proof that the Congress was of no value.

The coverup and the takeover had merged into a single project. For four years, the President's anger at his "enemies" had been growing. As his anger had grown, so had that clandestine repressive apparatus in the White House whose purpose was to punish and destroy his enemies. And as this apparatus had grown, so had the need to control the Cabinet departments and the agencies, and the other branches of government, because they might find out about it—until, finally, the coverup had come to exceed in importance every other matter facing the Administration. For almost a year now, the coverup had been the motor of American politics. It had safeguarded the President's reëlection, and it had determined the substance and the mood of the Administration's second term so far. In 1969, when President Nixon launched his Presidential Offensive, he had probably not foreseen that the tools he was developing then would one day serve him in a mortal struggle between his Administration and the other powers of the Republic; but now his assault on the press, the television networks, the Congress, the federal bureaucracy, and the courts had coalesced into a single, coördinated assault on the American Constitutional democracy. Either the Nixon Administration would survive in power and the democracy would die or the Administration would be driven from power and the democracy would have another chance to live. If the newly reëlected President should be able to thwart investigations by the news media, the agencies of federal law enforcement, the courts, and Congress, he would be clear of all accountability, and would be above the law; on the other hand, if the rival institutions of the Republic should succeed in laying bare the crimes of his Administration and in bringing the criminals to justice, the Administration would be destroyed.

Although the coverup was still unknown to the public, it had left no part of American political life untouched. The coverup was composed of concentric rings of participants, of which the innermost had a high degree of awareness of the truth and the outer layers had progressively less awareness. At the center was the hard core of the conspiracy: the men who knew everything except what they had deliberately chosen not to know. In the ring surrounding these men were men in government who knew a part of the truth and whose duty it was to find out more, but who did not, and allowed themselves to be used as instruments in the hands of the main conspirators. This ring included officials of the C.I.A. such as Richard Helms and Vernon Walters, and officials of the Justice Department such as Patrick Gray and Henry Petersen. Petersen, for example, had been informed by John Dean on December 22, 1972, that Gray had received material from Hunt's safe, and Petersen had not asked Gray about it until some two months later. Gray had denied the story, and Petersen had made no further investigation until another two months had elapsed and the coverup was blowing apart. Gray was one degree nearer the innermost ring than Petersen was, for he had knowingly lied to help the coverup along. He was one of many men who had suddenly been raised to prominence by the Nixon Administration and had then been asked to engage in criminal or improper activities. When Gray was first informed of his appointment as Acting Director of the F.B.I., he had been so surprised that he thought it was a joke. Vernon Walters, too, had been swiftly raised by the Administration from relative obscurity to his high post, and when he balked at carrying out White House instructions designed to advance the coverup, Ehrlichman suggested to Dean that Walters be reminded "where he came from." Petersen had likewise been promoted to his relatively high position by the Nixon Administration, and it was this fact that prompted Dean to remark to the President that one reason for Petersen's coöperativeness was that "this Administration has made him." In manipulating men like Petersen, the President employed both promises of promotion and threats of exposure of their involvement in the coverup. In early April, when the President began to receive Grand Jury information directly from Petersen, he dangled the post of Director of the F.B.I. before him, and at the same time he reminded him of the impropriety of his having given Grand Jury information to Dean in the summer and warned him that exposure of that fact could damage him badly. "I've got Petersen on a short leash," the President told Ehrlichman and Ziegler. In the ring outside Petersen and those like him were men in the Republican Party and elsewhere who had no special knowledge of the coverup but allowed themselves to be used as instruments or spokesmen of the conspirators. These were the men who angrily denied charges against the Administration without having any way of knowing whether their denials were true. In this ring, too, were all those who had no personal involvement in the coverup but kept silent out of fear of retaliation by the White House.

Finally, in the outermost ring were most of the press, most political figures in the country, and most of the public. This ring was absolutely essential to the success of the coverup, and it took in nothing less than the mood of the whole nation. If it is true that some Republican politicians parroted the White House line uncritically until the very last moments of the coverup, it is also true that by election time the public, including members of the opposition party, was in possession of a large body of facts that were, to say the least, suspicious, and that the public nevertheless returned the Nixon Administration to office by a landslide vote. The country's demoralized state was a complicated phenomenon, with a history that stretched back at least to the beginnings of the Vietnam war. It was compounded of a mistrust of all politicians, a feeling that citizens were helpless to change things, and a drastically lowered standard of conduct for public figures. The word "coverup" suggests conspiratorial action by a few people to deceive a multitude. It would be closer to the truth to say that the Watergate coverup was primarily a national atmosphere in which millions of people who had had nothing to do with the coverup in any narrow sense were able to make decisions that allowed the truth to go undiscovered— that the coverup was a temporary tacit national agreement to let the truth remain concealed and the conspirators stay in office.

But if the coverup encompassed the entire political nation, so did the investigation. At the core of the investigation were the men in the Senate, in the House, in the judiciary, and in the news media whose specific duty it was to discover the facts and to bring the criminals to justice, but in this endeavor, too, the mental state of the whole public—its hidden reserves of indignation and of loyalty to Constitutional principles—would have a decisive role. The Watergate conspirators themselves would to some extent be forced by the demands of the investigation to assume Constitutional obligations, for they, too, as officials of the government, were expected to pursue wrongdoers, and so were required, against their will, to take actions

317

that might be their own undoing. Even the President, around whom the conspiracy revolved, was under obligations he could not wholly avoid to—in effect—bring himself to justice. In other words, in the ordeal that lay ahead not one of those involved was wholly an investigator and not one was wholly a conspirator. All were influenced in some degree by both the imperatives of the attempt to uncover the truth and the imperatives of the attempt to keep the truth concealed.

President Nixon understood perfectly that, in the absence of a mood of division, a mood of political enervation and numbness in the country as a whole could be as important to the success of the coverup as anything that Anthony Ulasewicz might do in his phone booths, and therefore the President took positive steps to worsen the moral climate of the country still further. It became his aim not just to defame specific members of the opposition but to defame whole generations of American politicians. Of all the White House efforts to "discredit" one group or another, this was the most comprehensive. It was an attempt to discredit American history. The President's plan took the form of a public-relations campaign whose purpose was to show not that the Nixon Administration was innocent of the crimes of which it was accused but that all American politicians committed such crimes and always had. By creating an unfavorable image of American politics as a whole, President Nixon hoped to produce an atmosphere in which damaging revelations about his Administration would not seem shocking. (Similarly, his strategy in the 1972 Presidential campaign had been to degrade the opposition rather than to ennoble himself.) He was aided in this effort by his own apparently unfeigned low conception of American politics. It was, after all, this low conception that had allowed him to imagine in the first place that "enemies" of his were doing to him the things he really wanted to do to them. "Goldwater put it in context," he told Dean on September 15, 1972. "He said, 'Well for Christ's sake, everybody bugs everybody else. We know that.'" And the President added, "It's true. It happens to be totally true." Later, he asked Dean, "Don't we try to get schedules? Don't you try to disrupt their meetings? Didn't they try to disrupt ours?" As he saw things, there was a double standard in operation: misbehavior by the opposition was overlooked, but misbehavior by him was thoroughly investigated. And if this was the case, he thought, then all he had to do was to publicize the misbehavior of the opposition, and the public would become so demoralized that it would no longer care what his Administration or any other Administration might have done. In fact, in his estimation the public was already indifferent to political crimes. On March 13, 1973, he told Dean that Patrick Buchanan had been "viewing with alarm the . . . great crisis in the confidence of the Presidency, and so forth," and he went on to ask, "How much of a crisis?" Speaking in the loose, disconnected manner that was apparently habitual with him in this period, he answered, "I mean it'll be, it'll be in a newspaper . . . but the point is that everything is a crisis. I mean Christ, we've had—screw around with this thing for a while . . . it'll be mainly a crisis among the upper intellectual types . . . you know, the softheads, soft— our own, too—Republicans, Democrats, and the rest. Average people won't think it is much of a crisis unless it affects them." Then he added, ruefully, "But it'll go on and on and on." Dean agreed with the President, as he so often did. Dean had already said, on another occasion, that they were going to "put this thing in, in, in, uh, the funny pages of the, of the history books rather than anything serious." One man who the President thought might be helpful in damaging the reputations of past Presidents was William C. Sullivan, the man he hoped to use to "destroy Hoover's image." Sullivan, he believed, might have information showing that Lyndon Johnson and perhaps other Presidents had engaged in wiretapping for political purposes. Dean remarked that if such information could be brought out, it would "tarnish . . . the F.B.I. and a former President." "Fine," the President replied. Such revelations would "change the whole atmosphere of the Watergate hearings," Dean thought. The President wondered aloud whether Sullivan would be willing to coöperate with the Administration. Dean answered, "I think the quid pro quo with Sullivan is that he wants someday back in the Bureau very badly." "That's easy," the President said. He was willing to reward Sullivan with a high post in the F.B.I. for destroying the F.B.I.'s image. However, none of this information was in hand, and a few moments later the President noted regretfully that he had "nothing on the Democrats, and nothing, nothing on what the previous three Administrations did."

On March 24th, Hugh Scott, the Senate minority leader, emerged from a meeting with the President and reported that the President had told him, "Hugh, I have nothing to hide. The White House has nothing to hide. I repeat we have nothing to hide, and you are authorized to make that statement in my name."

In April, *U.S. News & World Report* printed an article on the way the President was now conducting White House business. "His 'inner circle' has narrowed," it noted. "Fewer people are getting assignments direct from the President. He is concentrating on strict discipline, exercised through channels of command. Cabinet meetings are being further downgraded. The atmosphere in the White House, never really casual, tends to be more formal than ever. 'What this means,' said an aide, 'is that the strong men of the first Nixon Administration are even stronger now.'" And the article noted that the President, in accord with a policy of establishing a mood of "peace at the center," was "seeing even his 'inner circle' a little less than before," and that the change left him with more time for "reflective reading"—all of which was "in keeping with his 'sense of history.'"

While the President was laying plans for a public-relations assault on the totality of American political life in recent years, the strictly legal end of the coverup was approaching a crisis. The President had always had difficulty grasping the coverup's legal implications. To him, it was above all an exercise in politics and propaganda. "That's what this is, public relations," he had told Dean in September. For that matter, there was almost nothing he had done during his years in office which he had not seen in one way or another as public relations. The coverup, however, was in trouble far less with public opinion than with the law. In March, three distinct threats to the coverup had emerged. One was the confirmation hearings before the Senate Judiciary Committee on the nomination of Patrick Gray as Director of the F.B.I. For the Senate, these hearings were a first chance to probe the scandal, and for the Administration they were an opportunity to experiment with strategy, to test the mettle of the Congress, and to get the machinery of the coverup in good working order for a more serious confrontation with the Ervin committee. It was in the Gray hearings, for instance, that the President tried out his assertion of an executive privilege that would cover all Presidential aides, including former aides. The decision to nominate Gray as Director had been a calculated risk. On the one hand, it could be very important for the success of the coverup to have one of the conspirators heading the F.B.I., and Gray's corruptibility had already been put to the test and had not been found wanting. On the other hand, there was some danger that the Gray hearings would give the senators a look at the coverup story. The second threat to the coverup was the Ervin committee, which was scheduled to open hearings in May. President Nixon regarded this threat as the most dangerous, because it was the proceeding over which he had least control, and because it could have a strong impact on the all-important area of public relations, particularly if its sessions were to be televised. Indeed he told John Dean in March that he would far rather have his aides go before a Grand Jury in secret, despite the legal dangers there, than have them go before the Ervin committee in public. This, to be sure, was partly because he believed he could manage Grand Jury proceedings to a considerable extent. ("We've got much more control there," he pointed out to Haldeman and Dean.) The third threat to the coverup came from Judge Sirica, who had deferred the sentencing of the Watergate defendants until March 23rd, and had said that the amount of coöperation a defendant gave the authorities would be taken into account at sentencing time.

In the latter part of March, the pace of events in this area of the coverup quickened. Under the pressure of the pending sentences, two of the conspirators were breaking ranks: James McCord and Howard Hunt. McCord, who had been threatening the White House with exposure since December, now wrote a letter to Judge Sirica telling what he knew of the coverup. Hunt, for his part, was angry because he and the other defendants and their lawyers had not been paid as much money as they wanted in return for their silence. In November, 1972, he called Charles Colson to remind him that the continuation of the coverup was a "two-way street," and shortly after the middle of March he told Paul O'Brien, an attorney for the reëlection committee, that if more funds weren't forthcoming immediately he might reveal some of the "seamy things" he had done for John Ehrlichman—an apparent reference to the break-in at the office of Daniel Ellsberg's psychiatrist. Shortly thereafter, O'Brien informed Dean of Hunt's demand. These events on one edge of the coverup had an immediate influence on the chemistry of the whole enterprise. On March 21st, John Dean, convinced now that the coverup could not be maintained, met with the President and related the story of it as he knew it from beginning to end. The President's response was to recommend that the blackmail money be paid to Hunt. "I think you should handle that one pretty fast," he said. And later he said, "But at the moment don't you agree that you'd better get the Hunt thing? I mean, that's worth it, at the moment." And he said, "That's why your, for your immediate thing you've got no choice with Hunt but the hundred and twenty or whatever it is. Right?" The President was willing to consider plans for limited disclosure, and the meeting ended with a suggestion from Haldeman, who had joined the two other men: "We've got to figure out where to turn it off at the lowest cost we can, but at whatever cost it takes."

Dean's session with the President put the President in a peculiarly difficult position. The conspirators in a coverup are caught in a web of powerful opposing forces. On the one hand, they need to keep themselves as closely informed as possible about the crimes that are being covered up and about the coverup itself, in order to be able to plan their moves. On the other hand, they need to keep themselves as ignorant as possible of these same matters, since the knowledge of crimes, if it is not reported to the responsible authorities, is itself a crime—misprision. When the conspirators are men in government with a special obligation to investigate and prosecute crimes, the tension between the need to know and the need not to know is particularly acute. In such a case, the multiplicity of roles assumed by each conspirator gives rise to a complexity of motivation so great as to befuddle even the conspirator himself. The conspirator who is a public official not only must know the facts, in order to get on with the coverup, while seeming not to know the facts, in order to escape indictment for misprision, but also must, in his public role as investigator, seem actively to seek the facts while secretly making sure he does not find them. When the sleuth and the criminal are united in one person, as they were in the person of the President during the Watergate coverup, one is presented with the spectacle of a man following his own footsteps in circles while taking care never to discover where they lead. President Nixon was well aware of the importance of remaining ignorant of some matters, and in late February, he said to Dean, "The main thing, of course, is also the, the isolation of the President from this." (There had been much discussion in recent years about the isolation of American Presidents from reality, but no one had suggested that a President might deliberately cultivate such isolation.) Now Dean, by laying out the story of the coverup in detail, was forcing the President to take some action, because if the President did not now act, Dean would be a witness to the crime of the President's inaction.

The defection of Hunt and McCord had upset the delicate balance of roles demanded by the coverup. Information that had to be kept secret began to flow in a wide loop through the coverup's various departments. Not only Hunt and McCord but Dean and Magruder began to tell their stories to the prosecutors. The prosecutors, in turn, relayed the information to Attorney General Kleindienst and Assistant Attorney General Petersen, who then relayed it to Haldeman and Ehrlichman, who in this period were desperately attempting to avoid prosecution, and were therefore eager to know what was happening in the Grand Jury room. Any defections placed the remaining conspirators in an awkward position. In order to get clear of the collapsing coverup, they had to become public inquisitors of their former subordinates and collaborators. Such a transformation, however, was not likely to sit well with the defectors, who were far from eager to shoulder the blame for the crimes of others, and who, furthermore, were in possession of damaging information with which to retaliate.

Notwithstanding these new tensions, the President sought to continue the coverup. In the weeks following his meeting with Dean on March 21st, his consistent strategy was what might be called the hors-d'oeuvre strategy. The President described the strategy to Haldeman and Ehrlichman after a conversation with Dean on April 14th by saying, "Give 'em an hors d'oeuvre and maybe they won't come back for the main course." His hope was that by making certain public revelations and by offering a certain number of victims to the prosecutors he could satisfy the public's appetite, so that it would seek no more revelations and no more victims. (This technique, which Ehrlichman, on another occasion, called a "modified limited hang-out," was also what Haldeman had had in mind when he suggested that they should "turn it off at the lowest cost" they could.) Hors d'oeuvres of many kinds came under consideration. Some were in the form of scapegoats to be turned over to the prosecutors, and others were in the form of incomplete or false reports to be issued to the public. By now, the country's appetite for revelations was well developed, and in the White House it was decided that no less a man than Mitchell was needed to satisfy it.

As Ehrlichman explained the new plan to the President, Mitchell would be induced to make a statement saying, "I am both morally and legally responsible."

"How does it redound to our advantage?" the President asked.

"That you have a report from me based on three weeks' work," Ehrlichman replied, "that when you got it, you immediately acted to call Mitchell in as the provable wrongdoer, and you say, 'My God, I've got a report here. And it's clear from this report that you are guilty as hell. Now John . . . go on in there and do what you should.' "

That way, the President could pose as the man who had cracked the conspiracy.

Shortly thereafter, Mitchell was called down to the White House, and Ehrlichman proposed the plan. Mitchell did not care for it. He not only maintained his innocence but suggested that the guilt lay elsewhere; namely, in the White House. Ehrlichman told the President when Mitchell had left that Mitchell had "lobbed, uh, mud balls at the White House at every opportunity." Faced with Mitchell's refusal to play the scapegoat, the President, Haldeman, and Ehrlichman next invited Dean to step into the role. Soon after Ehrlichman's unsatisfactory experience with Mitchell, the President met with Dean and attempted to induce him to sign a letter of resignation because of his implication in the scandal.

The President approached the subject in an offhand manner. "You know, I was thinking we ought to get the odds and ends, uh . . . we talked, and, uh, it was confirmed that—you remember we talked about resignations and so forth," he said.

"Uh huh," Dean replied.

"But I should have in hand something, or otherwise they'll say, 'What the hell did you—after Mr. Dean told you all of this, what did you do?' " the President went on.

Again Dean answered "Uh huh."

The President then related that even Henry Petersen had been concerned about "this situation on Dean," and Dean once more answered with an "uh huh."

"See what I mean?" the President asked the uncommunicative Dean.

"Are we talking Dean, or are we talking Dean, Ehrlichman, and Haldeman?" Dean finally asked.

"Well, I'm talking Dean," the President answered.

But Dean, like Mitchell before him, was talking Ehrlichman and Haldeman, too, and would not resign unless they also resigned. He did not want to be an hors d'oeuvre any more than Mitchell did.

And since Dean was in possession of highly detailed information that implicated not only Haldeman and Ehrlichman but the President as well, the President was unable to "bite the Dean bullet," as he put it, until he was also willing to let Haldeman and Ehrlichman go. Their turn came quickly. By now the President was under intense pressure to act soon. If he did not, he could hardly pose as the man who had cracked the case. On April 17th, the day after the unproductive conversation with Dean, the President said to Haldeman and Ehrlichman, "Let me say this. . . . It's a hell of a lot different [from] John Dean. I know that as far as you're concerned, you'll go out and throw yourselves on a damned sword. I'm aware of that. . . . The problem we got here is this. I do not want to be in a position where the damned public clamor makes, as it did with Eisenhower, with Adams, makes it necessary or calls—to have Bob come in one day and say, 'Well, Mr. President, the public—blah, blah, blah—I'm going to leave.'" But Ehrlichman was not willing to throw himself on a sword. The person he was willing to throw on a sword was Dean. "Let me make a suggestion," he responded. It was that the President give Dean a leave of absence and then defer any decision on Ehrlichman and Haldeman until the case had developed further. However, the President pursued the point, seeming at times to favor Haldeman's and Ehrlichman's resignation, and finally Ehrlichman did what McCord, Hunt, Mitchell, and Dean had done before him. He lobbed mud balls at the White House—which in this case meant the President.

If he and Haldeman should resign, Ehrlichman observed, "we are put in a position of defending ourselves." And he went on, "The things that I am going to have to say about Dean are: that basically that Dean was the sole proprietor of this project, that he reported to the President, he reported to me only incidentally."

" 'Reported to the President'?" the President inquired.

A moment later, speaking in his own defense, the President said, "You see the problem you've got there is that Dean does have a point there which you've got to realize. He didn't see me when he came out to California. He didn't see me until the day you said, 'I think you ought to talk to John Dean.'"

At this point, Ehrlichman retreated into ambiguity, and said, "But you see I get into a very funny defensive position then vis-à-vis you and vis-à-vis him, and it's very damned awkward. And I haven't thought it clear through. I don't know where we come out."

The hors-d'oeuvre strategy had now been exhausted. No one was willing to take on the role. Likewise, after considering several possible reports to serve the same purpose (such as a report by John Dean, a report that would reveal the origins of Segretti's crimes but not the origins of the Watergate coverup, a report to the public by Ehrlichman), and after considering possible forums to head off the Senate investigation (such as a specially convened Grand Jury, a Presidential panel that would look into the facts of the scandal, a special prosecutor who could perhaps be controlled by the White House), the President, as the coverup came apart, could not offer the public anything. Dragged down by the weight of his co-conspirators, he had been unable to change himself from criminal into investigator. He had told John Dean that he wanted to "take the credit" for Magruder's decision to talk to the prosecutors, but Dean had responded that he himself was the more responsible party. And the President had said to Dean, "You're to say, 'I told the President about this [the coverup]. . . . And the President said, "Look, I want to get to the bottom of this thing, period." ' See what I'm driving at?" But he had actually said nothing of the sort to Dean at the time, and now Dean had answered only "Uh huh." To Henry Petersen the President had said, "Let me say this. The main thing, Henry, we must not have any question, now, on this, you know, I am in charge of this thing. You are and I am. . . . You know, I want to stay one step ahead of the curve. You know what I mean?" Petersen had responded only with a noncommittal "I understand."

On April 17th, the President made a short public statement saying simply that there had been "major developments in the case concerning which it would be improper to be more specific now." He was unable to offer any diversionary reports on propitiatory victims to deflect the public's wrath at the forthcoming disclosures. He and his aides had talked over countless schemes, but all of them had foundered on the unwillingness of any of the aides to sacrifice themselves for him—or for "the Presidency," as he had asked them to do. The coverup was all one piece, and it cohered in exposure just as it had cohered in concealment.

But if the President's hours of discussion had not produced any strategy that would establish his innocence in the eyes of the public, they had apparently served to establish his innocence in his own eyes. He and Haldeman and Ehrlichman had spent the better part of their time over the past eight months doing what they had been best at doing for more than four years: making up scenarios. The scenario they were looking for this time was a false over-all version of events which combined real and invented occurrences into a plausible story demonstrating their own innocence. As the state of the evidence before the prosecutors changed, the scenario also had to change, to take the new facts into account. Soon the three men had to improvise new stories almost hourly. At times, the President was put in the awkward position of having to inquire of his fellow-scenarists what his own actions and thoughts had supposedly been.

"How has the scenario worked out? May I ask you?" the President inquired of Haldeman the day before the public announcement.

"Well, it works out very good," Haldeman answered. "You became aware some time ago that this thing [the Dean "report"] did not parse out the way it was supposed to and that there were some discrepancies between what you had been told by Dean in the report that there was nobody in the White House involved, which may still be true."

"How do I get credit for getting Magruder to the stand?" the President inquired shortly afterward. And a moment later he asked, "Why did I take Dean off [the case]?" Then, having been told that the scenario had him on record as having alerted the Attorney General to the coverup, he was obliged to ask, "This is very good now. How does that happen?"

What is perhaps even more surprising than the President's ability to make up stories in a steady, unbroken stream was his seeming ability to believe each of them almost instantaneously. It was one thing for him to tell Henry Petersen that "Dean was the one who told us throughout the summer that nobody in the White

House was involved when he himself apparently was involved," for that statement could have been a simple lie. It was another matter altogether for him to ask, in a phone conversation with Ehrlichman late at night, whether it was right to "fire a guy for a mistake"—namely, Haldeman—when Ehrlichman knew very well that the real moral question was whether the President was willing to fire a man for the President's own mistake. On this occasion, the President seemed to have thrown himself so wholeheartedly into his false role that in his private conversations he had begun to agonize over moral questions that were appropriate to the false role but wholly inappropriate to his real role. The President had apparently forgotten what his real role was. At one point in March, Ehrlichman had called a White House aide to ask for his "recollection" of the meeting at which Ehrlichman was said to have ordered Dean to tell Hunt to get out of the country, and the aide had answered, "I'll recollect anything you want me to." The President, too, had become adept at recollecting whatever was needed at a particular moment. By April of 1973, he and his aides were spending most of their time making up history out of whole cloth to suit the needs of each moment. Unfortunately for them, the history they were making up was self-serving history, and by April their individual interests had grown apart. Each of them had begun to "recollect" things to his own advantage and to the detriment of the others. As their community of interests dissolved under the pressure of the investigation, each of them was retreating into his own private, self-interested reality. The capacity for deception which had once divided them from the country but united them with one another now divided them from one another as well.

In the White House, the fabric of reality had disintegrated altogether. What had got the President into trouble from the start had been his remarkable capacity for fantasy. He had begun by imagining a host of domestic foes. In retaliating against them, he had broken the law. Then he had compounded his lawbreaking by concealing it. And, finally, in the same way that he had broken the law although breaking it was against his best interests, he was bringing himself to justice even as he thought he was evading justice. For, as though in anticipation of the deterioration of his memory, he had installed another memory in the Oval Office, which was more nearly perfect than his own, or anyone else's merely human equipment: he had installed the taping system. The Watergate coverup had cast him in the double role of conspirator and investigator. Though the conspirator in him worked hard to escape the law, it was the investigator in him that gained the upper hand in the end. While he was attempting to evade the truth, his machines were preserving it forever.

At the moment when the President announced "major developments" in the Watergate case, the national process that was the investigation overwhelmed the national process that was the coverup. The events that followed were all the more astounding to the nation because, at just the moment when the coverup began to explode, the President, in the view of many observers, had been on the point of strangling the "obsolete" Constitutional system and replacing it with a Presidential dictatorship. One moment, he was triumphant and his power was apparently irresistible; the next moment, he was at bay. For in the instant the President made his announcement, the coverup cracked—not just the Watergate coverup but the broader coverup, which concealed the underground history of the last five years—and the nation suffered an inundation of news. The newspaper headlines now came faster and thicker than ever before in American history. The stories ran backward in time, and each day's newspaper told of some event a little further in the past as reporters traced the underground history to the early days of the Administration, and even into the terms of former Administrations. With the history of half a decade pouring out all at once, the papers were stuffed with more news than even the most diligent reader could absorb. Moreover, along with the facts, non-facts proliferated as the desperate men in the White House put out one false or distorted statement after another, so that each true fragment of the story was all but lost in a maze of deceptions, and each event, true or false, came up dozens of times, in dozens of versions, until the

330

reader's mind was swamped. And, as if what was in the newspapers were not already too much, television soon started up, and, in coverage that was itself a full-time job to watch, presented first the proceedings of the Ervin committee and then the proceedings of the House Judiciary Committee, when it began to weigh the impeachment of the President. And, finally, in a burst of disclosure without anything close to a precedent in history, the tapes were revealed— and not just once but twice. The first set of transcripts was released by the White House and was doctored, and only the second set, which was released by the Judiciary Committee, gave an accurate account of the President's conversations.

As the flood of information flowed into the public realm, overturning the accepted history of recent years, the present scene was also transformed. The Vice-President was swept from office when his bribe-taking became known, but so rapid was the pace of events that his departure was hardly noticed. Each of the institutions of the democracy that had been menaced by the President—and all had been menaced—was galvanized into action in its turn: the press, the television networks, the Senate, the House of Representatives, and, finally, in a dispute over release of the tapes, the Supreme Court. The public, too, was at last awakened, when the President fired the Special Prosecutor whom he had appointed to look into the White House crimes. In an outpouring of public sentiment that, like so much else that happened at the time, had no precedent in the nation's history, millions of letters and telegrams poured in to Congress protesting the President's action. The time of letters sent by the President to himself was over, and the time of real letters from real people had come. No one of the democracy's institutions was powerful enough by itself to remove the President; the efforts of all were required—and only when those efforts were combined was he forced from office.

The struggle between the Nixon Administration and the other principal institutions of the Republic carried the policies of the Nixon Administration to a strange fulfillment. He had brought his own worst nightmares to life. Soon after taking office, he had become convinced that the Presidency was threatened with impotence by the machination of unscrupulous domestic "enemies," who gathered under the banner of "the Establishment." To deal with this supposed threat, he had launched what he called his Presidential Offensive, in which he sought to wrest power from "the Establishment," and so destroy it. He did to his opposition the things he had imagined that his opposition was doing to him. When he came to believe that the Senate was employing un-Constitutional power against him by rejecting two of his Supreme Court nominations, he retaliated by asserting un-Constitutional powers himself. When he came to imagine that the press was out to destroy him, he retaliated by trying to destroy the press. In reality, the "enemies"—the press, the television networks, the courts, the Congress, the federal bureaucracies, the non-profit foundations—had had little stomach for opposing him, and his power had grown steadily at their expense. As for removing him from office by any means other than defeating him in an election, the mere idea was outside the pale of respectable consideration throughout his first term. But by April of 1973, although neither he nor his "enemies" quite knew it, he was in fact threatened with a terrible fall at the hands of those "enemies." By his own actions, he had given substance to his worst imaginings. Now the Senate, the House, the courts, the television networks, and the press, merely by doing what they normally should do under the Constitution, really did threaten his Administration with destruction. Other actions of his Presidency fell into the same pattern of nightmare brought to life. For example, he despised left-wing extremism, yet in the 1972 Presidential campaign he sent out his men to promote it, the better to destroy the politically dangerous Democratic center. In another move that gave substance to his worst imaginings, he invaded Cambodia in order to check what he saw as a rise in "anarchy" at home—although the United States had been calming down at the time—and in so doing he provoked something like real anarchy into existence all across the nation. The President's fantasy was father to the fact. What the President imagined to be true soon was true, as the result of his own actions.

The Nixon men used the language of the theatre—"scenario," "script," "players," "orchestration"—to describe the way they ran the country, but perhaps the most apt analogy would be to the state of dreaming. From the human faculty of dreaming, it can be seen that every person has the power to invent a wholly imaginary world that is indistinguishable to him from the real world. A waking person confronts a world that is given, but a dreamer confronts a world that is of his own creation. He is the author not only of his own actions but of the world in which he acts. In him are united subject and object. It is he who arranges to be attacked from behind and he who jumps in surprise. The beast that chases after and the "I" who runs away are the products of a single mind. President Nixon, using the great powers of his office, organized his waking life on the same principle. His methods of propping up his surrogate world were various. Sometimes he would block a fact out of only his own awareness; sometimes he would attempt to block it out of the awareness of the whole nation; and sometimes he would simply wipe the offending fact off the face of the earth in a B-52 raid. The President was becoming the author of his own environment. He manufactured events and then he "responded" to them. He invented enemies and then he went to war against them. He gave the speeches and then he applauded them. He threw the rocks and then he ducked. He invented crises and then he made "great decisions" to resolve them. As for the rest of us, it became our fate to live for a half a decade inside the head of a waking dreamer.

On one occasion, shortly after his reëlection, President Nixon described to a reporter how he reacted when he received news directly from the outside world on his television set. "The great decisions in this office require calm," he said, and he went on, "I could go up the wall watching TV commentators. I don't. . . . I never watch TV commentators or the news shows when they are about me." He added, "The major weakness of inexperienced people is that they take things personally, especially in politics, and that can destroy you." And by early 1973 it was true that facts that might appear on television could literally destroy him, for by then the investigations into the Watergate scandal had begun. But until these facts intruded he lived in a closed world in which he rarely had any experiences he had not arranged for himself. As in a dream, some of the experiences he arranged were pleasant and some were gratifying and some were frightening. What he could not endure were unplanned experiences that came from without, and it was these which his television set brought before his eyes. Had he remained in power much longer, he would surely have put an end to such disruptions once and for all. Then no unexpected sights would have offended his gaze. What he saw would no longer have sent him up the wall. It would no longer have destroyed him. His communion with himself would then have continued uninterrupted, and the world he saw would have been co-extensive with his thought processes. There would have been only the sound of the programmed enemies and the sound of the surrogates praising him in words of his own devising. And, at the center, a perfect closed circle in which he talked to his tapes and his tapes talked to him.

VI.
CREDIBILITY

I N THE YEARS OF THE VIETNAM WAR, the United States experienced a systemic crisis, which reached its final stage when, under the Nixon Administration, the American Constitutional democracy was almost destroyed by its President. Then, as the Nixon Administration was forced from office, the nation seemed—for the time being, at least—to reaffirm its allegiance to its Constitutional traditions. After a period in which almost any situation called an emergency was considered reason enough for the executive branch to suspend the rights of citizens, to arrogate power to itself, and otherwise to distort or simply break the law, the nation seemed to rediscover its forgotten political principles. It was reminded, for example, that great power can easily be abused; that if one powerful man is allowed to rise above the law, the law as a whole is placed in jeopardy; and that a heavy reliance on secrecy is incompatible with democracy. All these principles were dealt with in millions of words in the press and

337

in hundreds of hours of television, and I will not be further concerned with them here. Instead, I will offer some thoughts on the particular conditions that made our time the one in which the most serious threat to liberty in American history could take place.

One school of thought has it that the nature of the various stages of the Vietnam period was determined largely by the background and character of the various men who occupied the White House in those years. According to this way of thinking, the great accumulation of powers in the Presidency served to expand the character flaws of the officeholders and their staffs into national disasters. In the Kennedy and Johnson years, it is said, government policy came to be dominated by a group of brilliant, overconfident, privileged men of an East Coast "Establishment," whose character flaws were soon writ large in the war in Vietnam. And in the Nixon years, it is said, government policy came to be dominated by a ruthless, unprincipled group of men, many of them from southern California, whose character flaws were soon writ large in "Watergate" (as President Nixon's attempt to seize power came to be called). And certainly the variations in the character of the men in the White House were reflected in the events of the time. However, what stands out much more sharply than any variations is the astonishing degree of continuity which binds the stages of the mounting systemic crisis together—the marked differences in character of the officeholders notwithstanding. The distortions in the conduct of the Presidency which deformed national politics in the Vietnam years— the isolation from reality, the rage against political opposition, the hunger for un-Constitutional power, the conspiratorial-mindedness, the bent for repressive action—knew no party lines. They were all as clearly evident on a small scale at the Democratic Convention in Chicago in 1968 as they were on a national scale in the Nixon Presidency. The Kennedy and Johnson men supposedly belonged to "the Establishment," and the Nixon men regarded themselves as enemies of "the Establishment" and wished to destroy it forever; yet in handling the policies that had the most direct bearing on the Constitutional crisis the men of the three Administrations made decisions that were strikingly alike. In fact, when it came to making contributions to the Constitutional crisis President Nixon seemed to pick up precisely where President Johnson had left off, as though there had been no change of party in the White House.

The most telling decisions were, by and large, in the area of "foreign affairs"—our anachronistic euphemism for the unlimited sphere of action which now encompasses the life and death of every soul on earth. For in the Vietnam years the exigencies of foreign policy, and particularly the exigencies of the nuclear dilemma, began to dominate the course of the nation's politics. In those years, Presidents consistently sacrificed the welfare of the nation at home to what they saw as the demands of foreign affairs; and in the domestic record of the period one finds only discontinuity and neglect. The Johnson Presidency embodied the dominance of foreign affairs in a tragic form. President Johnson was more interested in domestic affairs than in foreign affairs, yet it was foreign affairs that, in the shape of the Vietnam war, determined the fate of his Presidency, leaving his dreams of reform at home in ruins. Under President Nixon, the role of foreign affairs was even larger. Foreign affairs were his chief interest to begin with, and he looked on domestic politics almost entirely as a cheering section for his foreign policy and—what amounted in practice to the same thing— as an arena for his reëlection. His indifference to the substance of the most important issues facing the country at home was, apparently, complete. He came closer to destroying the American Constitutional system than any man or group of men had come before, yet he had no clear conception of a system to put in its place. In the domestic record of the Nixon Administration one finds, instead of rigid adherence to a system of ideas, a deliberate separation of the image of government policy from the substance of government policy, and also a chaotic veering from one policy to another under the pressure of political expediency. In fact, more often than not the promises that the Nixon Administration made to the public turned out to have been signals that exactly the opposite of what was promised was about to occur. At the beginning of his first term, President Nixon promised to work for national unity, but then he launched a drive to polarize national politics. In economic affairs, he portrayed himself as a champion of the system of free enterprise, but then he became the first President to impose wage and price controls for any reason other than war, and also set about transforming the Cabinet departments and the agencies of the federal government into instruments for the coercion and political control of businessmen. (The fact that some sixty million dollars was raised by his reëlection campaign committee, much of it from corporations and wealthy individuals, provides eloquent testimony to the success of his efforts.) In the field of social programs, he championed a major expansion of spending for social needs, in the form of his Family Assistance Plan—which never came to fruition—but then he initiated a highly organized drive to cut back even the existing programs. As for the question of a political philosophy, he preached the decentralization of federal power, but then he attempted to gather the whole power of the federal government into his own hands. From the moment of taking office, when he promised, in his first Inaugural Address, to build a "great cathedral of the spirit" and unify the nation, to the spring of 1973, when he had Senate Minority Leader Hugh Scott announce on his behalf, "We have nothing to hide," he filled the air with empty and intentionally misleading phrases—phrases that in both tone and content were without relation either to each other or to the actions of his Administration. In the domestic sphere, far from being guided by an unwavering vision of how he wanted things to be, he had no guiding purposes at all. At times, his statements were merely ridiculous, as when he promised "the lift of a driving dream," or promised a "New American Revolution," which would be "as exciting as that first revolution almost two hundred years ago," and then forgot about it immediately. But often the consequences were grave, as they were when, in the words of his political planning group for the 1972 campaign, he set out to "exacerbate" national problems solely in order to "divide the Democrats" in the 1972 Presidential primaries and then win "far the larger half" of the electorate in the general election —and so became the first President on record to establish a program consciously aimed at worsening the torments afflicting the nation. No issue was above exploitation—not the issue of race, not the issue of Supreme Court nominations, not the issue of social spending. All were to be exacerbated. It is true that themes emerged from time to time. President Nixon's feelings were closely attuned to certain deep-running resentments in American politics—resentments against the press, against the television networks, against black people, against the rebellious young, and against the ill-defined entity known as "the Establishment"—and in late 1969 and for most of 1970 he sought to make a partisan drive against these supposed menaces the central theme of national politics. But even this theme, so congenial to the President's temperament, was suddenly dropped from his public statements after the congressional elections of 1970, in which its political usefulness had been tested and found wanting.

In foreign affairs, the gap between image and substance was no less wide, and the sudden, unexplained reversals of policy were no less startling: as a candidate, in 1968, Richard Nixon promised an early end to the war, but then, as President, he continued the war effort for four more years; in 1969, he spoke of "great powers who have not yet abandoned their goals of world conquest," clearly referring to China and Russia, but then in 1972 he went to China and Russia and drank toasts of friendship with the leaders of those powers, while promising the world a "generation of peace." In foreign affairs, however, if one looks behind the surface of shifting images, the more constant concerns can be made out. If one examines the covert record, as it appears in the Pentagon Papers and in other secret memoranda, and ignores the public justifications that were put forward only for reasons of propaganda, a remarkable consistency of purpose emerges; and if guiding principles in government policy are to be found in the years in which the American democracy experienced its crisis, they are buried here, in the realm of strategic theory. For from January of 1961, when John Kennedy took office, until August of 1974, when Richard Nixon was forced to leave office, the unvarying dominant goal of the foreign policy of the United States was the preservation of what policymakers throughout the period called the credibility of American power. (And, indeed, since President Nixon's fall the preservation of American credibility has remained the dominant goal of United States foreign policy.)

The various policymakers phrased the aim in many ways. To have a formidable "psychological impact . . . on the countries of the world" is how the Joint Chiefs of Staff put it in a memo to Secretary of Defense Robert McNamara in January of 1962. To prevent a situation from arising in which "no nation can ever again have the same confidence in American promise or in American protection" is how President Johnson put it at a news conference in July of 1965. To "avoid humiliation" is how Assistant Secretary of Defense John McNaughton put it in a memo in January of 1966. To shore up "the confidence factor" is how Assistant Secretary of State William Bundy put it in a speech in January of 1967. To prevent "defeat and humiliation" is how President Nixon put it in a speech in November of 1969. To demonstrate America's "will and character" is how President Nixon put it in a speech in April of 1970. To prevent the United States from appearing before the world as a "pitiful, helpless giant" is another way that President Nixon put it in that speech. To maintain "respect for the office of President of the United States" is how President Nixon put it in a speech in April of 1972. To win an "honorable" peace or a "peace with honor" is how President Nixon put it from time to time. But, whatever words it was couched in, the aim was always the same: to establish in the minds of peoples and their leaders throughout the world an image of the United States as a nation that possessed great power and had the will and determination to use it in foreign affairs. In the name of this objective, President Kennedy sent "advisers" to Vietnam in the early nineteen-sixties, and President Johnson escalated the Vietnam war in secrecy and persisted in carrying on the war in the face of growing public opposition. In the name of this objective, also, President Nixon sent planes and troops into Cambodia, sent an aircraft carrier into the Indian Ocean at the time of the India-Pakistan war, mined North Vietnamese ports in the spring of 1972, and carpet-bombed North Vietnam during the Christmas season of 1972. In the pursuit of this objective, massacres were condoned, hundreds of thousands of lives were lost, dictatorial governments were propped up, nations friendly to the United States were turned into adversaries, the domestic scene was thrown into turmoil, two Presidents were forced from office, the Constitution was imperilled, and the entire world was repeatedly brought to the verge of war.

The doctrine of credibility, far from being a fanatical ideology, was a coldly reasoned strategic theory that was designed to supply the United States with effective instruments of influence in an age dominated by nuclear weapons. The doctrine did not take shape all at once but evolved gradually as the full sweep of American military policy, including, especially, nuclear policy, was subjected to a reëxamination, which got under way outside the government in the late nineteen-fifties and was carried forward within the government in the early nineteen-sixties, after President Kennedy took office. When Kennedy entered the White House, the nation's nuclear policy had remained all but unchanged since the end of the Korean war, in 1953. In fact, although the conditions under which men lived and conducted their politics were altered more drastically by the invention of nuclear weapons than by any previous single invention, nuclear weapons had never become the subject of intensive public debate. In the aftermath of the Second World War, the United States had made a brief effort at the United Nations to bring the new weapons under some form of international control, but the atmosphere of the Cold War had soon settled in and the effort had been abandoned. Then, in the nineteen-fifties, the nation's attention had been further distracted from the new peril by rising levels of consumption, which quickly climbed beyond the highest expectations. In the United States, unprecedented wealth and ease came to coexist with unprecedented danger, and a sumptuous feast of consumable goods was spread out in the shadow of universal death. Americans began to live as though on a luxuriously appointed death row, where one was free to enjoy every comfort but was uncertain from moment to moment when or if the death sentence might be carried out. The abundance was very much in the forefront of people's attention, however, and the uncertainty very much in the background; and in the government as well as in the country at large the measureless questions posed by the new weapons were

343

evaded. As far as any attempt to find a way out of the nuclear dilemma was concerned, the time was one of sleep. But in the late nineteen-fifties, as the reëxamination of the American military position gathered momentum, a few men began to think through the whole subject of nuclear strategy anew. Among them were two men whose writings proved to be of special importance, not only because the ideas expressed were influential in themselves but because each man was to take a high post in government in the years ahead. One was Henry Kissinger, who was a professor at Harvard during the nineteen-fifties and nineteen-sixties, and whose book *Nuclear Weapons and Foreign Policy* appeared in 1957. The other was General Maxwell Taylor, who was the Army Chief of Staff under President Eisenhower, and whose book *The Uncertain Trumpet* appeared in 1960.

Both men were disturbed by a paradox that seemed to lie near the heart of the nuclear question. It was that nuclear weapons, the most powerful instruments of violence ever invented, tended to immobilize rather than strengthen their possessors. This paradox was rooted in the central fact of the weapons' unprecedented destructive force, which made mankind, for the first time in its history, capable of annihilating itself. Nuclear weapons, Kissinger and Taylor realized, were bound to have a chilling effect on any warlike plans that their possessors, including the United States, might entertain. Wars were supposedly fought for ends, but a war fought with nuclear arms might well obliterate any end for which a war could be fought. Not only that but it might obliterate all means as well, and, for that matter, obliterate the only earthly creature capable of thinking in terms of means and ends. As Kissinger put it in his book, "the destructiveness of modern weapons deprives victory in an all-out war of its historical meaning." He decided that "all-out war has therefore ceased to be a meaningful instrument of policy." Thenceforward, the United States would be in the position of having to fear its own power almost as much as it feared the power of its foes. Taylor, in his book, described his doubts about the usefulness of nuclear weapons in somewhat different language. The notion that "the use or the threatened use of atomic weapons of mass destruction would be sufficient to assure the security of the United States and its friends," he wrote, was "The Great Fallacy" in the prevailing strategic thinking of the day. The new strategists were saying that nuclear weapons, instead of making the nuclear powers more formidable, appeared to be casting a pall of doubt over their military policies. The doubt did not concern the amounts of military power at their disposal; it concerned their willingness, in the face of the dread of extinction, to unleash that power. Kissinger wrote, "Both the horror and the power of modern [nuclear] weapons tend to paralyze action: the former because it will make few issues seem worth contending for; the latter because it causes many disputes to seem irrelevant to the over-all strategic equation"—which had to do with the victory of one side or the other. In strength, it had turned out, lurked weakness; in omnipotence, impotence.

Kissinger and Taylor, working separately, set out to frame a foreign policy that would take into account the implications of nuclear weapons. Each of them began to think through a policy that would accommodate two broad aims. One aim was to prevent the extinction of the world in a nuclear war, and the other aim was to prevent the domination of the world—naturally, including the domination of the United States—by Communist totalitarian forces. It was clear to the two men that these aims conflicted at many points. The aim of preventing human extinction, which was peculiar to the nuclear age, seemed to call for unprecedented restraint in military matters, but the aim of preventing global Communist totalitarian rule seemed to call for unceasing military efforts on an unprecedented scale. On the one hand, nuclear dread inhibited the United States from using its military power aggressively; on the other hand, the ambitions, ideals, and fears that have traditionally impelled powerful nations onto the world stage impelled the United States to use its military power aggressively. Kissinger wrote, "The dilemma of the nuclear period can, therefore, be defined as follows: the enormity of modern weapons makes the thought of war repugnant, but the refusal to run any risks would amount to giving the Soviet rulers a blank check." The aim of standing firm in the face of Soviet power, which, of course, corresponded to the broad aim of preventing world domination by Communist totalitarian forces, struck a responsive chord in the thinking of American politicians of the late nineteen-fifties. American political life had been dominated at least since the decade began by a conviction that the freedom and independence of nations all over the world was threatened by a unified, global Communist conspiracy that was under the control of the Soviet Union. Since then, "anti-Communism" not only had been the mainspring of American foreign policy but for a time—when Senator Joseph McCarthy hunted for Communists in the United States—had also been the central preoccupation of domestic politics. In this atmosphere, a reluctance to give Soviet leaders "a blank check" was quickly understood. However, the second aim recognized by Kissinger and Taylor—the avoidance of a nuclear catastrophe—was harder for the politicians of that time to grasp; and it was in championing this aim that the two men had to do the greater part of their explaining. (Something that helped them greatly in getting a hearing on the nuclear question was the fact that the anti-Communism of each of them was so strong as to be above suspicion.) The military, in particular, was difficult to persuade. The notion that an increase in military strength might, in effect, enfeeble the nation was a paradox not to the liking of the military mind. It was therefore difficult at first for the military to agree that, as Kissinger put it, in the nuclear age "the more powerful the weapons . . . the greater becomes the reluctance to use them"—in other words, the greater the power, the greater the paralysis.

Kissinger and Taylor, however, had an answer to those who were afraid that a recognition of the paralyzing influence of nuclear weapons might weaken the nation. While the two men were prepared to point out that reliance upon nuclear weapons might lead to a sort of impotence, they were far from willing to accept the condition. In fact, they were convinced that by failing to take cognizance of the danger the government was actually making the United States weaker in world affairs than it need be. In the late nineteen-fifties, the Eisenhower Administration was relying almost exclusively on the threat of nuclear attack to cope with military challenges around the world. As Kissinger observed, American military policy was governed by the belief that "the chief deterrent to Soviet aggression resides in United States nuclear superiority." The policy was deliberate, and had been framed in response to the nation's experience in the early nineteen-fifties, during the Korean war. At that time, the public had shown that it reacted unenthusiastically to the sacrifice of American ground troops in inconclusive small wars fought far from the United States for goals that were difficult to grasp; and in 1954, after the war was brought to an end, Secretary of State John Foster Dulles had established a policy of using the threat of nuclear retaliation to achieve the sort of limited, local objective for which ground troops had been used in Korea. In a speech in January of that year, he said that in responding to a Communist challenge in any part of the world the United States would "depend primarily upon a great capacity to retaliate instantly by means and at places of our choosing," and he pointed out that a policy of reliance upon the nuclear threat not only would keep the troops at home but would be less expensive than ground operations. The Dulles policy became known as the policy of "massive retaliation," and also as "brinksmanship." It required the United States to rush toward the brink of nuclear war each time a crisis broke out somewhere in the world, and then to draw back at the last moment, having, it was hoped, frightened the foe into complying with American wishes. The strategy assumed, of course, that the Communist movement was a single force, controlled by the Soviet Union, and that a threat of nuclear retaliation against the Soviet Union would serve to stop Communist moves in, say, the Far East. Kissinger and Taylor were no less firm believers than Dulles in the unity of World Communism, and they did not oppose the Dulles policy on this point. Their charge was that his policy ignored the implications of the all-encompassing destructive force of nuclear weapons. Kissinger, employing a word that was just beginning to come into vogue, observed that a threat to use nuclear weapons in each minor crisis around the world would lack "credibility." What worried him was not only that the United States might make a misstep at the brink; it was also that the Communists might not be adequately deterred by a threat of massive nuclear retaliation. He was afraid that the Communists would find it implausible that the United States should be willing to risk nuclear annihilation merely to serve some minor purpose thousands of miles from home, and that they would therefore be unafraid to oppose the United States. For in the strategy of massive retaliation the government seemed to take the use of nuclear force almost lightly, as though nuclear weapons were ordinary, readily usable instruments of policy rather than engines of doom. The danger was, as Kissinger saw it, that "every move on [the Soviet bloc's] part will . . . pose the appalling dilemma of whether we are willing to commit suicide to prevent encroachments, which do not, each in itself, seem to threaten our existence directly but which may be steps on the road to our ultimate destruction." Kissinger was attempting to work out the implications of the distressing fact that once both adversaries were armed with nuclear weapons, a decision to use nuclear weapons was as dangerous to oneself as it was to the foe, for the result might be "suicide." And a threat to commit suicide was not a very convincing way of deterring a foe. Kissinger was suggesting that the policy of brinksmanship menaced the world with both great dangers of the period: global totalitarianism *and* human extinction. On the one hand, that policy threatened to transform every small crisis into a major nuclear crisis, and, on the other hand, it left the United States without "credible" instruments of force in situations where the stakes were too small to justify any risk of "suicide." The need was for a policy that would steer a middle course between the two dangers—for a policy that would, in Kissinger's words, "provide a means to escape from the sterility of the quest for absolute peace, which paralyzes by the vagueness of its hopes, and of the search for absolute victory, which paralyzes by the vastness of its consequences."

A middle course was available, both Kissinger and Taylor believed, in a strategy of limited war. "A strategy of limited war," Kissinger wrote, "would seek to escape the inconsistency of relying on a policy of deterrence [that is, massive retaliation], whose major sanction involves national catastrophe." And Taylor wrote, "The new strategy would recognize that it is just as necessary to deter or win quickly a limited war as to deter general war." Kissinger, for his part, believed that even in the nuclear age the freedom actually to use force rather than merely to threaten the use of force was indispensable to the maintenance of international order. He derided "the national psychology which considers peace as the 'normal' pattern of relations among states," and, while granting that "the contemporary revolution cannot be managed by force alone," he maintained that "when there is no penalty for irresponsibility, the pent-up frustrations of centuries may seek an outlet in the international field." Therefore, "to the extent that recourse to force has become impossible the restraints of the international order may disappear as well." In his view, dangerous as the use of force was in the nuclear age, the United States would have to overcome its uneasiness and thus "face up to the risks of Armageddon." And limited war, he believed, was both a more acceptable and a more effective way of facing up to these risks than was massive retaliation. For a strategy of limited war would rescue the use of force from nuclear paralysis. It would provide "credible" means of threatening the foe. It would make the world safe again for war.

More specifically, there were, in Kissinger's view, "three reasons . . . for developing a strategy of limited war." He listed them as follows: "First, limited war represents the only means for preventing the Soviet bloc, at an acceptable cost, from overrunning the peripheral areas of Eurasia. Second, a wide range of military capabilities may spell the difference between defeat and victory even in an all-out war. Finally, intermediate applications of our power offer the best chance to bring about strategic changes favorable to our side." (By "victory even in an all-out war" Kissinger meant the survival after nuclear war of enough conventional forces in the United States to impose America's will on the surviving remnant of the Soviet population.) His reference to "the best chance to bring about strategic changes favorable to our side" had to do with what he saw as the possibility that on occasion limited war might be used offensively as well as defensively, and would place the United States in a position to reduce "the Soviet sphere." These aims—the defense of a perimeter, the attainment of "victory" in all-out hostilities, and the attainment of improved strategic positions that would reduce "the Soviet sphere"—were straightforward military aims of a traditional kind. They can be called the tangible objectives of limited war.

One aim of the strategy of limited war, then, was to free the use of military force from nuclear paralysis, so that the United States might still avail itself of its arms to stop Communism from spreading around the globe. But there was also a second aim. It was to help in preventing a nuclear war. It was Kissinger's hope that the new policy could "rescue mankind from the horrors of a thermonuclear holocaust by devising a framework of war limitation." Or, in Taylor's words, the new policy "is not blind to the awful dangers of general atomic war; indeed, it takes as its primary purpose the avoidance of that catastrophe." By assigning largely to limited war the achievement of the tangible objectives in the fight against Communist enemies, the policy opened the way to a crucial shift in the mission of the American nuclear force. Secretary of State Dulles had sought to use the threat of nuclear war to work America's will in small crises around the world, but if limited-war forces could take over this job, the nuclear force, relieved of its provocative, belligerent role, could be retired into the purely passive one of deterring nuclear attack. Thereafter, the role of the nuclear force would simply be that of threatening retaliation in order to dissuade the Soviet Union from using its nuclear force in a first strike. Neither Taylor nor Kissinger spelled out the possibility of this shift, but it was implicit in their writings, and was later adopted as policy, under the name of deterrence. The strategy of limited war was thus a necessary companion to the policy of deterrence. In fact, it had been designed, in part, to wean the United States from its perilous sole reliance on the threat of massive nuclear retaliation. The policies of nuclear deterrence and limited war represented a division of labor, in which nuclear weapons would take on the defensive role in military policy and the limited-war forces would take on the offensive role. Taylor, describing a proposal along these lines he had made to the National Security Council in 1958, wrote, "Our atomic deterrent forces would be the shield under which we must live from day to day with the Soviet threat. This shield would provide us protection, but not a means of maneuver. It was rather to the so-called limited-war forces that we henceforth must look for the active elements of our military strategy."

The limited-war strategy would dovetail with nuclear strategy in another way, too. It would give the United States a new opportunity to make demonstrations of its "will" or "resolve" to use force in the world. It would, that is, give the nation a chance to demonstrate its credibility. This objective of limited war can be called the psychological objective. In a passage setting forth some of the fundamental reasoning behind the policy of limited war, Kissinger described the importance of the psychological objective to the whole of American strategic policy:

> Deterrence is brought about not only by a physical but also by a psychological relationship: deterrence is greatest when military strength is coupled with the willingness to employ it. It is achieved when one side's readiness to run risks in relation to the other is high; it is least effective when the willingness to run risks is low, however powerful the military capability. It is, therefore, no longer possible to speak of military superiority in the abstract. What does "being ahead" in the nuclear race mean if each side can already destroy the other's national substance? . . . It is the task of strategic doctrine to strike a balance between the physical and the psychological aspects of deterrence, between the desire to pose a maximum threat and the reality that no threat is stronger than the belief of the opponent that it will in fact be used. . . . The reliance on all-out war as the chief deterrent inhibits the establishment of this balance. By identifying deterrence with maximum power it tends to paralyze the will. Its concern with the physical basis of deterrence neglects the psychological aspect. Given the power of modern weapons, a nation that relies on all-out war as its chief deterrent imposes a fearful psychological handicap on itself. The most agonizing decision a statesman can face is whether or not to unleash all-out war; all pressures will make for hesitation, short of a direct attack threatening the national existence. In any other situation he will be inhibited by the incommensurability between the cost of the war and

351

the objective in dispute. And he will be confirmed in his hesitations by the conviction that, so long as his retaliatory force remains intact, no shift in the territorial balance is of decisive significance. . . . The psychological equation, therefore, will almost inevitably operate against the side which can extricate itself from a situation *only* by the threat of all-out war. Who can be certain that, faced with the catastrophe of all-out war, even Europe, long the keystone of our security, will seem worth the price? As the power of modern weapons grows, the threat of all-out war loses its credibility.

A strategy of limited war would help overcome the deficiency in the psychological equation and restore credibility. By advertising America's strength to the world at levels below the brink, it would hold the world a few steps back from nuclear extinction and at the same time would deter the Communists from aggressive moves. New room for military maneuvering would open up. Whereas under the strategy of massive retaliation there was only one step on the ladder between peace and the holocaust, under the strategy of limited war there would be many steps, and at each step the superpowers would have the opportunity to take stock of each other's intentions, to send each other clear signals of their "resolve," and, perhaps, to draw back before things got out of hand. In a passage that compared the opportunities for demonstrating credibility which were offered by the strategy of massive retaliation (in which only threats were possible) with the opportunities offered by a strategy of limited war (in which actual military efforts were possible), Kissinger wrote, "It is a strange doctrine which asserts that we can convey our determination to our opponent by reducing our overseas commitments, that, in effect, our words will be a more effective deterrent than our deeds." Under the policy he was proposing, America's deeds—its actions in limited wars—would "convey our determination." Taylor similarly underscored the psychological importance of limited war, writing, "There is also an important psychological factor which must be present to make this retaliatory weapon [the nuclear deterrent force] effective. It must be clear to the aggressor that we have the will and determination to use our retaliatory power without compunction if we are attacked. Any suggestion of weakness or indecision may encourage the enemy to gamble on surprise." And the best way to prevent "any suggestion of weakness or indecision" from appearing, he thought, was to prepare for limited war. The strategy would, in his words, guard against the danger that "repeated [Communist] success in creeping aggression may encourage a Communist miscalculation that could lead to general war."

The psychological objective was to be sharply distinguished from the tangible objectives. The tangible objectives grew out of an effort to escape the paralyzing influence of nuclear strategy, but the psychological objective was part and parcel of the nuclear strategy. In the new scheme, the attainment of the tangible objectives would belong wholly to the limited-war forces, but the attainment of the psychological objective of maintaining credibility, though it was also an important aim of limited war, would still belong primarily to the nuclear retaliatory force. For it was the inherent futility of ever using the nuclear retaliatory force—a futility that threatened military paralysis—that had driven the policymakers to rely so heavily on credibility in the first place. It was dread of extinction in a nuclear war that had placed in doubt the "will" of the United States to use its undeniably tremendous nuclear arsenal. Of course, there were additional factors that might paralyze America's will to use its military forces. One was the element of isolationism that had long existed in American political life, and another was the natural revulsion of any peaceful people against warfare. Yet these obstacles had been overcome in times of danger in the past. The dread of nuclear war was a paralyzing influence of new dimensions. Now, even if the public should develop a will to victory, a clear upper limit had been placed on the usefulness of violence as an instrument in foreign affairs. The strategists were preoccupied with the question of how to demonstrate America's will—or "resolve," or "determination," or "toughness," as it was variously put. How to make demonstrations of credibility was, above all, a problem of public relations, since what counted was not the substance of America's strength or the actual state of its willingness but the image of strength and willingness. To put it more precisely, the substance of the nation's strength was useful only insofar as it enhanced the image of strength. In Kissinger's words, "Soviet re-actions to what we do will depend not on what we intend but on what the Soviet leaders think we intend." Or, as he also wrote, "until power is used, it is . . . what people think it is." The strategy of massive retaliation had been one way of maintaining credibility —the technique in that case being to attest to America's will to go to war by *almost* going to war—but it was in the doctrine of nuclear deterrence that the doctrine of credibility found its purest expres-sion. The deterrent force was real, but its entire purpose was to *appear* so formidable that the Soviet Union would hesitate to take aggressive actions that might provoke the United States into re-taliating. The deterrent was not meant for use, because its use would lead to the utter futility of mutual extinction. Appearances, therefore, were not merely important to deterrence—they were everything. If the deterrent was used, deterrence would have failed. If the image did not do its preventive work and there was a resort to action, the whole purpose of the policy would have been defeated, and the human race, with all its policies and purposes, might be lost. In the strategy of nuclear deterrence, the "psychological relation-ship" was the whole relationship. If power, until it was used, was what people thought it was, then nuclear power could never be anything more than what people thought it was, for its use was forever ruled out, except in retaliation. The strategy of nuclear deterrence presented the nuclear dilemma in the form of pure para-dox. It provided for weapons of limitless power whose whole pur-pose was to prevent their ever having to be used. It called for cease-less preparations for a war whose prevention was the preparations' whole aim.

This arrangement was what opened up the fissure dividing image and substance which characterized American policy in the Vietnam years. The United States, blocked by nuclear dread from using its military forces on a scale commensurate with its global aims, began to use its power to strike poses and manufacture images. In the strategy of deterrence, the very survival of mankind was made to depend upon an image. An image, however, was a dis-tressingly undependable thing on which to rest the species' hope of escaping extinction. And the image that was required in this case was even more undependable than most. In the first place, the system of deterrence was aimed at producing an impression of certainty in the minds of America's foes about the mental state of the American people; and mental states are inherently obscure. In the second place, the mental state involved was a future one, concerning what the United States *would* do *if* such-and-such a train of events chanced to occur; and therefore it was highly changeable. And, in the third place, the future mental state to be depicted in the image was a willingness to risk destroying the human race, and this willingness was in its very nature open to question. The policymakers might declare their willingness to "face up to the risks of Armageddon," but the meaning of such a declaration was far from transparent. After all, what *did* it mean to "face up" to the extinction of the race? And what did their willingness say about the men who declared it? Clearly, this intention was one of the least "credible" ones imaginable. The doubts became especially keen as soon as one tried to imagine what a President really would do once the Soviet Union had launched a first strike—once deterrence had failed. Would he retaliate, out of pure revenge, and risk completing the annihilation of the human race for no reason? And if he would not, then what became of the doctrine of credibility, which rested on the assumption that the President would do just that? Since the whole system was so shaky, with its cross-currents of belligerence and dread of annihilation, it was perhaps not surprising that the strategists turned in any direction they could, including the direction of limited war, to find theatres where the crucial but elusive quantity of "credibility" might be demonstrated. Certainly limited wars were among the last places where the appearance of "weakness or indecision" which Taylor feared so much could be tolerated. For, in this system, if the credibility of American power should be destroyed in a limited war, then the middle ground between global extinction and global totalitarianism would be lost, and the government would be forced once again to choose between the risk of giving the Soviet leaders "a blank check" and the risk of committing suicide.

In considering the origins and the character of the war in Vietnam, the extent of the theoretical preparations for limited war in general must be kept in mind. Today, the notion that the war was a "quagmire" into which successive Administrations were sucked, against their will, has won wide acceptance. The metaphor is apt insofar as it refers to the policymakers' undoubted surprise, year after year, at the way their policies were turning out in Vietnam, and to the evident reluctance of both President Kennedy and President Johnson to get involved there; but it is misleading insofar as it suggests that the United States merely stumbled into the war, without forethought or planning. In 1960, Taylor recommended the establishment of a "Limited War Headquarters"—and this was before the nation began fighting in Vietnam. Rarely has such a large body of military theory been developed in advance of an outbreak of hostilities. The war in Vietnam was, in a sense, a theorists' war *par excellence*. The strategists of the late nineteen-fifties were only slightly interested in the question of which country or countries might be the scene of a limited war. When they turned their attention to questions of geography—which they did only rarely—they tended to speak blurrily of "peripheral areas" around the Soviet Union and China which stretched from Japan, in the east, through India and the Middle East, in the south, to Europe, in the west. A reader in the nineteen-seventies of Kissinger's and Taylor's books is struck by how seldom Vietnam is mentioned. Today, the very word "Vietnam" is so rich in association and so heavily laden with historical significance that an atmosphere of inevitability—almost of fate—hangs over it, and it is difficult to imagine oneself back in a time when few Americans even knew of that nation's existence. Instead of speaking in terms of particular wars, whether in Vietnam or elsewhere, the theorists tended to speak in terms of types of wars. One type that came under discussion was limited nuclear war. The strategists drew a sharp distinction between limited nuclear war and all-out nuclear war. Kissinger devoted a chapter of *Nuclear Weapons and Foreign Policy* to limited nuclear war. What might be called the fear of the fear of nuclear weapons was one of the keystones of the policy he was proposing, and he wrote, "The greater the horror of our destructive capabilities, the less certain has it become that they will in fact be used"—a situation that he evidently contemplated with alarm, for he saw it as undermining American credibility. The use of nuclear weapons in limited war, he thought, would help to overcome this dangerous uncertainty. As he put it, "in this task of posing the maximum *credible* threat, limited nuclear war seems a more suitable deterrent than conventional war." Another way he suggested of combatting the paralyzing effect of the fear of nuclear arms was to fashion "a diplomacy which seeks to break down the atmosphere of special horror which now surrounds the use of nuclear weapons, an atmosphere which has been created in part by skillful Soviet 'ban-the-bomb' propaganda." Kissinger, however, was not strictly consistent on this point, for it had been precisely the "special horror" of nuclear weapons which had inspired him in the first place to recommend the shift from the policy of massive retaliation to the policy of limited war, and in another passage in *Nuclear Weapons and Foreign Policy* he wrote that "a thermonuclear attack may . . . become the symbol of the vanity of all human strivings"—a statement that might be thought to add to the atmosphere of "special horror" surrounding nuclear weapons. Another type of limited war that the new strategists recommended would rely on conventional forces that could be flown to troubled areas around the globe at a moment's notice in a fleet of special transport planes, whose construction the strategists counselled. In virtually all the planning for limited war, the speed of the American reaction was seen as crucial. The strategists of the time apparently believed that limited war would be not only limited but short.

Once one has worked out the strategy and the goals of a war, and has gone as far as to contemplate setting up a "headquarters" from which to fight it, the step to actual hostilities is not necessarily a very large one; in the early nineteen-sixties the abstractions in Kissinger's and Taylor's books came to life in the hostilities in Vietnam. John Kennedy found the arguments of the limited-war strategists persuasive, and in February of 1960, while he was still a senator, he stated, "Both before and after 1953 events have demonstrated that our nuclear retaliatory power is not enough. It cannot deter Communist aggression which is too limited to justify atomic war. It cannot protect uncommitted nations against a Communist takeover using local or guerrilla forces. It cannot be used in so-called brushfire peripheral wars. In short, it cannot prevent the Communists from gradually nibbling at the fringe of the free world's territory and strength, until our security has been steadily eroded in piecemeal fashion—each Red advance being too small to justify massive retaliation, with all its risks. . . . In short, we need forces of an entirely different kind to keep the peace against limited aggression, and to fight it, if deterrence fails, without raising the conflict to a disastrous pitch." Kennedy was saying that the limited-war forces would accomplish the two great objectives of policy that Kissinger and Taylor had set forth in their books: the prevention of global totalitarianism and the prevention of human extinction. By using limited forces to push back "limited aggression," the United States would be able to oppose the spread of Communism, and at the same time avoid confrontation at the brink. Kennedy, moreover, had become persuaded that the outcome of a limited war would be important not only for tangible objectives that might be attained but for the psychological objective of demonstrating America's "will" to oppose Communism, and after he became President he often referred to the hostilities in Vietnam as a "test case" of America's determination to protect its allies.

The spirit of the Kennedy Administration was activist, and the policymakers set about their tasks in a mood of high excitement. In April of 1961, three months after his inauguration, Kennedy made a speech to the American Society of Newspaper Editors in which he defined the nature of the challenge that lay ahead:

> We face a relentless struggle in every corner of the globe that goes far beyond the clash of armies or even nuclear armaments. The armies are there, and in large number. The nuclear armaments are there. But they serve primarily as the shield behind which subversion, infiltration, and a host of other tactics steadily advance, picking off vulnerable areas one by one. . . . We dare not fail to see the

insidious nature of this new and deeper struggle. We dare not fail to grasp the new concepts, the new tools, the new sense of urgency we will need to combat it—whether in Cuba or South Vietnam. . . . The message of Cuba, of Laos, of the rising din of Communist voices in Asia and Latin America—these messages are all the same. The complacent, the self-indulgent, the soft societies are about to be swept away with the debris of history. Only the strong, only the industrious, only the determined, only the courageous, only the visionary who determine the real nature of our struggle can possibly survive. No greater task faces this country or this Administration. No other challenge is more deserving of our every effort and energy. . . . We intend to reëxamine and reorient our forces of all kinds— our tactics and our institutions here in this community. . . . For I am convinced that we in this country and in the free world possess the necessary resources, and the skill, and the added strength that comes from a belief in the freedom of man. And I am equally convinced that history will record the fact that this bitter struggle reached its climax in the late nineteen-fifties and the early nineteen-sixties. Let me then make clear as the President of the United States that I am determined upon our system's survival and success, regardless of the cost and regardless of the peril.

One of the members of President Kennedy's staff was Maxwell Taylor, who had been appointed Military Representative of the President, and in the fall of 1961 he was sent to Vietnam to take stock of the situation there. In Vietnam, the strategists of limited war, who had been thinking mainly in global terms, found themselves face to face with the challenge of guerrilla warfare. They quickly set about devising techniques to meet the challenge. Turning to the manuals of the Communist foe for guidance, they came up with the concept of "counterinsurgency" war. Men in the Pentagon began to regard themselves as potential guerrilla soldiers, and soon they were repeating such Maoist phrases as "The soldiers are the fish and the people are the sea." And in the early nineteen-sixties it was not only in the military area that the theories of professors were being translated into governmental policy in the struggle against Communism. During that period, a new breed of professor, trained in the social sciences and eager to test theories in the laboratory of real societies, came forward to offer "models" of economic and social development with which the government could rival the Communist "model."

In spite of all the expertise that was being brought to bear on the war, however, the reports from the field in Vietnam, when they began to come in, were discouraging. The long, sad tale of optimistic predictions followed by military reverses, to be followed, in turn, by increasingly drastic military measures, began to unfold, and by the mid-nineteen-sixties it was plain that the war would be far longer and far more difficult to end than any of the professors or policy-makers had foreseen. The theory of limited war had been abstract and general, but Vietnam was a particular country, with a particular history and a particular society, and these particularities turned out to be more important than the strategists had ever dreamed they could be. Awed, perhaps, by the magnitude of America's global power and global responsibilities, the strategists had overlooked the possibility that purely local events, not controlled by a centralized, global conspiracy, might pose serious obstacles to their plans. Yet it was on the local events, and not on the balance of nuclear forces, that the outcome in Vietnam was proving to depend. For Vietnamese life had its own tendencies, which not even the power of the United States could alter. Moreover, the strategic theory had it that human beings behaved according to certain laws—that if people were punished sufficiently, they could be deflected from their goals, even if they had not been defeated outright. Accordingly, the strategists had fashioned a policy known as escalation, in which the level of violence would be raised, notch by notch, until the foe, realizing that America's instruments of pain were limitless and its will to inflict pain unshakable, would reach the breaking point and desist. The Vietnamese revolutionaries, however, did not behave in this way at all. Their will stiffened under punishment. And many Americans at home, too, behaved in an unexpected way. Their will to inflict the punishment began to falter. The material resources for inflicting punishment were indeed nearly limitless, but the capacity of the American spirit for inflicting punishment, although great, did have limits. The stubborn uniqueness of the situation in Vietnam was perhaps even more devastating to the plans of the theorists than the unexpected stiffness of the opposition. It meant not only that the war was going to be difficult to win but that it was not the war they had thought it was—that the United States might have sent its troops into the wrong country altogether. For if the Vietnam war was primarily a local affair, rather than a rebellion under the control of World Communism, then it was not a test case of anything. Then, instead of being one of those limited wars between global forces of freedom and global forces of totalitarianism which the theorists had foreseen in their books, it was just a civil war in a small country.

If the war had been planned only to achieve the tangible objectives that Kissinger assigned to limited war in 1957, the unexpected intractability of Vietnamese affairs and the revelation that the Vietnamese forces were not under the control of World Communism might well have inspired a reappraisal of the American effort, and perhaps a withdrawal. After all, even if Vietnam *had* been the right place to oppose World Communism, only a limited tangible advantage could have been gained there: at best, the freedom of one-half of one small country could be protected. And when the situation had deteriorated to the point where the possible strategic gains were outweighed by the manifold costs of the war effort, a strict accounting logic would have dictated that the United States should cut its losses and leave. In the mid-nineteen-sixties, that point was apparently reached. However, the war was not being fought only for the tangible objectives. It was being fought also for the psychological objective of maintaining American credibility—an aim that was bound up in the strategists' thinking with the prevention of nuclear war and the prevention of global totalitarianism. The war had a symbolic importance that was entirely separate from any tangible objective that might or might not be achieved. The policy-makers were divided on many points, but they were united on this one. In both their private and their public statements, they unwaveringly affirmed the absolute necessity of preserving the integrity of America's image in the fighting in Vietnam. For the Joint Chiefs of Staff, the importance of the war lay in "the psychological impact that a firm position by the United States will have on the countries of the world—both free and Communist," according to the memo they sent Secretary of Defense McNamara in 1962. For Assistant Secretary of Defense John McNaughton, writing a memo in 1965, the aim of the war was to "avoid harmful appearances which will affect judgments by, and provide pretexts to, other nations regarding how the US will behave in future cases of particular interest to those nations—regarding US policy, power, resolve, and competence." For President Johnson, in a speech in April of 1965, the United States was in Vietnam because it had "a promise to keep." He went on, "We are also there to strengthen world order. Around the globe, from Berlin to Thailand, are people whose well-being rests in part on the belief that they can count on us if they are attacked. To leave Vietnam to its fate would shake the confidence of all these people in the value of an American commitment and in the value of America's word. The result would be increased unrest and instability, and even wider war." By 1966, the aim of upholding credibility had become virtually the sole aim of the war. In January of that year, McNaughton wrote the memo in which he said, *"The present U.S. objective in Vietnam is to avoid humiliation.* The reasons why we *went into* Vietnam to the present depth are varied; but they are now largely academic. Why we have *not withdrawn* is, by all odds, *one* reason. (1) To preserve our reputation as a guarantor, and thus to preserve our effectiveness in the rest of the world. We have not hung on (2) to save a friend, or (3) to deny the Communists the added acres and heads (because the dominoes don't fall for that reason in this case), or even (4) to prove that 'wars of national liberation' won't work (except as our reputation is involved)." In this memo, McNaughton affirmed the aim of upholding credibility ("to preserve our reputation as guarantor") and specifically dismissed the tangible aims ("to deny the Communists the added acres and heads"). The aim of upholding American credibility superseded any conclusions drawn from a simple accounting of tangible gains and tangible losses, and it dictated that the war must go on, for it was on American credibility, the strategists thought, that the safety of the whole world depended. Secretary of State Dean Rusk wrote in a letter to a hundred student leaders in January of 1967, "We are involved in Vietnam because we know from painful experience that the minimum condition for order on our planet is that aggression must not be permitted to succeed. For when it does succeed, the consequence is not peace, it is the further expansion of aggression. And those who have borne responsibility in our country since 1945 have not for one moment forgotten that a third world war would be a nuclear war." Nor did the question of whether or not Vietnam was the wrong country to be fighting in matter much in this thinking. The fact that the United States was fighting there made it the right country; America's presence in Vietnam invested the war with the global significance that it lacked intrinsically, for if the United States involved itself in a war, its credibility was by that very action placed at stake. An analyst representing the Joint Chiefs of Staff wrote in commenting upon a draft paper of a Project Outline on Courses of Action in Southeast Asia, which had been prepared by a National Security Council "working group," "It is *our* judgment, skill, capability, prestige, and national honor which are at stake, and we put them there." And Secretary Rusk wrote in his letter to the student leaders, "We are involved because the nation's word has been given that we would be involved."

Limited war had been conceived in part as a way for the United States to do bold things in an age when nuclear dread made the doing of bold things—particularly if they were violent things—especially dangerous. But now all hope of *doing* anything was abandoned. That aim was now considered to be, in McNaughton's phrase, "largely academic." What remained was proving something, to friends and foes alike: America's will and determination. The tangible objectives of limited war had been completely eclipsed by the psychological objective. The war had become an effort directed entirely toward building up a certain image by force of arms. It had become a piece of pure theatre. The purpose of the enterprise now was to put on a performance for what John McNaughton called "audiences." In the memo in which he mentioned the need to avoid harmful appearances, he went on to say, "In this connection, the relevant audiences are the Communists (who must feel strong pressures), the South Vietnamese (whose morale must be buoyed), our allies (who must trust us as 'underwriters'), and the US public (which must support

363

our risk-taking with US lives and prestige)." The triumph of the doctrine of credibility had introduced into the actual conduct of the
war the gap between image and substance which characterized the
doctrine of nuclear deterrence. The whole aim of having a nuclear
retaliatory force for deterrence was to create an image of the United
States as a nation not to be trifled with, and so to forestall challenges
that could lead to a nuclear holocaust. Now a real and bloody war
was being fought for precisely the same end. As the paper of the
National Security Council "working group" put it, the loss of South
Vietnam could lead to "the progressive loss of other areas or to taking
a stand at some point where there would almost certainly be major
conflict and perhaps the great risk of nuclear war." Those who were
opposed to the war tirelessly pointed out the disparity between the
Johnson Administration's depiction of South Vietnam as a free country battling international Communist aggression and their own impression that the South Vietnamese government was a corrupt
dictatorship that, supported by foreign arms and foreign money,
was fighting a civil war against indigenous Communist forces. What
those opposed to the war did not know was that the Johnson Administration had largely lost interest in Vietnam *per se*. What
primarily interested the Johnson Administration from the mid-sixties
on was not what was going on in Vietnam but how what was going
on in Vietnam was perceived by what the Joint Chiefs referred to as
the "countries of the world." In fact, so important were appearances
in the official thinking that as things went from bad to worse on the
battlefield the policymakers began to dream of completely separating
the nation's image from what happened in the war, in order that
even in the face of failure the desired image of American "will"
might be preserved. The effort to rescue the national image from the
debacle conditioned the tactics of the war from the mid-nineteen-
sixties on. On one occasion in 1965, McGeorge Bundy, a special
assistant to the President for national-security affairs, discussing a
plan for "*sustained reprisal* against North Vietnam," wrote, "It may
fail. . . . What we can say is that even if it fails, the policy will be
worth it. At a minimum, it will damp down the charge that we did
not do all that we could have done, and this charge will be important

in many countries, including our own. Beyond that, a reprisal policy —to the extent that it demonstrates U.S. willingness to employ this new norm in counterinsurgency—will set a higher price for the future upon all adventures of guerrilla warfare." To Bundy, a disastrous war effort was better than no war effort, because even a disastrous war effort would "demonstrate" the crucial "willingness" to use force in the nuclear age, and so would enhance American credibility. John McNaughton, writing in the same vein in a draft of a memo to Secretary of Defense McNamara in March of 1965, advised, "It is essential—however badly SEA [Southeast Asia] may go over the next 1-3 years—that US emerge as a 'good doctor.' We must have kept promises, been tough, taken risks, gotten bloodied, and hurt the enemy very badly." McNaughton may have been one of the first military advisers ever to suggest that getting bloodied should in itself be an objective of an army in the field. (He was telling men that they must get wounded or killed even though they knew they could not win.) Only in a war fought for credibility could the question of victory or defeat ever seem so immaterial.

The men in charge of the government were struggling to work out what the uses of military force might be in the age of nuclear weapons. The dilemma in which they found themselves was expressed in a memo that Walt Rostow, chairman of the State Department Policy Planning Council, wrote to Secretary of State Rusk in November of 1964, in which he mentioned "the real margin of influence . . . which flows from the simple fact that at this stage of history, we are the greatest power in the world—if we behave like it." Rostow's qualifying phrase "if we behave like it" summed up the maddening predicament of the great power in the nuclear age. For in reality "the fact" that the United States was "the greatest power in the world" was not "simple" at all. It was endlessly complicated, and contained deep, and perhaps irreconcilable, ambiguities. The reality was that the United States could by no means "behave like" the greatest power in the world if that meant acting the way great powers had acted on the world stage in the past. And it was not only idealism or moral scruple that stood in the way (although one can hope that these factors, too, did have a restraining influence) but also the unprecedented destructiveness, and self-destructiveness, of nuclear war. In October of 1964, in a paper titled "Aims and Options in Southeast Asia," McNaughton wrote that the United States must create an appearance of success in its operations in Vietnam in order to show that the nation was not "hobbled by restraints." But, whatever appearance the United States might create in Vietnam, or anywhere else, the fact was that the United States *was* hobbled by restraints—the very restraints inherent in the possession of nuclear weapons which Kissinger and Taylor had tried to come to grips with in their books in the late nineteen-fifties. Indeed, it was these restraints that had given rise to the doctrine of credibility, which now dominated government policy. It is true that before the development of nuclear weapons powerful nations had sought to cultivate aspects of their power which were similar to what the American policymakers meant when they spoke of credibility. In military affairs, a nation would often make a show of force in the hope of having its way without resorting to arms. The appearance of a gunboat in a harbor might be used to bring a rebellious colony back into line, or a troop movement on a border might be used to deter an attack. But in any matter of the first importance the show of force would give way to the use of force. The situation of a great power in the nuclear age was altogether different. A nuclear power was stuck on the level of show. When nuclear powers confronted one another over an important issue, major use of force was ruled out, since the unrestrained use of force could lead to national "suicide," and even to human extinction. Nuclear powers were in the situation—unprecedented in military history—of always having more power in their possession than they were free to use. The question of "will," which in former times was a question of a nation's capacity for making great sacrifices in order to protect itself, now became a question of a nation's willingness to approach the point of suicide. For the closer a nation was willing to come to that point, the more force it could permit itself to unleash. According to the doctrine of credibility, a nation that wished to have its way in international affairs was obliged, in a sense, to make demonstrations of indifference to its own survival, for it was obliged constantly to show its willingness not just to unleash force on others but to put the gun to its own head and pull the trigger—its willingness, that is, to "face up to the risks of Armageddon." Perhaps for this reason, policymakers of the time often announced that it was an aim of American policy to cultivate a reputation for "unpredictability." The ultimate in unpredictability, of course, would be to blow up the world, oneself included. Leaving the question of unpredictability aside, the will to victory in the nuclear age was tempered by the realization that victory could be a worse disaster than defeat. This new circumstance had a shaping influence on every phase of the warfare in Vietnam— on the limits of the war effort, on the justifications for the war, and on the atmosphere engendered in the home country by the war. The nuclear predicament forced the great powers to take military action only within a narrowed sphere, and always to behave with extreme caution and trepidation, not because they were weak but because they were too strong, and it taught them to rely more on the reputation of power—on show—than on the use of power. Still, the level of show was not without its possibilities. It provided the military strategists with what they regarded as an entire new sphere of action—the image world, in which battles were fought not to achieve concrete ends but to create appearances. Through actions taken to buttress the image of the United States, the strategists believed, the nation might still lay claim to the "margin of influence" that flowed from being the greatest power in the world. The United States might still have its way in international affairs, they thought, by fighting the admittedly militarily useless but presumably psychologically effective war in Vietnam. The image world was not the world of borders defended, of strategic positions won or lost, of foes defeated in great and bloody battles; it was the world of "reputations," of "psychological impact," of "audiences." It was, in a word, the world of credibility.

In the late nineteen-sixties, the war began to come home. The very nature of the war aims made a political struggle in the United States inevitable. Any long war, and particularly one that is poorly understood and is a failure besides, is likely to stir up opposition in the home country. But when the war, in addition, is being fought to uphold the nation's image, the strife at home takes on a deeper significance. When a government has founded the national defense on the national image, as the United States did under the doctrine of credibility, it follows that any internal dissension will be interpreted as an attack on the safety of the nation. The strain of such a situation on a democratic system is necessarily great. An authoritarian government has the means to project a single, self-consistent image of itself to its own people and the world, unchallenged by any disruption from within, but the image of the government of a free country is vulnerable to assault from every side on the home front. In a democracy, where anyone can say whatever he wants to say, and can frequently get on television saying it, the national image is the composite impression made by countless voices and countless deeds, all of them open to inspection by the whole world. It is not only the President and his men who form the image but anyone who wants to get out on the street with a sign. If the Vietnam war was one aspect of the nation's image, then the political process at home was the very essence of the nation's image. After all, in the United States the public, and not the government, *was* the nation. If the standing of the United States as the greatest power in the world was conditional upon its behaving like the greatest power in the world, then the way the public, in its scores of millions, was seen to behave at home was far more important to the national defense than the way a few hundred thousand soldiers were seen to behave nine thousand miles away. The soldiers in Vietnam could hardly demonstrate that America possessed the "will" to use force freely in the world while America itself denied it. When a war is being fought as a demonstration of the nation's "will and character," as President Nixon put it, what better way is there to oppose the war than to mount a demonstration of one's own—a demonstration, for instance, in which thousands of people march through the streets of the nation's capital in protest against the war? What better way is there to oppose a public-relations war than with a public-relations insurrection? The anti-war movement was often taken to task for its "theatricality." The fact is that it was precisely in its theatricality that its special genius lay. The war had been conceived as theatre—as a production for multiple "audiences"—and the anti-war movement was counter-theatre, and very effective counter-theatre. The demonstrations at home, if they were large enough, said as much about the nation's will and character as the demonstrations that the government was staging in Vietnam with B-52s. And the "psychological impact" of the demonstrations at home was probably greater around the world than that of the demonstrations in Vietnam, because the ones at home were voluntary, whereas the ones in Vietnam were backed by the coercive power of the government. Officials of the government often objected that the demonstrations at home undermined the war effort by giving encouragement to the enemy and by spreading demoralization among the troops. The opposition denied the charges, but here the government was probably right. Yet even the government never fully articulated why domestic dissent had such a devastating effect on the war cause. The fact is that the demonstrations at home struck at the very foundation of the larger aims for which the war was being fought. They struck a crippling blow at the credibility on which the whole strategy was based. In considering the shattering impact of the anti-war movement on the government, and the drastic responses of both the Johnson Administration and the Nixon Administration, it is important to recall that the nation's credibility was not an afterthought of the strategists of national defense but, rather, the linchpin of the deterrence strategy on which the government rested its hopes for avoiding the alternatives of global totalitarianism and nuclear extinction. A blow to the image of "toughness" was not just a blow to the pride of the men in government, or a political setback for them, or a blow to the war policy; it was a blow to the heart of the national defense. The aim of the war was to say something to the "countries of the world" about America's willingness to use force in the world, but the demonstrations at home tended to show the countries of the world that Americans were unwilling to use it. The war was meant to show that America was "tough," but the anti-war movement tended to show that it was "soft." The purpose of the war to say one thing; the anti-war movement said the opposite thing. Some of the demonstrators took to wearing old Army uniforms, as though to parody the real Army; and they *were* a counter-army, which undid at home the work that the Army was doing in the field. (Certainly part of the special bitterness engendered by the war grew out of the fact that while people died in the field for the sake of an image, people at home who were not risking death could effectively undermine the image merely by talking on television programs or by marching in the streets a few times a year.) Under these circumstances, even if the war could somehow be won militarily, the whole purpose of the war would be destroyed: in the process of fighting the war abroad the all-important appearance of a willingness to fight many more wars of this kind would have been lost at home. On the other hand, if the public were to suffer the war in silence, or were to make some show of supporting the war, then even if the war should be lost militarily, the image of a "tough" nation, unafraid to use its power in the nuclear age, might still be salvaged from the debacle, and McGeorge Bundy's "new norm" might yet be established. In fact, if the public were to go on supporting a disastrous policy indefinitely, that might be the most impressive display of will there could be. What could be tougher than a nation that, as it loses one war, is eager for the next? In this war, it was literally true that the battle at home for public opinion was more crucial to the war aims than the battle in the field against the foe.

The uproar at home over the war took the Johnson Administration by surprise. None of the theorists or practioners of limited war had foreseen the domestic implications of their policy; their thinking had been restricted to the foreign sphere. President Johnson therefore attempted to cope with his domestic difficulties in a loose and improvisatory—and often a repressive—way, such as when he sent out the F.B.I., the C.I.A., and the military to spy on and harass the opposition. Yet, for all his rage at his opponents, when he saw that his war policy was threatening the fundamental health of the body politic he resisted the temptation to turn an election into a contest between the representatives of order in the White House and disloyal anarchists in the streets; instead, he made his decision to quit political life and offered to open negotiations on the war. Thus, Lyndon

Johnson remained devoted to the domestic well-being of the nation, even to the extent of being willing to risk reverses in foreign policy. It was not until President Nixon came to power that the full impact of the war policy made itself felt at home, and put the democratic system in jeopardy. For when President Nixon saw the domestic opposition to the war policy taking shape again, he accepted the challenge: he made national division the principal theme of national politics, and sought to reorganize the national life around the issue of the war and around such issues subsidiary to the war as the news coverage of the war and the protesters' response to the war. And when he saw that the domestic strife was starting to quiet down, he took covert steps to whip it up again: he launched his secret program of "exacerbating" divisive issues. Here was the basic difference between the two Presidents. President Johnson, a man of great cunning, vanity, and pride, who had no love for the rebels opposing him, and who was not above deceptions and manipulations of all kinds, and who remained convinced up to the end that his Vietnam policy was correct, nevertheless withdrew from politics and altered his course when he saw that, somehow, his policy was leading the nation toward a ruinous political crisis. President Nixon, when he saw the same crisis mounting, set about "exacerbating" it, and eventually had to be driven from office in mid-term.

The immediate question that the nation faced when President Nixon took office, was, at bottom, whether the President or the people would have the last word in the forum of public discourse. The Constitution required that it be the people, but strategic doctrine required that it be the President. For the doctrine of credibility, once it was challenged, could succeed only if the President was empowered to take sole charge of the nation's image. The democracy could survive, however, only if the people were allowed, in chaotic, uncontrolled democratic fashion, to demand what they pleased, and let the nation's image take care of itself. In fact, the impression that a democratic nation makes on the world can never, strictly speaking, be organized into an image. Image-making is by its very nature calculated and centralized, whereas the democratic process is by nature spontaneous and decentralized. By the time

Richard Nixon assumed the Presidency, the tension between the public-relations requirements of strategic doctrine and the Constitutional requirements of democratic practice had reached the point where the President had to choose either credibility or the Republic. At first, President Nixon seemed to choose the Republic, for he promised the openness, the decentralization of power, the easing of tempers, and, above all, the withdrawal from the war which a full recovery of the democracy required. But his commitment to the war, and to the doctrine of credibility that was the principle justification for the war, was deep, and before long he was speaking of "peace with honor," and the like, and the domestic strife was revived with a new fury. The President then embarked on his effort—which was to continue throughout his remaining years in office—to make himself the unchallenged scenarist of American political life. Vietnam was one stage on which the credibility of American power was being demonstrated, and American life, if he had his way, would be another. Under his Administration, the separation of substance and image which characterized nuclear policy, and had come to characterize the war policy, now grew to characterize virtually all the policies of the Administration, including its domestic policies. After all, what was the use of fighting a war abroad to establish credibility when that same credibility was under challenge at home? How could foreign governments be taught to have "respect for the office of President of the United States" when the Americans themselves had not learned to respect it?

President Nixon's anxiety that the powers of his office were inadequate was reinforced by another worry that grew directly out of the nuclear dilemma: his fear that the United States was threatened with impotence in world affairs. The fear of impotence was a recurrent one in his public statements. President Nixon dreaded that the country might "tie the hands" of the President, that it would "cut off the President's legs," that the nation would be turned into a "pitiful, helpless giant." If the separation of substance and image was the form that the doctrine of credibility took, the fear of impotence—of "softness"—was its content. Everywhere the President looked, at home as well as abroad, he saw "appeasement," "passive acquiescence," Americans inclined to "whine and whimper about our frustrations" and "turn inward." In the courts, in the schools, and in the home, no less than in foreign affairs, he saw signs that the will on which everything now depended was eroding. His uneasiness on this score led him to his belief that the Congress, the courts, the press, the television networks, the federal bureaucracies, and the demonstrators in the streets were usurping powers that were rightfully his, and it fed his apparently insatiable appetite for new powers—powers that would destroy the independence of the other branches of the government and cancel out the rights of the people. It also led him to try to attempt to compensate for the lack of will he found among the people with a fierce will of his own, which would operate independently of the people. Some observers tended to see the roots of President Nixon's fear of impotence in the psychological idiosyncrasies of his character, and certainly these abounded. He was, however, far from being the first occupant of the White House to fear that the Presidency was in danger of becoming crippled. The fear of executive impotence in world affairs had been one of the deepest themes of nuclear politics for some fifteen years, having been powerfully augmented by the fear of nuclear paralysis which had worried Kissinger as far back as 1957. Indeed, the whole policy of limited war, which became the principal issue between the President and his opposition, had been designed as a means whereby the United States could continue to use military force in a world threatened with extinction—a means whereby "our power can give impetus to our policy rather than paralyze it," as Kissinger put it. Only in the nuclear age was there any question, if one was a giant, of being pitiful and helpless. The Kennedy and Johnson men, too, had argued that the President needed expanded powers if he was to discharge the global responsibilities that were now vested in the office. Moreover, President Kennedy, in his 1961 speech to the newspaper editors, had said that the international challenge facing the United States would require that we abandon our "self-indulgent," "soft" ways and "reëxamine and reorient . . . our institutions here in this community." If a whole succession of Presidents seemed to attach virtually limitless importance to their continued ability to wage limited war, it was because in the prevailing scheme of national defense limited war had been assigned the burden of providing what Taylor called the "active" element in American military policy. In this scheme, to deprive the President of his power to wage limited war was to deprive him of the only instruments of force available to him, and so was to paralyze the Presidency.

There was one more characteristic of the Nixon Presidency which had its roots in the nuclear dilemma: President Nixon's apparent isolation from the world around him. Presidential isolation, like the Presidential preoccupation with images and the Presidential fear of impotence, had a history at least as long as the war in Vietnam. The fact that whoever was President was alone required to concern himself from day to day with the practical and moral problems of survival while his countrymen thought, for the most part, about pleasanter things was at the source of his isolation. The strategists in the White House regarded the war as one way of "facing up to the risks of Armageddon," but the public remained largely unaware of this function. The fundamental principles of the foreign policy of the time had grown out of an elaborate theoretical structure that was meant to accommodate the two broad aims of opposing the spread of Communism and coping with the risk of nuclear war, but the policymakers, in their public statements, tended to give the aim of opposing Communism far the greater emphasis. The aim of preventing nuclear war, when it was brought up at all, tended to be mentioned only in passing. This anomalous state of affairs, in which the government was cultivating a grim "resolve" to brave the risks of annihilation, and was preparing itself for terrible sacrifices and for getting "bloodied," while the public lacked any such sentiments, was partly of the government's own making. Kissinger had warned in his 1957 book that the policy he was proposing would require "a public opinion which has been educated to the realities of the nuclear age"—by which he meant a public that had been educated to accept the need for limited wars. But no such education ever took place. Instead, the executive branch sent American forces into the limited war in Vietnam by stealth while promising to stay out. One reason for the government's failure to apprise the public of the full importance of nuclear strategy in its war policy may have been simply the peculiar combination of abstractness and horror which made the subject so forbidding to think about. An aura almost of obscenity surrounded the calculations of how many millions might be killed and in what manner, and this may have helped cause public figures to shun the whole topic when they could. Another reason for their reticence, certainly, was the political vitality of the anti-Communist position, which made it very dangerous for any politician with national ambitions to suggest policies that smacked in any way of weakness or lack of resolve in the fight against Communism. It may have been that few politicians felt they could afford to maintain publicly that the dread of nuclear war should in any way be allowed to modify the nation's anti-Communist stand; as a result, a strategy such as the doctrine of credibility, which was in fact inspired in great measure by an enlarged respect for the dangers of nuclear war, had to be presented almost entirely as though it were only an improved method of opposing the Communists. But an even more important reason for the politicians' failure to give the public the necessary education in "the realities of the nuclear age" seems to have been intrinsic to the doctrine of credibility itself. For the doctrine included within it a ban of sorts on giving too much public emphasis to what Kissinger called the "special horror" surrounding nuclear weapons, the reason being that the efficacy of the doctrine depended upon maintaining an image of the United States as a nation that was unafraid to use its power—that would not shrink from "the risks of Armageddon." Too great an emphasis on the "special horror" could itself spoil the image. Therefore, although Kissinger's own appreciation of that horror was apparently great, he felt obliged to counsel a diplomacy that would seek to "break down" the atmosphere of horror. It was, after all, fear of a collapse of the image of strength and will that inspired the government to continue the war in Vietnam for so many years and to enter into protracted struggle with Americans who opposed the war. One might say that it was in the very nature of the doctrine of credibility that it had to be presented misleadingly to the public and the world. For to explain the policy fully would be to undermine it. As a result, in part, of these inhibitions, the government strategists and the public they were supposed to represent began to live in two different worlds, and to cease to understand each other.

In the second half of his first term, as President Nixon went on disengaging American ground troops from the fighting in Vietnam and inaugurated his policy of détente with the Soviet Union, hopes were raised that a spirit of disengagement and détente might come to prevail in the domestic wars, too. It had been these hopes, after all, that carried Mr. Nixon into office in 1968. But just the opposite occurred. The anger in the White House intensified, the President's isolation deepened, and the campaign to humble the Congress, the press, and the other powers in the society which rivalled the executive branch was stepped up. Once again, the public, never having been adequately informed about the imperatives of the doctrine of credibility, had failed to take them into account. For, according to the doctrine, if the President was going to risk American credibility by withdrawing from a war, it became all the more important to uphold credibility on the home front. A period of military retrenchment was no time to allow suggestions of "weakness or indecision" to crop up in domestic affairs. Instead, dramatic and unmistakable demonstrations of firmness were required. And the withdrawal itself could not be rushed or panicky. It would have to be stately and slow. It would have to be accompanied by many awesome displays of unimpaired resolve—displays such as the invasion of Cambodia, the invasion of Laos, the mining of the ports of North Vietnam, and the carpet-bombing of North Vietnam in the Christmas season of 1972. In an era in which the President was haunted by a fear of seeming impotent, a withdrawal was the most delicate of operations. Under no circumstances could it be allowed to appear an expression of weakness or loss of will. The Nixon Administration's resolution of its dilemma was the one suggested by John McNaughton and McGeorge Bundy years earlier—that of trying to maintain an image of toughness in the face of failure by mounting futile but tough-seeming military campaigns. McNaughton had written in 1965 that it was important for the United States to get bloodied even as it failed in Vietnam, and this is exactly what happened. The United States did fail in Vietnam, and it did get bloodied, in Vietnam and at home as well.

If withdrawal from ground operations in Vietnam increased the pressures for militancy in other spheres of Presidential action, the policy of détente increased them even more. The apparent contradiction between the militancy both in Vietnam and at home and the spirit of friendly coöperation at the summit conferences with the Russians and the Chinese baffled the public. For a moment, as President Nixon proclaimed that "America's flag flies high over the ancient Kremlin fortress" while Americans were dying in Southeast Asia in an attempt to counter the Kremlin's influence, the fighting in Vietnam came to look like something without precedent in military history: a war in which the generals on the opposing sides had combined into a joint command. But President Nixon's split policy was in keeping with the fundamental requirements of American strategy as they had been conceived by men in the White House at least since the time of President Kennedy. Throughout the sixties and the early seventies, White House strategists had sought to balance each move toward peace in the nuclear sphere with militancy in other spheres of competition with the Communists. In the early nineteen-sixties, the move toward peace in the nuclear sphere came in the shift from the provocative doctrine of massive retaliation to the passive doctrine of nuclear deterrence, and the balancing display of anti-Communism came in the adoption of the aggressive strategy of limited war. Now, in the early nineteen-seventies, an Administration was once again taking a step away from the brink in the nuclear sphere—this time by its conclusion of agreements on the limitation of strategic arms at the Moscow summit meeting of May, 1972—and was once again seeking out other spheres in which to shore up the President's reputation as a fierce anti-Communist: to give him opportunities for the expression of his "ruthless" side, to quote the fourth, and final, draft of the speech by Kissinger to Soviet Communist Party Secretary Leonid Brezhnev a few weeks before the summit meeting. In the framework of Kissinger's thinking, it made perfect sense to move toward the summit, and so toward peace, in the sphere of direct relations with the Soviet Union while simultaneously moving toward confrontation, and so toward intensified war, in the sphere of Vietnam policy. As far back as 1957, Kissinger had noted and deplored "the notion that war and peace, military and political goals, were separate and opposite." Now, under his guidance, war and peace were being pursued simultaneously. At the summit, the President would work for a relaxation of nuclear tension (what he now called a "generation of peace"), and in the "peripheral areas" he would continue to make demonstrations of his credibility (what he now called "respect for the office of President of the United States").

There were political considerations to be weighed, too. Although the politics of nuclear strategy were nothing if not complex, one broad rule seemed to be that the political right tended to give greater weight to the fear of global Communist totalitarianism and the political left tended to give greater weight to the fear of human extinction. The right, therefore, tended to favor policies allowing for the free use of military force, and the left tended to favor policies calling for military restraint. The Kennedy policy, belligerent as it was, conformed to this political rule. His Administration was slightly to the left of the Eisenhower Administration, and, accordingly, his military strategy gave a larger place to the fear of nuclear weapons than Eisenhower's had. The same split appeared—though in a different political context—in the Presidential contest of 1964, when President Johnson campaigned as a proponent of restraint in Vietnam and Senator Barry Goldwater campaigned as a proponent of a quick victory. For a man on the right, the political danger lay in seeming oblivious of the danger of nuclear war—as Goldwater then learned. For a man on the left, however, the political danger lay in appearing to have a "soft" attitude toward Communism. From a political point of view, therefore, the course followed by President Johnson in 1964 was probably the most advantageous that could have been devised at the time. By escalating the war somewhat during the campaign, he headed off the charge that he was soft on Communism, and by vowing that he would never take precipitate military action of the kind that Goldwater seemed to be recommending he signalled his determination to avoid a nuclear war. What the public did not know was that this apparently sensible middle course had dangers of its own—dangers that became clear soon after Johnson had been elected to office. President Nixon, too, saw himself as charting a middle course in his dealings with the Communist adversary. During his years in office, it became a cliché to point out that only a seemingly determined anti-Communist like President Nixon could afford the political risks of visiting China and of establishing a policy of détente with the Soviet Union. But even President Nixon, with his impeccable anti-Communist credentials, nevertheless felt obliged to reaffirm his militancy, and he and other members of his Administration often hinted darkly to journalists that a "humiliating defeat" in Vietnam might lead to a dangerous right-wing backlash at home. Politically as well as strategically, therefore, the policy of détente created a pressure to find places where the credibility of American power could be affirmed, and in the early nineteen-seventies those places were Vietnam and the domestic politics of the United States.

It has not been the purpose of these remarks to blame theorists of the nineteen-fifties for the calamities of the nineteen-sixties and the nineteen-seventies, or to suggest that when they devised the strategies that would rule American politics in the years ahead they should have foreseen the bizarre events that unfolded. Many Americans found these events all but unbelievable even as they occurred. Moreover, the strategists' attention was concentrated on a dilemma that overarched all particular events. This dilemma—the dilemma of nuclear warfare—remains entirely unresolved to this day. And it can also be said that the combined strategies of limited war and nuclear deterrence still seem an improvement over the strategy of massive retaliation, which to the contemporary eye seems to have been an exceptionally reckless and shortsighted way of handling the question of human survival. On the other hand, it is not the purpose of these remarks to in any way excuse the political actors of the period —some of whom were also key strategists—from responsibility on the

379

ground that they did what they did in the cause of human survival. All governments have their burdens to bear and their decisions to make, and if the heaviness of the responsibilities were to be considered justification for repressive action, no country would remain free. A free country does not place responsibilities in one of the scales and the liberties of the people in the other. It holds to the faith that only in an atmosphere of freedom can the responsibilities be squarely met. Moreover, precisely because the United States is a free country, choices were at all times open to the government in the Vietnam years. At each stage, alternative policies were offered— sometimes by men in high positions in the government. In the Kennedy and Johnson years, the names of George Kennan, William Fulbright, George Ball, John Kenneth Galbraith, and Clark Clifford are among those that come to mind. In the Nixon years, the name of Walter Hickel comes to mind. And, what was of greater importance, millions· of ordinary citizens, making use of their freedom, raised their voices to insist that the war be brought to an end. In fact, their voices finally prevailed. And of still greater importance was the broad political coalition that forced President Nixon from office. There is every reason to believe that if this coalition had not been successful, the United States, by then a Presidential dictatorship, would still be pursuing credibility in Vietnam. For nothing in the record suggests that President Nixon was anything but dead serious both when he promised President Thieu that the United States would "respond with full force" if the North Vietnamese attempted to take over the South and when he told John Dean, speaking of his struggle with his domestic "enemies," "This is war."

However, if the record of American statesmanship in the Vietnam years, with its sheer mendacity, fumbling, and brutality—not to mention the apparent dementia in the White House which first made its appearance in the Johnson years and emerged fully into public view in President Nixon's last days in office—has a tragic aspect as well, it lies in the fact that in those years the nation experienced the defeat of its first sustained, intellectually coherent attempt to incorporate the implications of nuclear weaponry into national policy. For today it is clear that the doctrine of credibility has failed. It has failed not only in the terms of those who opposed it but also in its own terms. The doctrine of credibility did not provide the United States with an effective means of promoting its interests and ideals at levels of violence below the brink of nuclear war; instead, it provided the notorious quagmire in Vietnam into which the United States poured its energy and power uselessly for more than a decade. The doctrine of credibility, though different from the doctrine of massive retaliation, did not spare mankind from confrontations at the brink between the nuclear powers; far from freezing hostilities at a low level of the escalatory ladder, it led the United States up the ladder, step by step, until, in May of 1972, President Nixon felt obliged to lay down a frontal challenge to the Soviet Union and China by mining North Vietnamese ports against their ships. Finally, the doctrine of credibility failed to enhance American credibility; instead of enabling the United States to "avoid harmful appearances" and to create "respect for the office of President of the United States," it engendered appearances that were supremely harmful to the United States—appearances not only of helplessness, irresolution, and incompetence but of duplicity and ruthlessness—and precipitated a wave of disrespect for a particular President which culminated in his forced resignation from office. Nor did the doctrine of credibility merely fail; it was a catastrophe in its own right, which led to the needless devastation of the Indo-Chinese peninsula and the assault on Constitutional government in the United States.

The only benefit to be salvaged from the experience, it appears, is whatever may have been learned from it, and particularly what may have been learned about the political implications of nuclear weapons—for the Vietnam years do provide the record of an attempt to come to grips with the nuclear question, and of the ways in which that attempt drove two Presidents into states of something like madness and led to the near-ruin of our political system. Among the hazards that were translated into reality was one that had been foreseen almost from the start: the tendency for whoever was given custody of the new weapons to gather into his hands a dangerous array of other powers. Something that had been less clearly foreseen was that efforts to bring the weapons under some form of control and to prevent their use would favor the concentration of power even more than the original grant of unlimited authority over their use had done. During the Vietnam years, there were, broadly speaking, two such efforts. The first was the shift from the strategy of massive retaliation to the strategy of limited war, which was inspired, in part, by the "special horror" of nuclear weapons. At first, the shift seemed to mean a reversion to types of warfare which, unlike nuclear warfare, could be brought under the control of Constitutional processes. In practice, however, the war-declaring power did not devolve back upon Congress, for the limited-war power remained a part of the broader military strategy in which the atmosphere of extreme emergency surrounding nuclear weapons prevailed, and the result was that the President gained the sort of discretionary control over conventional forces which he had already been given over the nuclear forces. The potential for immediate abuses was greater in this new grant of authority than in the grant of nuclear authority, for nuclear weapons were all but unusable, whereas conventional forces could be used easily. The second effort to bring nuclear weapons under control was the policy of détente. Détente, too, was inspired by the horror of nuclear weapons, and it, too, had the effect of extending Presidential power. For one thing, it meant that the President was continually moving about on a world stage, and so could utterly dominate the news in an election year. What was more important, though, was that it tended to draw a wide variety of governmental activities into the orbit of nuclear strategy. In fact, there was virtually no governmental activity in America which did not touch in some way on what President Nixon called "the structure of peace." After all, the leadership could ask, did the nation, having given the President the power, at his sole discretion, to effect the extinction of the human race in war, wish to curtail his power to make peace? Having given him the responsibility for framing and executing a global policy that would guarantee national and human survival, did the nation now want a host of others—congressmen, judges, newsmen, even teen-agers marching in the streets—to disrupt the carrying out of its parts? Should we save the Bill of

Rights but lose mankind? President Nixon put these questions to the country directly in the impeachment proceedings against him in the spring and summer of 1974. For as soon as he was threatened with removal from office, he repaired to the sanctuary of "national security" and informed the nation that an assault on "the Presidency" could fatally undermine "the structure of peace," on which, he claimed, the survival of mankind depended. He wished the country to weigh the crimes of his Administration and the dangers they posed for the Republic against the danger of human extinction. In that balance, he thought, the crimes would weigh lightly. He was offering the nation the spurious deal implicit in the conduct of his whole Administration: American survival at the price of American liberty.

Another unexpected political danger of the nuclear period which was revealed in the Vietnam years was the tendency for the government to enclose itself in a private reality. To begin with, the subject of nuclear weapons is confined by its very nature to the realm of theory. Since the principal aim of nuclear strategy is to guarantee that the nuclear deterrent forces will never be used, no body of direct experience can ever grow up against which the prevailing theories can be tested. (And probably if the weapons *should* ever be used no lesson will be learned, for the reason that there will probably be no one about to do the learning.) Yet in the postwar period an elaborate body of theory necessarily developed, and it was on the basis of this body of theory that the leaders of the nuclear powers were obliged to determine the shape of world politics. Never before, it seems safe to say, has pure, untested theory played such a decisive role in world affairs. Ordinarily, political men prefer to consult practice rather than theory, and are inclined to seek out men of broad experience to advise them, but on this one matter—the most important matter of all—they have been obliged to depend on the theorists themselves.

In the Vietnam years, the inherent unreality of the nuclear question was reinforced by the particular theories that the strategists relied on in framing their policies. One of these theories was the doctrine of linkage. Two kinds of linkage must be distinguished.

One kind was the linkage that was assumed to bind America's foes together into the single force of World Communism. It lost a great deal of its application to the postwar scene when the Russians and the Chinese turned against each other, with each becoming a more resolute foe of the other than either was of the United States, and lost even more of its application during the Vietnam war, when it became apparent that even in small nations the success or failure of a left-wing revolution depended far more on the strengths and weaknesses of local forces than on any "links" with the Russians or the Chinese. (If most of the nations of Eastern Europe were exceptions, that was because in their case the links were not hidden lines of influence but invading Russian armies.) The second kind of linkage was the kind that bound all the United States efforts to oppose Communism—or, indeed, to oppose anything or anyone else it might choose to oppose—into a single force. It was here that the doctrine of credibility came to play its decisive role. According to the doctrine of credibility, the President himself was the universal link: he bound all parts of the world together, for wherever he involved himself he placed the credibility of the United States at stake. The reason that American Presidents became convinced that a single setback anywhere in the world would jeopardize the whole structure of American power was not only that they believed World Communism to be indivisible but that they believed the credibility of American power to be indivisible as well. And what threatened the credibility of American power—the crucial image of will and determination on which the survival of man was now thought to depend— was not only the Communists but, even more important, the American people themselves. In this struggle, "only Americans" could "defeat or humiliate the United States," President Nixon said in 1969. For it was the *Americans'* "special horror" of nuclear weapons, the *Americans'* scruples about endangering the human race, and the *Americans'* revulsion against pitilessly unleasing the nation's force on a small country that were leaving America "hobbled by restraints," and were preventing it from behaving like the greatest power in the world, and were turning it into a "pitiful, helpless giant." A President determined to uphold American credibility at all costs would have to get free of the American people, and the only way he could do that was to destroy the democratic system that gave the people power over him.

The strategic doctrine of the day therefore drew the nation into a confrontation with itself which was quite distinct from any confrontation with World Communism. It made the country self-absorbed, and distracted its attention from the world—for this internal struggle had an integrity of its own, which did not depend on events elsewhere. Even while America fought a war in distant Vietnam, it was they themselves that Americans were interested in —their own "character," their own "reputation"—and the rest of the world, as far as they were concerned, was, in John McNaughton's words, "largely academic." And, finally, of course, the images on which the whole strategic system rested—the images that were meant to build American credibility—tended in themselves to draw the government into a world of fantasy, for the images, like the theories that had given rise to them, could not be tested against experience. The evidence of their efficacy lay in the impenetrable territory of people's minds. Ultimately, the reliance on images for the national defense drew the government into an interior world in which success and failure were determined not by visible results but by pure guesswork. The nuclear question, which revolved around the most concrete peril that the world had ever faced, was proving to be an elusive, phantom thing—the province of professors, psychologists, public-relations men, and other mind-readers and dealers in the shadowy, the insubstantial, the half real.

The fact that the inception of nuclear weapons coincided with the launching of a worldwide crusade by the United States against the spread of Communist influence; the fact that the President's exclusive control over the nuclear arsenal tended to concentrate other kinds of power in his hands; and the fact that nuclear strategy enclosed the White House in a hermetic world of theories and images which was all but impervious to real events and which fostered an atmosphere of unreality in the White House—all these were circumstances that belonged to a distinct phase of the nuclear story. The boastfulness, the hypocrisy, the hardheartedness, the ob-

session with outward appearance and the neglect of inward substance, and the nervous insecurity in spite of matchless power which
marred American policy in the Vietnam years may all be seen as
aspects of one contortion in the nation's writhing in the grip of the
nuclear dilemma. With the fall of President Nixon and the end of
the war in Vietnam, this particular episode in the story of the nuclear
dilemma has apparently come to an end, and, with it, some of the
special problems of that time may have come to an end as well.
What will not come to an end is the nuclear dilemma itself. Nor does
it seem likely that the decisive influence of the nuclear dilemma on
the American Presidency—whatever form that influence may take as
time goes on—will come to an end. For the advent of nuclear weapons has done nothing less than place the President in a radically
new relation to the whole of human reality. He, along with whoever
is responsible in the Soviet Union, has become the hinge of human
existence, the fulcrum of the world. He lives and works astride the
boundary that divides the living world from universal death. Sur-
veyed from where he stands, the living creation has no more
permanence than a personal whim. He or his Soviet counterpart can
snuff it out as one might blow out a candle. If Presidents in recent
years have lost touch with reality, bringing disaster to their Administrations and to the nation, may it not be because their grip on
what is literally human reality—on the continued existence of mankind—is so tenuous and shaky? When the whole of human existence
is trembling in one's grasp, it may be difficult to train one's attention
on each detail. And, measured against the extinction of the whole,
almost anything that does not contribute directly to the current
scheme for survival may seem to be a detail. If President Nixon,
then, slipped into the habit of treating the world as though it were
nothing but a dream, may it not have been because the world's
continued existence did rest on the foundation of his thoughts, his
moods, his dreams? And if a false atmosphere of emergency came to
pervade White House thinking on every issue that arose, surely it
was in part because the men there lived with a vast, perpetual,
genuine emergency. And, finally, if the President tended to gather
tremendous new power into his hands, to violate the rights of others,

to break the law, and generally to ride roughshod over every obstacle, the reason, at bottom, may have been much the same. He had discovered a rationalization without limits in the altogether real aim of protecting mankind from extinction. For what right, what law, what fact, what truth, what aspiration could be allowed to stand in the way of the imperative of human survival, in which all rights, laws, facts, truths, and aspirations were grounded? The first question of the age was how to guarantee survival. Another question was the one that the strategists asked themselves in the nineteen-fifties—how a great power can exercise its influence in the face of the paralyzing effects of nuclear dread. And still other questions that were posed by the ruinous experience of the Vietnam years were how, in the face of the nuclear imperatives, other human aims and human qualities, including freedom and sanity, could be preserved. For thirty years, the burden of nuclear weapons has rested upon the nation with a crushing weight. Their presence has corrupted the atmosphere in which the nation lives, distorted its politics, and coarsened its spirit. The questions they raised have all outlasted the Presidency of Richard Nixon and the nation's reaffirmation of its Constitution and its laws. They are questions on which the framers of the Constitution and all other counsellors from other centuries are silent. The questions are unprecedented, they are boundless, they are unanswered, and they are wholly and lastingly ours.

Notes
on
Sources

All of the information in this book has been derived from the printed public record. All of it has been checked for accuracy by Martin Baron of *The New Yorker* checking department, and I would like to take this opportunity to thank him for his inspired work and for the many invaluable discoveries of new material he made. These notes will by no means constitute a full bibliography of the already voluminous literature available on the Nixon years, nor will they be a full catalogue of the sources I have used in writing this book. Rather, they will merely list a few of the sources I happened to draw on most heavily, and will give references for a few facts that may be less familiar to readers than some others.

In putting together the chronology of the aboveground facts of the entire period, *The New York Times* was a basic tool of inestimable importance and a rich source of detail for many specific subjects.

I. UNITY

In preparing the account of the Nixon Administration's record in civil rights in the summer and fall of 1969, I relied mainly on Richard Harris's article "Justice," which ran in *The New Yorker* in November of 1969 and was later published as a book under the same title by Dutton in 1970. *Nixon in the White House*, by Rowland Evans and Robert Novak (Random House, 1971), was also useful on this subject. For an account of the Administration's crime policy in the same period, I relied again mainly on the Harris article. The interviews with Donald Santirelli and Egil Krogh on the Administration's crime policy are to be found in an article titled "The Krogh File," by Edward Epstein, which appeared in the spring issue for 1975 of *The Public Interest*. Most of the information on the Family Assistance Plan was drawn from Daniel Moynihan's account of the effort to pass that legislation, "Income by Right," which appeared in *The New Yorker* in January of 1971 and was brought out as a book under the title *Politics of a Guaranteed Income* (Random House, 1973). The memos on the Presidential Offensive are to be found in chapter four of *An American Life*, by Jeb Magruder (Atheneum, 1974). For information on Spiro Agnew, both before and after he became Vice-President, I have made use of *A Heartbeat Away: The Investigation and Resignation of Vice-President Spiro T. Agnew*, by Richard M. Cohen and Jules Witcover (Bantam, 1974) and *White Knight: The Rise of Spiro Agnew*, by Jules Witcover (Random House, 1972). Most of the internal White House memos on the press quoted in this and in subsequent parts of the book were first made public in 1973 by the office of Senator Lowell Weicker of Connecticut. In my discussion of the Administration and the press, I have also drawn upon "Shaking the Tree," by Tom Whiteside, which appeared in *The New Yorker* of March 17, 1975.

II. DIVISION

The account of the Carswell nomination relies mainly on "Decision," by Richard Harris, which appeared in *The New Yorker* in December, 1970, and was published as a book by Dutton in 1971. T'.e Buchanan memo on setting up a foundation to be secretly controlled by the Administration is exhibit no. 164 in the record of the hearings of the Senate Select Committee on Presidential Campaign Activities. The memo by Magruder on constructing an image of the Nixon men as "bright, young, well-educated men who *care*" is quoted in chapter five of Magruder's *An American Life*. A collection of President Nixon's speeches and public messages for 1970 and 1971 titled *A New Road for America* (Doubleday, 1972) contains useful documents on the subject of reorganization. The material on the attempted reorganization of the intelligence agencies is drawn from exhibitions introduced at the Senate Select Committee hearings (exhibits no. 35–42 were especially useful) and from the Commission on C.I.A. Activities Within the United States, which was chaired by Vice-President Nelson Rockefeller at the request of President Ford.

III. PEACE

The memo of Patrick Buchanan in which he wonders whether the President's image is consistent enough was first quoted by William Safire in chapter eight of his account of the Nixon years, *Before the Fall* (Doubleday, 1975). The fullest treatment of the attempt to destroy Daniel Ellsberg is to be found in the Statement of Information of the House Judiciary Committee's hearings on the impeachment of President Nixon.

IV. FOR THE REELECTION OF THE PRESIDENT

The best account of the Administration's sabotage of the 1972 election, including its fund-raising practices, its espionage, its infiltration of the opposition, and its many-sided program for the disruption of the Democratic Party primaries is to be found in the official record of the Senate Select Committee and in its Final Report. Of special interest are exhibits no. 171–194, which include the memos of Patrick Buchanan and his political planning group on how to divide the Democrats. The draft of the Kissinger confidential speech to the Soviet leaders is to be found in chapter five of part six of Safire's *Before the Fall*. It seems worth noting that this draft is one of the few internal documents of the Nixon Administration concerning foreign affairs that has yet come to light. The underground record of the executive branch in foreign policy during the Kennedy and Johnson years was made known through publication of the Pentagon papers, but the underground record in foreign affairs of the Nixon Administration remains mostly undivulged.

V. THE SCRIPT AND THE PLAYERS

A word on the publications of the Senate Select Committee and the House Judiciary Committee may be in order here. Generally speaking, the reports of the Senate Select Committee, which include the somewhat chaotic record of the hearings and the highly organized Final Report, give the best accounts of matters not necessarily directly related to the personal conduct of the President, such as the campaign abuses of 1972. The reports of the House Judiciary Committee, on the other hand, which include its Summary of Information, its Statement of Information (which documents the Summary of Information), its report, *Impeachment of Richard M. Nixon, President of the United States,* and its Transcripts of Eight Recorded Presidential Conversations, give the best accounts of matters having directly to do with the President's conduct, such as the plan to destroy Ellsberg, the attempts to make political use of government agencies to punish the Administration's "enemies," and, of course, the Watergate cover-up. In quoting from the President's taped conversations, I have used the Transcripts of Eight Recorded Presidential Conversations whenever possible, but otherwise have had to rely upon the much more copious but far less accurate transcribed excerpts which President Nixon offered to the Judiciary Committee, apparently in the hope that the Committee would desist from seeking actual tapes. For the account of the Republican Convention, I have drawn heavily upon reports published in the *Times,* including, especially, those of Charlotte Curtis and John Kifner.

VI. CREDIBILITY

All the quotations of officials of the Kennedy and Johnson years are taken from *The Pentagon Papers* (Beacon, 1971) which includes a useful chronologically arranged catalogue of public statements by government officials concerning the war. Henry Kissinger's *Nuclear Weapons and Foreign Policy* has come out in two editions—one brought out in 1957 by Harper & Row, and the other by Norton in 1969. The Norton edition is abridged, and readers who wish to have a full and accurate impression of Kissinger's thinking in 1957 should make sure to read the original edition.